The M&A Process

A Practical Guide for the Business Lawyer

Committee on Negotiated Acquisitions

ABA Section of
BUSINESS LAW
Practical Resources for the Business Lawyer

**Defending Liberty
Pursuing Justice**

The materials contained herein represent the opinions of the authors and editors and should not be construed to be the action of either the American Bar Association or the Section of Business Law unless adopted pursuant to the bylaws of the Association.

Nothing contained in this book is to be considered as the rendering of legal advice for specific cases, and readers are responsible for obtaining such advice from their own legal counsel. This book and any forms and agreements herein are intended for educational and informational purposes only.

Any statement made herein regarding tax matters may not be relied upon by anyone to avoid tax penalties and are not to be used or referred to in any publication or marketing materials.

Printed in the United States of America.

Library of Congress Cataloging-in-Publication Data

The mergers and acquisition process : what the business lawyer needs to know / American Bar Association, Section of Business Law, Committee on Negotiated Acquisitions.
    p. cm.
ISBN 1-59031-572-3 (pbk.)
    1. Consolidation and merger of corporations—United States. 2. Corporations—Finance—Law and legislation—United States. 3. Negotiation in business—United States. I. American Bar Association. Committee on Negotiated Acquisitions.
KF1477.M47 2005
346.73′06626—dc22   2005013844

Discounts are available for books ordered in bulk. Special consideration is given to state and local bars, CLE programs, and other bar-related organizations. Inquire at Book Publishing, American Bar Association, 321 North Clark Street, Chicago, IL 60610.

12 11 10 09 08 07 06   8 7 6 5 4 3 2

Summary Table of Contents

Table of Contents

Acknowledgements

The work of the Task Force on this Guide has been a labor of love for many of us over the five years of the project. In addition to the oversight of Co-Chairs Vince Garrity and Tom Thompson, Rob Ouellette has served as Reporter for the Task Force. While thanks are due to all of our firms, Rob's colleagues at Schottenstein Zox & Dunn Co., L.P.A., have had the heaviest lifting: collecting the submissions, doing the word processing, applying the conventions, reconciling conflicting styles and formats, and performing numerous other logistical chores.

Over the past year, the laboring oars have been pulled by a very hard working Editorial Committee of:

Neal H. Brockmeyer	Los Angeles, California
Robert G. Copeland	San Diego, California
William B. Payne	Minneapolis, Minnesota
Murray J. Perelman	Toronto, Ontario

Not only has this group spent a great number of hours editing and re-editing the Task Force's and each other's work (while suppressing their own pride of authorship and ego), these Editorial Committee members have also contributed a significant part of the original material making up this Guide.

In addition to the Editorial Committee, numerous Task Force members have contributed thoughtful chapters and subchapters, which have become the core of this Guide, or provided helpful comments and support throughout the project:

David L. Albin	Stamford, Connecticut
Howard J. Barnhorst, II	San Diego, California
Brian Belanger	Pittsburgh, Pennsylvania
David L. Benson	Seattle, Washington
Neal H. Brockmeyer	Los Angeles, California
Eric V. Brown, Jr.	Kalamazoo, Michigan
Charles H. Brownman	Denver, Colorado
Henri M. Bybelezer	Montreal, Quebec
John F. Clifford	Toronto, Ontario
Gordon E. Cooper	Toronto, Ontario
Robert G. Copeland	San Diego, California
Cecilia Ann Cordova	Seattle, Washington
John F. Corrigan	Providence, Rhode Island
Mark A. Danzi	Tampa, Florida
Byron F. Egan	Dallas, Texas
Vincent F. Garrity, Jr.	Philadelphia, Pennsylvania

David C. Gavsie	Toronto, Ontario
Jon T. Hirschoff	Stamford, Connecticut
Michael S. Jordan	Columbus, Ohio
Josef Keglewitsch	Columbus, Ohio
Lori L. Lasher	Philadelphia, Pennsylvania
Theodore W. Lenz	Nashville, Tennessee
Daniel H. Minkus	Birmingham, Michigan
Brian S. North	Philadelphia, Pennsylvania
Robert R. Ouellette	Columbus, Ohio
William B. Payne	Minneapolis, Minnesota
Murray J. Perelman	Toronto, Ontario
Ralston W. Steenrod	Louisville, Kentucky
George Malcolm Taylor	Birmingham, Alabama
Thomas M. Thompson	Pittsburgh, Pennsylvania
Thomas W. Van Dyke	Kansas City, Missouri
Dennis J. White	Boston, Massachusetts
Arthur J. Wright	Dallas, Texas
Norman A. Zilber	San Francisco, California

William Freivogel, Senior Vice President—Loss Prevention of Aon Risk Services, Professional Services Group, has contributed mightily by reviewing and commenting upon the ethical discussions and potential malpractice implications of our treatment of practices. While not a member of the Task Force, Joel Greenberg read the final draft of the Guide and made a number of very helpful comments and suggestions.

Corporate Service Company (better known to many of you as CSC) provided the Task Force with an extranet site *gratis* that was very useful in organizing the early phases of the process and demonstrating the utility of such sites in deal organization.

Finally, our thanks to Nat Doliner and Rick Climan, Chairs of the Committee on Negotiated Acquisitions during this project, and to Jacqueline McGlanery, Suzy Bibko, and Ann Poole of the American Bar Association Publication Staff for ongoing editorial support and encouragement to the Task Force.

Preface

This Guide grew out of a suggestion by J. Patrick Garrett, the first Chair of the Committee on Negotiated Acquisitions of the American Bar Association's Section of Business Law. Pat felt there was a need for a book on the merger and acquisition ("M&A") process that described for the young lawyer and general practitioner how experienced acquisition lawyers approach a deal and relate to the various players involved. The work of the Committee to that point had focused on a series of specific model acquisition agreements and commentary, as well as on the due diligence process. These models dealt with the way practitioners approach particular provisions of these agreements and ancillary documents and the substantive law behind the issues raised by or dealt with in those provisions. Pat's thought was that beyond these model agreements there remained a need for a book that addresses how experienced lawyers actually "do the deal." In 2000, Nat Doliner, Chair of the Committee, created a Task Force on the Manual on Acquisitions Practice and Procedure co-chaired by Vince Garrity and Tom Thompson to develop a publication addressing this need.

The development of the Guide also coincides with a need identified by the Section of Business Law to educate law students and beginning business lawyers in the practice of business law. We see this Guide as supporting that objective.

The Guide's primary target is the beginning lawyer embarking upon an acquisition for the first time. We also view this Guide as a valuable tool for the more experienced practitioner who may handle acquisitions only infrequently. We suspect that even the experienced M&A practitioner will find some pearls of wisdom in these pages, as few of us have experienced personally every task and challenge described in this Guide. While authored by American and Canadian practitioners and focused principally on the U.S. legal system as it impacts acquisitions, we believe much of what this Guide covers knows no borders and will be of value to M&A lawyers in any country.

Any effort such as this owes much to James C. Freund's excellent *Anatomy of a Merger*. However, it has been over 30 years since the publication of that entertaining and instructive work, and we view this Guide as addressing in even greater detail the technique and nitty gritty of transactional practice.

Several observations have grown out of the effort. First, much of what we do in an M&A deal is but a subset of the skills involved in any commercial, real estate, financing, or other business deal. Much of the process is the same. We would hope that many of the lessons in this Guide would have application in other areas of practice.

Second, it has become clear that there is not necessarily one right or wrong approach to many of the issues this Guide addresses. The Task Force spent many entertaining hours debating the merits of diametrically opposite approaches to common problems taken by equally respected acquisition lawyers from around the country. It became clear that the approach worked for each lawyer and that it would be a mistake to try to pick between them. To a large extent, the choice is often one of personal style. Where we have found these differences in approach, we have tried to present both angles and identify the merits of each without judging which is a "best practice."

The Guide from time to time recommends particular approaches to the resolution of a legal issue. This is not intended to suggest, yet alone establish, a professional standard of practice. There are several reasons for this: (1) as noted above, equally sophisticated and experienced M&A practitioners may advise their clients to assert a dramatically different position on a particular issue; (2) every deal is truly distinctive and diverse legal resolutions understandably occur, i.e., one size does not fit all; and (3) perhaps most importantly, the relative bargaining power of the parties can make a very substantial difference in terms of how they and their counsel grapple with the legal issues. For example, the negotiating stance of a terminally ill owner of a business (often the principal asset of his estate) that has been unsuccessfully "on the market" for some time will be considerably different from that of an owner under no compulsion to sell who has attracted numerous bidders in the range of his asking price.

This Guide is designed to be a guide for all customary structures of acquisition transactions (i.e., a merger, asset sale, stock sale, share exchange) and covers the purchase of both publicly and privately held businesses. Having said this, there is greater emphasis on private deals, and we have not attempted to address many of the more technical, substantive aspects of public deals.

While there is much substantive learning supporting the thinking on many of the issues, what we have tried to do is to identify issues and to point the practitioners toward other sources for answers. For example, we have not tried to provide definitive positions on issues such as the responsibility of the board of directors in acquisition transactions from state to state or the specifics of the current state of legal opinion practice. To quote the noted barrister Horace Rumpole, "knowing the law has almost nothing to do with being a lawyer." Where valuable resources are available on a particular topic (including other ABA publications and model agreements published by the Committee), we have described briefly the considerations and issues and have directed the reader to those other resources. We have made numerous references to two publications of the Committee: *Model Stock Purchase Agreement with Commentary* (1995), cited as "MSPA," and *Model Asset Purchase Agreement with Commentary* (2001), cited as "MAPA."

Sidebars. We have included sidebars to provide real life examples for some of the points made, as well as possibly adding some entertainment. Sidebars are designed to provide special insights on textual material through personal war stories provided by Task Force members, reported cases, and sample document extracts illustrating the advice contained in the Guide.

Glossary. The Guide includes a Glossary designed to give the new M&A lawyer a running start on dealing with the lingo of our craft. Our Glossary is not designed to be as inclusive as the M&A Dictionary scheduled to be published by the Committee soon after this Guide goes to press. The M&A Dictionary will be more comprehensive in addressing Delaware case law, public company practice, and contested transaction usages. The Glossary in our Guide is designed to introduce new practitioners to basic terminology in private M&A practice. Much of the Glossary is based upon a similar lexicon developed by Neal Brockmeyer of Los Angeles for use at the Heller Ehrman firm.

Usage of certain terms. Terms that are capitalized and not immediately defined in nearby text can be found in the Glossary. We have also assumed a general level of knowledge among deal lawyers, so many common terms of M&A practice are used without any special distinction. These common terms, like baskets and caps in indemnification provisions of acquisition agreements, also can be found in the Glossary.

Bibliography. We have also included a bibliography containing books, articles, and other resources our Task Force members have found useful over the years.

We hope that our efforts have resulted in a work that will be of practical use to lawyers. We hope the Guide will prove serviceable to deal lawyers as either a good read from cover to cover (if not at the beach) or as a resource read selectively as a lawyer works through a deal.

Vincent F. Garrity, Jr.
Thomas M. Thompson
Co-Chairs

Robert R. Ouellette
Reporter

CHAPTER 1

Context of M&A Transactions

The phrase "M&A" comes trippingly off the lips. Easy to say, harder to understand. Conventional wisdom, driven home by images in movies and television, would indicate that M&A is about power and prestige.

Recent history is not particularly helpful in trying to understand M&A. M&A activity in the 1980s triggered concern. Corporate raiders, cultural icons being acquired by companies from other countries, stable industries being uprooted and transformed, all caused stress and tension in the minds of many people. M&A activity in the 1990s was a different story. Deals generated attention, the stock market was climbing, new industries were being created, and magazines profiled new young millionaires who had developed and sold their businesses to larger more established buyers. Then the technology bubble burst. M&A activity in the 21st century? Although activity levels will no doubt fluctuate over time, there is no doubt that M&A will always be an important part of our economy—businesses will always be bought and sold.

This Guide can probably safely assume that its target audience knows that M&A involves the transfer of a business. It is also not a stretch to assume that its readers know that the lawyer's role in an M&A transaction is to assist the client achieve its objectives. Now that the lawyer's role is clear, delivering the skills needed to close the M&A transaction should be straightforward, right?

Is there a law of M&A? Why is it that when a lawyer looks for guidance in M&A, he might find decisions in hotly contested litigation issued by Delaware courts? Or rigorous explanations contained in securities law treatises? Or references to federal statutes regarding how many days' notice must be given if a plant will be closed? Or, even worse in the minds of many lawyers, the realization he may need to know something about accounting? Do M&A lawyers need to understand litigation, securities law, labor law, and numbers? Is that what M&A is all about?

The central theme of this Guide is to help lawyers gain a deeper understanding of the M&A practice. One cannot understand M&A only from current texts, contract forms, updates on legal developments, or business trends. M&A is not a narrowly defined body of law. M&A is certainly not a collection of preprinted forms. M&A is a *process*, the process of transferring a business from one owner to the next.

Because M&A is the transfer of a business, and businesses are inherently complex (whether looked at from a strictly legal or another perspective), an M&A transaction is complex. Take a simple type of transaction, a private company that wants to transfer one of its existing businesses to a newly created separate subsidiary. Even this seemingly simple non-arm's length transaction is fraught with complexity because the business and its assets, including its human capital, must be identified and legal constraints on its transfer must be identified. Are contracts assignable? Is the proper intellectual property being transferred? What are the employment implications of this transfer? What are the tax and accounting issues?

If M&A is the transfer of a business, what is a business? A business may be any asset that has produced revenues. At least the SEC has taken a very expansive definition of a business. In practical terms, the transfer of some portion of a business will often involve aspects of M&A. Even a classic real estate transfer may become an M&A deal.

When the transfer to a subsidiary described above, which is only a straightforward internal reorganization, becomes the sale of an existing business to a third party, additional considerations arise. An already difficult process of transferring a business is now subject to contractual obligations. At the beginning of the process, the seller puts the best face on the business it wants to sell. The buyer tries to assure itself that it is buying the business it thinks it is buying.

With these concerns come additional considerations as buyers and sellers surround themselves with advisors (both internal and external), and the timeframe to the closing stretches into months or even years. There are numerous legal issues to be dealt with pertaining to both the transaction and the operation of the business.

Lawyers usually do more than simply craft legal documents in an M&A transaction and their role may vary substantially depending on the sophistication of the client. They must understand the client's ultimate business objectives. Sometimes those objectives are best achieved by not completing a transaction. Often lawyers are in the best position to offer advice. A lawyer understanding the process knows and can offer the client a rich smorgasbord of options to best carry out the client's objectives. Lawyers, because of their experience, may have the best grasp of any of the client's advisors on the entire process and unique issues presented.

This Guide can be read cover to cover, section by section, or chapter by chapter. Because the M&A process is interactive and fluid, the reader will notice certain topics appear in more than one area of the Guide. This redundancy is intentional and necessary; the M&A process is simply not linear in nature. In fact, it is very hard to tell sometimes when is the appropriate time to address an issue in the M&A process, as the following sidebar illustrates.

How Much Are Those Assets in the Window?

In an asset purchase, price allocations are a determining factor of the parties' tax consequences. The allocation determines the seller's gain or loss on each asset. For a buyer, it establishes each asset's basis, which is important for depreciation. Failure to negotiate and consider the tax implications of the price allocations can result in unnecessarily disadvantageous tax consequences for a seller, a buyer, or both. For the buyer these consequences can last for many years after the closing.

In an asset purchase agreement, the parties' utmost concern in determining the total sales price was to ensure that the buyer could satisfy its debt service requirements. The seller and buyer were clear on the purchase price. The acquisition agreement was clear about the purchase price. However, the parties failed to see the importance of allocating the purchase price among the assets.

During the years after closing, the buyer reported depreciation deductions on its tax returns based upon post-closing asset appraisals amounting to nearly $5 million. However, the seller reported the asset purchase price allocation of $1 million as reflected in the acquisition agreement. Not surprisingly, the IRS issued the buyer a notice of tax deficiency. The court found no evidence of undue influence, which would have provided the buyer with a basis to challenge successfully the IRS's determination of tax liability. The parties simply failed to negotiate the price allocation.

The court held that the buyer was bound to honor the price allocation as outlined in the acquisition agreement, which resulted in lost depreciation deductions for the buyer amounting to hundreds of thousands of dollars. Ironically, if the acquisition agreement had been structured to be more tax advantageous for the buyer, the seller's tax result would also have been more tax advantageous.

It is important to understand that the M&A process is tremendously variable. The claim by a lawyer wearing the mantel of authority that "it is always done this way" is usually false. Because business itself is highly variable and because the law of M&A is essentially the law of contracts (what the parties agree to will generally be legally respected), there is no prescribed form or context in which deals are done. There are legal constraints of course, from state corporate law involving the duties of directors and requirements imposed on public companies to the common law of torts and contracts. But of all M&A transactions done each year, only a relative handful involve public company mergers. That is, most M&A deals involve negotiation for the sale of a privately held business. There is no particular regulatory framework that drives M&A, and so both the process and the agreements themselves are rich and varied.

Not all of the processes outlined in this Guide will be applicable to every situation. Not all will be followed. For the practitioner, it is important to understand, in broad terms, what may happen and what alternatives may be available. In M&A, there is usually not a "one-size-fits-all approach" to any problem, and understanding the art of the possible may allow the lawyer to add significant value to any transaction. M&A practitioners must think by analogy.

This Guide was put together to provide insight to a lawyer not experienced in M&A (either a new lawyer or one having a more general practice) or to refresh others on some aspects of M&A. To fully understand the M&A process, one must be involved in it. By touching on various aspects of the process, from forming the team, determining to sell, preparing the business for sale, finding a buyer and the process of sale onward, we hope to provide insight on what it is all about. Each chapter has been prepared to focus upon a particular component of the M&A process.

The Guide discusses key relationships in the acquisition process that need to be considered in most deals. Specific ethical concerns that appear in the M&A process are discussed. We explore the key components of finding buyers and sellers. We also discuss basic concepts of financial statements, accounting, and valuation.

And an M&A lawyer needs to understand all of the foregoing before he can even begin to negotiate and structure the deal and prepare the acquisition agreement. Due diligence is crucial to the process. As the M&A process unfolds, lawyers will need to understand how to properly document the transaction, a topic for which entire books have previously been published. This Guide tries to focus its contribution on the *process* of documenting the transaction, rather than particular substantive legal issues.

Once the acquisition agreement is signed, more tasks appear for the M&A lawyer. The deal needs to get to closing, and some deals disintegrate before closing. The closing itself has its own history and vocabulary. Finally, there are often post-closing steps that need to be taken and, sometimes, disputes that need to get resolved.

The M&A process will continue to evolve. Future judicial decisions, legislative innovations, and economic development will force lawyers to sharpen their legal and client counseling skills. The lawyers best equipped to help their clients with M&A will be the ones who inherently understand the M&A process and the constant pressures that affect each of its components.

CHAPTER 2

Managing the Client Relationship and Other Ethical Issues

This chapter is not an essay on legal ethics or an analysis of the ABA Model Rules of Professional Conduct or on any individual state rules of professional conduct. There are numerous current and informative sources of this information available elsewhere.[1] Rather, this chapter is about how to recognize in advance ethical issues that may confront a lawyer in an acquisition transaction. These issues include identifying the client, confronting actual or potential conflicts, documenting the engagement, preserving the attorney-client privilege, and simply communicating with the client and other participants in the transaction.

Who Is the Client?

Other than successfully completing a closing, there is perhaps no moment in an acquisition transaction quite as invigorating for a deal lawyer as the initial call requesting his services. This euphoria sets in whether it is a new client representation or one that may stretch back many years. When that call comes, it is natural to focus on the challenging substantive and procedural issues that may be involved in the deal being described. The euphoria often results in not carefully considering just "Who is the client?" It is important to make this determination early in the process because it will create a series of professional responsibilities, such as having to analyze any actual or potential conflicts, maintain communications in confidence, and preserve the work-product protection and the attorney-client privilege.

The reality is that the client is not necessarily a unitary actor, but often comprised of different constituencies, each with a distinct agenda. These nuances need to be recognized along with each actor's agenda. Because each transaction may also involve major changes in relationships among these entities and individuals as it progresses, counsel needs to take these changes into account in order to achieve the client's goals and objectives and carry out the duties and responsibilities required by the applicable rules of professional responsibility.

At a minimum, acquisitions usually involve two sides—the sell-side and the buy-side. Parties than the seller, target, or buyer may be involved on either side. Whether your representation falls on the sell-side or the buy-side, it is likely that the client(s) will be one or more of the following: the seller, target, buyer, investors and owners (shareholders, partners, or members), management, key employees, and sometimes lenders or key vendors. But, it is in the representation of the main actors where most ethical issues in the acquisition process arise—and the number of issues to be resolved usually is disproportionately greater for the lawyers on the sell-side of a transaction.

As if there were not already a host of issues for the seller's attorney to face in a deal—almost instant loss of leverage once a letter of intent is signed and the often substantial job of trying to bring the buyer's "reasonable first draft" of the acquisition agreement into a form that meets the quoted phrase—he will also have to recognize and solve some tough, often "moving target" ethical issues. Who does the attorney represent, initially and later as the deal unfolds?

The lawyer representing the buyer actually has an enviable position: he represents the party with the money (or so he hopes), he usually gets to come up with the first draft of the acquisition agreement, and he usually has very few ethical issues to face in representing the buyer. But, as we will see, there are exceptions, such as a management buyout or where the lawyer is also asked to represent one or more investors who are putting cash into the buyer to finance the acquisition.

For a better understanding of the possible situations that arise, look at the possible clients typically found in an acquisition transaction.

Sell-Side Representation

On the sell-side of a transaction, there is often a broader spectrum of issues involved in identifying the client. Trying to represent everyone on the sell-side is nearly impossible. Working through the analysis that is required to sort out conflicts and from whom waivers are required is time consuming, sometimes difficult to get paid for, and the effort ultimately may be futile as the landscape (and who is the client) shifts with changes in the deal.

For example, the owners of the business call you and say they have decided to sell. Who is the client? What kind of deal is being proposed? In an asset sale, the entity is the seller. In a sale of stock, the shareholders are involved as sellers. Moreover, you may have done the corporate work of the target, having been brought in by a major investor whom you represent in many other situations. The point: the identity of the client may not be obvious and representation may not be simple to determine.

Acquisitions come in many forms. In transactions involving parties of substantial size, nearly every involved player will have its own lawyer: the target, various target board members and officers, the investment banks, the buyer, and on and on.

If the target is a publicly traded entity, it is likely that counsel is expected only to represent the target and not its various constituencies. But even here conflict issues can arise if the public company is controlled by another company or group of individuals. It is not unusual for the principal shareholders to select counsel to represent the target. Another situation bringing this to the forefront is when, early in the deal, management attempts to engage company counsel to represent management in negotiating compensation and employment issues with the buyer.

For many privately held companies the demarcation is not simple either. Although the entity may engage counsel, the real parties in interest are often the owners or at least the group comprising the controlling shareholders. They could be common shareholders, preferred shareholders, general partners, limited partners, or a combination. One of the first questions should be: "Who made the decision to sell?"

Where a controlling shareholder decides to sell, the deal may not happen unless key management will commit to stay with the company and are satisfactorily remunerated by the company, the buyer, or both. In that situation, company counsel may really be representing the controlling shareholder, and separate counsel may be needed for the management team.

Similar issues can arise with venture-backed targets. Company counsel usually has ties to either the founding shareholders or the venture capital investors. In these situations, separate counsel may be needed for each shareholder group since they may hold separate classes or series of stock with different rights in an acquisition. The ongoing management team may also need separate representation.

In third and fourth generation family-owned businesses, it is not unusual for the passive shareholders to advocate a sale because most private companies do not pay substantial dividends. Thus, the passive shareholders may be at odds with the active shareholders or others who are managing the business. Those managing the business may prefer to cash out the passive shareholders by a stock redemption or a leveraged recapitalization, but too often the financing required for such a transaction can inhibit future growth of the business. The same counsel may not be able to represent these groups unless the varying interests and goals are reconciled. These same considerations can apply to partnerships and limited liability companies.

When the management team selects target counsel (whether it be existing company counsel or special counsel), other issues come into play depending upon whether the key members are continuing in the new regime or only in a transition phase. If management is essential to the buyer, the basic terms of the acquisition may need to be negotiated separately from management's deal, otherwise a claim might be made that management sold out for too little in order to enhance its own relationship with the buyer. Since the buyer may prefer to make payment with tax-deductible dollars in the form of compensation or may prefer a purchase price that is not charged against earnings, its interest in shifting purchase price to compensation may be difficult to predict. This is less of a problem for transitioning managers, unless the consulting contracts and/or noncompetition covenants could be considered excessive.

Buy-Side Representation

The scope of the inquiry is often easier on the buy side of an acquisition because there is usually a commonality of interest among the buyer, its ownership, and management regarding the objectives of the acquisition. Nevertheless, where more than one party is involved on the buy side, some issues can arise that may be more practical than ethical in nature.

Even if a lawyer is representing only the buyer, he may want to ascertain the goals and objectives of the others that have an interest in the transaction and determine whether there are any considerations that may be relevant to negotiating or closing a deal. Taking what might at first seem a simple example, if the buyer is a subsidiary of another entity, an acquisition may make perfect sense from the perspective of the subsidiary and its management, yet still conflict with overall goals and objectives of the parent for the entire organization. The converse is of course also true. Although counsel's initial contact, and most of his day-to-day dealings during the acquisition transaction, may be with the subsidiary's management, it would be helpful to understand the underlying objectives of the ultimate decision-makers (which may be the parent's board of directors or a lead investor) in order to evaluate and negotiate the proposed transaction. Unfortunately it is not unheard of for a subsidiary to spend significant money on outside counsel and accountants, plus hours of management and staff time, and proceed all the way to the closing table only to have the deal killed at the last minute by the parent for reasons that may be entirely unrelated to the merits of the pending transaction.

Counsel might want to determine whether there is a disconnect between the negotiating team and the ultimate decision makers. Early communication with knowledgeable decision-makers and representatives of the parent also will help identify any legal or practical limitations imposed on the parent by its lenders or its contracts or relationships with other third-parties, which may not have been routinely communicated by the parent to the subsidiary's management. The same considerations can apply to determining the authority of the persons with whom counsel is dealing. While counsel can rightfully assume that management, particularly officers, have authority to sign documents, sometimes embarrassing situations arise.

Who Has Authority?

The parties had engaged in protracted negotiations over the parent's guaranty of the selling subsidiary's indemnity obligations. At about 11:00 p.m. on the evening before signing the acquisition agreement, the subsidiary's negotiating team produced a letter signed by the Vice President of Finance of the parent confirming the parent's guaranty. The next morning, the General Counsel of the parent sent a fax to all hands advising them that the Vice President of Finance did not have the authority to agree to the guaranty.

Especially (but not only) where the buyer is family owned or otherwise closely held, consideration should be given to confirming the source of the authority to make the initial acquisition decision and the many business decisions that follow. Sometimes the smaller the ownership group, the greater the number of competing agendas, particularly where a family is involved.

This same issue may arise where a significant investor is directing the buyer or has been brought in for the purpose of helping fund the acquisition.

Which Side Are You on Now?

More complicated scenarios involving both the buy-side and the sell-side arise in the management buy-out, in which a group of managers put up their own funds with third-party financing to acquire ownership of the target. Where counsel has previously represented the target and also the target's parent or individual owners, he must carefully identify which of the parties is being represented in the transaction. In most cases, counsel will represent only the parent or its shareholders, or only the management team (or individual members of the management team), and separate counsel will be engaged to represent other parties. Where counsel is representing the management team as a whole, it should be made clear that he does not represent the team members individually and that each of them should consider obtaining separate counsel to advise them of the effect on them of the various ownership, compensation, benefits, and loan liability issues applicable to their participation in the transaction. However, the controlling members of the management team may expect the target's counsel to represent them individually as well, which may be acceptable if properly disclosed, agreed to, and the other managers have separate counsel.

Addressing the Conflicts

As can be seen, the identity of the client(s) can present various conflicts that will need to be resolved before the engagement can be finalized. This can occur with taking on a new client, continuing to represent an existing client or attempting to represent multiple parties as clients in the transaction. As the deal moves through the negotiation process, new assignments may emerge for the lawyer, raising additional possibilities for conflicts. The interests of the lawyer's clients, or some of them, may abruptly diverge. Some parties may need independent counsel. The lawyer may need to formally disengage from the representation of one or more of the parties.

Significant time can be spent resolving conflict of interest situations. However, resolution typically has to occur in short order. The motivated parties involved in the deal will not wait very long over legal diversions that they do not fully appreciate. Sometimes, resolution is not possible, or particularly desirable. And, no one is particularly interested in paying for the billable hours spent running these issues to ground. "After all, these are really just the lawyer's problem," more than one party involved is likely to grumble.

Obtaining Informed Written Consents

Throughout this chapter, reference is made to conflict waivers or consents,[2] whereby parties acknowledge the existence of conflicts and give their informed written consent to representation. Failure to obtain an adequate conflict waiver can have bad consequences: withdrawal from all representation, denial of the right to collect fees, disgorgement of fees, malpractice exposure, and professional sanctions against the lawyer and the lawyer's firm, just to name a few.

Conflict waivers are written documents, usually in the form of a letter, which are used by lawyers to obtain the informed consent of existing or potential clients in circumstances such as where:

- the representation of one client will be directly adverse or potentially adverse to another client;
- there is a significant risk that the representation of one or more clients will be materially limited by the lawyer's responsibilities to another client, a former client or third person; and
- the lawyer represents a client in a matter and at the same time in a separate matter accepts a client whose interest in the first matter is adverse to the client in the first matter.[3]

The waiver may disclose that if one or more actual conflicts arise, the lawyer may be disabled from representing the parties whose interests actually conflict and which of the parties, if any, the lawyer may seek to continue to represent in that situation. The consequences of disablement may be described, which could include the necessity for the parties to obtain separate counsel, that lawyers in the firm may be called as witnesses if a dispute arises and, finally, that information obtained during joint representation, at least that which relates to the matter in which the clients have a joint interest, may not be subject to the attorney-client privilege in an action between the mutual clients.

Some jurisdictions require that conflict waivers be in writing, and some do not.[4] It is almost always advisable to obtain conflict waivers in writing. To be effective, conflict waivers must be based on the informed consent of the clients. "Informed consent" is defined in Model Rule 1.0(e) to denote "the agreement by a person to a proposed course of conduct after the lawyer has communicated adequate information and explanation about the material risks of and reasonably available alternatives to the proposed course of conduct." Demonstrating "informed consent" will always be measured in hindsight; establishing this without a written waiver will always be a very heavy burden.

Taking on a New M&A Client

When a lawyer is presented with an opportunity to represent a new client in an acquisition, it is not uncommon to find that the potential client is or was involved in an actual conflict situation with another current or former client. The natural desire is to find a way to accept the new engagement.

First, the potential new client must be cleared through the lawyer's conflicts system. The fact that the potential new client is adverse to an existing client probably may be the end of the inquiry. Seeking the informed consent of an existing client to the representation of a new client that is actually adverse to the existing client seems at least politically challenging. Before representing the new client, the lawyer must obtain conflict waivers from both the new client and the existing client.

This situation also underscores the desirability of limiting information received from a potential new client until it has been screened through the conflict system. If representation of the potential new client is not undertaken, it could claim that it divulged confidential information to the lawyer in the initial exploratory discussion, which may be enough to disqualify the lawyer from continuing to represent its existing client in the controversy with the potential new client. The consequences of having to fight off such a challenge, explain the situation to the existing client, and face disqualification are ugly to contemplate.

Under the rules of professional responsibility, the very identity of an existing client is generally considered information that must be maintained in confidence by the lawyer and not be disclosed without the client's consent.[5] Therefore, just proceeding with the task of exploring the possibility of obtaining waivers is pretty daunting—a new client may quickly decide there is too much red tape getting you on board and an existing client being approached may have concerns about you or your firm's undivided loyalty.

If the prospective new client (or an existing client) seeks representation in a transaction in which a former client is on the other side, it should be possible to take on that representation, provided the lawyer is satisfied the new matter is not substantially related to the matter he handled for the former client and he does not possess confidential information of the former client relating to the new engagement.[6]

The lawyer may want to consider sending a prospective client, whose representation has ultimately been declined, a letter confirming that its representation has not been undertaken and that the lawyer was provided with no confidential information in the process; however, even if no lawyer-client relationship has developed, the lawyer may not use or reveal confidential information learned from the prospective client to its disadvantage.[7] Thus, the lawyer may be precluded from representing a new client (or an existing client) adverse to the prospective client.

Additionally, an often overlooked step in the attorney-client relationship is for the lawyer to consider the advisability to formally disengage from the further representation of a client when the engagement, for whatever reason, ends. The step of formally ending the attorney-client relationship has benefits and burdens. It may make taking on a matter adverse to the former client easier in the future. It dispels any argument that there are continuing duties to that former client. At the same time, it is inherently difficult for a lawyer to tell a client, effectively, "you are now history," especially if the professional relationship was satisfactory. But if prospects for further work seem limited, then disengagement in writing is worth considering, and usually may be documented in a cordial manner.[8] Short of formal disengagement, consideration should at least be given to closing the file to evidence the end of the relationship.

Accepting an M&A Project for an Existing Client

The lawyer needs to address with its client at the outset any conflicts that may exist as a result of representation of the client in M&A transaction. If the party on the other side of the transaction (whether the seller, target, or buyer) has been identified, the appropriate names need to be cleared through the lawyer's conflicts system. If that party is also a client, the lawyer will have to obtain conflict waivers from both clients if he wishes to proceed. Any conflicts identified as a result of a firm's conflict review procedure should be discussed with the client. But the lawyer must be careful not to disclose any confidential information of another client without its consent. If a waiver cannot be obtained or if the conflict cannot be waived, the lawyer will have to decline representing the existing client in the M&A transaction.

Taking on Multiple Clients

The bread and butter acquisition practice of many M&A lawyers consists of representing businesses in which the officers, directors, and shareholders are often the founding or family group directing the business or are actively involved in the day-to-day management of the business. It is very common for a lawyer representing the company to have done work for some of these officers, directors, and shareholders. Even if some of these parties had not previously been represented by the lawyer, they may very well ask him to represent them in the transaction. Usually the relationships of these parties absent a sale do not develop into an actual conflict unless, for example, an individually represented client is about to be terminated as an employee. A sale usually creates significant economic interests in most, if not all, of these parties. And these economic interests may vary a great deal among them. When that business becomes the target, these interests, often conflicting, will need representation. Enter the deal and in almost the blink of an eye, the well-established set of relationships with a client or group of joint clients is about to be torn asunder.

Here are some examples of conflicts that can arise in transactions where joint representation of the seller or target and all their shareholders is undertaken.

The buyer in an asset sale insists that the major shareholders of the seller join with the seller in the representations to be made to the buyer and in the indemnification obligations for breaches of these representations, most likely on a joint and several basis. The shareholders who are required to join in the representations and stand behind the indemnity will have interests different from other shareholders. The former may want concessions before becoming indemnitors. At the very least, they may want to have an agreement whereby the other shareholders agree to contribute to any losses or damages that the indemnifying shareholders sustain. How can the lawyer discharge the duty of undivided loyalty to each of these groups of clients?

Some of the shareholders may be big players in the target's operations, and the buyer may want their continued employment post-closing. Often obtaining employment agreements with these shareholders and other non-shareholder employees is made a condition of the closing by the buyer. These employment arrangements usually are given to the lawyer to review and negotiate for the prospective employees. Similarly, a buyer usually requires noncompete agreements from some or all of a target's shareholders. The lawyer is also typically asked to review and negotiate these agreements. Substantial compensation and noncompete consideration is often an element of these arrangements. How will the lawyer discharge the duty of undivided loyalty to those shareholders who are only receiving money for their stock in the deal, and who feel that the noncompete consideration other shareholders are to receive is excessive and is being done simply to put a lot more money in those shareholders' pockets? What if nothing is said about the noncompete consideration? Does the lawyer ask the other shareholders if they are comfortable with the noncompete payments? Would a lawyer do that in the discharge of his duty to vigorously represent some clients while giving the other clients his undivided loyalty? What about the lawyer representing all the shareholders in the sale and one shareholder individually in his employment arrangements with the buyer? What if the latter client is prepared to kill the deal rather than sign up a long-term employment contract?

The list goes on and on. The situations are typical and very tough to resolve.

Of course all of these unpleasant conflict situations could be avoided by passing on the chance to represent any of the shareholders. Are you kidding? First of all, long-term personal relationships are involved and no lawyer wants to needlessly toss a paying client overboard— but these conflicts issues need to be analyzed and resolved. Moreover, it is usually perceived to be a benefit to have one or a few lawyers representing one side of a deal rather than each member of a group on one side represented in the deal by a different lawyer or firm. Aside from the added cost, if everyone were to be separately represented on the sell-side, it would probably drive a buyer and its counsel crazy. To the extent the potential clients are willing and able to resolve on their own the issues as to which they have disparate interests, they may be able to instruct common counsel, preferably with written waiver of the resolved conflicts.

Who now are the clients? The target is. Who else? Often the shareholders or at least the majority shareholders will want the lawyer to represent them. What about the employee shareholders, the ex-employee shareholders, the extended members of the majority shareholders' family who own stock, a bank trust department, and possibly a guardian or custodian? As the interests become more diverse, the more difficult the dilemma.

A corollary to identifying the client is defining the scope of the lawyer's responsibilities. The lawyer may be prepared to provide all necessary services to the majority shareholders, but may not wish to do so for each selling shareholder. There may not be time to think through and try to document all of the conflicting interests and obtain appropriate informed consents from these parties. They all may not want to pay the lawyer's reasonable rates. Most significantly, some may have very different and additional interests and agendas in the transaction.

The point in each of these situations is that the separate interests of one or more selling shareholders will likely diverge from those of the rest. The more persons who are clients, whether for all or limited purposes, the more Herculean will be the job of managing the conflicts.

While rules of professional conduct may vary across the country on the issue of how a lawyer should deal with a potential conflict of interest, before undertaking the representation of joint clients whose interests potentially conflict, it might be worthwhile for the lawyer to obtain the informed written consent of such persons to representation, with an acknowledgment of the existence of the potential conflicts, and for the lawyer to consider whether representation may be provided competently and diligently to each affected client.

In some situations, such as where two groups of shareholders who are all clients have disproportionate indemnity obligations, waivers are unlikely to be easy to obtain. In fact, it may not be advisable to even seek waivers for at least a couple of reasons: first, the more parties who are involved, the more exhausting the job of creating and documenting the informed written consent; and second, if further events and circumstances occur in the deal or in the interests of the jointly represented parties, then further waivers may be needed or required. Above all, the lawyer must remain able to provide representation to his clients with undivided loyalty. So, realistically, it is often pretty easy to conclude that it is time to bring in separate counsel to represent one group of sellers in the negotiations. An alternative would be to have all shareholders suffer proportionately the liability for indemnification and hold back a portion of the consideration in an escrow as to which the buyer is limited for recovery. Sometimes, this may not be feasible because it may be appropriate to share the liability disproportionately for certain sellers and not for others.

In determining whether to undertake joint representation, the following practical points should be considered:

Start early—do not wait until the deal is well underway—and have a face-to-face meeting with those you might consider representing so you may judge for yourself, first hand, the people involved, hear them and read their body language. Sometimes there is little warning before the seller's lawyer inherits the prospect of group representation: A merger deal is changed into a stock sale and, in a heartbeat, a single seller becomes a group of sellers. If the lawyer has become familiar with the people early on, it will become much easier to determine how to handle joint representation when it is presented as an alternative.

The scope of representation for each member of the group should be defined. If some selling shareholders have a common issue (the buyer wants noncompetes and employment agreements from them), that group may need to be referred to other counsel to assist and represent them in those arrangements. This could, of course, lead to a cratering of the deal if the employment or noncompete issues become difficult to resolve. But the cratering occurs because the lawyer representing the group advises them to take a certain stand that the buyer refuses to accept and no one backs down. The lawyer who represents the target and the rest of the selling shareholders in the overall sale transaction could never make the same call. To do so would risk some of his clients claiming they had been sold out to protect the interest of other joint clients.

Informed consents to the joint representation will be necessary. Conflict waivers need to be detailed. Will the waivers prove to be detailed enough and/or accurate and fair later? Who bears the cost for the time spent analyzing and drafting the conflict waivers? Who pays the fees and costs for the project? In that connection, the following might be suggested.

- You will continue to bill the target for fees and costs. If the sale craters, the target just takes care of the bill in the ordinary course (hopefully, not just more receivables for the firm).
- If the sale closes, the buyer will likely insist that the selling shareholders pay the fees and costs for the services of the lawyer. At closing, the amount of the lawyer's bills are deducted from the sale proceeds.

When do the conflict waivers get signed? That will depend on the size and nature of the group, the ability of the controlling persons to orchestrate things, and the familiarity of the lawyer with the players. If a lawyer is brought in just to handle the sale, the waiver should be discussed early. After a reasonable time and efforts at follow up, if one or more members of the group have failed to sign the letter, they should be advised in writing that they are not being represented.

It's Nice to Be Appreciated

After a deal successfully closes, there are few things more instantly gratifying to the seller's counsel than to receive a call from the buyer's counsel or a member of the buyer's management asking if the lawyer would be willing to continue doing work for the target or commence working for the buyer.

Since the lawyer just kissed the target goodbye at the closing, this is a welcome call—or is it? At a minimum, the call will require some hard conflict analysis and some political decisions as well.

In principle, the lawyer should be able to accept the new assignment with the following caveats.

The selling shareholders in a stock deal and the seller in an asset deal presumably remain the clients of the lawyer. Some or all of them may be obligated to indemnify the buyer or target for various matters. There is the real possibility of an actual conflict arising between the buyer and target and some or all of these parties. At a minimum there are potential conflicts among these parties. In order to act, the lawyer must obtain the informed consent of all joint clients in this situation.

Perhaps the lawyer could obtain a conflict waiver with the commitment that he will not represent any of the parties if a dispute should arise. The risk is that this might be construed by the former client that the lawyer is "selling out," and is not often seen in practice. It is highly unlikely that the selling shareholders or the seller in an asset deal would agree not to utilize the services of their counsel who advised them generally on the deal and specifically on their indemnification of the buyer. The more common result is that the lawyer will obtain the consent of the sellers and the buyer for limited representation of each under carefully articulated parameters.

Occasionally, counsel who has in the past represented both a parent and the target subsidiary can successfully represent a management buy-out team for the transaction, and continue to represent the target and the parent going forward (on matters other than the acquisition). However, this can be achieved only by obtaining conflict waivers from the parent, the target and the management team members, and by having the parent retain independent counsel to represent it in the transaction. Counsel should make it clear in the conflict waiver that he could not, without appropriate consent, represent any of the parties in disputes arising under the transaction. The possibility for conflicts and confusion can be complicated even further if some of the management participating in the buy-out group are already shareholders, if seller financing will be involved, or if an ESOP or other non-management employee stock ownership is involved or will continue following the transaction.

Acting for Two Parties

A firm can continue to act for opposing existing clients after a negotiated acquisition with the proper written understandings. Our firm had acted as general counsel to both a foreign parent and a number of its United States-based subsidiaries we helped them acquire. When one of the subsidiaries proposed a management buyout, it requested of the parent that our firm represent it for the buyout, its financing, and after the closing. The parent was agreeable on the condition that our firm could continue to represent it after the closing on other matters. The transaction proceeded with separate counsel that had represented another subsidiary acting on behalf of the parent. In the conflict waiver, it was made abundantly clear that our firm could not act for either party if any dispute occurred after the closing involving the buyout. Fortunately only one issue was raised and it was resolved by the principals directly without the use of counsel. Thereafter, our firm continued to represent both companies for many years until both were separately acquired.

As another alternative, can the lawyer obtain from the buyer and target an effective agreement in advance to permit the lawyer to represent the selling shareholders in future disputes and proceedings with the target or buyer arising out of the deal and not to seek to later disqualify the lawyer? How about seeking to obtain the parties' agreement to the lawyer's representation of any of them in existing and future unrelated matters?

An advance waiver is worth considering where multiple party representation is more or less imperative.[9] Even if carefully crafted, when an actual conflict does arise in the future, one or the other parties to the advance waiver may urge or take one or more of the following actions.

- The buyer and target seek to disqualify the lawyer anyway.
- The waiver is litigated with a current client, which is definitely not a happy prospect to contemplate. No one will want to pay the costs or be enthusiastic at the delay involved, including in all likelihood the trier of fact.
- The selling shareholders view the situation as unmitigated disloyalty and hire another lawyer and seek recovery of their expenses from their first lawyer.
- The buyer or target claim the lawyer has confidential information directly involving the issue creating the conflict and the lawyer feels ethically bound, right or wrong, not to fight it and advises all affected clients that the conflict has disabled the lawyer from representing anyone.

The key is to go through the same steps in considering the post-closing representation of the buyer or target as was done in analyzing who could be represented in the target-seller group going into the sale.

While authorities and commentators addressing advance waivers recognize their validity, advance waivers likely will only work when the person giving it is sophisticated and there is adequate disclosure. Some courts have thrown out advance waivers because of their inadequacies under the circumstances, not because advance waivers as a concept are per se invalid.[10]

I Just Wanted to Help

Another tough call arises in the situation where some employees have been referred to you to assist them in negotiating their employment and noncompetition arrangements with a buyer. They may also be selling or exchanging shares they own in the target.

Your referral source is perhaps a friend. He has probably gone out on a limb with his client saying something to the effect that the employees need separate representation and the lawyer to whom I am referring the employees is a good guy and "won't make a mountain out of a molehill." (You can assume that the statements like this were made, because that is what clients are often told in these circumstances.)

In meeting with the employees and in defining the scope of representation in an engagement letter, do you say you are only retained to advise, review, and negotiate the employment and noncompete agreements and say nothing more or expressly disavow anything else? Or do you specifically disclaim any responsibility for such things as reviewing price, the representations, and other terms of the transaction? Do you nevertheless have an obligation to look into other aspects of the transaction? One would think not, unless it is understood that the scope of the representation is meant to be broader. What if one of the employees asks for your view about specific terms of the acquisition? Since these clients are owed your undivided loyalty and vigorous representation, you may at least need to discuss the alternatives that could be pursued by you on their behalf to raise these other issues if requested to do so. It may be the last referral for a while from your friend.

Other Relationships with the Client

Other situations that can pose conflicts of interest between the lawyer and a client include: the lawyer's firm owns securities of the target; the lawyer holds an office, such as secretary, in the target; or the lawyer's firm is owed a substantial amount by the target for services and costs billed in the normal course—an unintended, but very real investment of the firm in the client. These circumstances usually will trigger an analysis as to whether a conflict waiver by the client should be sought.

What do you do about firm investments in the target, firm persons acting as an officer for the target, or the big account receivable? The officer issue may be most simply resolved by a resignation. The existence of the other situations represent firm economic interests in the target that should be disclosed and acknowledged by the parties who become common clients. Most state professional rules require this kind of disclosure and acknowledgement.[11]

Documenting the Engagement

Having identified the client in the deal and analyzed the conflicts, it is important to establish and document an understanding with that client about the terms of the representation before starting work on an M&A transaction, particularly if you have not represented that client before in a transaction of this type. You need to understand your client's expectations with respect to your role in the transaction, and the client needs to understand how you will fulfill those expectations. Whose interests will you represent in the transaction? What will your role be? How will you staff the transaction? How will you be paid for your services? Is there a clear and common understanding by lawyer and client of the answers to these questions at the outset of the transaction? All these matters should be addressed between lawyer and client and appropriately documented.[12]

The terms of the legal engagement can best be reflected in a letter. In the case of a new client, the rules of professional conduct in many states will require, or at least recommend, a written communication regarding the fee.[13] The lawyer may want to consider an engagement letter for an existing client, particularly if the type of representation, the basis for the fee or some other term of engagement differs from past representation of that client. If a conflict exists with respect to representation of the client, the engagement letter can also serve to evidence the client's conflict waiver as well as any limitations on the scope of the lawyer's future representation of the client. It will serve to avoid any future misunderstanding, particularly if the engagement is on terms that differ from those associated with past representation. An engagement letter is also useful in defining the scope of representation and, perhaps more importantly, what is not within the scope of representation.

Identification of the Client

As previously discussed, there may be a number of parties other than the seller, target, and buyer that have interests requiring representation in an M&A transaction. To avoid confusion, you should make sure the client understands whom you are representing, as well as whom you are not representing. If there are related parties in the transaction that you are not representing, it is equally important to make sure they understand that you are not representing their interests. For example, if the lawyer is representing a target and its parent in a divestiture, the target's management needs to understand clearly that the lawyer is not representing their interests and that they should consider retaining separate counsel. It may be prudent to have this understanding acknowledged in writing. An example of an engagement letter where counsel is representing the shareholders in an acquisition, but some shareholders have special counsel for their employment and noncompete agreements, is attached as Appendix 2-A.

Often it is deemed expedient by a client that consists of a group, such as a group of shareholders, to use a single member as the point person or representative for communicating with counsel. This can alleviate and expedite communication issues with a group. If this technique is to be employed, it is worth considering the following: document the arrangement in the engagement letter, specify what communications between counsel and the representative should go to the entire group and how communications will occur, and deal with the authority of the representative to make decisions on behalf of the group. Also worth considering is whether or how often counsel should take steps to confirm that this procedure is working.

Role of Counsel

To ensure that the client's needs and expectations are satisfied, you will also need to reach an understanding on your role in the transaction. The level of a deal lawyer's involvement can range widely depending on the client's needs and preferences.[14] At one extreme, a lawyer could manage and oversee the entire transaction, coordinating the work of all the other professionals involved. At the other extreme, the lawyer's role could be limited to simply preparing and revising documentation as requested by the client.

Engagement letters represent important bulwarks against claims that the lawyer failed to protect or handle something that later costs the client. An example is carving out who is responsible for the tax work on the deal. If the engagement letter states that the seller's CPA or some other identified counsel is handling tax issues, a later problem in the tax area should be avoided because you were careful to narrow the scope of your representation. If the engagement letter is silent as to who will be responsible for those issues and there is a later tax-related problem for which the client sustains damage, as hard as it is to believe, the CPA may well try to shift the problem to you. The client will not care as long as it is made whole and the problem is solved.

Payment for Services

The arrangement for the payment of the lawyer's fees will be of paramount interest to the client and lawyer. Fee arrangements for M&A transactions can be structured in a variety of ways. Payment for services can be based upon the typical arrangement of the time spent by professionals at their usual hourly rates. This arrangement presents little risk for counsel because it ensures that you will be compensated for your services regardless of the outcome of the transaction.

Alternatively, an agreement can be reached on a fixed fee. This provides an opportunity to receive a higher fee than one based upon hourly rates if the lawyer can provide the services in an efficient manner. However, it also presents a substantial risk that circumstances and events outside the lawyer's control (such as the emergence of a competing offer or protracted negotiations) could result in the fixed fee being substantially less than the fee that would have been payable based the time spent by professionals at their usual hourly rates. In a fixed fee arrangement, increases or decreases should be considered in the event that the level of services required in the transaction differs significantly from that on which the fee was based.

One variation of the fixed fee is to provide estimates or fixed fees for each of the significant stages of a deal. This gives the client an appreciation of its economic exposure if the deal craters at various stages and makes it easier to pinpoint where and why an estimate got off the mark.

Another alternative arrangement is a discount in fees if the transaction is not successfully completed as well as a premium if it is completed. This arrangement can provide an incentive with respect to the outcome of the transaction that can at times diverge or be perceived to diverge from the client's own interests. For instance, if the lawyer discovers something material while conducting due diligence for a buyer that suggests it would be in the client's best interest not to pursue the transaction, the lawyer's own economic interests differ from the client's interests. With this type of fee arrangement, you and your client must be comfortable that you can provide objective advice under all circumstances.

Regardless of the fee arrangement selected, the lawyer and client should agree on the basis for the payment for legal services at the beginning of the transaction and spell it out clearly in writing. The lawyer also needs to reach a clear understanding with the client on reimbursement of expenses in the transaction and who should be initially responsible for significant costs.

Updating

It is probably a good idea to review the engagement letter often. It should be updated from time to time to reflect changes in the transaction itself and the related terms of the engagement. For example, the scope of the engagement may shift. One or more of the selling shareholders may decide to hire separate counsel, or the lawyer may be asked to examine new issues that fall outside of the carefully crafted provisions on the scope of the representation in the original letter. Updating the engagement letter also may offer the opportunity to reflect changes in the lawyer's hourly rates or billing arrangements.

Communications with the Client

Let us turn to a topic that probably seems so obvious that it is a wonder anyone would take much time to say anything about it—communications with the client. And, by the way, what does this have to do with ethics? Rules of professional conduct uniformly dictate that lawyers communicate with their client.[15]

This topic starts with a pretty startling statistic: failure by lawyers to communicate with their clients is a major source of client complaints about lawyers to bar associations, malpractice claims, and disciplinary proceedings. Another interesting, if not unsettling, observation is that serious post-closing claims for indemnification seem far more frequent than was the case a decade ago. The reasons behind this phenomena are not as important as the logical fallout—

the client against whom an indemnification claim is brought is likely to blame the lawyer for not protecting the client in the deal: "That is what I paid you all those fees for, wasn't it?"

It will help immeasurably if the lawyer can produce letters, e-mails, or memos to the client and to the file that have memorialized important events and circumstances, decisions, significant advice, or limitations on scope of representation, and instances where significant rejections of advice occurred during the transaction.

The suggestion is not to flood the client and paper the file with "CYA" letters and memos, but there are events in every deal that rise to the level of being significant, and documenting these in some fashion can be important in the future.

Keeping the client informed happens in many ways in the course of a deal. There will likely be many meetings and telephone conferences where the client is present. There also will be numerous instances where substantial negotiations and the preparation of documents will occur outside of the client's presence. Tell the client about it—e-mail has made this a cinch. Offer the client the opportunity to receive copies of all drafts you send or receive as well as other communications.

Of course, detailed invoices also communicate what has been done. It is the experience of many lawyers, however, that these detailed invoices wind up where most other invoices do—at the "bottom of the heap" so to speak—and are not read at all once the client has seen the total amount due. A cautionary note: Consider the detailed descriptions of the work undertaken in the invoices, keeping in mind that, for a business client, those invoices may go into the accounts payable department and be subject to examination by accountants, the Internal Revenue Service, and others, possibly affecting reliance on the attorney-client privilege. Some lawyers include both a summary invoice, showing the fees and detailing only the costs, and a detailed invoice, with the summary going to accounts payable and the detailed invoice being maintained as an attorney-client communication. Some lawyers provide only the summary.

The Attorney-Client Privilege and Similar Protections

One of the more troublesome problems related to the disclosure of confidential information during the due diligence process is how to provide the other party with enough information for it to make a meaningful evaluation without waiving any work-product, attorney-client, or similar protections.[16]

The work-product doctrine protects the work product, notes, research and written analysis prepared by an attorney in anticipation of litigation or for trial.[17] In most jurisdictions, a waiver of the work-product protection can occur where the protected communications are disclosed in a manner that "has substantially increased the opportunity for potential adversaries to obtain the information."[18]

The attorney-client privilege generally protects confidential communications (whether written, oral, or in another form) between a client and its attorney. Any disclosure of these communications to a third party who is not within the group as to whom the privilege extends will waive the privilege as to the entire subject matter of the disclosure. There does not appear to be a consensus on how to balance the buyer's reasonable request for adequate disclosure (concerning a lawsuit pending against the seller, for example) against the potential waiver of the privilege in the context of an acquisition transaction. Some parties utilize a joint defense agreement, but there is some question whether this will be effective to preserve the privilege. At the end of the day, if the buyer concludes that he will not do the deal unless the seller waives the privilege as to a particular matter, then the seller will have to make a business decision whether to waive the privilege or lose the deal. *See* MAPA § 12.6 for a discussion of this subject. The following discussion will be devoted primarily to the attorney-client privilege, which is where most of the problems arise in the context of an M&A transaction.

Who Holds the Privilege?

If the same lawyer has represented the target in the past and now represents the target as well as the selling shareholders, how does the attorney-client privilege work? If the target is to remain a client (although counsel is also representing the selling shareholders), and be billed and pay for services for convenience up to closing, then the engagement letter should make it clear that the billing arrangement is for convenience, and the communications and dealings between counsel and the selling shareholders are intended to be confidential, protected by the attorney-client privilege, and not subject to disclosure to anyone, including the target, without an appropriate waiver. The form of engagement letter attached as Appendix 2-A contains an approach to this issue.

In an asset acquisition, the seller holds the privilege both before and, in some states, even after the closing. In a stock acquisition, the buyer will own the target after closing. Does this mean that the buyer can require the lawyer for the target, who also represented the selling shareholders, to reveal the deep dark secrets about the target in hopes of finding indemnity claims against the sellers or to disclose all conversations and written communications among the lawyer, target and selling shareholders pertaining to a matter for which indemnification is claimed? The same problem can arise where the transaction is structured as a merger, since the privilege of the target that is no longer in existence belongs to the successor corporation.[19] Would it help to resign and disengage as counsel for the target concurrent with closing?

Since at best this is a murky area, consider the approach taken in the form of letter attached as Appendix 2-B, which is an attempt to resolve this issue with the informed written consent of the buyer, as well as to provide for the future representation of the selling shareholders in connection with any indemnification claims brought on behalf of the target (which is usually made part of the buyers' indemnitee group under most indemnification provisions) and buyer against the selling shareholders. The approach taken in Appendix 2-B, coupled with a written disengagement of the target effective as of the closing, may enable the lawyer to represent the seller shareholders post-closing in disputes with the target and buyer.

Unfortunately, there are few bright lines here for guidance. Often the only brightness is the headlight of the approaching train, called litigation, disqualification, and trouble, if protection of the attorney-client privilege and the ability to represent the sellers post-closing in disputes are not considered at the outset and made part of initial understanding with the buyer. The letter of intent stage is not too early to raise and deal with these issues, or they may be resolved in the acquisition agreement or left to document by some form of writing during the pendency of the deal. Flagging the need to resolve these issues and obtaining an agreement as to how they will be approached and resolved early in the deal, and before the sellers have lost precious leverage, is wise.

Preserving the Privilege

Preserving the attorney-client privilege is a paramount goal in any engagement.[20] It is a challenge in the acquisition context since so many discussions and communications occur and are often regularly documented and distributed to a wide array of participants in the deal.

Care must be taken to consider and recognize those communications that are intended to be subject to the privilege. The reason is obvious. Later if there are disputes related to the transaction, much of what took place in exchanges between a party and its lawyer could be significant in substantiating an opponents' claim or demonstrating conduct or intent helpful to an opponent's case.

In most instances it only takes one small foul-up to forfeit the privilege entirely. So it is important to consider going somewhat overboard in taking steps to protect the privilege.

Here are some of the techniques used:

Explain the privilege. The lawyer should consider explaining the privilege to the client. The explanation might add that communications in writing will be appropriately labeled and that, to protect against loss of the privilege, written and oral communications should not be shared with anyone other than those to whom the privilege extends without discussing it with the lawyer. It may be a good idea to document this kind of advice in a writing to the client.

Use a label. All written communications between counsel and client should be labeled with something like "Confidential Privileged Attorney-Client Communication."

Limit access. Access to privileged information should be limited only to persons as to whom the privilege extends, most likely only senior executives of the receiving party. Accountants and investment bankers will be considered to be outside the group. Consequently, they should not participate in conference calls or meetings during which privileged information is discussed.

Take a break. In meetings and telephone conferences, if a confidential communication between the lawyer and client appears necessary or is requested, adjourn or take a break and converse in a secure location.

Make a note. It is a good idea to note the fact that an all-hands meeting or conference call was recessed while this private conversation occurred (which would help later if it is asserted the lawyer and client discussed the matter at the meeting or in the call, which if true would blow the privilege).

Other situations where preserving the attorney-client privilege becomes challenging include those where:

- a party is conducting due diligence and wants to see all the information on pending litigation; and
- disclosures are being prepared by a party for the acquisition agreement or schedules to qualify the representations of that party.

In the first situation, the client's files may contain candid and frank evaluations by counsel of the pending litigation, indicating that the client faces serious trouble. In the second situation, the party must make enough disclosure to avoid being accused later of having failed to provide sufficient information in order that the disclosed material not be misleading.

In each situation, assume the deal is not yet done and may not eventually close. Disclosure of attorney-client privileged information could destroy the privilege not only as to the shared information, but potentially any other privileged information that involves the same subject matter as the shared information. This is obviously a terrible result if the other party in the pending litigation learns of the disclosure or the lawyer is faced with identifying and withholding attorney-client privileged information in a document production or deposition. This risk is magnified if, as a result of the disclosure, the buyer decides to terminate the discussions and walk away from the deal.

In these situations, the buyer's and seller's interests usually coincide. The seller cannot afford to lose the attorney-client privilege in the litigation. The buyer, who is by definition interested in acquiring the target, does not want the target to have an adverse result in the litigation and is equally interested in not having the seller waive the privilege.

If, as is typical, it is the seller with the issue of how detailed a disclosure must be, the situation often is resolved by the buyer magnanimously allowing the seller off the disclosure hook as long as the seller indemnifies the buyer against any fall out from the litigation. If it is the buyer with the disclosure issue, it may be advisable for the seller to review the letters between the buyer's lawyers and accountants, any correspondence between the buyer and its lenders and the buyer's SEC filings, if any.

Sometimes it is possible to arrange for a visit with a party's lawyers who are handling the matter and who may be often able to communicate a great deal about the matter without imperiling the attorney-client privilege.

Although there is generally a commonality of interests, buyers sometimes will not be satisfied by limited disclosure and will want to acquire complete information as to pending or anticipated litigation in order to properly assess the risk. The parties may then want to take advantage of the "common interest doctrine." This is a doctrine developed by the courts that provides an exception where the disclosing party and the receiving party have a common legal interest, such as where they are involved in or anticipate joint litigation. However, to come within the exception, "the key consideration is that the nature of the legal interest be identical, not similar, and be legal, not solely commercial."[21]

The application of this doctrine depends on a facts and circumstances analysis, but it appears that critical to this analysis are the steps taken to ensure that the shared communications remain confidential.[22] In addition to the general techniques for maintaining the privilege, it has been suggested that the disclosure be covered by a specific agreement that evidences the common interest and stipulates a common plan for litigation or at least a confidentiality agreement that requires, among other things, that the information be maintained in perpetuity, that the disclosing party be notified immediately about any disclosure that is legally required to be made, and that the receiving party be obligated to assent the privilege and cooperate in attempting to obtain a protective order against disclosure.[23] Consideration might also be given to the parties entering into a joint defense agreement to support the common interest exception. This type of agreement would show that the disclosures were made in the course of formulating a common legal strategy.

Another technique used to cloak important disclosures with the attorney-client privilege is through the use of experts. It is not unusual for a target to have one or more existing situations relating to its business, the details of which ultimately will have to be disclosed to the buyer regardless of who may wind up with financial responsibility for it after closing. Such necessary disclosures often relate to the physical condition of improved real estate and environmental matters.

If there is to be an investigation into the situation, having it done by an expert (e.g., a structural engineer or environmental consultant) hired by the lawyer (with the understanding the costs will be reimbursed by the client) should result in the information developed being covered by the work-product protection[24] and, when reported to the client, by the attorney-client privilege. If the client hired the expert directly, there would be no privilege protecting the information produced by the expert.

Even in the sacrosanct region of attorney-client privilege, the best laid plans may go awry: litigation fall out from an acquisition may involve allegations of fraud, and the court may invoke the fraud/crime exception to the privilege obviating it. Moreover, if a party goes into bankruptcy, its trustee may waive the privilege if it furthers the interests of the trustee in the administration of the estate.

Communication Issues and the Privilege

While on the subject of the attorney-client privilege, there are several communications-related topics worth remembering: the use of e-mail, the misdirected communication, and the use of cellular and cordless telephones and facsimile transmission.

Rules of professional conduct generally impose obligations on attorneys to maintain the confidences and confidential information of the client, which are usually subject to exceptions of various sorts. It is, however, almost universally the case that the disclosure of a client's confidences and confidential information obtained by the attorney from the client, even inadvertently, may cause the loss of the attorney-client privilege. This disclosure can occur in many different ways.

What Is Metadata? Why Should You Worry About It?

When a document is created in a computer, information about the document or the file itself is automatically generated and may be transferred with the computer file or document when it is e-mailed.[25] This information is called metadata or hidden data. It can appear in documents created with Microsoft Word, Excel, Power Point, and even in Adobe Acrobat pdfs and WordPerfect files.

Metadata can contain information on changes made to a document, including deletions (showing them), the names of persons who worked on the document, the number of revisions, its origin, and editorial comments like "Do we want to take a hard position on this?" that may have been inserted by someone reviewing the document and do not become part of the text.

Much of this information is potentially confidential client information, including clients unrelated to the current document but related to an earlier version that is being used as a template or form. Comments included in metadata may reveal admissions, attorney work product, privileged communications, or just plain embarrassing commentary.

Metadata can be stripped from a Microsoft Word document by translating it into rich text, pdf, or WordPerfect format. Microsoft offers a tool to strip metadata that may be downloaded from Microsoft's website. Other programs are available that purport to remove metadata.

Bar associations have only begun to warm to the metadata situation. The New York State Bar Association on Professional Ethics opined in 2001 that lawyers should not surreptitiously look at another's metadata.[26] Is it okay, then, to tell your opponent you are going to look at it? Is it a failure to act in a client's best interest not to look if there is any metadata in a document? Is it a violation of ethical rules to put bogus information into metadata? In 2004, the New York State Bar Association on Professional Ethics went a step further and opined that lawyers have a duty to use reasonable care when transmitting documents by e-mail to prevent the disclosure of metadata containing client confidences or secrets.[27]

> Maybe the best answer is to be aware of the risks that metadata poses and make sure you take advantage of technological advances in addressing these risks.

At the risk of evidencing paranoia, consider the following: unencrypted e-mail can be intercepted and read. Cellular telephone and cordless telephone calls can be intercepted. Facsimile transmission can be misdirected or intercepted. Confidential or private facsimiles may be sent to a general office number and read by any number of people. All of these forms of communication can be sent to the wrong place (or to a nonsecure location), except for telephone calls where realization usually would occur immediately that a wrong number was reached. But sometimes a voice mail system is not obviously the wrong one and messages could be left resulting in serious later consequences.

Now the bad news. The lawyer mistakenly sending the communication must tell the lawyer's client. If harm results to the client from the missent communication, it may be malpractice. A plaintiff's lawyer worth his salt could have a field day with this type of scenario.

Does the lawyer on the receiving end of such a communication have a duty to disclose the fact of receipt to the lawyer's client? How about the substance of what was received? Common sense would seem to say that you cannot use the information or inform your client about it. However, this is far from settled at present. Courts in many jurisdictions have considered the issue of whether an inadvertent transmission of communications that are intended to be confidential is admissible as evidence, will result in the loss of the attorney-client privilege and should be ignored by the recipient. They usually take one of the following three approaches to determining whether the disclosure waives any privilege (and, consequently, results in the potential admissibility of the subject of the disclosure into evidence):

- The "lenient approach" whereby the privilege must be knowingly waived, and the determination of inadvertence ends the analysis.[28]
- The "strict approach," sometimes called the "absolute waiver rule," whereby any document produced, whether inadvertently or otherwise, loses its privileged status upon production.[29]
- The "middle" or "moderate" approach, which requires a court to make fact-specific waiver determinations on a case-by-case basis.[30] Courts applying this approach consider the reasonableness of the precautions taken to avoid inadvertent disclosure; the time taken to rectify the error; the scope of the discovery in the particular case; the extent of the disclosure; and whether the overriding interests of fairness and justice would be served by absolving the party of its error. This approach is the majority rule.

In summary, the law relating to the privileged status of inadvertently disclosed confidential information varies significantly among jurisdictions. Given that, the lawyer must check local law. And in representing a client in an interstate transaction, the issues to be analyzed are compounded.

Besides being useful, a communication protocol for a deal helps establish that counsel took measures to preserve the attorney-client privilege and to carry out a client's communication requirements. Apart from listing all the players and their contact information, the contact list might contain specific communication instructions for the various parties. It is worth underscoring the point that a communication protocol for a deal probably should be an early item covered with the client.

If there is going to be a communication protocol, then it is especially important to identify the telephone numbers to which facsimiles should be (or must be) sent. It is equally important to ensure that every lawyer, paralegal and staff person working on the matter is well informed of any communication protocol and especially of correct facsimile numbers. Nothing will spoil a client relationship faster than failing to observe the client's wishes and instructions on communications. A missent fax (and many lawyers have had that experience) is usually an egregious act in the eyes of a client.

Making the Blood Run Cold

We were in the process of selling a third generation family-owned business to a private equity fund. The client was a classic Midwestern manufacturing business, in which the president sat in the middle of a huge sea of desks. There were no office walls dividing any of the administrative employees. Confidentiality was an obvious concern (this is before the days of e-mail), so the standing instructions between my firm, my secretary and the president of the client was that we were only to fax documents to him if he was able to walk immediately over to the sole facsimile machine and wait for the document to come off the machine. If he was unavailable, or could not be contacted, the facsimile was not to be delivered.

The sale of the business took almost a year to complete. Toward the end of the process, we prepared a document analyzing the labor force for the client post closing and the anticipated affects of the acquisition upon the various categories and compensation rates of employees.

My client called me later in the day, expressing his extreme dissatisfaction at what had taken place. He was sitting at his desk in the middle of the office, on the telephone, when he noticed a collection of employees had gathered around the facsimile machine. He was curious as to what the commotion was about, until three employees walked to his desk and dropped our letter, which detailed the implications of the transaction and its effects upon the labor force, onto his desk. The document had been faxed without following the pre-clearance protocol that had been in place for months.

Our relationship managed to survive this episode and this client and the acquiring private equity fund, have become among the firm's top clients after the transaction closed. But, longstanding attorney/client relationships can easily be damaged or destroyed by such a mistake.

Negotiation Ethics

In the often protracted process of negotiating a deal, there are three scenarios that are frequently repeated and give rise to knotty ethical issues: the conduct of negotiations by the principals without attorneys, a client lying or otherwise misleading the other side, and the lawyer discovering that the other side has missed something significant.

Avoiding the Lawyers

One of the principals of a party calls and speaks directly to a principal of the other party in an effort to resolve some important issue that may be holding up negotiations. Such a call usually occurs outside the times when the negotiations normally take place, and its occurrence is heavily dependent on the sophistication and preferences of the client. The caller gratuitously offers this as a chance for the business people to come to an agreement on issues that the lawyers have been unable to resolve or are otherwise fouling up.

When the client on the receiving end of the call cheerfully advises his lawyer he had a call from his counterpart and they were able to resolve the issue, it usually takes his lawyer awhile to come down from the ceiling, explain to the client what may have occurred and plan the repartee to the other lawyer. If the client suggested the approach, there is certainly nothing wrong with a principal-to-principal telephone or in-person conversation. Indeed, such an approach may be just what is needed to get over a thorny issue. The situation is more problematic if the instigator of the call is one of the lawyers.

At one end of the spectrum, a lawyer may suggest to the client that he may want to call or meet with his counterpart to discuss approaches to resolving an issue that has negotiations bogged down. That is to be contrasted with a situation at the other end of the spectrum where the lawyer suggests that the client contact the counterpart businessperson to discuss an issue having significant legal implications and provides the client with a script containing legal and other arguments for use in seeking to convince the other businessperson to adopt the client's position. This might include suggestions that opposing counsel has a lack of experience, has misapplied a legal principle or does not understand the financial aspects of the issue—all or any of which the client is prepared to clear up. It could also include a suggestion that the client, if successful, document the agreement by exchanging e-mails with the counterpart. This fairly extreme, but unfortunately not uncommon, tactic is sometimes called "ambush coaching."

Coaching a client to talk with the other businessperson and seek agreement on an issue, where he is known to be represented by a lawyer, and without getting that other lawyer's approval, may not only be bad form, it may also be a violation of the rules of professional conduct.[31] The reason is simple—there really is no difference between a lawyer communicating with another lawyer's client outside the other lawyer's presence directly or through a coached android.

To reiterate, a lawyer suggesting that his client contact the counterpart on the other side to try to find and reach a middle ground on some issue is fine and, if the principals are up to it, it is often a way through a problem that has stopped progress in the negotiations. To avoid criticism and hard feelings, even in this situation, one should consider first securing approval of the other party's lawyer.[32]

Is the Client Lying?

The next situation is where the client flat out lies to the other side or says things that are intentionally misleading and the client's lawyer knows it or finds out about it later. What is the lawyer to do?

Here the rules of professional conduct in various states answer that question, but the answer differs on what is expected of counsel. In most jurisdictions and under the Model Rules, there are exceptions to the obligation of a lawyer to maintain information relating to representation of a client in confidence. Model Rule 1.6 permits a lawyer to reveal information of a client to the extent the lawyer reasonably believes necessary to, among other things, "prevent the client from committing a crime or fraud that is reasonably certain to result in substantial injury to the financial interests or property of another and in furtherance of which the client has used or is using the lawyer's services." Disclosure is not required under these circumstances, but the lawyer may not counsel the client or assist the client in conduct the lawyer knows is criminal or fraudulent. In such circumstances, the lawyer may have the right to withdraw from the representation under Model Rule 1.16. A few states require the lawyer to blow the whistle on the client.[33] Under Model Rule 1.6, if the lawyer only discovers the crime or fraud after the fact, he may also disclose information to the extent he reasonably believes necessary to prevent, mitigate, or rectify substantial injury to the financial interests or property of another that has resulted from the crime or fraud.

But the client says it was only "puffery"—only exaggeration. The lawyer should warn the client about such conduct and its potential for leading to dire consequences in the transaction and beyond. One precept worth remembering is, "If you always tell the truth, you will never have to remember what you said."[34] Now, hopefully, the lawyer is very concerned by a lying client and is all over the client as to the possible consequences of lying or creating a misapprehension, as well as how repugnant and dangerous it is to engage in that type of conduct. But if the client is unrelenting, unrepentant, and refuses to clear up the matter by a disclosure to the other side, the lawyer under the professional conduct rules of some states may be unable to say anything, even if the conduct is an ongoing course of criminal or fraudulent conduct by the client.[35]

The Opposing Client Makes a Big Mistake

Basically, the same rules apply where it becomes apparent the other side has missed something important due to a misleading statement or action by you or your client. Common sense screams out that where, because of a misrepresentation by a party, the other side has missed something significant or thinks something is true, the lawyer should encourage the client to clear up the misapprehension or misrepresentation. If the client refuses, about the only way out is to resign.

Lawyer Conduct

This discussion has so far focused primarily on client conduct that creates an ethical dilemma. But what about the lawyer? A lawyer should never lie, seek an advantage by creating a misapprehension or affirmatively mislead the other side and should never knowingly assist a client in that type of conduct. This can be actionable civilly,[36] as well as being malpractice and violative of the rules of professional conduct.

When all is said and done, while a lawyer may be known as tough and smart, it is being known as a straight shooter, honorable, and of the highest ethics that really count in what kind of a reputation a lawyer has among his peers and within the business community. Those who practice extensively in the M&A area are relatively few in number, and consequently it is not at all unusual to repeatedly deal with some of the same lawyers, accountants and investment bankers. If for no other reason, that is why one's reputation is so very important. It does not take much of a misstep to irreparably damage that reputation and adversely affect working relationships with others engaged in the practice.

Practice in Other States

The past decade has witnessed a proliferation of law firms and lawyers practicing and serving clients across state lines and across national boundaries. The expansions of client businesses and law firm consolidations have driven this phenomena. Lawyers want to continue to serve their clients for economic as well as other valid reasons. There have always been methods for litigators to be admitted by motion to practice in connection with a case pending in a court in another state, but until recently nothing had been done about transactional lawyers practicing across state lines.

A wake-up call came about from a case in 1998 in which the California Supreme Court held a lawyer not licensed in California could not recover legal fees from a client for work performed by the lawyer in that state.[37] This has led to some fall out, some good, some not so good.

A reaction to this case came out of the work of the ABA Ethics 2000 Commission and later the ABA Commission on Multijurisdictional Practice in the form of Model Rules 5.5 and 8.5, which were adopted in 2002. Model Rule 5.5(c)(4) permits a lawyer admitted in another jurisdiction to provide transactional legal services on a temporary basis in the subject jurisdiction that arise out of or are reasonably related to the lawyer's practice in a jurisdiction in which the lawyer is admitted. For corporate counsel, the rule also permits transactional legal services to be provided to the lawyer's employer or its organizational affiliates. Model Rule 8.5 deals with disciplinary authority and the choice of law for rules of professional conduct in situations involving practice in other states.

Other states have begun to take notice that lawyers who are not licensed are practicing law within these states. So far 15 states have adopted the Model Rules or a variation of them, and a number of other states have initiated reviews of the ABA's multijurisdictional practice provisions. Since the Model Rules are not universally adopted, care must be taken to consider the implications of representing a client in a deal where significant activity takes place in a state where the lawyer is not licensed—and given a large deal, this could wind up being in several states.[38] The next step will be to identify circumstances in which lawyers from other countries can practice temporarily in the U.S., as several states have already done.

What are some of the ethical issues this unsettled state of affairs presents? Two obvious ones come to light. First, a sophisticated, unscrupulous client might seek to avoid paying for services based on the fact that its lawyer performed services for it in a particular state without being licensed. One solution to this difficulty is to associate local counsel. Model Rule 5.4(c)(1) permits a lawyer admitted in a jurisdiction to provide legal services on a temporary basis in the subject jurisdiction that are undertaken in association with a lawyer who is admitted to practice in that jurisdiction and who actively participates in the matter.

A second more profound set of issues could result in a lawyer having two diametrically opposed sets of rules of professional conduct apply to his conduct, which could leave a lawyer with a Hobson's choice of deciding where he had the least liability in violating one set of professional rules or the other.

What is a lawyer to do when a client makes a misrepresentation that is relied on by the other side and two separate professional standards could apply? Say, for example, that the state in which the lawyer is admitted imposes a duty to maintain client confidences inviolate, and the lawyer is performing services for a client within a state that has adopted the Model Rules. Under the one set of rules of professional conduct he cannot and must not do anything to reveal client confidential information. All the lawyer can do is quietly withdraw. To act otherwise could subject the lawyer to professional discipline and malpractice liability. On the other hand, the Model Rules may require that the lawyer clear up the matter or affect a noisy withdrawal. Failure to do so could create liability to the parties in the transaction, who claim they relied on the misrepresentation and that the lawyer owes them a duty to clear up the issue as any lawyer licensed in that state would have to do.[39]

As in most endeavors, advance planning will help prepare the lawyer and client for a deal that will be conducted over state lines. The lawyer should become familiar with local rules and, where practical and cost justified, perhaps local counsel should be retained to assist and advise. And "know thy client," which is a uniformly good rule to follow, seems like an especially good thing to observe in this area.

APPENDIX 2-A
Form of Engagement Letter for Joint Representation

[*Date*]
[*Names and addresses of selling shareholders*]

Re: **Agreement for Legal Services**

Dear Ladies and Gentlemen:

By way of background, we have been asked by Mr. [*name*] (the "Seller Representative") to represent the interests of all shareholders (the "Sellers") of [*target*] (the "Company") in the possible sale of their shares to [*buyer*] (the "Buyer"), including the negotiation of an acquisition agreement to effect such sale and to perform such services as are customary and necessary to complete the sale on the terms and subject to the conditions set forth in the acquisition agreement and related documents (the "Transaction"). Initially, we set up our engagement as between our law firm (the "Firm") and the Company for convenience in tracking and invoicing our services.

As you are aware, Messrs. [*names of shareholders*] (the "Continuing Employees") have consulted with [*name of attorney*] of [*name of law firm*] for the purpose of receiving advice concerning their respective (and prospective) employment and noncompete arrangements (collectively, the "Ancillary Agreements") with the Buyer. By signing this letter, the Continuing Employees confirm that they did consult with [*name of attorney*] (or other counsel not related to this Firm), and that they have not received nor do they expect to receive any advice concerning the Ancillary Agreements from this Firm.

By signing this letter, each Seller confirms receipt of copies of drafts of the acquisition agreement, and related agreements and exhibits, to have read them and to have had an opportunity to meet with lawyers of this Firm to discuss and ask questions concerning the drafts of the acquisition agreement, and these related agreements (other than the Ancillary Agreements) and exhibits. We are now at a point where we must clearly document our engagement with each of you.

We are very pleased to have the opportunity to be of service to each of you, and appreciate your decision to have retained us in this matter. We believe a clear understanding regarding the terms of representation is fundamental to a good relationship between attorney and client. Accordingly, this letter will confirm the terms of our representation of you in this matter, and we will ask that, if these terms are acceptable, you sign and return a copy of this letter to indicate your agreement to them.

Joint representation issues

To the extent any of you provides us information relevant to the common interests of all shareholders, we will disclose it to the Seller Representative. Otherwise, it is understood and agreed by each of you that we will not be under any obligation to any of you to divulge confidential information relating to any of you to the others. No party signing this letter will request that we make any disclosure of one client's confidential information to the other. However, by signing this letter each of you acknowledges and understands that California Evidence Code Section 962 provides as follows:

> Where two or more clients have retained or consulted a lawyer upon a matter of common interest, none of them, nor the successor in interest of any of them, may claim a privilege under this article as to a communication made in the course of that relationship when such communication is offered in a civil proceeding between one of such clients (or his successor in interest) and another of such clients (or his successor in interest).

Thus, if there later is a civil proceeding between any of you about the subject of our joint engagement, the attorney-client privilege may be unavailable to prevent the disclosure of communications made to us as your common lawyers in a matter of common interest. We have not performed any particular analysis of the Section 962 issue, however, because such an analysis would require attempting to predict disputes that might in the future arise among you.

The simultaneous representation of each of you raises the potential of our representing conflicting interests of more than one client. Rule 3-310 of the Rules of Professional Conduct of the State Bar of California provides, in part, as follows*:

(C) A member shall not, without the informed written consent of each client:

   (1) Accept representation of more than one client in a matter in which the interests of the clients potentially conflict; or

   (2) Accept or continue representation of more than one client in a matter in which the interest of the clients actually conflict; . . .

                         *   *   *

(E) A member shall not, without the informed written consent of the client or former client, accept employment adverse to the client or former client where, by reason of the representation of the client or former client, the member has obtained confidential information material to the employment.

In order to concurrently represent the interests of each of you with respect to the Transaction, by signing this letter you each acknowledge that (i) our current representation of Mr. [*name*] and the Company in matters in which none of the other Sellers or Continuing Employees are directly involved does not cause an actual conflict of interest, and (ii) we may continue to represent Mr. [*name*] or members of his family and the Company in all matters, so long as such representation does not require our Firm to represent any of you in a situation in which any of your interests are actually in conflict with Mr. [*name*] or members of his family or the Company. Further, each of you acknowledges that at the termination of this joint engagement, Mr. [*name*] or members of his family or the Company may choose to engage the Firm as counsel in various matters, and other joint clients in this engagement will be former clients. You each agree that the Firm may represent Mr. [*name*] or members of his family or the Company in any matter adverse to other former joint clients so long as (i) the Firm has not actually received confidential information related to the matter from the adverse joint client, or (ii) the Firm establishes an ethical wall to prevent attorneys who actually received confidential information from the adverse joint client from disclosing it to the attorneys involved in the adverse engagement.

In the event (i) actual disputes or conflicts arise between any two or more of you and/or (ii) it becomes necessary for our Firm to take adverse positions on behalf of one of you with respect to the interests of any other of you, by signing this letter, you acknowledge your understanding that we may be disabled from continuing any further representation without a further waiver from the parties involved in such actual conflict. Indeed, no such waiver may be possible or practical, in which case each party to any such matter may be required to obtain the services of other counsel. In this paragraph, "adverse" refers to any matter in which one of you deals with the other at arm's-length and with potentially competing or conflicting goals or interests. "Adverse" is not limited to circumstances in which there is a dispute or controversy.

Scope of services to be provided

We have represented and will continue to represent each of you in connection with the sale of the shares you own, respectively, in the Company, including services related to finalizing the acquisition agreement, amending the acquisition agreement and consummating the closing of such sale.

Reporting
Staffing
Fees and costs
Statements

Up to now, we have sent our statements to the Company. In the future, we will deliver statements for fees and costs as the Seller Representative directs. We issue statements within approximately the first two weeks of each month for services and costs posted during the preceding month. Services and costs not posted as of the monthly closing date will appear on a subsequent bill. Recognizing that most legal services are performed outside of the view of the client, it is our policy to describe in our invoices the services performed in some detail, so that a reader will understand fully the work we have done and the charges for that work. Statements are due upon presentation. By execution of this letter, you each acknowledge that the Seller Representative is authorized to approve, contest and/or compromise our statements in his absolute discretion and his decisions in that regard will be fully binding on each of you.

In the event that any statement is not paid as required by this agreement, or as otherwise agreed to by us, you agree that we will have the right at any time to discontinue further services on this matter and on any other pending matter for you, and to withdraw as your counsel. In connection with any such withdrawal, you agree that we will have the right to file a copy of or otherwise disclose this fee agreement in any proceeding. Please be aware that it is our normal policy to discontinue further work in the event of nonpayment.

For the present and until changed by agreement between the Seller Representative and the Firm, payment of our invoices will be made by the Company.

As of the closing, it is likely there will be accrued and unpaid fees and costs, and that additional services will be necessary after the closing. It is our understanding that in connection with the closing, the Seller Representative will have disbursed to him in that capacity a sum that will be deducted from the cash purchase price and that such sum will be used to pay our fees and costs, both as then accrued and unpaid as well as those that may arise after the closing. The Buyer has agreed to pay one-half of the Seller's legal expenses in the Transaction. Should the Buyer fail to make such payment, the obligation to pay our fees remains that of the Sellers. Assuming that the Buyer performs as requested, this will be a substantial benefit to all of the Sellers.

Trust deposits
Charge on past due balances

Intellectual property maintenance
Termination of representation
Arbitration
Governing law
Venue; submission to jurisdiction
Approval

Although we have set out the terms of our representation in the form of a letter, you should understand that the agreement set out in this letter is a binding legal contract. If this agreement meets with your approval and accurately sets out your understanding of the terms of our representation, please sign and return a copy of this letter in the enclosed return envelope. This letter sets out our entire agreement, and no modification of the terms of this agreement will be effective unless set out in writing and signed by each of you and by us. It will take effect when it has been signed by each of you or when we first perform services, whichever is earlier.

Again, we thank you for asking us to represent you. If you have any questions concerning our fees and costs arrangements or procedures, or the scope of the legal services we will provide, you should feel free to call at any time. We welcome the opportunity to be of service to you.

Sincerely,

[*Name of firm*]

[*Signing partner*]

Acceptance and Approval
    The undersigned each accept and approve of the foregoing agreement for legal services.

SELLERS
    [*Date*]   _____
    [*Date*]   _____
    [*Date*]   _____
    [*Date*]   _____

SELLER REPRESENTATIVE
    [*Date*]   _____

*Not all states require citing professional rules in engagement letters.

APPENDIX 2-B
Form of Consent to Future Representation

[*Date*]
[*Name*]
[*Title*]
[*Company*]
[*Address*]

Re: **Waiver**

Dear [*name*]:

As you are aware, our law firm (the "Firm") has represented [*target*] (the "Company") and all the selling shareholders (the "Sellers") in the transaction provided for in the Stock Purchase Agreement dated December 28, 200_ (the "Stock Purchase Agreement") between [*buyer*] (the "Buyer") and the Sellers.

On behalf of the Buyer, and its present and future subsidiaries, affiliates and related entities of all kinds, you agree that the Firm is hereby authorized and entitled to represent the Sellers, or any of them, after the closing described in the Stock Purchase Agreement, in any and all matters, disputes and proceedings (the "Proceedings") that may arise between any of the Sellers and the Buyer.

Further, the Buyer waives any and all rights to disqualify the Firm and agrees that it shall not seek to disqualify the Firm in any such Proceedings for any reason, including but not limited to the fact that the Firm has represented the Company or the Sellers, one or more of its attorneys may be a witness in the Proceedings or one or more of its attorneys may possess or have received confidential or privileged information of or from a party whose interests are adverse to any party represented by the Firm in any such Proceedings. For this purpose, confidential or privileged information includes, without limitation, financial information, trade secrets and matters subject to the attorney-client privilege.

Without limiting its other purposes, this letter is a blanket consent to the Firm's future representation of the Sellers, or any of them, in Proceedings in which an adverse party or parties is or are former clients of the Firm under the terms of Rule 3-310(E) of the California Rules of Professional Conduct, any successor thereto, and any similar rule of any other jurisdiction or authority. Because it is represented by its own counsel, and the purpose of this letter agreement is to allow Sellers to continue to enjoy the services of their chosen counsel after closing under the Stock Purchase Agreement, the Buyer waives any right to require Sellers or the Firm to provide any information about the potential disadvantages of entering into this written consent. The Buyer accepts all responsibility, with assistance of its chosen counsel, to inform itself regarding the meaning and potential consequences of this consent.

Please indicate the Buyer's agreement to the foregoing by signing and returning the enclosed copy of this letter to me.

Sincerely,

[*Name of firm*]

[*Signing partner*]

Agreed to and accepted on ⎯⎯⎯⎯⎯⎯⎯⎯⎯⎯⎯⎯⎯, 200_.

[*Buyer*]

By: ⎯⎯⎯⎯⎯⎯⎯⎯⎯⎯⎯⎯⎯⎯⎯

⎯⎯⎯⎯⎯⎯⎯⎯⎯⎯⎯⎯⎯⎯⎯

Name and Title

CHAPTER 3

Forming a Team

When you are being engaged in an M&A transaction, an understanding should be reached with the client as to your role. The level of involvement can range widely depending on the client's needs and preferences. At one extreme, a lawyer could manage and oversee the entire transaction, coordinating the work of all the other professionals. This is often the role assumed for a privately held client with little, if any, experience in M&A transactions. At the other extreme, the lawyer's role could be limited simply to preparing and revising documentation as requested by the client. This more limited role might be for a client with an in-house legal staff that is frequently involved in M&A transactions.

What will the role be? Will you lead the transaction team with overall project management responsibility or simply be one member among many professionals on the team? Will you be responsible for all substantive legal areas including tax, antitrust, environmental, labor and employment, or only for the preparation and negotiation of the documentation? Will you have any responsibility for conducting due diligence? What role will you play in the negotiations?

If you are to manage the transaction, you will need to assemble the necessary resources within your firm or law department or elsewhere to make sure the client's needs are satisfied and interests protected. Putting the team together may be quite simple in a smaller transaction for a privately held client. The amount of support required may be limited, perhaps involving at most several other lawyers or non-legal advisors. It is the larger transactions for the more complex businesses that will require more diligence in obtaining the right people for the team and greater management skills to bring the project to a successful conclusion. Whether your role will be that of managing the transaction or a supporting role as a member of the team, it is important to understand the relationships among team members and the dynamics of working together.

The need to assemble a team can occur at various stages of an M&A transaction. It may be that the client is proposing to sell its business and is interested in preparing for a sale with no particular buyer identified. Or the client has already been approached and is in the process of negotiating with a potential buyer. The composition of the team will also depend on the nature of the transaction and whether the lawyer is representing a seller, buyer or target.

Background Information

Whatever the stage or nature of the transaction or the type of representation, the deal lawyer should have a good idea of the client's objectives and have background information on the client's business and industry before assembling the team. It may be that this is a long-time client, in which case its objectives are clear and there may be no need to gain any additional information. Quite often, however, the relationship with the client is new for the firm, the lawyer or both. This will require that the lawyer spend a considerable amount of time in getting up to speed. Equally important is the need to gather background information on the target or the potential buyer, as the case may be, if it has been identified. Is the target engaged in basic manufacturing with owned facilities throughout the country, or is it a service business, perhaps a financial institution or insurance carrier, that is subject to extensive regulation? This will make a significant difference in determining what legal and other resources may need to be engaged in the project.

For public companies and many private companies, a good deal of information is readily available through their web pages and elsewhere on the Internet.[40]

You Never Know What You May Find

A prominent publicly traded company was negotiating a significant control investment in a privately held high-tech company. Our client's engineers had checked out the viability of the technology and the terms of the deal were almost completed. However, when our client followed its standard practice of ordering a background check of the principal owners of the high-tech company, it discovered the SEC was currently investigating them with respect to other transactions unrelated to the high-tech company. Our client terminated all discussions because from a public and investor relations point of view, it could not be associated with anyone even allegedly engaged in questionable practices. Today, with easy access to so much information on the Internet, a preliminary check on the Internet would seem to be a first step in similar situations. Indeed, a background criminal and litigation check on management of the party on the other side of the negotiating table may be something worth considering before getting too far down the road.

The periodic reports of public companies, including their annual and quarterly financial statements and other detailed financial information, can be accessed through the webpage of the SEC and private services.[41] For many private companies, it is more difficult to acquire information, but the audited financial statements and related notes, if made available, can be a good start. Often the books[42] that are prepared by investment banks to market companies for sale provide a good deal of helpful information, but it is important to remember that these are sales documents.

The Client Team

While life might seem simpler if lawyers could do deals just within their own law firm or law department, reality is that M&A deals involve a number of players, beyond just the lawyers and may involve lawyers from more than one firm. First and foremost, there is the client and the cast of characters within the client's organization.

Gatekeepers

An important agenda item at the first meeting with the client is to identify the key contact person who is to interface with the senior outside counsel. Depending on the working relationship with the client, consider suggesting to the client the need for a funnel with a senior, respected client manager to act as gatekeeper. On most successful deals, both from a timing and cost point of view, having the right client contact who understands and plays the gatekeeper role is critical. Just which individual is chosen will depend on the size and importance of the deal to the client, the client's deal experience, the client's management style, and the scope of authority given outside counsel.

The key specifications for a gatekeeper are:

- authority to make most decisions or quick access to the decision-maker;
- enough clout to cause necessary specialists and custodians of data within the company to be responsive;
- availability; and
- a good working relationship with the lawyer-side contact.

While other specialists at the law firm and the client will often have their own channels of communication, the point persons on the law team and client team need to be kept current on all developments and issues. The client's choice, depending on its organization and the nature of the deal, could be the CEO, CFO, general counsel, a head of corporate development, a manager of the business unit or other managers, depending on the situation. The title is less important than meeting the specifications listed above.

Chief executive officer. In larger companies, the CEO usually delegates the gatekeeper role to another person. It can be useful to keep the CEO distanced from the day-to-day issues of the deal so that, when sticky issues arise, the CEO can deal with a counterpart on the other side. Just as important, the CEO needs to continue to run the business. In smaller companies or when the CEO is a key owner or there are a small number of executives, this is harder to do. Impress upon the CEO that he will be the problem solver ultimately, and arrange for briefings as often as he would like. Sometimes a daily five-minute call is all that is needed. On the other hand, in family-owned businesses, the CEO is often the gatekeeper and is very much a hands-on participant in most aspects of the transaction.

General counsel. There has to be a good working relationship and frequent communication between outside counsel and, where one exists, in-house counsel for a deal to get done properly, on time and within budget. The general counsel is often the gatekeeper and, if experienced in M&A activity, this could be a great advantage or a significant problem. An experienced, deal-savvy general counsel with extensive knowledge of the client and a willingness to partner with outside counsel can be an enormous asset to a deal.

An Outside Counsel Testimonial to In-House Counsel

My best experience with a general counsel was on a late Friday afternoon during the summer on a large acquisition. I had never met her. She was an experienced general counsel. She convened a meeting of the senior department heads of her company to meet with me and some of my firm's key lawyers representing the company in the acquisition. She acted as chair of the meeting. In her opening remarks she summarized the deal, gave the anticipated time schedule explaining regulatory delays, and quickly said, "I am now introducing lead outside counsel who will be in charge of the acquisition from this point forward." Within a half hour, the members of the client team knew what was expected of them and who they would be working with from the outside, established a weekly meeting schedule for the whole group, and knew exactly to whom trouble or issues should be reported.

At the other extreme, a "know it all," "been there, done that" general counsel can be a Monday morning quarterback, blocking all messages, concerns, questions, and other communications to and from other business people.

In some companies, the general counsel may not have M&A experience and will prefer to continue to run the day-to-day legal aspects of the business and happily leave management of the deal to outside M&A counsel. In this situation, particularly with a target, the general counsel remains a valuable resource and a needed facilitator but is less involved in the M&A process.

At the other end of the spectrum, for some buyers and sellers, a general counsel with extensive M&A experience and a staff with broad experience may lead the transaction with little involvement from outside counsel.

Chief financial officer. In many deals, the CFO is the client gatekeeper. On the buy side, the CFO often will oversee, if not direct, the due diligence of the target's financials and their underpinnings and provide insight into the financial impact of due diligence and other discoveries. Even if not the gatekeeper, the CFO will usually keep in close contact with the process, especially where there are financial issues or disclosures that have to be explained, or where the CFO feels a need to know the target's business to ensure proper financing is obtained or integration achieved. The target's CFO will often serve as point in providing financial due diligence, fielding any number of questions and preparing the schedules.

Head of corporate development. In recent years, many large companies have created corporate development officers and staffs that are responsible for divesting and acquiring businesses and product lines that coincide with the corporate strategy. They are often quite experienced in the acquisition process, many having come from financial or investment banking backgrounds, and are usually heavily involved in the negotiation, due diligence, and documentation of all the divestitures and acquisitions. Where present, the head of corporate development or other members of the staff can be very helpful as gatekeepers.

Client Specialists

Depending on the nature of the transaction and the parties, there often will be additional members of the client team who will be responsible for particular aspects of the deal. These may include specialists in employment law and benefits, risk management, and information technology/MIS, as well as in tax, environmental, or real estate matters, and those who will be responsible for integration of the target's business and operations.

Employment and benefits. A senior human resource/benefits specialist from the client is often an important part of the team. In a multi-jurisdiction transaction, laws governing severance and termination vary widely. How do different benefit plans equate? How to handle a pension surplus, or worse, an under-funded pension plan for transferring employees? How to deal with post-retirement benefits for retired employees of the target when the seller wants to close up shop or there are collective bargaining issues? Personnel issues are often the thorniest to deal with in an M&A setting. On transitional issues, having a human resource/benefits specialist is very helpful.

Risk manager. The client, particularly a strategic buyer, should know the "hot button" risk issues. Someone familiar with insurance issues, how to meld coverages, and how to address uninsurable risks will be critical to both sides, particularly in asset deals.

Information technology/MIS. One of the most perplexing management issues for most companies is the selection, implementation, and operation of the information technology/management information systems. In the context of an acquisition, this becomes even more difficult. Even if the target is to continue as a stand-alone operation with its own internal systems, its operations often will need to be integrated with the financial reporting systems of a buyer. Specialists can evaluate the adequacy of a target's systems and, if necessary, compatibility with the buyer's systems. In some cases, the target's systems will be phased out, so that arrangements will have to be made for conversion and for running parallel systems until the conversion is successfully completed.

Implementation leader. Numerous transitional and implementation issues will have to be discussed between representatives of the seller and buyer who know the business and industry better than any lawyer involved in the transaction. In some deals, a separate implementation team is set up to bring out the points to be covered in the transitional or implementation agreements. These agreements often provide for continuation of certain services, such as information systems, human resources and employee benefits, accounting and tax, sales support and marketing and insurance and risk management.[43] Key to the team are people knowledgeable about both the target and the buyer, so that closing of the deal will be as seamless as possible to customers and suppliers of the target's business.

The Law Firm or Law Department Team

Because the transaction involves the purchase or sale of a business, all legal aspects that could pertain to that business are appropriate fodder. Exactly how they might be applicable to a particular transaction is tremendously variable. Normally the team, on either the buy or sell side, is comprised of an experienced M&A lawyer assisted by other lawyers playing various roles, divided between the supporting cast and the specialists. The process for assigning and delegating duties to other corporate/M&A lawyers who are members of the supporting cast is not unlike any other transactional matter handled by the firm or law department. It is the involvement and coordination of specialists that will require the most attention.

Legal Specialists

Types of specialists needed. The legal specialists required and the extent of their involvement depends on numerous factors, such as the profile of the target (type of industry and whether regulated), the risk tolerance of the buyer and the significance and form of the transaction. The possible permutations and combinations with respect to legal specialists are daunting. The following are some of the areas of specialization that may be required:

- tax
- securities
- ERISA/benefits

- litigation
- environmental
- antitrust and Hart-Scott-Rodino
- labor/employment law
- immigration
- intellectual property
- lending/financing
- real estate
- regulatory
- estate planning
- foreign or local counsel

While it would be unusual to have all of these specialists on any deal, involving a half dozen or more would not be unusual. There seems to be a need for benefits, environmental, employment, tax and, increasingly, intellectual property lawyers in most every deal. Particular client needs, often in regulated industries, may require additional specialists. The greatest concern will be buy-side representation, but often specialists interact with their counterpart specialists on the sell-side as well.

These specialists could come from the same law firm, but they are frequently drawn from various outside firms representing a buyer in particular areas, from the buyer's own internal legal staff, and from non-legal advisors providing specialty services, such as tax advice from accounting firms. Larger transactions tend to require more specialists (and lawyers in general).

Increasingly, larger corporations handle the entirety of an M&A transaction in-house, particularly on the sell-side, but often on the buy-side as well. The following observations remain applicable whether addressed to an outside or inside team.

Selection of specialists. The actual selection will depend on the exigencies of the situation. What specialists are needed? Are the regular specialists working for a client available? What is the role to be played—advisor, negotiator, or other? What is the timeframe for a particular deal?

Numerous factors affect the selection of specialists. An experienced buyer will usually have its own in-house team. A long-standing client may have specialists that it has relied upon within the same law firm and who would be most appropriate to be involved in the transaction, particularly where knowledge of existing client practices is important, such as in the benefits area. More difficulty arises when a client uses specialists from other firms because determining whether and how these other specialists will be involved is less certain. Clients often understand that using a specialist from the lead lawyer's firm may allow greater responsiveness. For example, a client may use a boutique intellectual property firm to resolve key IP issues, but may be willing to allow the lead firm to do IP due diligence and negotiate the IP representations.

Role of specialists. The roles of specialists vary. For example, a litigator would almost always be used to help a buyer understand the risk of pending or potential litigation, but in a particular transaction, such as a public deal, litigators may be asked to advise on the legal risk associated with certain actions or perhaps just to stand by if there is litigation. In other instances, a specialist may be asked to take responsibility for negotiating particular provisions of the acquisition agreement or of various ancillary agreements.

Some clients will rely on non-legal specialists, such as accountants, for tax planning. In these circumstances, it is appropriate to have an understanding with the client as to the respective roles to be played between the accountants and the tax lawyers. Are the tax lawyers and the accountants part of a combined team? Do the tax lawyers have any role at all (or are they relegated to reviewing the tax representations)? Even when an accounting firm has been given complete responsibility over tax issues, some lawyers will still want the reasonableness of the position confirmed, informally, by tax lawyers in their firms. It may be appropriate, as part of the engagement letter, or separately once the roles have been defined, to prepare a letter to the client specifying the roles of the lawyer's firm and the accounting firm.

A number of practices are followed in the actual negotiation of an acquisition agreement. Sometimes the assignment for negotiating all deal terms and the precise form goes to the lead M&A lawyer. Sometimes the M&A lawyer's role becomes more limited—deal terms are negotiated by others, with the legal aspects (such as representations and covenants) being negotiated by the lawyer. But the legal aspects are often divided among the lawyers. Specialty lawyers, such as those engaged in tax, benefits and environmental law, may negotiate the representations (and related indemnification) with their counterparts on the other side. The problem with the handoff is that too often those provisions are negotiated in a vacuum, without an understanding of client objectives and risk profile or conventions used in the acquisition agreement. On the other hand, some specialists (such as in the executive compensation areas of some law firms) are devoted to the M&A aspects of their specialty and understand precisely what needs to be done on a particular matter.[44]

Even with an extremely experienced specialist, there is risk that things head in the wrong direction. A discussion between the lead M&A lawyer and the specialist is always important to set common objectives and the lead M&A lawyer should generally understand the specialist issues and keep informed as to the related negotiations. An exception to this might be where the specialist works directly with the client and the client has a set way of doing things, such as an experienced buyer that always handles its benefits matters in a particular way. The key is that the lead M&A lawyer needs to understand that these are the ground rules.

When to Involve Team Members (Generally Earlier, Not Later)

The process of assembling the legal team and involving team members is a complicated process. Most buy-side deals are tentative. Of possible deals that a potential buyer might be interested in pursuing, only one of dozens usually gets very far in the process. If a lawyer's first involvement is the review of a proposed confidentiality agreement, it usually would be foolish to try to assemble and engage a full blown team at that time. Even for sell-side representation, trying to find team members, when the role and seller's counsel and timing is unknown, is often not productive. For most law firms, trying to reserve other lawyers for some indefinite time period just does not work. Nevertheless, it is usually worth the effort to attempt to identify team members and establish their availability even before there is work for them to do.

Despite the difficulties, it is highly desirable to organize the team as soon as appropriate, particularly as the pace of a deal accelerates and certain bridges have been crossed. The lead lawyer should ideally attempt to organize the team once some level of probability has been achieved. It is not necessary to identify the precise role to be played by each person. The beginning exercise is usually to find the needed expertise with time availability. How the roles play out will depend on how the transaction unfolds. Having a team in place early on enhances client service and better assures that the legal issues are surfaced and addressed at an appropriate time.

It may not be necessary to put together a full blown team in one fell swoop. Some specialists, such as tax advisors, may be brought into the picture at the talking stage, when structure may be more important than the details. Others may become involved when a letter of intent is being negotiated, depending on the elements of the deal being discussed. Some need not be involved until the acquisition agreement is being drafted or negotiated (or even later), particularly on the sell-side.

But once a deal has expanded to due diligence (at least on the buy-side), it is appropriate to put a full team in place. The need for specialty lawyers continues in the documentation phase. The trick is determining when a broad-based effort may be required. Sometimes there is no warning—a client may announce that it is interested in buying a particular company and wants a team on the ground in a distant city the following day. In deals where the letter of intent precedes due diligence, sending out the letter of intent is often the point when the lead lawyer goes to work in putting the team together. At other times, the client may simply signal needed assistance in the due diligence process, as for example, participation in an auction. But if the client is the most logical buyer of a particular business, developing the team even at an early stage may be appropriate.

On the sell-side, just when the team is assembled may very well depend on the role of the lawyers. Depending upon the sophistication of the seller and its other advisors, some sellers feel that lawyers need not be involved in putting together a data room or in otherwise assisting the client in determining which documents will be provided.

Obstacles to Working with the Legal Team

Your own law firm (or law department). The difficulty of providing effective, quality client service in an M&A context cannot be overstated. In virtually any transaction, the client (in addition to any internal legal staff) will have a number of businesspersons working on the matter, from top executives on down. The client will also have a number of external advisors, such as investment banks and accountants. The legal team may be only one of several sets of advisors. Unlike the well-oiled professional football team, the client team and advisors will have been pulled together on the fly, may not even know each other and may not have had M&A experience. Often knowing the assignments is difficult, compounded when they are to be carried out by people having differing relationships.

Even in the happy circumstance where the legal team members are all from the same outside law firm (or in-house department), there can be difficulties in serving the client.

First, team members will always have a differing knowledge about the client. Some members may never have worked for the client. Others, while working for the client extensively, may only have a vague idea of the strategic imperative for a particular deal. There are always differences in what is important to the client and what sends the client over the edge.

Second, team members will always have differing understandings of how to approach the deal. Often team members look at transactions through the prism of their own practices, so that some specialists can view an isolated matter as a terrible legal problem. While no one would advocate sloppy practice, most experienced M&A practitioners realize that there are often trade-offs and it is impossible to button down all of the loose ends in a transaction. An M&A lawyer who can participate in the specialist negotiations may bring special value to the representation.

Third, team members have differing experiences and styles. There is no one best practice that applies to each element of an M&A deal. Lawyers working on a matter will have their own unique experiences, and based on those experiences, will approach tasks in differing ways. While no one would suggest that M&A practitioners must be stamped out of the same mold, it may be necessary to attenuate some behaviors in the interest of best serving the client. For example, some lawyers are not always good at meeting deadlines. When working one-on-one, deadlines may not be as meaningful and the eccentricities of a lawyer can be worked around. In a deal context, the lawyer late in making a required contribution to a document becomes the weakest link, affecting the entire team.

Fourth, team members have differing norms of timing and service. Other than perhaps a hearing on a temporary restraining order, there are few areas of law practice that involve such time pressures as an M&A deal. Often team members are drawn from other disciplines, where deadlines come with long lead times and where legal work is focused on a regulatory scheme rather than negotiated language.

Some of these factors may be less applicable to an in-house legal department, but there is an element of truth in each. For example, the first factor talks about differing knowledge of the client—in-house law department members have an inherent advantage in understanding the company they work for. But there are always differing understandings of how a particular deal fits the needs of the company.

Law department (when team leader is an outside lawyer). The relationship between an outside team leader and an in-house lawyer can be complex. Inside lawyers, quite naturally, will have a reporting responsibility elsewhere and will look first to that relationship in providing guidance. An in-house lawyer may not have particular deal experience, so being the keeper of the keys to a particular area may mean that the negotiating process is delayed as the in-house lawyer gets up to speed or gets internal direction. On the other hand, an experienced in-house lawyer who knows how the company always does deals can be an immense resource. Finally, the distraction of other responsibilities cannot be overlooked. The internal benefits specialist asked to work on a deal will still have a day job requiring attention. Sometimes, the general counsel or other lawyer designated to manage the internal legal role will interface with these in-house specialists, which may help in terms of setting priorities. The tone of cooperation set by general counsel will go a long way in assuring a good working relationship between the team leader and in-house lawyers.

Managing the Legal Team

Given the obstacles, the barriers to success in managing the legal team are formidable. Not only will some team members not have worked together or worked for the client, but they also will bring varying levels of experience to the team and their methods of practice and service may differ considerably.

Management approaches, as would be expected, vary, from letting the chips fall where they may to an active team building process. Some practitioners may simply nominate other lawyers for team membership, their names go on the distribution list and all are expected to exhibit appropriate professional behavior. Alternative approaches involve immersing all team members in client objectives, communicating what the deal is all about and noting appropriate service objectives, such as standards of timeliness. For example, the "chicken little" lawyer may be misunderstood by some clients, either because the client understands the risks or because the hue and cry overwhelm normal expectations.

Applying management approaches when some team members are outside the law firm or law department can be even more difficult, particularly if other law firms are involved. In those circumstances there is even greater need to adopt appropriate practices to make sure that all team members are on the same page.

The handoff versus the consulting approach. It may not be necessary to have a team at all— tasks in a deal could be carried out through individual handoffs of particular assignments with the team leader providing enough information for the assignee to complete the task. For some limited assignments this may be the preferable approach, but for larger transactions this has some drawbacks—it is inefficient, it denies the benefit of interaction, and it is ultimately less satisfying as a way to practice law. Unless the team leader has superhero attributes, the deal can often bog down if, for whatever reason, the leader is overwhelmed, distracted, or otherwise unavailable.

How do seniors and juniors, specialists and M&A lawyers, insiders and outsiders work together? There are as many approaches as there are personalities. Lawyers, particularly experienced specialists who may have a preexisting relationship with a client, may chafe when it is suggested that they are working for the lead M&A lawyer. Working as part of a team may only mean that a specialist does his own thing in connection with a transaction. For junior lawyers, handing off an important area of unsupervised work is fraught with peril. In those circumstances, the lead lawyer would normally expect the junior to continue to work under his supervision. But even the deepest of specialties should not be operating in a vacuum. Issues that concern particular specialists may be tradeoffs in other areas. The input of specialists may affect overall design and structure. It is usually more fun to be part of a team rather than isolated in your office working on a narrow sliver of a deal. The consulting approach to M&A has its own rewards.

Team meetings. Some believe that an initial team meeting is important. They can foster a sense of commitment and camaraderie to a deal. Because there will be a discussion and an opportunity to ask questions, they provide the best assurance that client demands will be understood. The team leader might explain the overall process and what is expected of the team. For those team members new to the client, some explanation of the business and overall objectives can be helpful. An explanation of the need for timelines would be explored—team members are more likely to deal with what appear to be unreasonable demands if they understand the need. The downside is the cost to the client of wide participation at an hourly time charge. While there are benefits to in-person meetings, conference calls can be effectively used, particularly when team members may not be in the same physical location.

Organizational techniques. A key to effective team behavior is an understanding of the tasks to be accomplished. Team leaders often rely on some of these techniques:

- Working group lists, so that everyone understands who is on the team and how to make contact.
- Time and responsibility (T&R) schedules, in which various tasks are specified and the date for completion and name of the responsible team member is listed—in other words, who needs to do what by when. These lists are reviewed and updated as the deal progresses. Regular updates are a reminder of the objectives and help align the team. An example of a T&R schedule is attached as Appendix 3-A.
- Issue lists, which may be observations and concerns arising out of due diligence or the negotiation of an acquisition agreement.
- Standard formats for due diligence reports, to better assure that all concerns are addressed and decision makers have the information they need in the format they desire.
- Standing dates and times for meetings or conference calls.

Communication devices. Communication is imperative for team effectiveness. Information must be communicated in such a way as to permit an entire team to do its job most productively. Communication is two way, not merely a broadcast. While general distribution of information and expectations is necessary, it is the communication coming back up the chain that establishes superior performance.

To most effectively serve the client, the lead lawyer must know, at least in general terms, what is going on and should be kept apprised of significant issues and decisions. When team members are negotiating matters with the other side, the status and positions taken need to be communicated to the lead lawyer. To be sure, there are some areas where an expert or a team is just given the mandate to accomplish a particular task and nothing else is expected.

It will not be appropriate to provide an open forum for discussion of all aspects of a particular deal. That would be inefficient. Similarly, it is probably not necessary for all of the specialty lawyers to understand all of the details of a particular transaction. There will always be a need for communications among team members on a one-to-one basis. Generally the efficiency of communication and the desirability of assuring that everyone is on the same page need to be balanced against the costs and delay of mass communications. The team leader must appropriately manage the communications to make sure that pertinent information is available, but that excessive resources are not being consumed.

Sometimes the situation can be dealt with by adding the law team members to part of a larger communications network established for the entire team, either formally or informally. At the risk of a client perception (often correct) that many team members means higher costs, it is relatively easy to contribute the names of team members to distribution lists, e-mail groups, and extranet sites.

It is relatively easy for a law team to create internal e-mail distribution lists, to make sure that all team members are included in memos, or to utilize a wide variety of electronic tools that are available for collaboration. But, make sure that these devices are used appropriately. Everyone does not need to know everything. It is important for everyone who can access a communication network to understand what is appropriate behavior and the importance of avoiding flip comments and locker-room language.

Recently, electronic means of communications have become available, such as extranet sites maintained by a law firm, company, or financial printer where information may be stored and accessible to team members (or to everyone working on a particular deal). Often these are used for due diligence, where a number of people may need access to some of the same documents. The existence of these sites compounds the need for effective team interaction and communication. It was easier when documents existed only in tangible form; when new documents were made available, those documents were directed to the appropriate person and directions were given (*e.g.*, "Review these documents to determine whether there are change-in-control clauses that could impact our deal."). When new documents are posted on an extranet site, the implication of that posting needs to be implicitly understood by each of the team members, often not an easy task, or one designated person needs to assure that there is follow-through.[45]

Any circulation of information, either by old fashioned or electronic means, involves considerations of security, control, and contractual obligations. As many have unhappily learned, it is all too easy to distribute information through an e-mail to unintended recipients.

E-Mail Discloses Confidential Information

In the April 10, 2002 issue of *The New York Times*, it was reported that, while more than 50 companies expressed confidential interest in acquiring Global Crossing, their identities were no longer secret to one another. According to the story, an e-mail message had been sent to the potential bidders by an employee of the law firm that was serving as Global Crossing's counsel in its bankruptcy proceedings. Although the message included only routine information on bidding procedures, it inadvertently named each of the more than 50 recipients by copying their e-mail addresses at the top of the message.

It was reported that all the companies included in the message had signed confidentiality agreements in the last two months with Global Crossing's financial advisor, expressing their interest in studying a bid. The companies that signed confidentiality agreements were identified by the e-mail addresses of their representatives listed in the message.

While the story indicated that only a handful of the companies mentioned in the message were expected to submit serious offers for Global Crossing, many of the companies whose names were included were surprised by the mistake, their representatives said. Others were reported to have played down their inclusion, pointing out that it did not necessarily mean they were preparing a bid.

The accessibility of extranet sites brings with it concern for appropriate security, not only for the particular deal but for other information accessible through the site. It is probably the concern for those safeguards that make extranets not terribly popular—often it is just too hard. Confidentiality agreements must also be respected. Broad-brush confidentiality agreements are now often supplanted by ones providing a nuanced approach to who receives access to documents. With such an agreement, broadcast e-mails and access to extranet sites will need to be tailored. Confidentiality and security concerns are heightened. Public discussions (such as on elevators or the use of cell phones) and public display of laptops with confidential information need to be guarded against. Depending upon the nature of the matter, it may be appropriate to adopt extraordinary measures, such as password protection of documents and use of code names.

Need for particular attention to deadlines. Attention needs to be paid to the timing for completion of assignments. M&A deals are fast moving, often contrary to the experience of many team members. Team members need to understand exactly what the deadlines are and that they are not artificial. Many lawyers discount deadlines because a client artificially sets them and because they reflect the client's sometimes unilateral preferences. Overcoming those preconceptions is crucial. Detailed communications on particular assignments is important. Too often the team leader (probably justifiably) assumes that the specialists brought into a transaction understand what they are supposed to do. Being explicit avoids these problems.

Interfacing with the business side. There are significant obstacles to effectiveness in an M&A transaction. It is often not clear who is in charge, how the legal and business risks are being sorted out and the weight that is being given to legal concerns. Because of the quick pace of deals, a hierarchical communication pattern may be supplanted with numerous cross links between various lawyers on the legal team and their business contacts at the client. Understanding the advice that has been given to the client and making sure that it is properly weighed becomes difficult. A command to communicate through the lead lawyer may begin to solve that problem, but at the cost of slowing down what needs to be a fast moving process. An instruction to copy the team leader on all correspondence, or to summarize any advice given, faces the exigencies of a particular situation.

Establishing the appropriate level of service. The previous discussion assumes common objectives. But it is important that the level of service be appropriate. It is crucial that the M&A lawyer understand the level of service for which the client is willing to pay. Service is often measured in terms of timeliness. Some consumers of legal services might always demand that cycle times be reduced. But speeding up the belt has consequences (not the least of which is establishing inappropriate client expectations). M&A deals go fast, but the one-day wonder is a thing of the past. They will be done over a finite period of time. While the deal goes on, it is often an all consuming, 24-7 matter. To maximize effectiveness, the troops need to be rested.

Spending significant energy to meet artificial deadlines, particularly for only modest pieces of the puzzle, will affect the ability to get other aspects accomplished.

"Level of service" may also imply "scope of service." For example, in assisting with due diligence, what contracts are to be reviewed and for what purpose? Client interests may not be served by the review of insignificant contracts. Some clients may want the lawyers to review and summarize the business terms of contracts; others may want only a warning of particular legal risks. There should be an understanding of expectations.

Outside Non-Lawyer Advisors

The purchase and sale of a business is an involved process, beginning perhaps years before vigorous lawyering activity commences and typically involving many players other than lawyers. What must be done on the buy and sell sides, while complementary, is not always equal in burden. The types and number of advisors and their respective roles will vary depending on the size, capabilities and deal sophistication of the parties. The same roles are played by different categories of advisors in different deals. For example, the lead negotiator in a transaction could be, depending on the deal and client, the outside lawyer, general counsel, CEO, CFO, corporate development executive, or investment banker. Due diligence could be shared by lawyers, accountants, investment bankers, client employees or specific experts (e.g., environmental consultants).

Whether they contact the lawyer or the lawyer contacts or recruits them, non-lawyer players are part of the picture in putting together the team. Often, in sizeable transactions, an investment bank or an accountant who has been planning the business side of the transaction with the client for some time makes the first contact with the lawyer. The investment bank may have already graded the deal as "doable" before the lawyer is called, and has also developed a scheme to finance the deal. The accountants may have also been involved for some time answering financial and sometimes tax questions for the seller.

Types of Advisors

The following outside professionals could be on the deal team of one side or the other.

Investment advisors. Investment banks and other investment advisors can play an important role in M&A transactions.[46] On the sell-side, an investment advisor can assist the seller to better understand its business and to package and sell the business, often leading the effort as an intermediary to identify potential buyers and pitch a transaction to them. The investment advisor also can assist a seller to understand and distinguish between competing bids for the business and advise a seller on the best financial structure having regard to its objectives and needs.

An investment advisor can play a similarly important role for a buyer. The advisor can assist with due diligence, assist the buyer to learn about and understand the strengths and issues associated with the business, and advise on financial and other structuring issues. The investment advisor can also assist a buyer to arrange financing for the purchase.

If investment advisors are to be involved in the transaction, it is important to identify and retain them early in the process. The transaction attorney may have a key role to play in recommending potential advisors.

Accountants. Accounting firms can play a broad range of roles in acquisitions, which will depend on the relationship of the company to the accounting firm, and the mix of other advisors and their historic roles with the company. In addition to assisting with tax planning, financial structuring, *pro forma* preparation, and due diligence, an accounting firm may often be helpful to a buyer on issues such as purchase price allocation, pre-closing and post-closing audits, and other accounting issues. The seller may find an accounting firm helpful in responding to requests for due diligence information, as well as for tax planning, financial structuring, and post-closing operational issues.

The accounting firm should be engaged early in the transaction planning process. In transactions involving public companies, Sarbanes-Oxley[47] considerations might require engagement of an accounting firm other than the regular auditors of the client, depending on the scope of services to be rendered. Accounting firms usually cannot assist with valuation issues in public transactions involving their audit clients. Where the client is privately held, an accounting firm that has an existing relationship with the client will normally advise on the transaction.

Human resource, benefits and pension specialists. Employee issues, including compensation and other benefits, are common to almost all acquisitions. Buyers and sellers alike look toward mitigating their financial exposure. Personnel issues are often the most difficult of all the issues to be addressed. Experienced outside advisors, especially job counselors, can be extremely helpful in assisting with employee issues that could be deal breakers. Benefit consultants can help in smoothing over differences between a buyer's and a target's benefits and compensation plans, often dealing with retired employees and their benefits. Pension consultants often, very knowingly, deal with pension deficits or surpluses regarding employees to be transferred with a business.

Valuation firms. Whether it is an initial valuation of a business or of particular assets, a financing or a fair value issue, experts in valuations of one sort or another are common. Valuation firms are sometimes engaged by a party that is contemplating the sale of a business in order to get an idea, given the prevailing market conditions, of how the business might be valued by a buyer and an appropriate asking price. These firms can also determine an appropriate allocation of the purchase price among the assets being acquired, or justify values of particular assets, for purposes of recording these values in the buyer's financial statements under purchase accounting.[48] In public company situations and in some private deals, valuation firms are retained to provide an opinion as to the fairness, from a financial point of view, of the consideration to be received by a party in the transaction.

Lenders. If third party financing is required to complete a transaction, lenders (and their counsel) will likely become key players. Well-advised buyers will assemble a team (legal and business) to work on the financing simultaneously with the acquisition process and will require coordination between the two teams. Sometimes, the basic terms or structure of the original deal have to be changed to make both the deal itself and the financing work. Lenders may have a role to play on the seller's side if their consent is required in order to complete the transaction.

Proxy solicitors. Proxy solicitors are often involved in widely held public company situations involving shareholder votes on the acquisition or on a related equity financing. Counsel will want to coordinate with the proxy solicitors on the substance of their message as it impacts legal exposure, and be sensitive to the timely needs for the solicitation to be effective. They are also concerned with timing issues, i.e., mailings to meet deadlines, so it is important to keep them informed about issues that impact timing.

Management or integration consultants. Management or integration consultants often are called agents of change. Combining the buyer and seller may create issues about how best to combine the parties' assets, liabilities, and people. Usually there is a consultant available for every category, but the hardest to deal with can be the people issues. On any business combination, individuals are always worried about their jobs, their positions or status, competition with the other party's employees, and being subject to new senior management. Generally, these concerns become more apparent as the closing approaches. Being able to shunt these issues off to a consultant, often one who works in the management change field, leaves counsel free to deal with legal issues and management free to focus on running the business.

Other advisors. There are a multitude of other advisors that a seller or buyer might wish to retain in order for it to understand due diligence issues or to assist with regulatory processes. The work of these other advisors often is in support of completing the transaction, particularly if the advisor is assisting in obtaining regulatory clearances (e.g., Hart-Scott-Rodino antitrust clearance).[49]

If the advisor is assisting counsel with an aspect of the transaction and maintaining the confidence of the advisor's work is important, counsel should consider retaining the advisor directly and put in place appropriate mechanisms to ensure the advisor's advice and work product is covered by the attorney-client privilege.[50] Examples of advisors that typically are retained by counsel rather than the client include:

- *Economists.* Economists can be vital to any transaction that has competitive significance. A seller and buyer, jointly or separately, might retain an economist to provide economic advice about the transaction and its competitive consequences, some or all of which advice might be used by counsel in their dealings with antitrust agencies.
- *Environmental consultants, risk managers, and insurance experts.* Through disclosure or due diligence, business risk issues will become apparent—a land site that was used for heavy industrial operations or other environmentally sensitive usage, toxic torts, product liability, or claims made against the target with uncertain insurance coverage. If the transaction includes an environmentally compromised property or if there may have been improper disposal of hazardous wastes, environmental consultants can assist to investigate the extent of the issues and evaluate the risks. Risk managers and liability insurance experts can then help the parties to minimize the risks identified by the environmental consultants.

Managing Outside Advisors

Doing even a simple M&A deal is tough sledding. The combination of owners, managers, and outside advisors is difficult to manage. With success fees and egos driving transactions, there may be competing interests. Some advisors may be "doing their own thing" without understanding the jobs of others. There are varying degrees of experience, skills and desire of each participant.

How this is handled may very well depend on the phase of the transaction and whether the representation is on the buy side or sell side. Generally, the deal team is created for a particular deal and, with isolated exceptions, will not have worked together as a team. There will be both insiders and outside advisors on the team, and the insiders will usually have a variety of reporting relationships. Under these circumstances, it is always difficult to manage the team.

There are exceptions of course. The experienced buyer may have a standing deal team. Any buyer with in-house corporate development capability may be able to manage the transaction through its own personnel.

Similar to managing the other team members, devices to manage the outside advisors include the preparation of working group lists showing participants on both sides of the transaction (often prepared by the investment banks), time and responsibility schedules, virtual data rooms and other communication devices. The lead M&A lawyer may be part of a smaller executive group in charge of a particular transaction. Regularly scheduled meetings of the key client personnel with the outside advisors, in person or by conference call, keep everyone who needs to know in the loop and well informed.

Certain phases of the transaction may lend themselves to better management than others. For example, a buyer during the due diligence phase will assemble its due diligence team, which is usually comprised of representatives of the buyer, lawyers and outside advisors. Assuming that the review is done onsite (rather than through a virtual data room), the physical presence of the team and ability to meet face-to-face can be a tremendous advantage in understanding and implementing common objectives.

Unique Role of In-House Counsel

Much of the discussion in this chapter applies whether the deal is being led by outside counsel or a deal team consisting exclusively of in-house lawyers. There are, however, roles in the process and perspectives that are unique to in-house counsel.

Understanding the Target

The need on the buy side to understand the target is critical for a successful acquisition. Many buyers will have an experienced acquisition team, but integration with the business unit that will operate the business being acquired is necessary both to understand the target and to sell the deal internally. The in-house attorney will understand better than an outside attorney the buyer's legal concerns in operating the target. In-house counsel can play a critical role in this process by identifying key legal issues or trends that affect the target. For example, are there product liability issues or does the target conduct its business in a unique manner that creates legal risks? The business people performing due diligence on a target will understand its business and industry, but the in-house attorney will better understand the legal issues that are unique to the target or its industry.

On the sell side, the in-house counsel, even if not leading the deal, will likely have an understanding of the target critical to structuring, negotiating the representations and seeing that steps are taken to comply with covenants and be better equipped than outside counsel to identify the right people to prepare and review the schedules and comment on key operational representations.

Institutional History and Lessons Learned

Every company has an embedded history of lessons learned from past transactions. There are institutionalized hot points for successful deals or deals gone bad. Similarly, individuals in the process have issues learned from past deals. These issues may or may not be entirely rational or properly evaluated as to their importance. However, they may be relevant. The historical experiences have to be identified and dealt with in every transaction. Whether in drafting or responding to the acquisition agreement, in-house counsel is often a critical source of this institutional knowledge.

Deal Structure

Once the business case for the deal is understood, the buyer needs to establish the acquiring entity and decide on a deal structure. The in-house attorney on the buy side may better understand structuring issues unique to the buyer or the target, as well as the traditional factors such as tax and successor liability. Many times there are specific company or industry related regulatory or liability issues that will influence a deal structure. The in-house attorney who is usually involved in the deal very early should consider the traditional areas that affect deal structure. For example, are there specific tax issues unique to the buyer or target that could drive the transaction?

The in-house attorney is in a position to make sure that the deal stays on track, and he can be a bridge between the lawyering and the accomplishment of business objectives as they are understood.

Involvement of In-House Lawyers

Many in-house attorneys have substantial acquisition experience, while others do not. Even if the business unit attorney does not have deal experience, he should usually be part of a team because of his intimate knowledge of the business and the industry. The attorney and the businessperson with lead responsibility must manage the process both with in-house and outside professionals in areas such as tax, employee benefits, health and safety, and environmental.

When forming the buy-side deal team and performing due diligence, thought should be given to capturing and retaining information that would be beneficial in managing the business in the future. The in-house counsel can be very helpful in this coordination between the deal team and the business unit. The business unit that will assume responsibility for the new business should be involved—both to buy into the deal and to be able to quickly manage the acquired business. Understanding the contractual commitments and actual physical operations should be a key goal of the due diligence team. Finally, the team that does the due diligence must share responsibility for reviewing the final schedules and conveyance documents. In-house counsel should be part of this review on both sides of the transaction.

Foreign Counsel

In the globalized world of the 21st century, cross border transactions are commonplace and even a seemingly domestic transaction may include international aspects. International transactions can be a dynamic and refreshing change for the U.S. attorney accustomed to dealing only with domestic issues. They will give rise, however, to a variety of thorny and sometimes novel issues for the M&A attorney who has a key role in identifying and effectively managing the international aspects of the transaction. And, it should never be assumed that the practice and legal framework of another country are the same or similar to that to which the transaction attorney is accustomed. Some of these issues and practices have been summarized in Appendix 3-B.

The introduction of foreign elements to a transaction will require further inquiry by the U.S. attorney and perhaps the involvement of foreign counsel. The need for foreign counsel and extent of involvement will be dictated by the significance of the international aspects of the transaction. For example, a transaction involving an entity that has nominal sales into a foreign country may not warrant involvement of the foreign attorney. There also may be circumstances in which the relevance (or lack of relevance) of the foreign law is known to the deal lawyer because of prior experiences with transactions involving that country. It should also be noted that in many European jurisdictions, accountants play a more significant role than their U.S. counterparts in due diligence and tax planning.

In general, foreign counsel should be contacted very early in the process to identify for the lead attorney the issues that might arise, including regulatory requirements such as labor and antitrust filings that might be required.

When Does a Transaction Have International Ramifications?

A transaction, even if between two U.S. companies, can have international ramifications if any part of the transaction, or a party to the transaction, is affected by or could be subject to laws of a jurisdiction outside of the United States. International considerations typically arise if the parties or the subject matter of the transaction have a connection to a foreign jurisdiction. Types of connections that can create international issues include:

- The parties are from different countries.
- The stock to be acquired is stock of a non-U.S. company, or a U.S. target to be acquired holds interests in entities that are incorporated or otherwise formed outside of the United States.
- The target's stock is listed on a foreign stock exchange or shareholders of the publicly traded target are resident outside of the United States.
- Assets to be acquired from a U.S. seller or any of its affiliates are located outside of the United States. This may be obvious if the seller has established branches or liaison-offices abroad, but more remote possibilities should also be considered (*e.g.*, trademarks registered abroad).
- The target has significant commercial dealings with non-U.S. entities. For example, due diligence on the target reveals that it exports products from the United States, is using distributors or sales agents abroad or has entered into a joint venture or cooperation agreement with a foreign partner.
- Lenders or other investors that reside outside the United States finance the domestic acquisition.

How Different Can It Be . . . ?

U.S. attorneys must be on the lookout for connections to foreign countries and determine the relevance and impact of foreign laws or practice on the transaction. It can never be assumed that things are done the same in other jurisdictions. Here are a few examples.

- In July 2001, the European Commission announced that it had determined to prohibit a proposed merger of General Electric Company and Honeywell International, Inc. The Antitrust Division of the U.S. Department of Justice had previously reached an agreement in principle with the companies that resolved its antitrust concerns, and the Canadian Competition Bureau had informed the companies that it would not take action to challenge the merger. This action demonstrated some fundamental differences in doctrine between the United States, Canadian and European Union merger regimes.
- In Canada and many European countries, employees must be provided substantial severance benefits upon termination and buyers must give new employees substantially the same benefits as provided by the seller.
- In civil law countries, such as France and Germany, a party can be liable for terminating negotiations if it is thought to have acted in bad faith or negligently.

Locating Foreign Counsel

There are many ways to locate foreign counsel to assist on an international transaction. The starting point should be the client, who may have existing relationships with counsel in the foreign jurisdiction. Failing that, the attorney could seek referrals from colleagues at his own firm, other firms, or other clients. If appropriate foreign counsel cannot be identified through personal referrals, legal directories, and other publications that identify and provide information about counsel in foreign jurisdictions might be consulted.[51] Directories that provide a qualitative assessment of foreign attorneys and firms can be particularly useful.

Engaging Foreign Counsel

In engaging foreign counsel, a discussion should be undertaken early on by the lead attorney or client about the fee arrangements. If the client is ultimately responsible for payment of the fees, this should be communicated to the foreign counsel, and the lead attorney should ensure there are no unique provisions in the foreign laws that might impose liability for fees on the referring firm. For example, according to regulations governing European attorneys, counsel referring work to a colleague may in some circumstances be held liable if the client does not pay. Also, the lead transaction attorney could consider whether to require the foreign counsel to provide a budget of its fees on the transaction and commit to stay within the budgeted amount. It may come as a surprise to the transaction attorney, and a particular surprise to the client, to receive a significant bill from foreign counsel after completion of the transaction that reflects its practice and involvement, but exceeds the expectations of the client that may not have had any direct interaction with the foreign counsel.

Once the fee and other aspects of the engagement have been resolved, the lead attorney may wish to confirm the arrangement in writing. While a formal written retainer agreement may not be appropriate in all circumstances, it is good practice to document and confirm the arrangement by letter or e-mail. In some countries, such as Germany, a direct engagement letter with the client is required. Among other things, the writing can confirm the billing rate and billing arrangements (e.g., monthly billing or bill upon completion of the transaction), confirm whether the foreign attorney is being retained by the transaction attorney's firm or the client (it should be the client if the client will bear ultimate responsibility for the fees) and that the foreign attorney's firm has no conflict of interest representing the client in the transaction. If particular laws of the foreign jurisdiction have relevance to the retainer, this too could be confirmed in writing. For example, in some countries fees are set by statute and may consist of a lump sum, the amount of which depends on the value of the transaction.

Managing the Engagement

The lead M&A attorney should proactively manage relations with foreign counsel. Communication is key. It is good practice to provide explicit instructions so that the foreign counsel clearly understands its role in the transaction and the scope of its work. Clear communication also ensures that the lead transaction lawyer identifies the expected deliverables and delivery dates from the foreign counsel. Communication typically will bring to light language and cultural differences that could have an impact on the success of the transaction. For many foreign counsel, English will not be their first language and communicating foreign legal concepts with clarity in the English language might be a challenge. Likewise, transaction practice in a foreign jurisdiction might be conducted quite differently, and in some, but certainly not all, jurisdictions with less intensity, than that to which a U.S. attorney is accustomed. It is therefore vitally important that the scope of foreign counsel's work is communicated clearly and is well understood, and that key dates for deliverables are agreed upon.

Role of Foreign Counsel

The particular role played by foreign counsel will be dictated primarily by the significance of the connection with the foreign jurisdiction and the relevance of foreign laws to the transaction. Foreign counsel might be asked only to conduct searches for liens against the assets located in the jurisdiction. The size of the foreign operations, however, may be so significant that foreign counsel might be required to conduct significant due diligence of the foreign operations, negotiate transaction documents with foreign counterparts, or prepare and submit local antitrust, competition, or investment screening filings.

A common experience is for the lead lawyer to prepare the primary transaction documents and request that foreign counsel review them to ensure that nothing is inconsistent with the foreign law or might prejudice the position of the client in that jurisdiction. The review of representations and covenants related to employment and tax matters can be particularly important. In addition to local law requirements, representations and covenants also may be affected by the results of due diligence conducted by the foreign counsel. To effectively advise on the transaction documents, foreign counsel should be provided with drafts as early as possible and kept informed of all changes to the documents as they are negotiated. Adding foreign counsel on the primary distribution list for revised documents is the best way to ensure that this occurs. To the extent that foreign counsel has particular concerns about the content of a document that reflects local requirements or practice, the lead attorney should consider having the foreign attorney negotiate those particular provisions with the foreign counterpart on the other side on the transaction.

When seeking legal opinions from foreign counsel that a U.S. lawyer might consider routine, it is important to be aware that lawyers in other countries have widely differing approaches, styles, willingness, and outlooks on providing legal opinions.

Differing Roles of Professionals

It is important in the retention and use of foreign counsel to understand the differences in local rules governing the legal profession in the various jurisdictions. These might not often be obvious or predictable, so the lead attorney should ask about differences in approach. For example, correspondence exchanged among French attorneys is confidential, but if a French attorney who authored the correspondence permits his counterpart to share the correspondence with his client, there is no further ability to keep the correspondence confidential. In some countries, there is much less protection afforded to attorney-client communications with in-house counsel than the level of protection to which a U.S. attorney is accustomed. For this reason, the U.S. attorney should be sensitive to potential differences and, if maintaining the confidence of certain information or documents is of particular importance to the transaction or the client, not disclose that information or documents to the foreign counsel without assurance as to how they will be treated in the foreign jurisdiction.

Local and Special Counsel

Even in a purely domestic U.S. acquisition, the differences in certain substantive areas from state to state will sometimes necessitate retaining counsel in a particular locale to handle identified aspects of the transaction. In addition, there may be specialized legal issues with which neither the in-house legal department nor the outside law firm has expertise.

Among the common situations necessitating retaining local or special counsel are the following.

- Where the transfer of real estate or other significant real property issues are involved, it will likely be necessary to involve real estate counsel from that jurisdiction given the differences in conveyancing and other real estate practices from state to state. Sometimes unique issues relating to the enforcement of noncompete covenants or other employment issues necessitates special expertise.
- Where the lead law firm or in-house law department has no intellectual property expertise, special counsel may be necessary where intellectual property is a key element with the target.
- Local environmental counsel is sometimes retained where there are specific thorny issues related to the transfer of real property in a state where the other lawyers involved in the deal do not practice.

Many of the same issues discussed with regard to retaining foreign counsel are applicable when retaining local or special counsel. An outside law firm should pay attention to whether its client already has a preferred working relationship with a firm in the geographical locale or specialty area involved. Similarly, the client ought to at least consider whether more weight should be given to local or special counsel than an ongoing working relationship with the lead outside law firm. A working relationship and history with local or special counsel can be highly valuable and reduce surprises arising out of unique billing practices, standards of timeliness, and quality issues.

An outside law firm and its client will need to make a judgment whether local or special counsel should be retained by the client or by the firm. When there is a relationship with the outside law firm, it may be quicker if the retention is between those two firms. However, the outside law firm should consider whether it is taking on a payment obligation for the local or special counsel's fees in the event that difficulty with its client should arise.

Local or special counsel should recognize the same degree of urgency with regard to the transaction deadlines as the client and lead lawyer likely share. Given that the particular tasks assigned to local or special counsel may well be relatively minor as compared to the significance of the deal to the lead outside law firm, it is sometimes necessary to build a fire under them when the final crunch time of a deal arrives. By the same token, whoever is leading the transaction needs to promptly communicate with the local or special counsel any changes in the schedule and the deadlines for performance. It is not unheard of for a client and outside law firm to neglect to tell local or special counsel that a deal has cratered and later find themselves facing a bill for work done in good faith that no longer has any value.

Appendix 3-A
Time and Responsibility Schedule

Date	Activity	Responsibility
Day 1	Perform tax and accounting analysis	Seller/Seller Counsel/ Seller Accountants
Day 1	Perform Hart-Scott-Rodino/antitrust analysis	Seller Counsel
Day 3	Review material contracts for assignment or "change-in-control" provisions	Seller/Seller Counsel
Day 3	Begin and coordinate due diligence examination of Seller	Buyer/Buyer Counsel/ Buyer Accountants
Day 5	Begin preparation of asset purchase agreement	Buyer/Buyer Counsel
Day 15	Circulate first draft of asset purchase agreement to all hands	Buyer/Buyer Counsel
Day 15	Distribute first draft of asset purchase agreement internally to specialists (tax, ERISA, etc.) as necessary; begin preparation of disclosure schedules	Seller Counsel
Day 15	Begin preparation of ancillary agreements (employment agreements and noncompetition agreements)	Buyer/Buyer Counsel
Day 20	Meet internally to discuss first draft of asset purchase agreement	Seller/Seller Counsel
Day 25	Provide written comments on first draft of asset purchase agreement to Buyer Counsel	Seller Counsel
Day 27	Distribute internally draft of disclosure schedules	Seller/Seller Counsel
Day 30	Meet to negotiate asset purchase agreement	All hands
Day 32	Obtain internal comments on draft of disclosure schedules	Seller/Seller Counsel
Day 36	Send revised draft of disclosure schedules to Buyer Counsel	Seller/Seller Counsel
Day 37	Circulate revised draft of asset purchase agreement to all hands	Buyer Counsel
Day 38	Provide comments on draft disclosure schedules to Seller Counsel	Buyer/Buyer Counsel
Day 42	Conference call regarding asset purchase agreement	All hands
Day 44	Circulate revised draft of asset purchase agreement to all hands	Buyer/Buyer Counsel
Day 45	Begin preparation of proxy statement	Seller/Seller Counsel
Day 45	Provide comments on draft disclosure schedules to Seller Counsel	Buyer/Buyer Counsel

Day 45	Circulate drafts of ancillary agreements to all hands	Buyer Counsel
Day 45	Begin preparation of HSR filing	All hands
Day 46	Prepare resolutions for Buyer board of directors approving asset purchase agreement	Buyer/Buyer Counsel
Day 50	Conference call regarding ancillary agreements and asset purchase agreement	All hands
Day 51	Prepare resolutions for Seller board of directors approving asset purchase agreement; prepare form for third-party consents	Seller/ Seller Counsel
Day 51	Draft joint press release	Buyer/Seller
Day 51	Conference call regarding outstanding issues on asset purchase agreement	All hands
Day 51	Circulate draft of proxy statement to all hands	Seller Counsel
Day 52	Finalize asset purchase agreement, disclosure schedules, and ancillary agreements	Buyer/Buyer Counsel/ Seller Counsel/Seller
Day 53	Hold meetings of boards of directors of Seller and Buyer to approve asset purchase agreement	Buyer and Seller
Day 53	Sign asset purchase agreement, with disclosure schedules and forms of ancillary agreements attached	Seller /Seller Counsel
Day 53	Issue joint press release	Seller/Buyer
Day 54	File Hart-Scott-Rodino notifications	All hands
Day 55	Provide comments on proxy statement to Seller Counsel	Buyer/Buyer Counsel
Day 65	Mail proxy statement	Seller
Day 70	Circulate closing memorandum	Buyer Counsel
Day 75	Circulate drafts of closing documents, including deeds, bills of sale, and assignments	Buyer Counsel/Seller Counsel
Day 80	Obtain third-party consents and estoppel certificates and deliver to Buyer Counsel	Seller
Day 84	Preclosing review of closing documents	All hands
Day 85	Hold Seller shareholder meeting	Seller/Seller Counsel
Day 85	HSR waiting period expires	
Day 85	Deliver estimate of closing date working capital	Seller
Day 86	Closing	All hands
Day 86	Commence preparation of closing balance sheet	Buyer Accountants
Day 86	File charter amendment changing name	Seller Counsel
Day 86	Pay severance/retention bonuses	Seller
Day 116	Determine closing date working capital and pay balance of purchase price, if any	Buyer/Buyer Accountants

Notes:

This is a simplified time and responsibility schedule (T&R schedule) for a sale of the assets of a privately held company to another privately held company for cash. The form, timing, and action items will vary depending on the form of transaction and whether the companies are privately held or publicly held.

Most T&R schedules contain a key that lists the various participants by name and then provides the manner in which they are designated in the schedule. For example, the law firm of Evans & Smith, which represents the seller, might be designated as E&S.

The date column normally will be filled in with the actual dates on which the action is to be taken or by which it is to be completed. Sometimes a calendar showing the months in which the project will take place is set forth at the outset of the T&R schedule for the convenience of the participants.

Appendix 3-B
Selected Issues Arising from the International Character of a Transaction

The lead attorney in a transaction with international characteristics should consider whether any laws of all relevant foreign jurisdictions are applicable to the transaction and the impact of those laws and related practices on the transaction.[52] The following are some of the laws and practices that may be applicable.

Due diligence. Appropriate due diligence should uncover whether the transaction has international aspects. The due diligence checklist will usually cover the residency of shareholders, the place of organization of the target and its subsidiaries, the location of the target's assets, the source of sales and whether foreign merger filings have been made by the target or its parent in the past. A close review of the auditors' report on the target also may reveal international aspects of the transaction. Special attention may need be paid to the handling by the target of currency exchange risks, the list of foreign subsidiaries, the depth and quality of the foreign subsidiaries' financial statements and inter-company transactions, such as transfer pricing and loans.

A transaction with international aspects will impose particular burdens on the lead counsel to organize, supervise and assess the results of the diligence review of the target and its foreign assets and operations. Assistance of foreign counsel often is required to assist with the diligence on foreign operations.

Tax and accounting issues. An international transaction must be harmonized with the international tax planning of the buyer, and special attention may need to be given to the tax aspects of transaction financing and associated leveraging. Additionally, international transfer pricing methods may contain substantial tax risks. Where the foreign target uses its own national accounting standards, readjustments when converting into U.S. generally accepted accounting principles or international accounting standards may complicate the acquisition process and purchase price determination.

Regulatory approvals. Many countries have regimes that require antitrust notifications to be made if specified financial thresholds (e.g., asset values or revenues) are exceeded. In some countries, filings must be made very early in the process (e.g., Brazil requires notification within seven days of the parties signing any agreement). Others require that a notice be filed and the relevant agency complete its review before the transaction can be closed. The thresholds for notification and filing differ greatly from country to country. Penalties for noncompliance can be severe. For example, under European and German law, the failure to notify can result in the acquisition agreement being declared void. The laws of relevant foreign countries also may require investment screening or other filings or clearances before a transaction can be completed. Some regulatory approvals take considerable time to obtain. These foreign time requirements and associated costs should be taken into account in planning.

Governing law. Often, the law of the jurisdiction where the target has the most significant presence is chosen as the law governing the contractual framework of the transaction. If the parties are unable to agree on either target's or buyer's jurisdiction as a choice of law, the law of a neutral jurisdiction may be chosen. It is not uncommon for the law of the United Kingdom to be chosen to govern contracts relating to transactions in common law countries outside of North America. Similarly, the laws of France or Germany may be chosen for transactions in civil law jurisdictions, and many transactions involving Middle Eastern parties often are governed by Swiss or Swedish law. As between several choices, there may not be a right or wrong jurisdiction. However, the attorney should ensure that the law of the chosen jurisdiction has some relevance and is sufficiently understood and predictable so that he can properly advise the client on the process for and predictability of enforcing the agreements in the chosen jurisdiction. The transaction attorney must be satisfied (perhaps by an appropriate opinion of foreign counsel) that the choice of a particular law to govern the acquisition agreement will be enforced in relevant foreign jurisdictions.

Special attention should be paid to the applicability of international treaties to the purchase of goods, such as the Hague Convention[53] and the United Nations' Convention on the Sale of Goods, also called the Vienna Convention.[54] While neither convention applies to the sale of stock and participations in corporate entities, they could apply to a cross-border sale of assets unless specifically excluded.

Choice of mechanisms to resolve disputes. Courts may not always be an appropriate forum to resolve disputes between the parties. Because of negative perceptions resulting from large damage awards and perceived unpredictable jury trials, parties located outside of the United States often will resist having disputes settled in U.S. courts. U.S. parties accustomed to pretrial discovery may find it very surprising to learn that in many continental European countries civil rules of procedure do not contemplate pretrial discovery and that judges play a much more active role in running the proceedings. For these reasons, it is not uncommon for international agreements to include provision for disputes to be resolved by arbitration, provided, of course, that the arbitral award, if made, will be recognized and enforced in relevant countries.

An arbitration may be *ad hoc* (i.e., conducted according to rules set by arbitrators selected by the parties) or conducted under the rules of an organization such as the American Arbitration Association[55] or the International Chamber of Commerce.[56] If arbitration is preferred by the parties, appropriate provisions will need to be included in the transaction documents to define matters such as the scope of disputes to be arbitrated, rules of the arbitration, how arbitration panels are to be chosen, the number of arbitrators, the language of the arbitration (and related documents), the place of arbitration, and the like.

The attorney should consider whether an *ad hoc* arbitration would be more appropriate than an institutional arbitration for disputes relating to technical, economic, accounting, or other specific issues. In many cases, expensive litigation or arbitration proceedings may be avoided by submitting the issue to a technical or financial expert, who acts as arbiter and whose decision is final and conclusive on the parties. Accounting issues, in particular with a view to international accounting standards and consolidation issues, are often referred to an expert, usually by choosing an international accounting firm. Disputes regarding technical issues, such as whether milestones for further investment obligations and the like have been met, also can conveniently be referred to a technical expert for resolution.

Choice of language of contract/binding translations. Where the parties to a transaction are from different jurisdictions, the language of the transaction agreements might be an issue. In some cases, local laws require that agreements be written in the language of the country where they are to be implemented or enforced. For example, agreements between a Polish company and its foreign shareholder must be written, or translated, into the Polish language; agreements that have to be recorded by a notary public in France must be written in the French language and the province of Quebec requires that certain agreements be in the French language unless the parties expressly agree otherwise. In many countries, tax administrators insist that an agreement written in a foreign language be translated into the official language of the country concerned or the agreements will have to be translated if enforcement is sought in a local forum.

Contract formalities. Many national laws prescribe particular form requirements for the valid conclusion of agreements, or the transfer and assignment of title to stock or assets. And, in some countries stamp duties or transfer taxes are imposed when stock or assets are sold. In order to find out whether a deed, notarization, authentification and legalization of signatures, registration procedures, administrative approvals, or the like are required, or whether special taxes or other levies might be payable, it is very important to verify the requirements applicable in the country where the target is organized or its assets are located. Similar inquiries should be made in any jurisdiction where assets are being secured to support financing of the transaction.

Breaking off negotiations. In civil law countries, such as France and Germany, a party to a transaction may be held liable for damages if it acts in bad faith or negligently when terminating negotiations. A choice of law clause may not deal with the issue adequately in situations where relevant national law allows an action for damages on the grounds of tort law, if negligence can be proven. The risk can be mitigated, however, by addressing the issue in a letter of intent or memorandum of understanding. For example, the letter of intent could provide that particular approvals (such as board or shareholder approvals) or financing is required before closing of the transaction and that the parties may terminate negotiations any time prior to the occurrence of those events. Also, in some jurisdictions a binding contract is deemed concluded upon reaching agreement on the price and identification of the assets to be acquired, leaving the fixing of the other details to statutory law or to the decision of a court of justice.

CHAPTER **4**

Dealing with Other Constituencies

In addition to the transacting parties themselves (i.e., the buyer, seller, target, and their respective equity holders), a host of additional stakeholders or constituencies can profoundly affect, and be affected by, an acquisition. These potentially affected parties include employees, customers, suppliers, creditors, and the entire panoply of counter-parties to licenses, leases, or other contracts with the transacting parties, as well as communities and charitable organizations. These are a matter of concern for the acquisition lawyer and the legal team in at least three respects.

First, it is the responsibility of the legal team to identify, early in the process, any contractual, statutory or other rights that other constituents may have vis-à-vis the parties to the transaction. For example, if the target is unionized, what are the responsibilities of the target to notify the union, and what are the responsibilities of the buyer in recognizing the union? The assessment of these rights and corresponding duties will, in turn, affect, and be affected by, the structure of the transaction, and the roles that these parties are expected to continue to have with the target or buyer following completion of the transaction. The results of this due diligence investigation will form the basis of drafting, negotiating, and allocating, as between the transacting parties, the costs and liabilities associated with these constituencies.

Second, since these other constituencies often drive the value of the business as a going concern, the lawyer should be in a position to advise the client as to structures and methods that will best preserve—to the extent practicable and desirable—the existing relationships, both for the benefit of the buyer (in the event the transaction closes) and for the benefit of the seller (to ensure that closing conditions are satisfied or in the event that the deal busts). Managing and preserving these relationships involves the application of both law (e.g., ensuring that any "change of control" or anti-assignment clauses in relevant contracts are complied with, or appropriate consents obtained) and psychology (e.g., assuring suppliers and customers that their relationship with the successor will be as beneficial as the relationship previously enjoyed with the target) and, in all events, require timely and effective communication with the affected parties.

Third, to the extent that action by the board of directors is necessary to approve the transaction, the lawyer should be in a position to advise the board with respect to its fiduciary duties, including whether and to what extent the interests of the various constituencies should be taken into consideration in approving a transaction or approving one deal over another. The ability and willingness of the board to consider these other constituencies is largely dependent upon whether it is a public or private deal, whether there are competing bidders, whether management has put the company into play, and whether management and/or the equity holders have particular ties to their employees and/or communities, as well as the law of the applicable jurisdiction of incorporation.

The lawyer representing the seller must also keep in the back of his mind that the deal—no matter how well it is going, or how close it is to closing—may nonetheless fail to close. In this case, the seller may need to continue to depend on its employees, customers, suppliers, and other constituents on a long-term basis, potentially due to a perception of damaged goods in the industry. This dependence can be awkward following a busted deal and can have deleterious effects on the business.

Even in the absence of any legally enforceable obligation to do so, it is not uncommon for boards of directors (at least on the sell-side and particularly in privately held, family-run businesses) to consider—out of moral, ethical, or similar considerations—the effect of a transaction on certain non-shareholder constituencies. It is often incumbent upon the transaction attorney to advise the board on its duties in connection with an M&A deal, including the ability of the board to consider these constituencies. Whether or not the board has that ability will largely depend on whether the applicable jurisdiction has adopted a constituency statute.

Constituency statutes are a group of state laws promulgated beginning in the 1980s[57] that permit (and in one case require) the board of directors of a corporation to consider the interest of non-shareholders constituencies, such as customers, suppliers, employees, and communities, when taking any action, particularly in the context of dispositions and changes of control.[58] These statutes, which are a subset of so-called "anti-takeover" statutes, were enacted in some states largely in response to a perception that hostile takeovers of a corporation based in that state would soon be followed by significant employee layoffs and possibly relocation of headquarters or other facilities to another state, either of which might have an adverse effect on the local economy. Constituency statutes were also drafted against the backdrop, and in some cases to specifically reject, the principles espoused in certain Delaware cases that imposed a heightened standard of review on boards in implementing anti-takeover defenses in the face of hostile bids,[59] and limited or prevented boards, in the context of the sale of a company or a change of control, from considering interests other than maximizing short-term shareholder value.[60] Many institutional investors were critical of these statutes.

Constituency statutes are most frequently invoked in support and defense of actions taken by boards of public companies in the face of hostile takeovers. However, these statutes can also be relevant to garden variety negotiated acquisitions, even private deals. Whether a constituency statute (even if otherwise available) is relevant, is heavily dependent upon the context.

Employees

The employees are almost always the most visible and obvious constituency, and the ones that are most likely to be affected by an acquisition. While there are innumerable employee and labor-related issues that must be taken into consideration in structuring and executing an acquisition, some of the more salient considerations are discussed below.

Severance Issues and Resulting Liability

Whether and to what extent the target's employees are going to be hired and/or retained may depend on whether the transaction involves a financial buyer,[61] which may not have any existing workforce and, therefore, may be more likely to take on the existing workforce *en masse*, or a strategic buyer, the primary incentive of which may be the anticipated benefits from combining workforces and eliminating redundancies. In any event, layoffs, large and small, are an unpleasant but not uncommon feature of M&A. With layoffs come costs and potential liabilities, which can range from quantifiable pre-negotiated severance pay under individual employment contracts, standard employee policies, or collective bargaining agreements, to potential lawsuits for wrongful or discriminatory termination. The transacting parties will carefully negotiate, and allocate in the acquisition agreement, responsibility for these actual and potential liabilities as between the buyer and seller.

Responsibility for the termination of employees can be affected by the structure of the transaction. For example, in a stock sale or reverse triangular merger, the employees will simply remain with the target under its new ownership. By contrast, in an asset sale, there must generally be some affirmative action by the buyer to offer or continue employment of the seller's employees. There is a tension between the transacting parties that arises not only from the potential liabilities that are associated with any terminations, but also with the visceral and emotional desire (and in particular, of sellers who have ties to the community) not to play the role of bad guy.

In any event, it is important—where layoffs are anticipated—that the rights of workers are understood and dealt with, including contractual rights (e.g., employment agreements, employee personnel policies, and collective bargaining agreements), common law rights (e.g., applicability of the at-will employment doctrine), and statutory rights (e.g., the need to offer temporary health care coverage under COBRA). In some circumstances, the lay-offs (or related plant closings) may be so significant, in terms of the number of affected employees, that it is necessary for the seller to comply with the notice and related requirements of the WARN Act[62] or similar state laws.

Retaining/Binding Key Employees

In most transactions, there will be certain employees of the target whose continued employment will be critical to the ongoing business, and whose willingness to continue employment may be a condition to the buyer's obligation to close the transaction. There may also be another set of employees who, while not having a long-term future with the buyer, are nonetheless necessary to bring the transaction to the closing and/or to assist with post-closing transition and integration. Generally, the determination of who falls into which category is made by the business people. Once this determination is made, however, the legal team can and should assist in ensuring that the appropriate structures are put in place to sufficiently incentivize these employees to fulfill those expectations.[63] A seller may insist that a buyer of a business expressly agree to retain all of its employees for some limited (say six months) period after closing at their current compensation levels. Whether that undertaking is enforceable by those employees against the buyer is addressed in Chapter 11.

Shifting Loyalties

Another significant concern of a seller is the tendency of its employees—at all ends of the spectrum, but especially problematic among key employees—to begin looking to the potential buyer as their employer. This shift in loyalty can impair the ability of these employees to effectively negotiate with the buyer and can impair their ability to provide unbiased advice to the seller and to its outside counsel and other professional advisers. As a result, sellers often try to limit the interaction of their employees with the buyer, including prohibiting the buyer from negotiating or entering into contractual relationships with the employees until shortly before or even after the closing, although there are frequently countervailing considerations. A distinct but related issue can arise in the context of post-closing disputes, where the buyer is making a claim against the seller based on pre-closing statements made by seller's employees or on allegedly false representations made in the acquisition agreement that were prepared with the assistance of these employees, who are now employed by the buyer and moreover are potential witnesses.

Unions

Targets that are unionized present special issues in the M&A context and, accordingly, an acquisition attorney faced with a unionized workforce should promptly enlist the assistance of an experienced labor attorney. There are, of course, some fundamentals with which even the non-specialist acquisition lawyer should be generally familiar. The two primary sources from which rights of unionized workers emanate are the NLRA and the applicable collective bargaining agreement. The collective bargaining agreement tends to have a more immediate impact on the acquisition process, and it is here that the review of rights and obligations should begin. The obligations under a collective bargaining agreement are more of a concern for the seller, unless the buyer has agreed to assume the agreement or is considered to be a "successor." The seller is in privity with the union and can therefore be sued for breach of its obligations. The agreement may also contain a successors and assigns clause that forbids the seller from selling the business unless it has caused the buyer to agree to assume the agreement.

Employee Benefits and Human Resources

Next to the question of "Am I going to still have a job," the question that will most likely be on the minds of employees is "What are the terms of my employment, including benefits." The terms of employment are a business issue that will be decided primarily by the buyer (although its ability to dictate these terms may be limited by existing agreements, including collective bargaining agreements). The seller may, nonetheless, exert some influence on the terms of employment. For example, it is quite common for a seller to insist that the target employees be given credit, under the buyer's benefit plans, for their years of service with the seller.

In addition to the determination of what benefits are being offered, there is an issue of how, mechanically, the transition of employment and employee benefits is going to occur. This is sometimes less of a concern in the case of those stock sales or mergers where the infrastructure of the selling entity may be staying in place. It can be a logistical nightmare, however, in the sale of a division or other asset sales, or transactions in which the target will be integrated into a strategic buyer, where the buyer needs to fold the continuing employees into its own system and/or to create a new system. In addition to the integration mechanics, there is the question of culture clash and the corresponding effect on employee morale when transitioned employees are faced with the new employer's plans and policies that differ from the former plans and policies.

Fortunately, for the lawyers, the respective benefits and human resource personnel of the buyer and seller usually work out these mechanics and integration issues. One aspect that the lawyers are frequently called to deal with, however, is a potential gap that exists between the closing and the time at which the buyer is able to implement its benefit plans. Not infrequently, the buyer will not be able to get in place by closing all of the health insurance, workers compensation, paycheck processing and other functions that are necessary for the transitioned employees. In such circumstances, the seller and buyer may enter into a transitional services agreement whereby the seller (or certain of its personnel) will agree to continue to provide various human resources functions and support, and sometimes even benefits, for a period of time following closing.[64]

Effective Communication and Confidentiality

Effective and appropriately timed communication is critical to maintaining good employee relations during what is inevitably a stressful and uncertain time period in their lives. The respective human resources personnel of the buyer and seller typically handle these communications, with limited input from the lawyers, except perhaps in the public company context. However, the legal team needs to be cognizant of the sensitivities associated with employee communications, including the need to vigilantly maintain the confidentiality of the transaction prior to its announcement to employees. In most cases, particularly with privately held companies, an announcement of a potential sale is deferred until relatively late in the process. By the same token, it is a rare deal in which rumors and suspicions of a sale have not begun to be circulated around the water cooler before the official announcement is made. These rumors are often fueled when carloads of bankers and lawyers and other "suits" suddenly show up at seller's place of business to conduct due diligence or plant tours. At a certain point, the rumors may be so disruptive that it is necessary for the seller to come clean with its employees. Employees are often more at peace having the clear knowledge that their employer is being sold (and even that they will likely lose their jobs), than having to deal with uncertainty and innuendo.

Customers and Suppliers

Next to employees, customers and suppliers comprise probably the second most visible and important constituency in the M&A context. The acquisition lawyer, in conjunction with the appropriate business personnel, will need to analyze the respective rights and obligations of the target's customers and suppliers as they relate to the transaction, as well as the strategic importance of certain customers and suppliers to the business—and, thus, to the buyer. As with employees, existing customers and suppliers are often among a company's most valuable assets and these relationships need to be protected and preserved throughout the transaction process. Of course, in some circumstances, these relationships can also be liabilities. For example, the seller may have a long-term supply contract containing take-or-pay provisions that either conflict with the buyer's strategic plans or are no longer economically viable. In most cases, however, the goal is to prevent the loss or impairment of these relationships.

Although there may be formal contracts with key customers and suppliers, the relationship is often less defined by contract and more by relationship, which is to say that customers may simply choose to stop buying and suppliers may choose to stop supplying, even if there is otherwise a contractual framework in place. To a large degree, this is a question of economics and is commercially driven. On the other hand, certain non-economic variables may come into play in the M&A context, including whether existing customers or suppliers have concerns with the buyer over quality or over whether it will continue to support the target's products. The customer or supplier might also be a competitor, or otherwise unwilling to do business with, the buyer for other reasons.

PeopleSoft's Customer Assurance Program

PeopleSoft Inc. adopted a customer assurance program after a hostile bid was received from Oracle Corporation. Under the program, customers of PeopleSoft would be entitled to two to five times the cost of software license fees if PeopleSoft were to be acquired and the acquiring company were to discontinue supporting its products. It claimed that the program was to ease customer's fears over their investment in software applications and supported its ongoing sales efforts. Oracle claimed that it had more to do with entrenchment of management than with customer assurance. Oracle published a "PeopleSoft Customer Commitment" in which it committed to support the PeopleSoft product line and not to force customers to migrate to Oracle applications or databases.

When to Notify

A question that will almost always arise is when to notify customers and suppliers of the proposed transaction. The answer to this question is driven by a number of factors, including:

- the buyer's need and desire to contact suppliers and customers as part of its due diligence;
- the existence of rumors in the marketplace that a transaction is in the works and the need of the target to assure nervous customers and suppliers;
- the need to obtain a consent or waiver under contracts containing anti-assignment or change of control provisions; and
- the need to obtain contractual amendments to accommodate particular aspects of the transaction (e.g., customer purchases in an area in which the buyer has an existing exclusive distributor that prevents direct sales).

In most cases, the buyer will try to gain direct access to the seller's significant customers and suppliers as early in the process as possible, both to get feedback on their current relationship with the target and to determine if the transition to the buyer will be well received. The seller, by contrast, will generally try to limit or delay alerting customers and suppliers to the proposed sale until at least after the acquisition agreement has been signed and the buyer is, albeit conditionally, locked in to doing the deal. Even after that point, there is often a reluctance to allow the buyer to make contact, at least without the active participation of representatives of the target.

Who Bears the Risk of Lost Relationships?

There is an inherent conflict between the buyer, which will want to receive assurances that customers, suppliers, and other third-parties will not cease or limit their relationships as a result of the transaction, and the seller, which will often try to avoid having its customers and suppliers learn of and/or focus on the transaction, especially if there is a real risk of an adverse reaction. This conflict relates to the question of which party should bear the risk of a loss of key customers or suppliers or other third-party contractors during the period of time between signing and closing. Sellers will frequently demand that the acquisition agreement be drafted in a manner (typically through carve outs to the definition of material adverse change) that the loss of key customers or suppliers resulting from knowledge of the transaction will not give the buyer a walk right. The buyer will often strongly resist these tactics.

Other Contracting Parties

There are a host of other third parties that are important to the seller (and to the buyer) in the M&A context, including landlords, tenants, licensors, licensees, distributors, sales agents, consultants, and other service providers, all of whom may have important contractual rights and obligations vis-à-vis the transacting parties. To the extent that these relationships are assets of the selling entity, the same concerns exist regarding preservation of relationships and allocation of risk as are discussed with respect to customers and suppliers. There are, however, some significant differences among the various categories of contracts. For example, the interpretation by a court of an anti-assignment clause contained in a lease, which is governed at least in part by real property law and its corresponding disdain for restraints on alienation, may differ significantly from the interpretation of an anti-assignment clause in a license of patent rights. Nonetheless, there are common threads to all these contracts.

Anti-Assignment and "Change of Control" Clauses

A central issue to all contractual relationships in an M&A context is whether the counterparty has any consent (or, perhaps, termination) rights with respect to the proposed transaction as a result of an anti-assignment or change of control provision and, if so, whether a consent should (and can) be obtained. The failure to obtain consents can result in the loss of contract rights, the acceleration of monetary obligations or an action for breach of contract. In some cases, the consequences may not be realized for a significant period of time after the closing (and perhaps after contractual remedies against the seller have expired). For example, in an asset sale, the seller might assign its insurance contracts. The buyer might not make any claim under the insurance for a significant period of time following the closing, only to find out that the insurance carrier refuses to pay based on the failure to obtain an appropriate consent to the assignment.

In some cases, the failure to obtain a consent can result in a violation of law. For certain regulated industries or entities (e.g., a registered investment adviser) consents may be required by statute even in the absence of contractual provisions. Similarly, contracts with the federal government, by force of statute, can generally not be assigned and require a novation.

The determination of what consents may be required is primarily a question of legal due diligence and contract interpretation. In most asset sales, the sale constitutes an assignment of contracts. In most stock sales, the transfer of stock may trigger a change of control clause, but not an anti-assignment clause. In some jurisdictions, a merger that results in the merging corporation's contracts being vested in the surviving entity is not deemed to constitute an assignment, even where the contractual language prohibits assignments "by operation of law or otherwise." In other jurisdictions, a merger (even a reverse triangular merger) may be deemed to be an assignment. The analysis for determining whether an assignment has occurred will vary from jurisdiction to jurisdiction, with some focusing on the vesting language of the merger statute and others on more subjective factors, such as whether the transfer would result in an increased risk to the counterparty.

Letting Sleeping Dogs Lie

In some cases, the buyer and seller will make a strategic decision not to request a particular consent even where it may be technically required under the terms of a contract. In many cases, the contract may be immaterial and it is unlikely that it will be terminated after the transaction is closed. This decision may also be made for any number of other reasons, but the most common is that the risk of getting a negative reaction from actively seeking consent is higher than the risk of not asking for consent and having the contracting party seek to enforce its contractual remedies for failure to obtain a consent. There is rarely a down side to this strategy for a seller, although for a buyer failing to get a consent prior to closing squarely places the risk of adverse consequences in the buyer's court. The reluctance to seek consents in certain circumstances is also a product of the tendency of contracting parties to use any request for a consent as an opportunity to extract concessions or to otherwise renegotiate the terms of the contract. Electing not to obtain a consent may not be an option in all contexts, however, such as where it is required by statute.

In some situations where a consent has not been obtained, the parties will negotiate elaborate procedures whereby the target will subcontract to the buyer the services or rights otherwise inuring to it under the contract. Similar treatment may be required in the sale of a division where the seller has a contract that relates both to that division and to the seller's retained business—so-called "dual use" contracts. There is no magic to dealing with these situations, other than using common sense and careful drafting.

Creditors

The term creditors encompasses a wide range of persons or entities to which the party in question (and most importantly in the M&A context, the target) is indebted. These debts may be secured by liens on certain (or all) of the target's assets or not secured. There are, of course, other types of creditors, including voluntary creditors (e.g., landlords, suppliers, current, and former employees) and involuntary creditors (e.g., personal injury victims, judgment, and statutory creditors).

Treatment of Creditors

All of these creditors will have certain rights under contract, statute, or common law, against the target that will need to be dealt with in an acquisition. To the extent that a transaction is structured as a forward merger, creditors of the seller (and their corresponding rights to payment) will transfer by operation of law as debts of the surviving or continuing entity, unless paid-off or otherwise released prior to closing. Similarly, in a stock sale or reverse merger, the creditors will (unless paid-off or otherwise released prior to closing) remain creditors of the existing entity under its new ownership. In an asset sale, the debts do not become liabilities of the buyer unless they are assumed, expressly or otherwise. However, certain laws, including bulk sale and fraudulent conveyance laws, may render the buyer liable to the seller's creditors (at least up to the value of the property acquired) even in the context of an asset sale.

A central focus of the buyer's due diligence will be to identify existing creditors and the amount of the liability. This process can be difficult where the debts are contingent or unliquidated. Once identified (to the extent practicable), these liabilities can be fully fleshed out in the agreement or dealt with in some other fashion. The liabilities to banks and other institutionalized credit providers typically are secured and the credit agreements have broad anti-assignment and change-of-control clauses that will be triggered by most M&A transactions. It is important to remember that an assignment of indebtedness will not, absent a novation (which typically requires action by the party to whom the obligation is owed), relieve the assigning party of the obligation, but will only make the assuming party an additional party against whom the debtor can proceed. Of course, the assignor will have rights against the assignee if it fails to discharge those liabilities.

Duties to Creditors—In the Vicinity of Insolvency

In most circumstances, the duty of the board of directors is to the corporation and its shareholders, and there are no fiduciary duties owed to creditors. Creditors are expected to rely on their contractually bargained for rights to protect themselves. One recognized exception to this rule, however, is where the corporation is insolvent, in which case, under a trust theory, the directors of the corporation are deemed to hold the assets of the corporation in trust for the benefit of its creditors. This doctrine has been expanded in recent years and in certain jurisdictions, most notably Delaware,[65] such that the fiduciary duties of the board of directors (and potentially of its officers) shifts to include the corporation's creditors as the corporation approaches or is "in the vicinity" of insolvency (even where it is not otherwise technically insolvent). Where this shift has occurred, the directors can become personally liable to creditors for failing to properly discharge these duties.

This potential shift in duty needs to be kept in mind by directors (and the attorneys who advise them) when contemplating a sale, recapitalization or similar transaction at a time when the corporation is near insolvency or could be rendered insolvent by the particular transaction.

The Directors' Dilemma

A corporation is near insolvency and its directors have made a decision to sell the business through an auction process. The auction has resulted in two final offers. The first, which is not subject to any material contingencies, would pay only enough to cover the company's creditors and the winding up of the corporation. The second offer, by contrast, would result in some payout for the common shareholders, but that offer is subject to several contingencies (due diligence, financial or otherwise) that reduce its likelihood of successful completion. In such a context, and depending on the jurisdiction, the directors may have to consider their duty to creditors in accepting an offer.

This is a developing area of the law. The law is unsettled in many jurisdictions and there are significant variations from jurisdiction to jurisdiction where the expansion has otherwise been recognized.

Communities and Charities

There may be relationships that are important to a seller, including communities and charitable entities, which, in turn, may have non-contractual expectations that need to be considered. Many companies have long-standing ties with the communities in which they operate. In some cases, the relocation of facilities can have a devastating effect on the local economy. It is important to anticipate these concerns and develop a strategy to deal with them, possibly involving promises by the buyer to remain in the community.

Hershey Experiences Community Objection to Sale

The Hershey Trust Company, which controlled about 77% of the stock of Hershey Foods Corp., decided to diversify its holdings and wanted Hershey Foods to explore a sale. It was reported that Hershey Foods employed about 6,200 workers, most in Hershey, Pennsylvania, a town the candy maker founded and once totally owned. Hershey Foods later announced it had been informed that the board of directors of Hershey Trust Company had voted to instruct Hershey Foods to terminate its sale process.

With the support of unions, local politicians, and other community leaders, the Attorney General of Pennsylvania had been successful in obtaining an injunction against the sale in an effort to prevent a loss of local jobs and tax base. The Hershey Trust Company indicated that its decision was due to unsatisfactory offers, not local opposition to the sale.

Similarly, there may be charitable entities that are particularly near and dear to family-owned businesses that have been rather free with the corporate funds in furtherance of these favored charities. It is not unheard of in the acquisition of a family-owned business for a condition of the sale to be that the buyer agree to the continued funding of specified charities, or charitable trusts, for a specified period of time on the same basis that the seller has historically done so. Of course, at the end of the day, everything comes down to dollars, and any such requirements effectively are factored into the purchase price.

CHAPTER 5

Planning for a Sale

The preparation for the sale of a business can raise a host of legal issues, but lawyers often are not engaged until late in the process. Clients often view the lawyer's job as executing the deal after a potential buyer or seller has been identified and the financial terms are settled. In many cases, a seller will have received unsolicited inquiries from a potential buyer or an intermediary and negotiations will have been conducted without the seller exploring other alternatives. This scenario might even have included the execution by the parties of a form of confidentiality agreement that the lawyer has not had an opportunity to review. Yet lawyers, as counselors to business clients, may well have more experience in buying and selling businesses than the owners or the executives that operate the business on a day-to-day basis and can guide their clients in how best to approach a potential transaction and protect their interests. A lawyer's past experience with intermediaries and even potential buyers or sellers can serve as an invaluable resource.

Once the decision to sell a business has been made, planning should be undertaken to organize the process in a manner designed to achieve a successful conclusion. This process will include an examination of the target, assessing the need for and selecting intermediaries, preparing marketing materials and implementing arrangements to retain key employees. In addition, it is important to understand the motivation of a seller and to apply that understanding to selecting the type of buyer.

Conducting a Presale Examination

Since the marketing of a company necessarily involves telling the target's story to prospective buyers, a prime responsibility of the lawyer is to put the target in the best possible legal condition in contemplation of a sale. At the outset, as discussed in Chapter 10, it is advisable to conduct sell-side due diligence to determine whether any issues exist that may concern a prospective buyer and affect a sale.

Action items for the target and its attorney might include:

- Corporate
  - Update minute books to ensure that they contain minutes of all meetings, completely executed consents and a current copy of the charter, bylaws, and other governing documents.

- Review records reflecting securities issuances and transfers, including stock books and option records, to determine the status of outstanding securities.
- Examine documentation for securities issuances to determine the rights of security holders.
- Prepare written contracts or amendments to reflect the manner in which the target conducts its business and to support payments being made by the target for any property or services used in its business.
- Obtain required authorizations and permits and complete foreign qualification in required states.
- Environmental
  - Consider obtaining an environmental audit to determine the existence of significant environmental issues.
  - Prepare or review reports, notices, and other disclosures required under applicable environmental laws.
- Labor and employment
  - Review union contracts and resolve any outstanding grievances or other issues with unions.
  - Prepare or update employment agreements, confidentiality agreements, and noncompetition agreements with key employees.
  - Determine whether the target is in compliance with minimum wage, withholding, and similar laws.
  - Review immigration law compliance.
  - Determine whether the target is in compliance with anti-discrimination laws and health and safety regulations applicable to the workplace.
- Supply chain
  - Review agreements with major suppliers, examine procedures administered by the purchasing department, and determine whether alternative supply sources exist.
- Sales and distribution
  - Review documentation related to distribution, including agreements with major customers.
  - Examine pricing policies and other business practices to determine whether the target is in legal compliance.
- Contract termination rights
  - Determine whether a sale of the target will trigger a right of a major supplier or customer to terminate its contract with the target.
- Intellectual property
  - Review intellectual property registrations and licenses to determine ownership and other rights.
  - Examine agreements with owners, employees, and consultants to determine whether they provide adequate protection of intellectual property rights.

It is sometimes difficult to convince a client that this type of examination is in its best interests and worth the expense. Yet it is much better to discover and attempt to cure problems than to have them brought to the client's attention by a potential buyer. Some of these matters can also dictate a particular structure of the transaction, which is important to know at the outset. At the very least, once a problem is known an explanation and analysis can be agreed upon in advance in an attempt to alleviate the concerns of potential buyers.

Assessing the Need for and Finding an Intermediary

The decision to engage an intermediary in the marketing process is purely a business decision. Some clients, particularly in the smaller transactions, may believe that they know the likely buyers and be perfectly comfortable with determining the value of the business and conducting negotiations without the use of an intermediary. For other clients, an understanding of the different types of intermediaries, what they do and the basis of their compensation is essential to enable a lawyer to properly advise the client.

Sellers often choose to engage an intermediary to access a level of expertise that is absent in their own company. Intermediaries generally have access to the most current information in the M&A marketplace and possess a broad base of experience to draw upon in marketing the target and advising on valuation. They can also be helpful in negotiations, not only because of their experience but also due to the fact that their involvement creates a buffer between the seller's principal decision makers and potential buyers. Engaging an intermediary may also provide extra protection to the target's board if the transaction is later challenged on the grounds that the board breached its fiduciary duty in approving a transaction (especially if the intermediary renders a fairness opinion).

The exact services that an intermediary provides will differ from transaction to transaction and will depend on the type of intermediary engaged by the seller. However, common to all intermediaries is the introduction of the target to potential buyers.

It should be kept in mind that the bulk, if not all, of an intermediary's compensation is earned only if the transaction closes. So, while the attorney's role includes identifying and evaluating potential risks and problems to protect their clients, intermediaries have an economic incentive to minimize problems and find solutions to those that threaten the deal. To use intermediaries to the best advantage, clients must understand their role and perspective.

Types of Intermediaries

Most transactional lawyers have engaged in deals with business brokers, finders, investment banks, and other professionals that participate in the marketing of businesses. What do these different types of professionals actually do and what distinguishes one from another?

A business broker is an agent that may only represent one side in a transaction and may not receive compensation from the other party. Usually a broker represents the seller and, as the seller's agent, its goal is to obtain the highest price and best payment terms. A seller will usually list the business for sale with the business broker, the broker will field inquiries from potential buyers and ultimately will put one or more potential buyers in contact with the seller. Business brokers will usually provide valuation advice and participate in negotiations.

A finder is not an agent of either the buyer or the seller. Finders represent the deal rather than a party and, unlike brokers, can be paid by both parties or either party. Finders are not involved in the negotiations between a buyer and seller, but merely seek to introduce willing parties to one another and act to maintain the contact between them. Unlike business brokers and investment banks, they are usually not subject to licensing requirements.

An investment bank is a full service financial advisor that can generally provide advice regarding valuation of the target (including rendering a fairness opinion), conduct the marketing process, advise on the appropriate structure for the transaction, participate in the negotiation of financial terms and even raise funds to finance the transaction. An investment bank, like a broker, is an agent of the party engaging it and may not receive compensation from the other party.

Factors to Consider

Determining the type of intermediary appropriate for a particular deal is a function of the services the seller needs. If the seller will generate its own marketing materials, conduct its own negotiations and value its own enterprise, then it need not bear the expense of a full service investment bank. On the other hand, if it needs an intermediary to establish and conduct the marketing process and provide expert advice on valuation, then the experience of an investment bank will most likely be required. In addition, the size of the transaction may dictate the type of intermediary that is appropriate. Just as a global investment bank will not accept an engagement to sell a small local retail establishment, neither is a local business broker best suited to advise and market a large enterprise to potential buyers that may include large publicly traded companies and investment funds.

Listed below are some factors to guide clients in the process of choosing the appropriate intermediary for the sale of a business:

- cost
- size of the transaction
- required services, including participation in negotiations and advice on valuation issues and negotiating tactics
- familiarity with industry and competitive dynamics
- transaction experience in the target's industry
- tradition of representing companies and/or deals of same size and profile
- possible conflicts of interest (i.e., does the intermediary have established relationships with potential buyers)

Many of these same factors are also applicable in choosing an intermediary to assist in finding businesses that a client might acquire.

Finding an Intermediary

Once a seller settles on the type of intermediary appropriate for the deal, it will often compile a list of potential candidates and conduct interviews to determine which one best fits its needs. Counsel can be a valuable resource based upon his experience with various intermediaries and having seen firsthand their strengths and weaknesses. There also may be others whose experience with intermediaries can be drawn upon, such as directors, accountants, or other advisors.

After a list of potential candidates is agreed upon, a representative of the seller (which may be the target's founder, a member of the executive team, its counsel, or the party referring the candidate) should make an initial contact to gauge the intermediary's interest in representing the target. Once the candidates have been contacted and narrowed to those interested in the possible engagement, interviews are conducted with each candidate. This process is often referred to as the "mating dance" in which the target sells itself to the prospective intermediary and vice versa. It is generally appropriate to obtain a confidentiality agreement from prospective intermediaries. The intermediaries may schedule formal presentations in which they prepare and present elaborate marketing materials containing descriptions of their organization and experience in the relevant industry in so-called "dog and pony shows." As part of the seller's due diligence, references supplied by the intermediary can be checked.

Terms of the Engagement

Regardless of the type of intermediary used in a particular transaction, the terms and conditions of the engagement should always be memorialized in a written agreement, which is usually in the form of a letter referred to as an engagement letter. The engagement letter will define the services that the intermediary will perform and the scope of the engagement, describe the fees it will receive and who will be responsible for payment, and address the consequences of termination of the engagement. Counsel's role in the engagement of the intermediary is the most visible at this stage since he is normally asked to review and advise the client on the terms of the engagement letter. The intermediary or its counsel typically takes the primary drafting responsibility for the engagement letter, but the final terms of these agreements can be and usually are negotiated, sometimes heavily.

Services to be Performed. The first material issue addressed in an engagement letter is the services that the intermediary will provide. Listed below are various types of services that may be performed by an investment bank:

- review with the board and management the target's financial plans, strategic plans and business alternatives;
- review and analyze historical and projected financial information provided by the target;
- assist the target's board and management in valuation of the target's business;
- advise the target regarding the financial structure and terms of a transaction that might be realized in the current market environment;
- prepare a confidential offering memorandum, identify potential buyers and market the target to potential buyers, including conducting an auction;
- provide a fairness opinion to the target's board; and
- assist in structuring and negotiating the financial aspects of the transaction.

Compensation Arrangements. The second material issue addressed in an engagement letter is the compensation of the intermediary for its services. The fee structure will usually include a "success fee" that is computed as a percentage of the total transaction or enterprise value and may also include a retainer as well as a separate fee for delivering a fairness opinion.

The success fee is normally contingent on the transaction closing and is payable at that time. The retainer fee might be payable monthly during the engagement, upon signing the engagement letter or upon signing a binding agreement to sell the target. The retainer and fee for a fairness opinion are often applied as credits to any success fee that becomes payable. Finally, intermediaries will request reimbursement of all out-of-pocket costs and expenses incurred in performing the services, including the fees of their counsel. All these fees can be, and usually are, negotiated and should not be accepted by the target merely because the intermediary says that the fee structure is standard and customary in the industry.

For many years, investment banks used the so called Lehman Formula for calculation of the success fee. This is a sliding scale, generally a 5-4-3-2-1 formula, where the intermediary would receive 5% of the first $x million of total transaction value, 4% of the second $x million, 3% of the third $x million, 2% of the fourth $x million and 1% of the balance. Although still used today, other variants are common, particularly in larger transactions, such as a fixed percentage of the total transaction value, or a fixed percentage for the first $x million of total transaction value and a higher percentage in excess of $x million. The latter arrangement is intended to provide an incentive to the intermediary to seek a price at the higher end of the anticipated range. If any potential buyers have already been contacted by the target and have expressed an interest, they might be excluded or a reduced percentage may be applied. In many cases, a minimum fee is specified regardless of the total value of the transaction, which is considered an opportunity cost for the time and effort devoted to the project by the intermediary. It is also not unusual to see a flat fee in the sale of a division or subsidiary.

Where the fee is expressed as a percentage of the total transaction or enterprise value, the parties should agree upon the structure of the transaction and what should be included in the determination of the amount of the fee. Most intermediaries will include in the draft of an engagement letter an expansive description of the possible transactions on which a fee will be payable (e.g., a sale of stock or assets, a merger, a lease, a joint venture, a recapitalization, and an investment). The structure of the transaction and what is being sold (e.g., the stock of the target or only certain assets with the retention of liabilities) can significantly affect the amount of the fee. In addition, intermediaries will often attempt to include the consideration for noncompetition covenants, consulting agreements, and employment agreements, on the theory that these are part of the purchase price. In addition to the consideration received or to be received in the transaction, the amount of any debt assumed, acquired, or to remain outstanding is often included because it is either part of the purchase price or of the enterprise value of the target.

If the transaction will include seller or carryback financing or payment in kind, such as equity in the buyer, the seller may wish to negotiate a flat fee for the services to avoid the burden of having to determine the total transaction value upon which the intermediary's fee is paid. Also, if the buyer will pay some of the consideration in installments, the target might attempt to negotiate payment of the intermediary's fees in installments to match the timing of payments to the intermediary with receipt of funds from the buyer. The same approach can be taken with respect to an earnout, rather than treating the earnout as if it had been earned at the closing.

Impact of Changes in the Deal on the Transaction Fee

An investment bank was retained to assist the shareholders in a sale of all the shares of an S corporation. The investment bank's written fee agreement provided that it would receive a fee based on the amount received by the shareholders in the transaction. The shareholders had identified the buyer and discussions had taken place before the investment bank was contacted. Furthermore, the investment bank never produced the offering memorandum, or book, that it had promised.

The S corporation had made several distributions prior to closing to allow the shareholders to pay their estimated taxes, as they had historically done. Not long before closing, the shareholders were told by the investment bank that the buyer had determined it would be highly desirable for it to make an IRC §338(h)(10) election, thereby allowing it to treat the transaction as an asset sale for tax purposes. The shareholders agreed to amend the acquisition agreement to permit the buyer to make the election as long as it would be "tax neutral" to them. The buyer agreed. At the closing, the buyer "grossed up" the purchase price to cover the increased income taxes that would be incurred by the shareholders as a result of the tax election.

The investment bank claimed entitlement to its fee based not only on the agreed purchase price, but also on the amount of the S corporation distributions and the tax "gross up" payment. The shareholders rejected the claim and it was submitted to binding arbitration before a single arbitrator.

The arbitrator determined that no fee was payable on the S corporation distributions since they were not in connection with the purchase, but that the investment bank was entitled to a fee based on about one third of the tax "gross up" payment.

Lessons learned:

- If the deal changes and someone's fees are based in part on the transaction value received by the party it represents, it would be a good idea to revisit the fee agreement to determine how it would be applied to the revised transaction and reach a new agreement, if necessary, before the closing.
- Consider that in binding arbitration of issues relating to transaction fees, it is not uncommon for the arbitrator to split the award so that neither party prevails completely.

Fairness opinions. Clients will often ask whether a fairness opinion is really needed in a transaction. In the typical fairness opinion, the intermediary will opine that the consideration received in the transaction is fair, from a financial point of view, to the seller. This does not mean that the transaction or the price paid in the transaction is the best available or that it would be unreasonable for a seller with full knowledge not to accept the deal. Instead, it means that, from a financial point of view, the consideration received is not below the minimum level that a reasonable person in the position of the seller should accept.

In making the determination whether to obtain a fairness opinion, the client should be advised that it can be very useful protection for the board and even controlling equity holders against claims from minority holders based on an alleged breach of fiduciary duty, and can also be useful when the approval of equity holders is required to authorize a sale and in transactions where equity holders can exercise dissenters' rights. While a fairness opinion may not be appropriate in many transactions, the cost of obtaining a fairness opinion may be justified depending upon whether risks of the type described above are present. In the final analysis, the decision to obtain a fairness opinion is protection versus cost.

Because of the potential liability associated with delivering fairness opinions, intermediaries may try to charge a large fee for the opinion in addition to the other deal fees. In other cases, clients have successfully negotiated delivery of a fairness opinion as part of the standard fee arrangement. The inevitable conflict of an intermediary is even greater to the extent the total fee for a fairness opinion is conditioned on closing the transaction. As a result, some boards of directors, after Sarbanes-Oxley, have begun to insist that the fairness opinion be delivered by an investment banker other than the one engaged for the transaction itself, with the fee to be paid regardless of the conclusion reached by the investment banker providing the fairness opinion or whether the transaction closes.

Indemnification. The third material issue addressed in an engagement letter is indemnification protection provided to the intermediary by the seller or the target, depending on the structure of the transaction. This is one provision that often seems very one-sided in favor of the intermediary. Intermediaries face the risk of having to pay significant amounts in damages in any given transaction. As a result, they will demand that the seller or target indemnify them against any claims, losses, and expenses arising out of the engagement. Whether the indemnification language is contained in the letter itself or, as in many cases, in an exhibit or attachment to the letter, it will often be difficult to negotiate substantial changes. The businesspeople will usually have limited authority to make changes, and requests for changes may have to be referred to the intermediary's legal department.

The indemnity provision typically will carve out claims arising from the intermediary's gross negligence or willful misconduct. Intermediaries may try to limit this carve out further by providing that such claims must arise "primarily" from the intermediary's gross negligence or willful misconduct. In addition, language disclaiming any duty to the equity holders of the target is becoming more prevalent, although its effectiveness may be in doubt. Finally, intermediaries will include a right to contribution to protect them against a court's refusal to enforce an indemnification provision. These contribution provisions generally provide that the sharing of liability between the target and the intermediary is based on the relative benefits gained in the transaction (i.e., the consideration paid in the transaction as compared with the fees collected by the intermediary) with a cap on the intermediary's liability equal to the fees that it actually receives.

Termination. The fourth material issue addressed in an engagement letter is the termination provision. The intermediary will include a so-called tail provision in the termination language providing that if the engagement is terminated and the target consummates a transaction with any party within a certain period of time after termination, then the intermediary is still entitled to its fee. The key components of this provision are the time period over which the tail will operate and the universe of potential buyers covered. The intermediary will usually push for as long a tail as possible, perhaps up to two years, and will attempt to sweep into the tail any buyer, whether or not the intermediary had contacted it. Sellers are often successful in reducing the tail to between six and 12 months and limiting its application only to those potential buyers that the intermediary actually contacted and with respect to which the intermediary expended effort in marketing the target. The intermediary can be required to notify the seller in writing on or shortly after termination of the engagement of each potential buyer it has contacted so the seller will have a record in the event of any later dispute.

It is not uncommon for intermediaries with which clients had passing conversations regarding a potential deal to demand fees after a particular transaction is closed. It is advisable for clients to keep a log of inquiries and correspondence and answer every unsolicited letter by rejecting offers of purchase or engagement and keeping copies of all of this correspondence to minimize the risk.

A common situation occurs where intermediary A refers a potential buyer to the client which is initially pursued but then dropped and intermediary B revives and closes a deal with the same buyer. If this is not covered in the engagement letter with intermediary A or the arrangement with intermediary B, state law will control the issue and the client may end up owing fees to both intermediaries.

Marketing Materials

In larger transactions, especially where an auction is used, and in some smaller transactions, the primary marketing document for the target is an offering memorandum, also called the book. This document serves to introduce potential buyers to the target, its industry, business and management team. Since the primary focus of the book is marketing, it tends to differ from a securities disclosure document, which is also often known as an offering memorandum.

An intermediary, if one is engaged, will generally assume primary responsibility for preparation of the book. The intermediary will meet with management to conduct an investigation into the target and to obtain the information it needs to put the book together. Counsel frequently has little involvement, if any, in the actual drafting of the book outside of producing information or documentation from its files that may be required for its preparation and perhaps supplying disclaimer language with respect to the information supplied in the book. This process is primarily an exercise for the intermediary and the target's management.

Counsel's Role

Counsel should review the book prior to its distribution and pay particular attention to issues that may impact upon antitrust concerns, including the Hart-Scott-Rodino filing, if clearance may be required, such as commentary about the target's market, industry concentration and distribution and pricing methods and strategies. A discussion of the Hart-Scott-Rodino notification requirements is contained in Chapter 12. Also, distribution of the book should be limited through use of a numbering system, and potential buyers should be prohibited from distributing the book other than to their representatives (e.g., disclosure of information in the book by recipients should be on a need to know basis). This can be covered by a legend in the forepart of the book or separately in a confidentiality agreement.

Buyers may attempt to incorporate the book into the representations contained in the acquisition agreement, essentially requiring the target to represent and warrant that all the information contained in the book is accurate. Counsel should vigorously resist this demand and in fact disclaim in the book, as well as in any confidentiality agreement or other transaction document, any and all liability for any inaccuracy of the information contained in the book.[66] This is so for the following reasons, which are usually persuasive:

- As noted above, the book is a marketing document and not a disclosure document.
- The buyer should have ample opportunity to conduct its own due diligence and should be charged with relying on its due diligence efforts to determine whether to pursue the deal.
- Many months may pass between the generation of the book and closing. The target should not be charged with continuing to update the book.
- The book will generally contain projected financials which, if required to be represented and warranted, would constitute future performance guarantees.

Content of the Book

The book will generally contain an executive summary, an industry description, a description of the target, a discussion regarding the opportunities for potential buyers, a description of the target's management, and historical and projected financials.

The executive summary contains a short description of the target's business and industry, recent and projected financial performance, and management. The goal of the executive summary is to focus the potential buyer's attention on the business opportunity.

The description of the target's business and industry serves as an in-depth introduction of the target to the potential buyer. The matters covered are generally the same as the business description in a prospectus for a public sale of securities or in a private placement memorandum. The narrative will explain the business conducted by the target and the business it intends to conduct on a segment-by-segment basis. This discussion will typically include a description of the products and/or services offered or in development, the work force and facilities, the process of manufacture and/or delivery, the use of intellectual property, seasonality of the business, identity of major customers and a description of competitive conditions. The goal of this portion of the book is to introduce potential buyers to the target's industry (including the size of the industry and growth prospects), the target's place in the industry, its material properties and other similar company specific information to familiarize potential buyers with the target in advance of due diligence and the management presentations.

The portion of the book discussing opportunities for potential buyers will focus on the various strategies open to the universe of strategic buyers and financial buyers to extract value from the target business. In addition to discussing industry trends (i.e., growth and consolidation), the target will generally discuss the entry opportunity for near market participants (i.e., those potential buyers that compete in a related market either by industry type or geography), the associated synergies that may exist through an acquisition by a strategic buyer and the cash flow and liquidity opportunities available for a financial buyer. The purpose of this portion of the book is to explain to different types of potential buyers the benefits that they could derive from the acquisition.

The book will also contain biographical material on the executive management team, including industry experience and educational background. This section, along with the introduction to senior executives in the management presentation, is an important first introduction for those, such as a financial buyer, that will rely on the target's existing management to continue to operate the business after closing, since they will be undertaking the risk that existing management will continue to operate the business successfully as part of the buyer's organization.

Historical financial information usually will include, to the extent available, year end financial statements for the last three fiscal years and interim financial statements for the most recent period available compared with the same period of the prior year. The year end financial information presented in the book is usually audited while the interim financial information is unaudited. These financial statements will usually be accompanied by *pro forma* statements showing adjustments to reported income for certain distributions that have been made to the owners, whether as compensation, management fees, or similar items and for the elimination of other nonrecurring items, such as arrangements commonly present in closely held businesses that a buyer would not continue. Sometimes adjustments will be made to the reported income to eliminate or minimize the impact of a one-time blip in results. All of these adjustments should be described in the introduction or notes to the *pro forma* statements. It is also helpful to provide management's discussion and analysis of the financial condition and results of operations to assist the reader in analyzing the target's finances and trends. The target's accountants will often take the lead in providing much of this information to the intermediary for inclusion in the book.

Projected financial information will generally include income statements and balance sheets for a three- to five-year period after the closing and will show the projected cash flows for the target business on a year-by-year basis (and sometimes even a quarter-by-quarter basis) for that period. In addition, a discussion of the assumptions used in the preparation of these projections will be included. The target's financial personnel and the intermediary will generally take the lead in preparing this portion of the book.

Employee Retention Arrangements

When a seller begins the marketing process and the employees become aware of this fact, even if the target might be sold to an employee group, the employees will become concerned about job security. In most transactions, there will be certain employees whose continued involvement in the business is critical and whose willingness to continue employment may be a condition to the buyers' obligation to close the transaction. There may also be another set of employees who, while not having a long-term future with the buyer, are nonetheless necessary to bring the transaction to close and/or to assist with post-closing transition and integration. This issue can be more important for financial buyers that often do not have operating management within the target's industry and the necessary infrastructure in place. Generally, the determination of who falls into which category is made by the businesspeople. Once this determination is made, however, the lawyers can assist in ensuring that a retention program is established to sufficiently incentivize these employees to remain with the target for the desired time period. Among the factors affecting the design of the arrangements for these employees will be their existing pay packages, their wealth from independent sources or potentially from the acquisition, the desirability of their having a role in the post-acquisition organization, their skills and prospects of other employment. and the existence and enforceability of noncompete covenants.

Frequently, key employees will already be subject to employment agreements, or at least confidentiality and noncompetitions agreements, which may effectively discourage them from voluntarily leaving their current employer or its successor (although, in some states, there are limitations on enforceability or the ability of a company to assign employee non-compete agreements in the context of a sale). These agreements and provisions should be reviewed to determine their applicability and sufficiency as to the desired ends in the transaction. Where circumstances dictate, the seller and/or buyer may consider offering key employees new employment agreements, stay bonuses, separate severance arrangements, or other contractual incentives to ensure that they remain for the necessary time period. In some cases, severance arrangements might already be in place for key employees in the event of a change of control of the target or simply giving them some protection in the event of involuntary termination. A stay bonus program, however, is generally instituted only when the marketing process for a sale begins. The use of a stay bonuses and severance arrangements are not exclusive. Often both of these methods will be used to retain key employees. There are innumerable variations on these retention arrangements, and the amount of consideration and the timing of any payments will be dictated by the particular circumstances. The buyer and seller may ultimately negotiate the question of which will bear responsibility for these retention payments.

Stay Bonuses

A stay bonus program specifically motivates key employees to remain with the target through a sale and perhaps for a period after a sale. The target pays the key employee a bonus equal to a portion of the employee's current salary (usually between three to 12 months salary) in a lump sum at a specified time or times so long as the employee does not terminate employment. The payment often is split with a portion of the stay bonus being payable at the closing of the sale and the remainder being payable if, within a specified period of time after the sale, the buyer terminates the employee or the employee terminates his or her employment for good reason, which generally includes relocation, demotion or decreases in compensation.

The use of stay bonuses will allow the target to utilize the assistance of the key employees in the sale process (especially in management presentations and the preparation and collection of due diligence materials) because the target's confidentiality concerns regarding disclosure of the impending sale to the key employees is reduced. In addition, the target might use stay bonuses to secure a noncompetition covenant from key employees after the sale (usually lasting six to 12 months). Potential buyers will be acutely sensitive to the risk associated with potential key employee defections. Use of a stay bonus with a noncompetition covenant will negate the leverage key employees may otherwise have to hold up a sale in order to negotiate higher compensation. The enforceability of noncompetition covenants as a matter of state law is beyond the scope of this discussion, but as a good rule of thumb, the noncompete period should match the portion of the key employee's annual salary paid under the program (i.e., a six month non-compete for a stay bonus equal to six months of the key employee's salary). Including a confidentiality provision that prohibits the employee from discussing the existence of the stay bonus and the prospect of a sale of the target with others except at the target's direction might also be considered.

Severance Arrangements

The primary issues in negotiating a severance arrangement with a key employee are the description of the event or events triggering a payment and the tax implications to the target and the employee. The size of the payment can range from a portion of the employee's annual salary to a multiple of his annual salary and bonus. The table below summarizes the various forms of triggers typically used in these agreements:

Type	Description
Single trigger	The employee receives payment if (i) a change of control occurs (i.e., a merger, sale of majority control or an asset sale) and (ii) the employee thereafter terminates employment for any reason. Single trigger agreements are not common and reserved for senior management, if used at all.
Double trigger	The employee receives payment only if (i) a change of control occurs and (ii) the buyer thereafter terminates the employee's employment without cause or the employee terminates his employment for good reason.
Modified double trigger	These agreements use the double trigger provision during a transition period after a change of control (often between six and 12 months), with a single trigger for a set period of time after the transition period. This allows the employee and buyer to determine whether a long-term relationship is desired and encourages them to either agree on employment terms or part ways after the transition period.

Severance agreements generally contain noncompetition covenants similar to those discussed with respect to the stay bonuses. In addition, these agreements may contain a provision obligating the employee to attempt to find a new job, which reduces the payments by the amount of any other compensation earned during the period severance payments are made.

Tax Considerations

Payments to the employee under a stay bonus program and a severance agreement are taxable as compensation to the employee and deductible to the employer. The target will generally be responsible for payment of any stay bonuses that it can treat as a pre-sale expense for tax purposes. Severance agreements generally provide that the buyer is obligated to make the payment or the target itself is obligated after the sale. A buyer usually will take this additional liability into account in negotiating the purchase price. In addition, Section 280G of the Internal Revenue Code limits the deductibility of severance payments (aggregated with other payments caused by the change of control) in certain circumstances if they exceed 2.99 times the employee's average annual compensation over a five year period; if this limit is exceeded, amounts in excess of one times average annual compensation may not be deductible and may be subject to a 20 percent excise tax, payable by the employee. Many severance agreements will contain a provision reducing the amount of the payments to the maximum amount deductible under this limitation, but others will increase the payment to reimburse the employee for the tax.

The Type of Buyer

A decision will have to be made at a fairly early stage as to the type of buyer that would be best suited for a client that wants to sell its business. This determination will depend in large part on the client's motivation for selling. Once the motivation becomes clear, consideration can be given to the various types of potential buyers and the extent to which they might satisfy the seller's objectives. The decision might be to discuss a potential sale with employees of the company, to explore the possibility of selling to third parties, either strategic or financial, or to embark on any combination of these approaches.

Understanding a Seller's Motivation

A decision to sell a business can occur for many different reasons. Understanding the client's motivation, and the circumstances relating to that decision, is essential to counseling on the best fit between the client and a buyer. Some clients are motivated entirely by the financial gain and a desire for liquidity, in which case the search may turn to buyers having the potential to offer the highest price in cash. Other clients may be motivated simply by a desire to retire or to pursue other interests. This desire could be caused by advanced age, health concerns, disputes among owners or the lack of a successor to carry on the business. The price therefore may not be as important as timing and being relieved of any further responsibility for the business.

Tensions in Family-Owned Businesses

One fairly common situation involves family-owned businesses where, upon the death of a founder, ownership has passed to members of later generations. This can create significant tensions because some family members may continue to operate the business while others are not involved in operations. Questions are often raised as to the performance of those family members operating the business, the level of their compensation and the payment of dividends to the owners, some of whom otherwise may have limited sources of income. Whenever considerable value has been created, there can be added pressure by some to sell the business or realize value in some other manner, while others may prefer to continue the business in the same tradition.

Freedom Communications, Inc., a publisher of daily newspapers and weekly publications with a libertarian editorial philosophy, was founded in the 1930s and was run by R.C. Hoiles until his death in 1970. A dispute ultimately arose among the family members, some of whom wanted the company to be sold while others preferred a transaction whereby the company could stay in the family but those who wanted to sell their shares for cash could do so. It was reported that there were 10 potential suitors, including other newspaper publishers and financial buyers. The result was a recapitalization that closed in May 2004, providing liquidity for some family members and affording other family members continued control over the company.

Some businesses are sold because of a need for additional resources to grow and remain competitive, such as capital, professional management or more advanced technology. This may lead to consideration of only strategic buyers who have these resources and a familiarity with the business and industry. Sometimes financial problems or regulatory issues can lead to a sale, and again timing might be more important than the price. It can also make a difference as to whether the owners want to continue working for the buyer or to at least find a decent home for those key employees who have helped build the business. Most owners have considerable pride in what they have built up over the years and therefore may have to balance their personal goals against finding a buyer that will be a good steward for the business and support its continued growth.

Selling to Employees

Prior to exploring a sale to third-party buyers, a seller might look to the target's own employees. A sale to employees may take many forms, including a sale to management (called a management buyout or MBO) or to an employee stock ownership plan (called an ESOP).

Factors to consider. The table below lists some of the advantages and disadvantages of a sale to employees as compared with a sale to a third-party buyer:

Advantages	Disadvantages
• Greater familiarity with the business	• Creates distractions and an adversarial relationship
• Possible limited need for full representations and indemnities	• Lack of financial resources and deal experience
• Increased prospect of employee retention	• Employee defections if unsuccessful
• Seller can maintain control over the process	• Difficulty in simultaneously marketing to third-party buyers

A primary advantage of selling to employees is their familiarity with the business. A third-party buyer will be less willing to assume the risk of the unknown because it simply is not as knowledgeable about the target's business as the employees. As a result, third-party buyers may demand and receive more robust representations and indemnities. The allocation of this risk to the seller can erode the value of what it might receive in the transaction.

A sale to employees can allow the existing owners to maintain a positive connection with the target and possibly fulfill a moral obligation to long-time employees. It is not uncommon for key employees to have the expectation, whether explicit or implicit, that they ultimately would have an opportunity to own the business when the current owners disengage from day-to-day operations or otherwise want to sell the business. Employees understandably get nervous about their future prospects when a disruptive event like a sale takes place, and a sale to them may alleviate these fears and enhance the prospects for employee retention. This concern magnifies the need to formulate strategies to retain employees throughout the marketing and acquisition process when considering a deal, a subject that is covered earlier in this chapter.

The personal involvement of management and employees in the acquisition process can disrupt the daily operation of the business and erode value. Disruption inevitably occurs in any transaction, but in this particular scenario the key employees may be less likely to concentrate on operating the business because they are trying to put a deal together. They can become disgruntled and leave, causing significant employee morale and retention issues if a sale to them falls through.

Another key disadvantage is the creation of an adversarial relationship between the employees or management and the owners in this type of transaction.

Founders' Motivation

The founders of a business through the years had developed differing goals and decided it was time to part ways. One founder, along with other investors, wanted to buy out the other founder. The other founder refused, reasoning that he would not engage in an adversarial negotiation over the value of the target and insisted on a sale to a third party. An investment bank was engaged to conduct an auction and a strategic buyer was found that eventually paid far more for the target than what the founders thought they would realize. In this instance, the motivation of a founder to avoid having to negotiate a sale within the organization became the basis for the entire structure of the sale and a resulting windfall.

In addition, if the employees are competing with third parties, they may not be inclined to cooperate in any efforts by these parties to evaluate the business in order to make a proposal.

A sale to a third party can afford a seller greater control over the presentation of information to potential buyers as well as their access to the business. However, once a buyer is chosen, it will generally seek and obtain control of the process, including drafting the documentation, conducting additional due diligence and timing the closing.

A sale to employees may take more time than a sale to a well-financed third party because of the inexperience of the buyer, the need for third party financing and the general complexity of financing structures. A possible benefit of a relatively simple sale to a third party is the potential for reduced transaction costs.

Financing the sale. Because of the special nature of an employee buyout, no discussion of this topic would be complete without commenting on the means of financing these types of transactions. In a sale to employees, financing may be the primary concern since the employee group among themselves will almost never have the resources to complete an acquisition without some form of third party financing. The three types of financing structures for an employee buyout explored below are: seller financing, an ESOP and a financial sponsor, which may be used independently or in combination.

Seller financing, or carryback financing as it is also called, can take many forms but essentially represents the portion of the acquisition price that the existing owners agree to finance themselves, whether in the form of debt or equity. Seller financing usually consists of unsecured subordinated debt or even junior preferred stock, depending on the use of senior and mezzanine debt and third party equity in the transaction. On occasion, seller financing can be combined with and become subject to the same payment terms and security as senior debt. Some of these transactions can be structured as "bootstrap" acquisitions, in which part of the equity interest of the owners is purchased by the target for a note and the remainder is purchased by the employees for cash, so that the employees end up as the sole owners and the note is repaid by the target over a period of time using its cash flow. In effect, the acquisition is financed by the target itself rather than by third party financing.

Use of an ESOP is a popular technique to effect an employee buyout. An ESOP is a tax qualified employee benefit plan, which together with an ESOT, a tax exempt trust that holds assets for the benefit of employees of the sponsoring employer, is formed as the acquisition vehicle for the target. Third party financiers will loan the purchase price to either the target (which will in turn loan this amount to the ESOP) or to the ESOP itself (in which case the target will usually guarantee the loan), the ESOP will purchase the equity of the target for the benefit of the employee participants and the third party financier will take the purchased equity as collateral. The target then makes cash contributions to the ESOP to service the loan. As the loan is repaid, the purchased equity is released from the collateral pool securing the loan. These transactions are generally quite complex by nature, but the basic fund flows are diagrammed below:

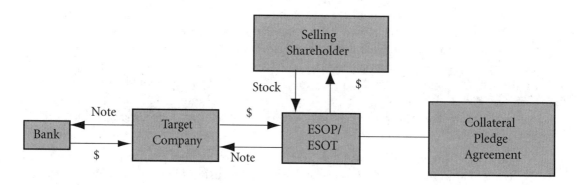

Use of an ESOP can provide very favorable tax treatment to the sellers if they effect a rollover of the proceeds of the sale into replacement securities in accordance with Section 1042 of the Internal Revenue Code. These rules are very technical and participation of a tax lawyer specializing in this area is strongly advised when counseling clients on this type of transaction. The technical advice required and the difficulty in valuing the purchased equity and locating suitable third party financing, together with the expense associated with meeting these requirements, are disadvantages to the use of a leveraged ESOP to finance an employee buyout.

Another possibility is the use of a financial sponsor, in combination with the employees, to acquire the business and provide the needed financing. In this type of transaction, the purchasing group, generally key members of management, will usually engage a private equity firm with an investment fund as a lead financial sponsor. The investment fund will provide all or a portion of the funds necessary to complete the acquisition by itself or, depending on the size and complexity of the transaction, may include a syndicate of commercial banks and investment funds to provide the senior debt, mezzanine debt and equity to complete the acquisition. The employee group will operate the business and receive a portion of the common equity in the purchasing entity. These transactions will have many of the same characteristics as any other acquisition by a financial buyer.

Selling to a Third Party

A sale to a third-party buyer, *i.e.,* a buyer other than the target's employees, may take many forms, including a stock or asset sale or a merger. The particular buyer may be a competitor of the target, a company in a related market looking to expand into the target's market, an investment fund or a wealthy individual. The search for a third-party buyer may begin after determining that a sale to employees is not feasible or while those discussions are ongoing.

Before embarking on this process, it is important to understand the types of third-party buyers, which generally fall into two categories—strategic and financial. This distinction can be important because the motivations of these buyers differ dramatically and may not align with the objectives of the seller.

The table below summarizes the general characteristics of strategic and financial buyers:

Strategic Buyer	Financial Buyer
• Uses cash and/or equity as consideration and often does not require financing	• Uses cash as consideration and leverages with significant acquisition debt. May seek to pay part of the consideration with notes.
• May have a limited role for existing management	• Requires management continuity and provides strategic and financial oversight
• Cultural issues and synergies are important elements in determining price and are used to enhance a strategic buyer's market value	• Pricing is generally cash flow driven and the investment horizon is typically short term
• Operates the business as part of its organization on a stand-alone basis or integrates it into its existing business	• Usually owns other portfolio companies unrelated to the target's business
• May have considerable familiarity with the target's business	• Often has somewhat limited knowledge of the target's business

Strategic buyers are operating companies that focus on the synergies created in an acquisition to determine the desirability of a target and its enterprise value. Conceptually, a strategic buyer will look to the added capabilities a target can provide, whether it is run as a stand-alone or is folded into the buyer's existing operations, to determine whether the target will enable it to do things it could not otherwise do and vice versa. Aside from a pure financial analysis, the culture of the target is very important to a strategic buyer since it will need to integrate the target's business into its own in order to achieve the synergies that form the basis for the transaction. As a result of these motivations and knowledge of the target's business, strategic buyers may pay a higher price than financial buyers, but pricing of deals between strategic buyers and financial buyers can fluctuate over time.

Financial buyers acquire companies with a view to growing the business and selling it or taking it public, typically within a three to seven year period. Most financial buyers are investment funds managed by private equity firms. Investment funds are private pools of capital contributed by high net worth individuals and large institutional investors such as pension funds, charities, insurance companies, and similar organizations. They usually will require that existing management continue after the sale, incentivizing them with equity participation, because they are not interested in managing day-to-day operations but only in providing strategic and financial oversight. An exception would be a financial buyer that is involved in a consolidation play, where it acquires separate operating companies within a single industry segment and therefore has available other management resources.

Financial buyers generally value a target based upon a multiple of discounted cash flows and will model the acquisition based upon the estimated value at sale to determine a projected internal rate of return for the investment. The internal rate of return, or IRR, is the rate at which cash inflows exceed cash outflows from a particular investment over a given period of time. The distinction between strategic and financial buyers can sometimes become somewhat blurred when financial buyers are consolidating separate companies within an industry segment. However, while strategy and synergies are a factor in these types of acquisitions, the financial objectives remain the same in terms of finding an exit for the investment in the near term as described above.

CHAPTER 6

Embarking on the Sale Process

At some point early on, a decision will have to be made as to how the sale process is to be conducted. Once that decision is made, a plan for identifying potential buyers has to be developed. In this chapter, we will discuss the principal methods by which a business can be sold, including consideration of the advantages and disadvantages of these methods, and offer some suggestions as to how potential buyers, or potential sellers in the case of acquisitive companies, might be identified.

The lawyer's role in the decision as to the method of sale and in finding a buyer or seller will vary considerably, depending in large part on the sophistication of the client, the experience of the lawyer, and the involvement of an investment bank or other intermediary. It is certainly not unusual for a client to inform the lawyer of the name of the potential buyer with whom discussions have already taken place. As a matter of fact, some practitioners will say that they very seldom have anything to do with the identification of potential buyers. Nevertheless, it is important to understand the process for those situations in which the lawyer's expertise and experience will be sought.

Selecting the Method of Sale

Most businesses are sold in direct negotiations with potential buyers on a one-on-one basis. Another strategy for selling a business is an auction. This process can range anywhere from a controlled auction, in which negotiations are conducted with a limited number of potential buyers without any specific time constraints, to a formal auction, in which multiple potential buyers are approached or a proposed sale is publicly announced and the bidding and time parameters are highly structured.[67] In some cases, an auction is conducted in an effort to satisfy the fiduciary duty of directors[68] and in others it is simply thought to be the best means of maximizing value. The advice of intermediaries and counsel who have experience in the sale of businesses can be very helpful to the client in making this decision.

The following are the principal advantages and disadvantages of selling a business in an auction as compared with a negotiated transaction.

Advantages	Disadvantages
Possibility of enhancing value	An unsuccessful auction can inhibit selling the business for some time

Maximizes bargaining leverage through competitive bidding	More difficult to maintain confidentiality
Greater control over the process	Susceptible to disruption
Greater say in fixing the terms of the acquisition	Can consume more time

To a seller, the principal advantages of an auction are the prospects of enhancing value and of maximizing bargaining leverage through competitive bidding. An auction also permits a seller to compare offers in a systematic fashion and affords it greater control over the entire process, including the ability to control the timing of the negotiations and closing. By submitting its own form of acquisition agreement, the seller can have more say in fixing the terms and can minimize the likelihood of renegotiation by a buyer once a bid is accepted.

There are, however, a number of risks in undertaking an auction. Since a number of potential buyers may be contacted, it may be more difficult to maintain confidentiality. Disclosure that the business is for sale can affect relationships with suppliers and customers. A prospective buyer may leak word about a sale or, for that matter, make contact directly with key customers or suppliers in violation of confidentiality agreements. Similarly, word can get out among employees of the target causing serious morale problems. An auction can create more anxiety among management and key employees than a negotiated transaction with a known buyer. Uncertainty as to the identity of the bidders or, if known, which of them might be successful, can leave management and the employees with concern over their future throughout the entire process. That is why stay bonuses or severance arrangements are often put in place prior to an auction to help prevent defections. The other aspect of confidentiality in an auction is that proprietary or sensitive information concerning the target will have been more widely disseminated, and thus there is a greater degree of risk that the information may be improperly disclosed or used.

Of course there can be no assurance that an auction will generate an acceptable offer, or that negotiations with a successful bidder will result in acceptable terms. Since an auction can seldom be conducted on a confidential basis, all the participants and others will be aware that the auction failed. Not only the auction itself but also a failure may be publicized in business and trade publications. Regardless of the reason for the failure, whether stated or not, rumors will abound and there will often be a suspicion that there was something uncovered that caused bidders to back away. In any event, it may be very difficult after a failed auction to remarket the business until a significant period of time has elapsed. Of course somewhat the same result can occur in a negotiated transaction that is not consummated, particularly if this becomes known publicly or in the trade.

The auction process can consume more time than simply identifying a potential buyer and engaging in direct negotiations, although well-structured auctions can be completed within a relatively short period of time. Auctions are susceptible to disruption caused by unforeseen events or by bidders. If exclusivity is granted to a bidder, there is a risk that the seller is leaving itself open to an attempt to renegotiate the price offered. Renegotiation is seldom blatant without a stated reason, which is usually the discovery of new facts in due diligence. This highlights a fundamental problem with auctions—competitive bids are submitted by a number of potential buyers having somewhat limited information about the target. Sellers want to minimize disclosure of their proprietary information during the early stages of the process, and bidders want to minimize their deal expenses until it is clear that they have a good chance of being selected.

The Risks of Game Playing

Illustrative of the potential disruption to the process caused by a bidder was an announcement in 2003 by General Electric Co. that it would no longer offer its properties to private equity firms in open auctions, but would deal exclusively with a small group of firms that it selects to better control the process. GE blamed private equity firms for some of its failed auctions, because it believed that some tried to circumvent the process. It mentioned an auction in which one bidder caused other bidders to drop out, but then the high bidder lowered its bid citing concerns arising from its due diligence. GE claimed that this firm never intended to pay the initial amount bid, but rather used its bid to drive other suitors away.[69]

In spite of the efforts that are made to structure the bidding process, it is also not unusual to encounter preemptive or unsolicited bids, or even higher bids by a participant after being advised that the process is concluded. This is particularly true with public companies, even after an acquisition agreement has been fully negotiated and signed. This can pose a dilemma for directors if they do not accept a higher bid (potentially triggering claims by shareholders that the directors have breached their fiduciary duty) and possibly result in claims by the successful bidder if the seller disregards the announced auction process.

While auctions have become increasingly acceptable in the marketplace, some may refuse to participate. If the bidders are properly identified, the process should theoretically result in full value being paid. Some buyers have an aversion to engaging in competitive bidding, either because they will have limited control over the process and often an inability to engage in face-to-face negotiations with management, at least early in the process, or simply because the auction can lead to irrational behavior of some bidders who hate to lose and therefore overpay, in which case the whole process can be a waste of time and resources. Additionally, some financial buyers may be reluctant to participate unless they are granted exclusivity at an early stage due primarily to time and expense concerns. As a practical matter, however, a significant amount of the deal flow for financial buyers comes from auctions, as distinguished from so-called proprietary deal flow in which the financial buyer is able to convince a seller not to shop the company.

Identifying Potential Buyers

If the decision is to explore selling to third parties, a procedure has to be developed to identify and evaluate potential buyers within that group. This process, which is common to both negotiated sales and auctions, begins by looking through the universe of strategic and financial buyers to find those that might be interested in the target.

In order to identify these potential buyers, the seller or its representatives will generally conduct a search-and-screen process in-house or in conjunction with an intermediary or other advisor. The process begins by identifying the target's industry and reviewing industry literature (especially reports on merger and acquisition activity) to find those that are active in making acquisitions or are known to be considering acquisitions. At the outset, using the target's and related S.I.C. codes (Standard Industrial Classification), the seller can search through the S.I.C. database to develop the list of industry participants and near industry participants. Identification and contact with the target's trade associations and attendance at trade shows is another source of information. Other fruitful sources of company-specific information are the filings with the SEC for potential buyers that are subject to the public reporting requirements and *Dun & Bradstreet* reports for potential buyers that are private companies.

The goal of the search at this point is to identify and categorize potential buyers as strategic or financial candidates and to develop a system to determine the best fit between the target and the candidate based on the seller's motivation. One of the objectives of the search is to allow the seller to rank in order the universe of potential buyers. Categorization in this search-and-screen process focuses on the characteristics of potential strategic buyers and financial buyers. An important contribution of counsel is to assist the client in assessing antitrust risk with potential buyers.

The most important resource a lawyer has in this particular context can be his own contacts. Financial buyers establish networks of professionals and intermediaries, as well as other financial buyers, that serve to pinpoint potential opportunities. This network creates deal flow for the particular fund and is vital to its existence. A lawyer can assist a seller by making inquiries of those in the lawyer's network that may be interested in acquiring the type of business that is being sold. However, the lawyer must think through all of the possible conflict of interest scenarios that may arise when assisting a client in the process of identifying potential buyers. If the potential buyer is or was a client, the lawyer may find himself conflicted out of the transaction. Chapter 2 contains a discussion of the potential conflicts of interest that can arise in this context.

Identifying Potential Sellers

Much of the discussion in this chapter regarding the search for a buyer is also applicable to finding a target for an acquisitive client. Lawyers for acquisitive clients, whether operating companies looking for strategic acquisitions or financial buyers looking for acquisition opportunities, may be called upon to assist in locating potential acquisitions.

The process for finding a seller, as for finding a buyer, can include engaging an intermediary to identify potential acquisition targets, searching through listings of a local business broker or using a network of business contacts, depending on the size and nature of the business that the buyer wishes to acquire. The website of the International Business Brokers Association, Inc., located at www.ibba.org, is a very useful resource for locating a business broker in a particular locale and even identifying many types of large and small businesses for sale in a particular industry and geographic area. Accountants and financial planners often represent owners of small businesses that are potential candidates.

Financial advisors such as investment banks and business brokers can be useful to buyers searching for acquisition targets. These intermediaries can assist a buyer in the conduct of the search-and-screen process and approach potential targets about whether they might be willing to sell without having to disclose the identity of the interested party.

As in the case of finding a buyer, the lawyer can assist an acquisitive client by contacting others within his network that may own or know about the type of business that the client seeks to purchase.

Maintaining Confidentiality

During this process, and particularly when potential buyers and sellers have been identified, confidentiality becomes a critical issue. There are two aspects of confidentiality that need to be considered in the context of an acquisition. The first is maintaining confidentiality of the fact that the business is for sale, as well as the status of the negotiations and identity of the parties, and the second is maintaining confidentiality of the information that the seller and buyer will be disclosing to each other or to others involved in the process.

Maintaining Confidentiality of the Deal

Maintaining confidentiality of a proposed sale and related information can be controlled to some extent by implementing procedures to ensure that the group involved, whether employees or outside advisors, is kept to a minimum on a need to know basis and that precautions are taken with respect to the distribution and display of documents and the manner and location for holding meetings. Within a seller or target, the importance of maintaining this information in confidence should be stressed and the employees involved should be admonished not to make inadvertent slips or comments to their coworkers or others. Outside the target, the advisors, whether investment banks, attorneys or accountants, will usually have their own procedures for maintaining confidential information. Some parties will require that their business brokers or investment banks sign a fairly simple confidentiality agreement. In an effort to maintain confidentiality, the participants will often adopt code words to identify the project and the parties.

Maintaining Confidentiality of Shared Information

Both aspects of confidentiality as applied to third parties are typically covered by written agreements that are usually the first legal document to surface in the sale process. The target (and often the buyer) will be justifiably concerned over the potential disclosure or misuse of its confidential or proprietary information that is provided during the due diligence process, particularly where there is a strategic buyer that could potentially use the information for competitive purposes if the transaction is not consummated. Understandably, it is quite common for a target to insist upon a confidentiality agreement very early in the process before any confidential or proprietary information is disclosed. This can be a unilateral agreement, restricting disclosure or use of information provided by the seller, or bilateral, restricting disclosure or use of information provided by either party to the other.

While attorneys can provide critical guidance on the content of confidentiality agreements, in many cases they are not consulted. To be sure, some companies who have been through the acquisition process may pull off the shelf a perfectly good form of confidentiality agreement that they have tailored to their particular sensitivities. By contrast, the following are some other common scenarios:

- The buyer proffers its standard form of agreement that appears sufficiently legalistic to the seller, so it chooses not to start the meter running by calling outside counsel.

- The seller pulls off the shelf a generic form of nondisclosure agreement that it has used when customers, consultants, bankers, etc., are being given sensitive information in other types of commercial or financial transactions.
- The seller foregoes requiring a confidentiality agreement and decides it can deal with all this later if the buyer shows a real interest.
- The seller proffers a full metal-jacket agreement carefully crafted by its counsel, or a "standard form" used by its investment bank, but which hamstrings the unrepresented buyer in many ways it never anticipated when the deal craters.

Because these agreements often will be prepared or reviewed by both buyer's and target's attorneys, it is important to become familiar with the issues to be considered. A form of confidentiality agreement with detailed commentary is contained in the Ancillary Agreements to MAPA. As discussed in the commentary to MAPA, the confidentiality agreement may be superseded by a separate provision in the acquisition agreement.

Content of confidentiality agreements. Confidentiality agreements are negotiated between a potential buyer and seller in the context of a specific acquisition and therefore will describe the proposed transaction, acknowledge that the information to be transmitted is proprietary in nature and limit its use to an evaluation of the transaction in question. As with any agreement, the confidentiality agreement should carefully identify the parties. Sometimes these agreements are prepared and distributed on the letterhead of an investment bank, which enters into the agreement as agent and on behalf of the seller or potential buyer.

From the point of view of a target, the agreement should describe the confidential information as broadly as possible to include all material provided to a potential buyer in written or electronic form and all information communicated orally or in any other way to the potential buyer, including any notes, analysis, and other documents that are prepared by the buyer utilizing information provided by the target. Some agreements require that documents to be treated as confidential must be stamped as being proprietary or confidential, and that to protect any information disclosed orally, its confidentiality must be confirmed in writing within a specified period after disclosure; that approach presents the seller with a significant risk of inadvertent failure to cover some information. In addition to information provided to the potential buyer, the agreement often treats as confidential that the parties are considering a potential transaction, that confidential material has been provided and any other information concerning the discussions of the parties or the proposed transaction.

A potential buyer will want to limit the information treated as confidential as much as possible by excluding:

- information that is available to the public other than as a result of disclosure by the recipient;
- information that was already known by the recipient on a nonconfidential basis prior to its disclosure to the recipient;
- information that otherwise becomes available to the recipient on a nonconfidential basis from a source that is not bound by a confidentiality agreement or other contractual, legal or fiduciary obligation; and
- information that is independently developed by the recipient without use of the information disclosed.

In addition, most agreements deal with the circumstances in which a potential buyer is required or (and this aspect is negotiable) requested by a court or governmental agency to make available information or documents, and require that advance notice be given to allow the seller to obtain a protective order or other appropriate remedy.

A potential buyer will wish to share the confidential information with its agents and advisors who are involved in the process and in deciding whether to proceed. That list may include the buyer's directors, officers, employees, attorneys, accountants, investment bank, and consultants. It may also include financing sources and the financing sources' advisors and agents. Accordingly, the agreement may provide that, if confidential information is disclosed to the agents and advisors, the buyer will be responsible for informing them of the terms of the agreement and for enforcing the agreement as to them. Some sellers require that the buyer obtain a separate agreement from its agents and advisors to be bound by the confidentiality agreement so that the seller can enforce the agreement against them directly.

One of the matters that is often covered is the process by which a potential buyer obtains the confidential information. Often a seller, for its protection, will designate one person to be contacted with respect to requests for confidential information.

Targets often include language in confidentiality agreements disclaiming any responsibility for the accuracy of information or materials provided to potential buyers other than as set forth in an acquisition agreement and to the effect that buyers should not rely on the accuracy of such information or materials. However, in two recent cases, *A.E.S. Corp. v. Dow Chemical*[70] and *Marram v. Kobrick Offshore Fund*,[71] courts have found that at least in a stock sale these provisions will not preclude causes of action under the federal securities laws in connection with the sale of securities. Other cases are to the contrary.[72]

Another topic is the term or time period during which the buyer is required to keep the information confidential. Of course, sellers would like to have the term be unlimited and buyers would like to limit the term as much as possible. Many buyers will ask to limit the duration to a relatively short period of time—often one to three years. The reason for the limitation is the concern by buyer's counsel that the obligation of the buyer not go on forever and that a date certain is necessary so that it need no longer police its employees against inadvertent disclosure.

Confidentiality agreements will deal with the return or destruction of the confidential information in the event that the transaction is not consummated. The agreement often provides that if the discussions between the parties are terminated, the confidential information will promptly be returned to the seller. As a practical matter in this cyber age, returning the disclosed information is much more difficult because much of it is stored electronically. Therefore, it is common to provide that the confidential information must be deleted from all computers and that an executive officer certify that all confidential information (including notes and summaries prepared by the buyer) have either been returned to the seller or destroyed. Indeed, deletion may be difficult for any organization that regularly conducts data backups. As a practical matter, certification of destruction may make more sense than insisting upon a return of material, since a party that would be deceitful or sloppy about destruction in all likelihood could not be trusted to return all copies of the documents. Sometimes counsel for the buyer will request that one copy of the confidential information be retained by the potential buyer or, more appropriately, its counsel as proof of the extent of the confidential information should there be a claim at a later date for disclosure violating the terms of the agreement.

Another common point of negotiation is the question of choice of law and choice of forum should there be litigation. A seller may want to have its local law used as the governing law for the agreement and the local courts be the sole venue for any litigation should there be a breach of the agreement. Virtually all confidentiality agreements provide that money damages are insufficient and specify specific performance or other equitable relief as a remedy. Of course if sensitive information has already been disclosed, equitable relief may be of little benefit. Because of the urgency of preventing the disclosure or use of confidential information, these agreements seldom provide for arbitration or similar dispute resolution mechanisms.

If a public company, a target may require that a potential buyer agree to a "standstill" or agreement for a specific period of time not to acquire any of the target's securities or to commence a tender offer or otherwise to seek to obtain control of the target.

In recent years, it has been fairly common for confidentiality agreements to contain provisions restricting the hiring or solicitation of employment of the target's employees. This inclusion is to address a concern that a potential buyer may become familiar with the abilities and expertise of key employees of the target and, if the transaction is not consummated, will offer them employment. These provisions are generally applicable for only a specified period of time, sometimes specify the management or supervisory level of the employees covered and often make distinctions between solicitation by the potential buyer and the response to a general advertisement by a key employee.

Negotiating confidentiality agreements. As confidentiality agreements have become more standardized, the issues raised and the outcome have become fairly predictable. Since the same comments will be made, counsel can develop fairly standard responses and language that will be acceptable to the client. When the form of confidentiality agreement originates from the intermediary for a seller, potential buyers will usually pass their comments along to the intermediary, which will then either respond itself, based upon prior discussion with counsel to seller, or seek the advice of counsel to the seller. Counsel will determine what changes would be acceptable and provide the wording to the intermediary. If an impasse is reached, the negotiations might be conducted directly between counsel.

The Negotiated Sale

The traditional process for most of those parties selling a business is the negotiated sale. The owner may have determined that this is an opportune time to sell the business and prepare for a sale in the manner discussed earlier. In some cases, someone who is interested in buying the business approaches an owner who may not have seriously considered a sale. This potential buyer might be a group of managers, a private equity firm, or a competitor, supplier, or customer. Negotiations can commence and a sale be completed without the owner ever checking to see whether there are others that may be interested in buying the business. Some owners, once they are approached about a sale of the business and warm to the idea, may want to see whether there are other potential buyers that might better meet their objectives.

An owner who is inclined to explore the field will go through the process of identifying potential buyers. Once a list is prepared and the potential buyers are ranked in order, the next step would be to contact several of the preferred candidates to gauge their interest. It is common for preliminary discussions to be conducted with several prospects at the same time. While the seller may make each of the potential buyers aware that it is negotiating with one or two others, the process still does not rise to the level of an auction. Nevertheless, it may proceed in somewhat the same fashion.

As in any sale, there are many variations on the theme. The intermediary or the target itself can make the initial contacts depending on how the seller wishes to proceed. These contacts might be made one at a time in series, or several contacts might be made simultaneously, depending on the strategy that is adopted. Unless there is already a personal relationship, contact is normally attempted with those at the top of the organization chart—the chief executive officer, the chief operating officer, or the chief financial officer. The conversation should be as general as possible and focus on providing information about the target's business and personnel and the desire to discuss the possibility of a transaction between the two organizations. When an intermediary makes contact, a call may be preceded with a letter and a brief outline of the opportunity.

If the prospects are strategic buyers, they may be familiar with the business and the target so the process can be fairly informal, beginning with a confidentiality agreement and leading to preliminary negotiations. If the process is to be more structured, the next step may be to send a book to those prospects who have expressed an interest. Those who are to receive the book are asked first to execute a confidentiality agreement, or they may suggest that their form of confidentiality agreement be used. The ease with which this agreement is finalized can sometimes be an indication of what is yet to come with that particular prospect. In many cases, each copy of the book is separately numbered and a log is maintained with a copy of the confidentiality agreement for each party.

If there is continuing interest, it may be time to meet face-to-face. The initial meeting is generally held at a neutral site such as a law firm or at an intermediary's offices to maintain confidentiality. The goal of this initial meeting is to provide a potential buyer with a greater sense of the target and its operations and to determine whether the potential buyer is truly interested and there is a likelihood of arriving at an agreement on a transaction.

If it is determined from the initial meeting that the potential for a deal exists, the parties will establish an action plan to move forward with further discussions. When the negotiations reach a point of basic agreement, the parties will often enter into a letter of intent or term sheet, which is covered in Chapter 8. Whether incorporated in this document or dealt with separately, the seller will typically be required to afford the potential buyer exclusivity for a period of time while due diligence is being conducted and an acquisition agreement is being drafted and negotiated.

Once exclusivity is granted by the seller, it will engage in one-on-one negotiations to arrive at a satisfactory acquisition agreement and any discussions with other prospects will be terminated. Often at this stage or sometimes when the acquisition agreement has been executed, a time and responsibility schedule, such as that described in Chapter 3, will be prepared. This schedule will list the various tasks to be performed through the closing, assign responsibility and set times by which the tasks are to be completed. Preparation of the schedule is usually undertaken by the buyer's counsel since the buyer will most likely be in control of the process and will want to be sure that the various tasks are adequately covered and are completed on a timely basis. This is the stage where a bit of client management may be necessary. Clients will normally want to close the transaction as soon as humanly possible, but the time schedule that is established needs to be realistic, particularly where consents of third parties or governmental filings and clearances may be required. A judgment will have to be made whether to risk possible unhappiness of the client at the outset when a realistic estimate of time to closing seems too long or later when unrealistic time deadlines keep slipping.

Preparation of the acquisition agreement and related documents, including the roles of counsel to the seller and buyer, is discussed in Chapter 11. The roles of counsel and some of the other participants will be different in a controlled auction, which is discussed below.

The Controlled Auction

A typical controlled auction is conducted in stages—identifying potential bidders, making contact with prospects, soliciting indications of interest, narrowing the prospects, and selecting a buyer. The procedure can be structured in a variety of ways, and those responsible for establishing the procedure should try to anticipate potential issues and build in as much flexibility as possible. However, there may be some limits, particularly in the public company context, to discriminating among bidders. The concept of fairness and creating a level playing field may require, for example, that all bidders be provided the same financial and other information.

Need Auctions Be Fair?

Safeway Inc. conducted an auction in 2003 for the sale of Dominick's Finer Foods Inc., and Yucaipa Cos. was one of the bidders. It was reported that Safeway refused to allow Yucaipa to participate in the bidding process unless it agreed to use its best efforts to procure collective bargaining agreements with Dominick's unions regardless of whether it wound up acquiring Dominick's. Yucaipa was later informed that Safeway planned to sell Dominick's to another bidder, and Safeway asked Yucaipa to abide by its agreement with respect to the unions. Yucaipa filed an action claiming that Safeway planned to use Yucaipa as a "stalking horse" to gain union support for anyone but Yucaipa, and did not conduct a fair and impartial bidding process. Safeway said that it had conducted a fair auction and Yucaipa was not the winning bidder. It filed a counter-claim against Yucaipa alleging that it had not documented its funding sources and behaved poorly during the auction process. Yucaipa announced that it would abide by its agreement if the investment bank for Dominick's could prove that the winning bid exceeded that of Yucaipa. Safeway later decided to take Dominick's off the market.

The following discussion will describe the typical auction procedure with some of the variations, and assumes heavy involvement of an investment bank representing the seller.

Roles of the Participants

Depending on the particular state law applicable to the company, the ultimate authority to make decisions on behalf of a seller might rest with the board of directors of the company or its parent, its controlling shareholders, or a special committee comprised of disinterested directors. Special committees and their advisors can wield significant control over the sale process, including the conduct of an auction.[73]

Those representing a seller in an auction will take on somewhat different roles than in the normal negotiated transaction. In most situations, an auction will require the services of an investment bank that will design and control the process. This will include assistance in identifying those to be contacted, establishing the timing and procedure, coordinating communications among the parties and management, evaluating bids and negotiating terms. It can also determine the likelihood of the various potential buyers closing a deal, and analyze and compare the consideration and terms offered by different bidders to determine which is the superior offer. In selecting an investment bank, the seller will want to inquire about the extent of its experience with the auction process and particularly the successful conclusion of auctions that it has conducted. It can also be more important in an auction that the investment bank have considerable knowledge about the target's industry, since it will often be required to play off one sophisticated bidder against another. Finally, one should not forget that investment banks are compensated largely on the basis of a success fee. They sometimes have relationships with the potential buyers, so that their interests may therefore not be entirely aligned with those of the seller.

The seller's counsel will play an expanded role in an auction. This role sometimes will include reviewing the offering memorandum and assisting in the development of the procedures and documentation for the solicitation of bids. In most auctions, seller's counsel will prepare the first draft of the acquisition agreement for distribution to potential bidders, and then negotiate the terms of the draft with bidders and their counsel toward the latter stages of the process. In dealing with multiple parties, it is more practical to have bidders work off a single draft of the acquisition agreement that contains what the seller would find satisfactory, than for the seller and counsel to have to compare and respond to a number of different forms of agreement submitted by the bidders.

Whatever familiarity the seller's counsel has with the target, it will usually require some due diligence in order to identify the critical structural and other issues and to address them in the draft. Failure to address these issues may severely limit the pool of potential buyers interested in investing the time and resources necessary to make an offer or may cause them to revise their offers after the completion of due diligence. In preparing the draft, counsel needs to consider whether being overly protective of the client will discourage potential bidders. This is not unlike the risk of killing a deal when buyer's counsel prepares an overly one-sided agreement to present to a seller in a negotiated transaction. For more information on considerations relevant to the preparation of the acquisition agreement, see Chapter 11.

The role of seller's counsel can be more difficult in an auction in that he is required to respond to due diligence inquiries from multiple parties, particularly inquiries that relate to pending litigation and regulatory matters. The sharing of information in a manner that protects the attorney-client and work-product privileges may not be as easy as in one-on-one negotiations. Finally, seller's counsel can be instrumental in identifying potential antitrust or other regulatory or legal issues that might affect the timing or likelihood of closing a transaction with a particular bidder.

Management will typically make more presentations and engage less in negotiations in an auction, leaving most of the negotiations to the investment bank. One concern that often arises is the extent to which management's bias or conflicts can impact the process. If members of management have no economic incentive to achieve the highest price and expect to continue managing the business after the sale, their presentations and other disclosures might be slanted in order to favor certain bidders and their loyalties can quickly change. This can become even more difficult if members of management would like to form a group in order to participate as a bidder. In that case, a decision will have to be made at the outset as to whether they will be permitted to bid and, if so, the type of controls that might have to be imposed on their participation.

Identifying Potential Bidders

As described above, considerable time will be spent in researching potential buyers and narrowing the list of those that will be contacted. Management often will have significant input, identifying those with a strategic interest in the business and eliminating some competitors or others where, for antitrust or other reasons, contact should be avoided. Investment banks will have insight into both strategic buyers and financial buyers that might have an interest in the business or the industry, while management can add others that have previously expressed an interest. In the larger transactions, it is common for consortiums of potential buyers to be formed to make a joint bid, sometimes at the suggestion of the investment banks.

Contacting Prospects

Once a list of potential buyers has been agreed upon, the investment bank will contact each, possibly on a no-name basis and sometimes after sending out a brief sketch of the opportunity, commonly referred to as a teaser. If an interest is expressed in response to that inquiry, the investment bank will send a confidentiality agreement that usually will identify the business for sale. It is often based on a form used by the investment bank, prepared on its letterhead, and signed by the investment bank on behalf of the seller or target. It is important to the auction process that bidders be prohibited in the confidentiality agreement from exchanging information with other bidders during the process or even if they drop out of the auction.

Once a confidentiality agreement is signed, the next step will be to send out an offering memorandum or book. As previously discussed, the book serves to introduce potential buyers to the target, its industry, business, and management team. Since this is a marketing document, it will also contain a discussion regarding opportunities for potential buyers. An analysis of the tax benefits that could accrue to a buyer might also be included.[74]

Sellers may want to arrange for stapled financing (*i.e.* a pre-determined package that will be made available to a buyer). Stapled financing is usually offered by the investment bank working on the transaction. In some cases it may be offered by more than one investment bank. The stapled financing package will be put into place by the lending arm of the investment bank and will indicate its view on the appropriate debt level for the business based on the industry characteristics, business profile, historical, and projected financial results and other factors. Buyers are not obligated to use the stapled financing. In many cases where it is offered, financial buyers will investigate various financing sources in order to obtain higher leverage. This approach will give the provider of stapled financing the incentive to deliver an aggressive proposal. The purpose of stapled financing is generally to level the playing field and increase the number of participants who can compete in the auction. It also helps give the seller confidence that the deal can be completed. Some buyers may use the stapled financing as a form of bridge financing. Usually an initial communication at the start of the auction will indicate that such financing will be available, the leverage level being offered, the minimum equity contribution required and the interest rate ranges. For final round bidders who indicate an interest in using the financing package, detailed commitment documentation, to be customized to the buyer, will be provided. The seller may wish to closely review this documentation to minimize conditionality.

Soliciting Indications of Interest

At some point during this process, the participants will be asked to submit initial nonbinding indications of interest in order to narrow the field to those that appear to be within an acceptable price range and are otherwise able to complete a transaction within a reasonable time period and with minimum conditions. An example of a letter from an investment bank describing the process and soliciting indications of interest is attached as Appendix 6-A.

At this stage, the information about the target that is provided may be limited to that contained in the book. Sometimes prospective buyers will be afforded an opportunity to conduct some degree of due diligence before being asked to submit an indication of interest, with assurances that they can engage in more complete due diligence after the list of participants is narrowed. During this process the seller should avoid providing only favorable information and delaying or downplaying unfavorable information concerning the target. While more of a tactical rather than a legal concern, having more informed indications of interest, and later bids, will help to avoid surprises and ultimately renegotiation.

Letters soliciting indications of interest vary in form, but will usually request some or all of the following information:

- the amount of consideration the prospective buyer, based on the information received, would be willing to pay;
- an indication of any additional information required to complete due diligence;
- the sources of financing required, its status, and any contingencies or material conditions;
- a description of any approvals or consents required and an indication of timing;
- any material contingencies, conditions or assumptions upon which the indication of interest is based; and
- the proposed timing and any requirements regarding the closing date.

Narrowing the Prospects

After evaluating indications of interest received, the seller and its advisors will select a limited number of parties to participate in the next phase of the process. It is best not to make this group too large, because some bidders will be unwilling to spend the additional time and incur the cost unless they think they have a reasonable chance of succeeding. Those selected and their representatives (counsel, accountants, and specialists) will be permitted to engage in extensive due diligence, which will include management presentations, facility visitations, and more intensive discussions with selected members of management. An example of a letter to those remaining about arrangements for facility visits, data room visits, and review of the accountants' workpapers is attached as Appendix 6-B.

The more sensitive aspects of due diligence, such as contacting key customers or suppliers or examining proprietary technology, are usually deferred until near the end of the process. The documents that are thought to be relevant to the transaction are organized and made available for inspection in data rooms, or by providing virtual data rooms where documents are made available on CD ROM, extranets or other web-based systems. For more on due diligence, see Chapter 10.

Once further due diligence has been completed, the participants will be asked to submit formal bids in written form. The letter requesting these bids is similar to that used in soliciting indications of interest, with added encouragement for bidders to submit their best and final price and terms, and an indication that any proposal that is conditioned on further due diligence or a financing contingency may place the bidder at a significant disadvantage. An example of a follow-up letter from an investment bank to potential bidders soliciting binding proposals is attached as Appendix 6-C.

Letters requesting formal bids typically contain protective provisions that negate any obligation to accept a proposal, and reserve the right to:

- terminate the process at any time;
- modify the procedures at any time;
- reject any or all proposals for any reason;
- negotiate with any prospective buyers at any time and in any manner; and
- enter into a definitive acquisition agreement with any party.

They also make it clear that no proposal will be deemed to be accepted, or obligation undertaken, until the execution and delivery of a definitive acquisition agreement.

It is fairly common for the formal solicitation of bids to be accompanied by the draft of an acquisition agreement prepared by seller's counsel. Bidders are asked not only to address the purchase price and material terms of purchase, but also to make any changes they would propose in the draft. The request is most often that the bidders return an electronic copy of the draft agreement that is marked to show their proposed changes and in a form that they will be willing to sign. It should not be assumed, however, that this request will be honored. It is not uncommon for bidders to submit a memorandum specifying the changes they would make in general terms rather than revising the draft agreement, or to expressly indicate that they are not precluded from making other changes. If a bidder is too aggressive in its changes or its changes are not sufficiently described, it of course runs the risk of being dropped from the bidding process. There is a question, however, as to whether an extensive mark up will work against a bidder if the price is attractive. More likely, the mark-up will be used to give some indication of the extent of the bidder's interest and the difficulty and probability of getting the deal done.

Sometimes the distribution of the draft acquisition agreement is accompanied by a set of the disclosure schedules referenced in the agreement. While this might move the process along more quickly, it does change the dynamics somewhat since it would require that time be devoted by the bidders to reviewing the schedules rather than dealing with significant deal issues.

At this stage, the investment bank is often in constant contact with the bidders to give some guidance and provide additional information or insight that might produce a higher price. After formal bids have been submitted, clarification might be sought from the bidders in an attempt to isolate the leading bids for a last round of discussions. This is a critical stage in which the investment bank can be helpful in playing off bidders against one another by seeking the resubmission of bids. Sometimes an extension will be granted to allow bidders more time to arrange financing or to conduct additional due diligence, with a view to keeping more in the mix during this final round. The resubmission of bids may become necessary when there has been a significant downturn or improvement in the results of the business.

Selecting a Buyer

In selecting a buyer, sellers may have some leeway to take into account factors other than price, such as the timing and likelihood of closing or other considerations that are thought to be important. This may depend on the extent of the fiduciary duty of the directors of a corporate seller in these circumstances under state law. It might also depend on whether the seller had made it clear in the process that it would take into consideration factors other than price.[75] One concern for the seller would be the possibility of claims being made for misleading or deceptive business practices under state statutes, the scope of which seems to be expanding.

At some point, the leading bidder will expect to be afforded a right to exclusive negotiation. The seller needs to appreciate that this will dramatically shift the negotiating power to that bidder, and sometimes the seller will keep two bidders alive until one signs an agreement. If the bid is fairly detailed and changes have been provided to the form of acquisition agreement, the final negotiations might progress fairly rapidly to an acquisition agreement. In some situations, an attempt might be made to hold the successful bidder to the terms of its offer that the seller has accepted. In any event, there is always a chance that the leading bidder will want to renegotiate or that the parties will fail to reach agreement over some significant remaining term. Every effort should be made to avoid this possibility, because it is usually very difficult to reopen the process and go back to those whose bids had been rejected. One possibility to maintain some negotiating power would be for the seller to keep two bidders active well into the final negotiations, followed by a shortened exclusivity period or another final round of bidding. To encourage both bidders to continue in the process, it may be necessary for the seller to offer reimbursement of expenses or a set fee to the losing bidder.

APPENDIX 6-A
Letter Soliciting Indications of Interest

[*Date*]

[*Name*]
[*Title*]
[*Company*]
[*Address*]

Dear [*name*]:

On behalf of [*target*] (the "Company"), we would like to express our appreciation for your interest in exploring the possible acquisition of the Company. We are now writing to invite you to submit a preliminary, nonbinding indication of interest to acquire the Company ("Proposal"). This letter sets forth the procedure and timing with respect to your submission of a Proposal, as well as summarizing the general process which the Company will employ.

We acknowledge receipt of a faxed copy of your signed Confidentiality Agreement. Enclosed is a copy of a Confidential Memorandum describing the history of the Company, its business and management, and containing historical and projected financial data. In this phase of the process, the only information about the Company to be made available will be that contained in the Confidential Memorandum, with clarification, if any, supplied only by us in response to your inquiries. The Company recognizes that you and other potential buyers will want to conduct detailed due diligence prior to submitting any final, binding proposals, and wishes to assure that, to the fullest extent practicable, all bidders believed to be qualified and seriously interested will be given an opportunity to undertake their due diligence investigations before submitting any such proposals. At the same time, we intend to conduct the process in a way that will minimize the disruption to the Company and its business.

Your Proposal should be in writing and submitted to us via facsimile or courier to the address listed below, to arrive by [*time and time zone*] on [*day and date*]:

[*Name, address and telephone and facsimile numbers*]

In order to be able to fully evaluate your Proposal, it should include the following:

- a description of the transaction that you would propose, including the cash consideration, stated in U.S. dollars, that you would be willing to pay for the Company based on the information received to date;
- details of the key assumptions pertaining to the transaction that you have made in order to derive the proposed cash consideration, including separate identification of the value you attribute to any tax benefits resulting from a purchase of assets or a Section 338(h)(10) election;
- the identity of the prospective buyer and other participants, if any, in a potential transaction;
- an indication of the additional information that you would require to complete your due diligence investigation of the Company, including any specific topics that are of particular significance or documents that you would like to review before submitting a binding proposal;

- a description of the proposed source(s) of financing, and to the extent your proposal contemplates external financing, the status of any arrangements, any contingencies or material conditions relating thereto and the proposed timing;
- a description of any corporate, stockholder, regulatory or other approvals or consents that may be required to consummate a transaction, together with an indication of the timing anticipated in obtaining such approvals or consents, and the commitments you would make with respect to such approvals or consents to ensure a transaction would be consummated expeditiously;
- a description of intended strategy with respect to the Company's management, employees and facilities;
- a description of any material contingencies required to complete a transaction or material conditions on which you are basing your Proposal, and an indication of the anticipated timing when such contingencies or conditions can be satisfied;
- the extent, duration and general terms of any transitional services or supply agreements that you will require as part of any transaction;
- a list of any outside advisors (including your investment bank, accountants and outside legal counsel) who you expect to work with on these matters; and
- a list of the names, direct telephone numbers and facsimile numbers of the persons within your organization with whom we may clarify any issues with respect to your Proposal.

While the Company has specified cash consideration, it would be willing to consider other forms of consideration that would provide comparable economic value. Similarly, in terms of structure, the Company favors a sale of stock, but is open to variations in the structure so long as it can receive at least equivalent value on an after-tax basis.

After evaluating the Proposals, the Company expects to select a limited number of parties to be invited to participate in the next phase of the process. In making this determination, we may seek clarification of the information received in some or all of the Proposals. The Company will consider a variety of factors, such as the preliminary indications of the economic value of the consideration a party may be willing to provide, the party's financial and operating strength and reputation and its ability to consummate a transaction in an expeditious manner.

Shortly after completion of this phase, we will notify all parties who have submitted Proposals as to whether they will be invited to participate in the next phase. The Company reserves the right in its sole and absolute discretion to accept or reject any or all Proposals, and to amend, modify or terminate these procedures at any time without notice and without specifying the reasons therefor. Those parties invited to participate in the next phase will be given the opportunity to meet with the Company's management, tour the facilities of the Company, and visit a data room which has been established to assist in the due diligence process.

Upon completion of the due diligence phase, we will solicit final, binding proposals for the acquisition of the Company. It is contemplated that participants will be provided with a proposed form of acquisition agreement specifying the terms and conditions upon which the Company will be willing to enter into a transaction. The Company will, with our advice and assistance and that of its legal advisors, promptly evaluate the Proposals submitted, including a mark-up of the acquisition agreement, with the objective of entering into a acquisition agreement with the party that submits a Proposal best satisfying the Company's objectives. We will be available to consult with potential buyers in order to answer questions or requests and to provide guidance as to the appropriateness of Proposals.

Please do not hesitate to call me at [*telephone number*] or [*name*] at [*telephone number*] with any questions regarding these procedures, the information to be provided in the Proposals or the process in general. We ask that you, and any of your advisors, not contact anyone at the Company without our prior consent. We appreciate your interest in the Company and look forward to receiving your Proposal.

Sincerely,

APPENDIX 6-B

Letter Regarding Facility Visit, Data Room Visit, and Review of Accountants' Workpapers

[*Date*]

[*Name*]
[*Title*]
[*Company*]
[*Address*]

Dear [*name*]:

As a follow-up to our telephone conversations, the management presentation for [*target*] (the "Company") will be held at the [*off site location*] (the "Hotel") starting at [*time*] _.m., local time, on [*day and date*] in the meeting room reserved under the name of [*investment bank*]. The Hotel is located approximately [*elapsed time*] minutes from the [*airport*] (see attached directions).

We envision that the presentation will last approximately [*elapsed time*] hours with lunch to follow. During the working lunch, management will answer any additional questions that were not addressed during the presentation. We encourage you to bring your entire team to the management presentation, including any financial advisors, lenders, accountants or other members of your team, as appropriate. After lunch, we will provide a tour of the Company's facilities. However, to maintain confidentiality, we would like to limit the number of facility tour participants to three or four representatives. An agenda has been attached to this letter for your convenience. Your team should schedule flight departures for no earlier than [*time*] _.m., local time.

Also in accordance with our conversations, we have scheduled your data room visit for [*time, day and date*], the day following the management presentation, at the offices of [*law firm*] in [*city*] (see attached directions and suggested hotel accommodations). Prior to your team's data room visit, we will be forwarding an index of the information that will be made available in the data room (noting the documents for which copying is not permitted) so that you can appropriately allocate resources to that effort. Accompanying this letter are data room procedures that outline additional details related to your team's visit to the data room. Upon arrival, please ask to be directed to [*contact person*].

Also on [*time, day and date*] we have scheduled the Company's accountants, [*accounting firm*], to be available for a review of the audit workpapers at its [*city*] office (see attached directions). The accountants require that their standard workpaper review release be signed by both [*prospective buyer*] and its accountants, prior to a review of workpapers. Please contact [*contact person*] at [*telephone number*] in order to facilitate this process.

In preparation for these due diligence activities, please provide us with a list of the names, titles and firm affiliations of those individuals who will be: (i) attending the management presentation, (ii) visiting the data room, and (iii) reviewing audit workpapers, by facsimile at [*fax number*] or by phone at [*telephone number*].

Following the management presentation, facility tours, data room visit and audit workpaper review, we would anticipate receiving your final acquisition proposal. We will be forwarding additional instructions with respect to the timing and our expectations for your final proposal when we forward a draft of the acquisition agreement following the management presentation. We would anticipate that your acquisition proposal will indicate that your due diligence is complete and that all required financing is committed.

Prior to entering this stage of due diligence, we would like to request that you remind each member of your team that no direct contact should be made with employees, management, customers or suppliers of the Company without our direct authorization.

Once again, we appreciate your interest in the Company and look forward to working with you and your team on the prospective acquisition. Please contact [*contact person*] at [*telephone number*] or myself at [*telephone number*] with any questions.

Sincerely,

Attachments

APPENDIX 6-C
Letter Soliciting Binding Proposals

[*Date*]

[*Name*]
[*Title*]
[*Company*]
[*Address*]

Dear [*name*]

On behalf of [*target*] (the "Company"), we would like to express our appreciation for your interest and time invested in the potential acquisition of the Company. We would now like to invite you to submit a final, definitive and binding proposal ("Offer") to acquire the Company. This letter sets forth the procedure and timing with respect to your submission of an Offer.

Your Offer should be in writing and submitted to us via facsimile or courier to the address listed below, to arrive by [*time and time zone*] on [*day and date*]:

[*Name, address and telephone and facsimile numbers*]

Any Offer received after the time and date set forth above may be rejected. In evaluating your Offer, the Company will focus on its key objectives, which include obtaining the highest possible value for the Company, maximizing the certainty of consummating a transaction and consummating a transaction as expeditiously as possible.

In order to evaluate proposals on a comparable basis, each Offer must comply with the terms and conditions outlined below. Submission of the Offer shall constitute your acceptance of these provisions.

- The Offer should specify the identity of the prospective buyer and other participants, if any, in a potential transaction.
- The Offer should be executed by an officer authorized to bind the prospective buyer to its terms and a statement indicating that the Offer has received all necessary internal authorizations, including if necessary the approval of your board of directors.
- The Offer should state the consideration, stated in U.S. dollars if in cash, that you are offering, with any of the details of any key assumptions pertaining to the transaction that you have made in order to derive the proposed consideration.
- The Offer should describe your plans for financing the transaction and, to the extent you contemplate external financing, give the names of the lending institutions and equity participants providing your financing, together with contact names, telephone numbers and executed commitment letters or other relevant documentation related to your financing. Financing sources are expected to have completed their due diligence prior to your submission of an Offer. You should make known to us and resolve any remaining due diligence issues related to financing prior to submission of your Offer.
- The Offer should describe any corporate, stockholder, regulatory or other approvals or consents that may be required to consummate a transaction, together with an estimate of the timing for receiving such approvals or consents. You should discuss with us prior to submission of an Offer any potential problems or issues with, or factors that may delay the receipt of, such approvals or consents.

- Attached is a form acquisition agreement (the "Agreement"). Your Offer should include the Agreement marked to represent a form that you are willing to execute. To the extent that you would prefer to provide an electronic markup of the Agreement, please call [*name and telephone number*], so that we may forward an electronic version of the Agreement via e-mail. If you provide an electronic markup, please ensure that the document can be altered to show the form of the Agreement both with and without your revisions. Please do not provide conceptual comments and do not retype the Agreement. Technical questions or clarifications regarding specific legal terms of the Agreement should be sought prior to submission of your Offer, and you or your legal counsel are encouraged to contact [*contact information for legal counsel*], the Company's legal counsel prior to the deadline. Your revisions to the form of Agreement will be an important component of your Offer and any substantive changes may disadvantage consideration of your Offer.
- The Offer should state whether you have completed your due diligence and, if not, what specific issues or documents remain. The Agreement does not include a provision that makes the purchaser's obligation to close the transaction conditioned upon completing further due diligence. Furthermore, any outstanding due diligence items will negatively impact the Company's assessment of your Offer.
- The Offer should include a description of any material contingencies required to complete a transaction or material conditions on which the Offer is based, together with an indication of the timing anticipated in satisfying any such contingencies or conditions.
- The Offer should contain a statement regarding the proposed timing of a transaction and any requirements regarding the closing date of a transaction.
- The Offer should include the names and telephone numbers for your personnel and advisors who will be available to us and the Company to discuss or clarify any aspect of your Offer. The Company and its advisors reserve the right to discuss with any potential buyer the terms and conditions of any Offer submitted by that potential buyer for the purpose of clarifying the terms of such Offer.

In order to facilitate a thorough evaluation of your Offer, it should remain in effect until [*date*]. You will be notified by us of any action taken by the Company with regard to your Offer.

As of the deadline, we will assume that all parties have submitted their best Offer. All Offers will be reviewed by the Company and its advisors. The Company reserves the right, in its sole and absolute discretion, to amend, modify or terminate these procedures and the terms and conditions set forth in the Agreement at any time and without notice, and to select any Offer or to reject any or all Offers without providing any reason therefor. The Company also reserves the right in its sole discretion to consider any and all factors in the determination of the successful Offer, to negotiate with one or more prospective buyers at any time and in any manner, and to enter into an agreement for the sale of the Company without notice to other prospective buyers. You should not assume that you will be given an opportunity to revise your Offer. The Company will not have any liability to any prospective buyer as a result of the rejection of any or all Offers or the acceptance of another Offer.

You should be prepared to negotiate and execute an acquisition agreement in [*location*] upon request and should have present at the negotiations all employees, advisors and representatives necessary to make decisions or grant approvals on your behalf. The Company shall not have any obligation to any prospective buyer other than those set forth in a definitive, executed agreement, if any, between the Company and such buyer. Nothing in this letter is to be deemed a contract of any kind between the Company and any other party, and an Offer will be considered formally accepted only when an acquisition agreement has been executed and delivered by the Company.

Please do not hesitate to call me at [*telephone number*] or [*name*] at [*telephone number*] with any questions regarding these requirements or the process. We ask that you, and any of your advisors, not contact anyone at the Company without our prior consent. We appreciate your interest in the Company and look forward to receiving your Offer.

Sincerely,

Understanding Accounting Principles, Financial Statements, and Business Valuation

An M&A lawyer need not be a financial analyst or certified public accountant, but should have a rudimentary understanding of accounting principles and terminology, financial statements and the methodologies used in valuing a business. The following are examples of why this knowledge can be important in representing an M&A client.

- Before deciding how much to ask or offer, accept or pay for a business, the seller and prospective buyer must judge its value. The pricing of the deal is often based upon valuation models that utilize financial statements, particularly the statement of cash flows.
- A buyer will be keenly interested in the manner of accounting for the acquisition and its effect on its financial statements.
- Post-closing purchase price adjustments and earnouts, which are drafted by counsel, require an understanding of accounting terminology and principles.
- Acquisition agreements usually contain representations with respect to the target's financial statements, the underlying accounting books and records, certain assets (e.g., accounts receivable and inventories) and the absence of certain liabilities.[76] Accounting terminology and principles will apply in the negotiation and drafting of these and, most likely, other representations.

This chapter contains an overview of these matters and concepts.

Accounting Principles and Financial Statements

It has often been said that accounting is the language of business. The content and presentation of financial statements is governed by accounting principles, usually referred to as GAAP. GAAP originally referred to policies and procedures that were widely used in practice, but the term more recently has come to refer to pronouncements issued by accounting bodies. In the United States, these pronouncements have been issued (and are periodically updated) by the Financial Accounting Standards Board (FASB), which is the successor to the Accounting Principles Board.[77] In addition, the Auditing Standards Board of the American Institute of Certified Public Accountants (AICPA) issues pronouncements setting forth standards for audits performed by independent auditors, which are called generally accepted auditing standards, or GAAS. In 2002, the Public Company Accounting Oversight Board (PCAOB) was created by Sarbanes-Oxley to adopt auditing and related standards and rules that apply to public accounting firms that audit the financial statements of publicly owned reporting companies.

Accountants are sometimes referred to as mere bean counters. Nothing could be further from the truth. The preparation of financial statements in conformity with GAAP requires many estimates, judgments and assumptions by management, and in many cases GAAP permits alternative approaches. These have to be evaluated by the accountants, who will have to apply their own professional judgment. Absolute, mathematical precision is neither expected nor achievable in financial statements, whether audited or unaudited. A fair presentation of the financial information in all material respects is the goal.

It's a Judgment Call

The following are a few of the areas in which the exercise of judgment can significantly affect a company's financial position and results of operations:

- *Revenues.* When are revenues from a transaction realized or realizable and earned such that they can properly be recognized? This has been a significant issue for some public companies and many have been required to restate earnings due to a misapplication of GAAP.
- *Goodwill.* When does goodwill become impaired so that it has to be written down?
- *Accounts receivable.* What is the degree of risk that accounts receivable will not be collected and how large a reserve should be established? Does this require an analysis of each account or is historical experience adequate to establish an adequate reserve?
- *Inventories.* At what point do inventories become obsolete requiring a write off? Differing approaches to this question can have a significant impact on the price and other aspects of an acquisition.
- *Self insurance.* How can potentially incurred but unreported claims be estimated? Are historical trends and experience sufficient to project ultimate losses?

As this demonstrates, accounting is an art and not a science. Accordingly, the evaluation of a target's financial statements and the manner in which GAAP has been applied requires extensive attention and due diligence by a buyer and its advisors.

Accounting for Business Combinations

Among the pronouncements of the FASB are those dealing with the accounting for business combinations.[78] Beginning in July 2001, business combinations are required to be accounted for by the "purchase method," and the alternative "pooling-of-interests method" for accounting for qualifying business combinations was eliminated. Under the purchase method, goodwill is recognized as an asset in the buyer's financial statements. This asset is initially measured as the excess of the cost of the acquired business over the sum of the amounts assigned to identifiable assets acquired at their fair value less the liabilities assumed. Intangible assets that do not have a finite life are also included in goodwill. Goodwill and indefinite lived intangible assets are required to be tested for impairment and written down if their fair value declines below the amount at which they are carried on the books. Previously, goodwill and intangible assets were amortized over their life not to exceed 40 years.

Financial Statements

Management is responsible for the preparation of the financial statements and for maintaining effective internal control over financial reporting. The financial statements of publicly held companies and many substantial closely held businesses are audited. This means that an independent accountant has conducted an audit and, on the basis of that audit, it has issued a report stating that the financial position, results of operations and cash flows are presented fairly in conformity with accounting principles generally accepted in the United States.[79]

Interim (other than fiscal year end) financial statements are usually unaudited, but typically provide that they include all adjustments necessary for a fair presentation of the results for the interim periods, subject to normal year-end audit adjustments. Sometimes the unaudited statements are compiled or reviewed by accountants, in which case they have followed certain specified procedures.

The financial statements that are typically the most significant to acquisition attorneys are the balance sheet, income (or profit and loss) statement and statement of cash flows.

Balance Sheet. Simply stated, the balance sheet is often referred to as a snapshot, as of a particular date, of the assets, liabilities and net worth (or financial position) of a business. The assets are listed on a balance sheet in order of liquidity, starting with current assets. Cash is first, followed by accounts receivable and inventories. Next are noncurrent assets such as equipment and buildings. Liabilities are listed in the order in which they are due, with those having the nearest maturity first and those having the most remote maturity last. They are generally divided into short-term and long-term liabilities with the former due within one year from the balance sheet date and the latter longer than one year. Equity items (e.g., common and preferred stock) are classified in their decreasing order of permanence.

Income Statement. The income statement reflects the operating profit or loss (or results of operations) of a business over a period of time, such as a fiscal year or quarterly period. It shows all income and expense accounts, either by each line item or condensed, and generally measures profitability of the business.

Statement of Cash Flows. The statement of cash flows consists of three parts: (i) the cash provided by (or absorbed in) operations; (ii) the cash provided by (or used in) investing activities, and (iii) the cash provided by (or used for) financing activities.[80] Projected operating cash flows are usually discounted to present value, which is commonly referred to as the Discounted Cash Flow or DCF, as discussed later in this chapter. A multiple of EBITDA is often used in the pricing of a business. Operating cash flow and EBITDA will, of course, differ from profit (or loss) on an income statement.

These financial statements can be presented in several different formats:

- Consolidated financial statements combine the accounts of a parent with those of its subsidiaries in which it owns a majority of voting equity interest, while eliminating intercompany transactions.
- Consolidating financial statements show separate line items for each member of a consolidated group.

- Combined financial statements contain the accounts of several businesses that may be related (e.g., brother-sister corporations) or are otherwise economically linked, without a controlling equity interest.

Notes to Financial Statements

Financial statements prepared in accordance with GAAP are required to contain additional financial detail and certain types of disclosures in the notes. The notes will include a summary of significant accounting policies, the impact of recent accounting pronouncements, a breakdown of certain assets and obligations, and a description of capitalization and of certain commitments and contingencies. Some say that the notes to financial statements are "where the bodies are buried."

Among the loss contingencies described in the notes are those arising from pending or threatened litigation. Accountants are required to book a contingency that may result in a loss (i.e., reflect a particular amount as a liability), when it is both probable that the liability has been incurred and the amount of the loss can be reasonably estimated. If one or both of these conditions are not met, disclosure of the contingency is required in the notes to the financial statements when there is at least a reasonable possibility that a loss may have been incurred. An example of this type of disclosure is an excerpt from a note to financial statements of Exxon Mobil Corporation set forth in Appendix 7-A, which deals with the grounding of the Exxon Valdez in 1989.

Accounting Terminology

A number of accounting terms may be referred to in an acquisition agreement or otherwise come up in the negotiations or due diligence. Some of these terms are set forth below, and these and some other terms are included in the Glossary.

Working Capital, Current Ratio, and Net Worth

Working capital means the total amount of current assets less the total amount of current liabilities and is ideally, in most industries, a positive number. Current assets include cash and those other assets that are expected to be converted to cash within one year, such as accounts receivable. Current liabilities are those liabilities that are expected to be paid within one year, which would include the current portion of a long-term liability such as bank debt. The current ratio is the total amount of current assets divided by the total amount of current liabilities. Working capital and current ratio are measures of the liquidity of a business, i.e., its ability to turn its current assets into cash so that it can pay its liabilities as they become due. These liquidity measures are critical to lenders and suppliers who are extending credit to the business, as well as to potential buyers. Another term often encountered is net worth (also referred to as net equity or shareholders' equity), which is total assets less total liabilities.

Accruals and Deferrals

Accruals and deferrals are two sides of the same coin. An accrual is made when an event should be recorded for accounting purposes during a current period even though payment will not be made until some future period. A deferral is made when an event should not be recorded for accounting purposes until a later period even though payment is made in the current period. Accountants will accrue a liability on the balance sheet for an obligation, such as vacation pay, which has been incurred with respect to the current accounting period even though the obligation will not be paid until a future accounting period. Revenue is also accrued by recording accounts receivable on the balance sheet to reflect that sales have occurred in the current accounting period for which the cash will be received in a future accounting period.

The recording of obligations and revenue can also be deferred based on the particular facts. A payment made in the current accounting period for an obligation due in a future period (or alternatively viewed as a benefit spreading over a future period), such as pre-paid insurance, would be recorded as an asset on the balance sheet. Alternatively, a payment received, such as a down payment or deposit received by a contractor for services to be performed in a future period, would be recorded as a liability, namely deferred revenue, until the contractor performs the services with respect to which the payment has been received.

Deferred Revenue

Sports teams (such as the Steagles)* that sell season tickets will often receive significant payment from customers months before the start of the season. Those cash receipts are accounted for as deferred revenue when received and represent a liability of the team until the games are actually played and the revenue is earned. If a players' strike or owners' lockout occurs, the team would be obligated to refund that money for games not played.

* The Steagles were a combination of the Philadelphia Eagles and Pittsburgh Steelers that played in the NFL for a short time during World War II.

Depreciation and Amortization

Another area worth noting is the treatment of assets purchased by a business. Suppose a business on the first day of a fiscal year pays $1,000 for a piece of equipment that is expected to benefit the business, i.e., have a useful life beyond that fiscal year. Accountants would capitalize that asset. If the asset is expected to benefit the business, say, for five years, it will initially be recorded on the balance sheet at its $1,000 cost and will be depreciated using, for example, the straight line method, at the rate of 20 percent of its cost per year. This $200 annual depreciation is a non-cash charge (or expense) on the income statement for that first year. The balance sheet at the end of that year would reflect that asset at its cost of $1,000 less the $200 first-year depreciation, or $800 net after depreciation. However, if the asset is not expected to benefit the business beyond that fiscal year, its entire $1,000 cost would be expensed on that year's income statement. Amortization is a similar concept applied to intangible assets, whereby book value is reduced with a charge to income over their useful lives.

Financially Oriented Provisions

Some provisions of an acquisition agreement not only use accounting terminology, but are dependent upon the application of various accounting principles. Examples are purchase price adjustments, earnouts and certain representations.

Purchase Price Adjustments and Earnouts

An acquisition agreement often contains one or both types of provisions that can impact the ultimate purchase price that is paid. One is an adjustment (sometimes referred to as a true-up) that is, at least facially, balance sheet oriented and typically is based on changes in net worth or working capital of the target. Even though the purchase price is often based on its projected earnings or cash flow, the parties often agree upon a net worth or working capital adjustment in order to reflect a change in the financial position of the target between the date of its most recent balance sheet (identified in the target's financial statement representation) and the closing date of the acquisition.[81] If the adjustment is based upon changes in net worth, the amount usually approximates the amount of the target's profit or loss during the period between these two dates, effectively implicating an income statement approach. Sometimes the comparison is made with the average of net worth or working capital over a period of time. This type of post-closing adjustment is discussed in more detail in Chapter 8.

The other is an earnout, which is usually income statement driven. The earnout, which is discussed in more detail in Chapter 8, usually involves a potential increase in the purchase price for the business based upon post-closing results of operations or other factors. To the extent a portion of the purchase price is deferred or placed in escrow, the earnout can result in a reduction in or return of part of the purchase price.

Representations

The following are some of the representations that are based upon financial statements and accounting principles, and which usually lead to a fair amount of negotiation.

Financial statements. A virtually universal representation requested by the buyer relates to the target's financial statements, whether the transaction is a stock or asset deal or a merger. The essence of that representation is that the (identified) financial statements of the target "fairly present, in all material respects" the financial position and results of operations of the target as of the respective dates and for the periods ending on such dates, all in accordance with GAAP.[82] As a result of the SEC certification rules under section 302 of SOX, a variation of that representation is becoming more common (at least with respect to "reporting" companies) which substitutes "*and* have been prepared in accordance with GAAP" for "all in accordance with GAAP," in effect treating GAAP and fair presentation as two separate concepts. Incidentally, this language is similar to the operative language that would be in the report furnished by the target's independent auditors with respect to audited financial statements. While this representation relates to the financial statements viewed as a whole, the typical acquisition agreement also will contain representations with respect to individual line items of the balance sheet, such as accounts receivable and inventories. Those line item representations are intended to provoke a discussion about the seller's accounting for these types of assets.

Counsel to the parties should recognize the implications of fairly present. The term does not mean that the financial statements are perfect, *i.e.,* that they purport to reflect every single transaction of the target applicable to the relevant date or period. While this may be somewhat oversimplified, it may be helpful for counsel to think of fairly present as meaning that the financial statements, taken as a whole, are materially accurate.[83]

A zealous buyer's attorney may serve up a draft representation to the effect that the target's financial statements are "true and complete," thus seeking the perfection that is not implicit in fairly present. A target's attorney would normally object to this language for obvious reasons.

Books of Account. The buyer's attorney may request a representation by the target that its books of account and financial records are complete and correct.[84] While these books and records are intended to reflect every one of the hundreds of thousands of transactions of the target over its business life, they are obviously never perfect or complete. In this case, the target's attorney will propose language such as "complete and correct in all material respects," while reminding the buyer's counsel that the representation as to the target's financial statements (which are themselves based upon the underlying books and records) customarily utilizes the fairly present language.

Absence of Liabilities. A buyer's attorney may also seek a representation to the effect that the target has no liabilities except for those reflected or reserved against in the most recent balance sheet or incurred thereafter in the ordinary course of business.[85] The target's attorney normally will request a materiality or knowledge qualifier, or both, or a restatement of the representation to the effect that all liabilities required to be set forth on a balance sheet prepared in accordance with GAAP are so reflected or reserved against. The term *liability* is very broadly defined in the typical acquisition agreement and would include all the target's contractual obligations, but these obligations would not be required to be included on a balance sheet prepared in accordance with GAAP. Yet they would have to be disclosed as exceptions to the representation in the original formulation.

Accounts Receivable. Accounts receivable reflect the amounts owed to the target for goods or services sold to a customer. The total amount of all accounts receivable as set forth on a balance sheet is usually reduced by a reserve for uncollectible accounts. The buyer often seeks an unqualified representation by the target that these receivables will be collected or are at least collectible (after giving effect to the reserve) within a particular period following closing, failing which the buyer would be reimbursed to the extent of the shortfall.[86] The uncollected accounts are often reassigned to the target or seller. Should the target resist this and, if so, how? The target's lawyer will necessarily be involved in this negotiation.

Inventories. Inventories, generally speaking, consist of raw materials (materials purchased for the manufacture of a product), work in process (a product in the process of being manufactured, utilizing the raw materials) and finished goods (the completed product ready for sale to a customer). The buyer usually requests a representation to the effect that all items of inventory "consist of a quality and quantity useable, and with respect to finished goods, saleable in the ordinary course of business" while allowing for obsolete or below-standard quality items.[87] Although this requested representation should trigger substantive input of the accountants for both parties, their lawyers, who are responsible for the language of the acquisition agreement, will be significantly involved.

Valuing a Business

Lawyers generally do not have the training and experience to be a client's primary advisor on valuation, and yet they are often called upon to be involved in the valuation process. The lawyer's role in valuations will vary widely from one transaction to another. At one extreme, the sellers of a family business, who have never bought or sold a business before, may expect their lawyer to advise the family on valuation issues. At the other extreme, the client may possess valuation expertise or may retain an investment bank to assist in the valuation analysis or render a fairness opinion.[88] But even in that case, the client may look to the lawyer for help in interpreting the analysis, and in assessing whether it is well informed and objective. If the lawyer takes the lead in negotiations, he may need to respond to and advance positions couched in terms of the value of the target business. Valuation issues also arise in litigation regarding a proposed or completed transaction, and in connection with the exercise of appraisal rights by shareholders of the business being sold.

If the target's stock is publicly traded, with a sufficient float and adequate public disclosure, the market price of the stock may be a starting point for valuation of the business. But a buyer of the entire public company will typically pay a premium over the market price of the stock. If the target is closely held, there will be no reliable market price for its stock. There is a market in which closely held businesses are bought and sold, and information regarding recent transactions can be useful in valuing a target. In some industries, there may be customary or standard methods that are used as a rule of thumb for determining value. For example, value may be related to a multiple of revenues for an insurance agency, a price-per-bed for a hospital or a multiple of book value for financial institutions. But there is no "blue book" available for purposes of valuation. Businesses, unlike most used cars, are unique.

In selling a business, it may be risky to start with a high price, being prepared to lower the price until indications of interest are received. Some sellers have unrealistically high price expectations. If a seller sets and maintains an unrealistic price, it is likely that potential buyers will be discouraged from spending the time and effort to evaluate the business and eventually it will have to be taken off the market. Advertising a company for sale can be damaging to customer and employee relations, especially if no sale occurs. Sellers who are willing to take these risks might give serious consideration to using an auction to sell the business, which is described in Chapter 6.

Regardless of the method the seller uses in the search for a buyer, it needs to know not only what price it would be willing to accept, but what range of offers to expect. It therefore needs to ask the same question a prospective buyer would ask: What is this business really worth?

In one sense, a business, like a used car or a parcel of real estate, is worth whatever price an informed, willing buyer will pay. But it is important to distinguish pricing from valuation. Just as one who wants to sell a used car will first check its blue book value, negotiations for the sale of a business should not be undertaken without an objective idea of its value. Moreover, a negotiated price will be affected by a number of factors in addition to the parties' respective perceptions of the target's value. These factors may include other terms of the deal, such as:

- the extent of representations and scope of indemnification;
- the allocation between the seller and the buyer of synergistic benefits (such as the potential for reducing overlapping employee expenses), the opportunity for which will vary from one potential buyer to another;
- reliability of the historical and projected financial statements;

- overpayment resulting from inadequate due diligence;
- overbidding in auction situations;
- deal structure, including tax issues; and
- the negotiating skill of the parties.

What, then, does the lawyer aspiring to an M&A practice need to know about business valuation? It is far beyond the scope of this chapter to be a definitive discussion of valuing businesses. Fortunately, there are other sources that are available.[89] But we hope that this chapter will serve as an introductory guide to valuation issues.

Going Concern Value

A fundamental proposition in valuing a business is that it is worth the greater of its liquidation value (what the separate assets could be sold for after the business is terminated and its liabilities paid) or its going concern value. Unless the business has failed as an economic enterprise, it is unlikely that its liquidation value will exceed its going concern value. Most business acquisitions involve a going concern, and are valued as such.

The value of a going concern is customarily defined as the price at which the business would change hands between a willing buyer and a willing seller, both being fully informed and neither being under a compulsion to buy or sell. This rubric is of little help, however, in actually determining a fair price. Numerous terms are used in reference to the value of a business, such as fair market value, fair value, book value, investment value, intrinsic value and enterprise value. Once the total value of an enterprise is determined, debt less cash is subtracted to arrive at the value of the equity. In valuing a block of stock, the equity value attributed to those shares might be discounted for lack of marketability, lack of control or both. Fortunately, the valuation process is more straight forward when an entire business is being sold.

Statistics measuring the prices realized from sales of businesses are reported on the basis of the relationship that the price bears to historical revenues, earnings or cash flow. The period selected for measurement may be the last fiscal year, the last four quarters or the most recent 12 months. The earnings measured are usually before or after taxes, EBIT or EBITDA. While this may be instructive, it of course assumes that historical results are predictive of future performance, which is not necessarily the case. One cannot simply take these multiples and apply them to the historical financial results of a company that is to be sold as representative of value. Multiples vary widely within an industry, and will depend on the size of the business, the general market and economic conditions and factors intrinsic to the particular business, such as growth expectations, management and possession of proprietary intellectual property. Consequently, other methodologies have been developed to determine the value of a business enterprise in the context of an acquisition.

Valuation Methodologies

In some markets and for some buyers, the value of a business to the buyer is based on the stream of cash flows that the business will produce. As a result, factors such as earnings and cash flow are more significant in arriving at a valuation than net asset value, net book value and replacement cost. Investment bankers or appraisers engaged to value businesses or give fairness opinions typically employ a variety of methodologies or approaches, such as discounted cash flow, comparable companies and comparable transactions, and then weigh the applicability of the methodologies used to the particular company and combine the results to produce a value or, in most cases, a range of values.

Discounted Cash Flow. As an introduction to cash flow valuation, consider the methodology used in valuing a bond. Assume a bond with a principal amount of $100 that pays interest at 10 percent per annum and matures in five years. What is it worth? Using standard methodology, we ascertain the appropriate rate of interest for the bond in light of financial markets and the risks associated with the issuer's business, and use that rate to discount future principal and interest payments (the only returns the investor will ever realize from the bond unless it is sold) to their present values, adding those present values together to arrive at the value of the bond.[90]

Computing the Present Value of a Bond

Assume that for our bond, the appropriate interest rate, given market conditions and risks associated with the issuer, is 8%. To value the bond, we discount its future returns to their present value. Those returns are $10 at the end of each of the next five years (the interest) and $100 at the end of the fifth year (the principal). Using a present value table,[91] an appropriate calculator or a computer, we discount each of those six numbers to present value, using a discount rate of 8%. The present value numbers are $9.26, $8.57, $7.94, $7.35, $6.81 and $68.10, for a total of $108.03, which would be the value of the bond. Alternatively, and more simply, we could treat the interest payments as a five year annuity of $10 per year, discount those to their present value of $39.90 using the present value table and an 8% discount rate, and then add the discounted present value of the principal, which we have already determined to be $68.10, for a total of $108. (The difference between the two computations is a rounding difference.) This demonstrates a simple lesson regarding bond prices: when interest rates go down (10% to 8%), the value of the bond goes up. Conversely, when interest rates go up, the value of the bond goes down.

The standard DCF methodology for valuing a business is based on the same principles as those applicable to valuing a bond, although the process involves many more steps and judgments. In valuing a bond, we do not ask what the investor paid for it initially. We are interested only in future returns to the bondholder and the discount rate appropriate to the level of risk associated with those returns. In valuing a business, we are interested in the same two things: the future returns the investors may expect, and the risks associated with those returns. What the present owner paid for the business, and what the business paid for its assets, are beside the point, although obviously relevant to determining the profits or losses realized by investors and the target.

The process for business valuation is more involved than that for valuing a bond for a number of reasons. First, the ownership interest in a going concern, unlike a bond, does not specify the amounts or timing of the future returns, which therefore must be predicted. Second, the determination of an appropriate rate of return or discount rate is more difficult than in the bond context. Third, a going concern, unlike a bond, will have cash outflows as well as inflows. Finally, a going concern has no maturity and therefore some value has to be attributed to the continuing operations beyond the period of the projections and into the future.

In predicting future returns of a business, one customarily begins with its historical returns from its financial statements. As discussed earlier in this chapter, an M&A lawyer must be generally familiar with the reading and interpretation of financial statements. Our purpose here is to illustrate, through the simplest of examples, how financial statements are used as the starting point in projecting future returns of a business. The example assumes only the most basic familiarity with accounting principles. We also assume, for the sake of simplicity, a closely held business.

A family owns the target. Its net income, as shown on its financial statements, has increased by 10 percent in each of the past three years. Its manufacturing operations are carried on in a plant purchased five years ago. The target employs several members of the family in management positions. Its competitive position is good historically, although management must consider whether recent technological advances may make investment in new machinery and equipment advisable.

The first step in valuing the target is to project its future returns. This process involves determining its historical returns and then using other information to make a judgment as to how future returns are likely to vary from those past returns. Typically, an analysis is prepared for a period of five years or a full business cycle. It is important to recognize that we are not interested in the target's net income. The prospective buyer wants to know the cash returns that the target will generate for its new owners. We are assuming that its cash returns are all distributed as dividends. Even in publicly held companies, it is the future dividends that are regarded as the relevant return for DCF valuation purposes.[92]

In order to determine past cash returns, we must add back non-cash expenses that entered into the computation of net income. The principal non-cash expenses are usually depreciation and amortization. This is the means by which accountants allocate expenses among fiscal periods, where the benefit (or detriment) of those expenses will not all be realized in the current period.

Treatment of Non-Cash Expenses

The target manufactures a single line of products, which is the subject of a strong patent application. These products will become obsolete in five years, but until then the target will generate positive cash flows. In each of the next five years, it will realize $5 million in sales. It will incur, in each year, $4 million of cash expenses, principally for the purchase of raw materials, rent and labor. It will also spend, at the beginning of its first year, $200,000 for research and development and $200,000 for patent counsel and other expenses related to obtaining its patent, and $600,000 for the purchase of machinery and equipment.

In presenting its annual results of operations, the first year's results would be distorted, relative to the second through the fifth years, if the entire $1 million of the additional expenses were deducted in the first year. But unless these are taken into account as an expense, the five-year net income number would be $1 million too high. Accountants therefore capitalize these expenses and deduct them from income over an extended period of time. The investment in tangible assets (the machinery and equipment) would be subtracted from income through a depreciation charge, and the investment in intangible assets (the expenses for the patent and the research and development) would be subtracted from income through an amortization charge. If this was done on a straight line basis assuming a five-year life, the depreciation and amortization charges would be $120,000 and $80,000 per year, respectively.

Because capitalized items are shown as an asset on the balance sheet, at a number that is reduced over time by depreciation or amortization charges, and because that declining number is referred to as the book value of the asset, casual readers of financial statements are sometimes tempted to conclude that the balance sheet number reflects the value of the asset and the depreciation or amortization charge is intended to reflect diminution in the value of the asset. This temptation must be strongly resisted. The book value of an asset is its historical cost, reduced by depreciation or amortization charges, which are intended to allocate the expense incurred to acquire the asset (i.e., its historical cost) against income over an extended period. For valuation purposes we are interested in the discounted present value of the cash returns that will be produced by the assets of the business, not in their historical cost. And since the book value of the equity is equal to the book value of the assets (not their market value) less liabilities, it is not a reliable guide to the actual value of the business.

Returning now to the target, we can determine its historical cash returns by adding to its net income items of non-cash expense, such as depreciation of its plant and other tangible assets and amortization of its intangible assets, because these did not represent outflows of cash. For this purpose, we can use the income statement, or statement of operations, but an experienced analyst would use the statement of cash flows, if one exists, for this purpose. If our net income number is after taxes, we will also add back income taxes paid by the target and deducted from net income, because the value of the target's business as a going concern does not depend on the target's tax situation, which may well differ from that of a prospective buyer (the buyer would, of course, need to take its own tax situation into account in determining the net cash flows that it would realize from the target's business). And if we are seeking to determine the value of the target to all investors (holders of both debt and equity), we will also add back interest expense, because from this point of view it is part of the return to investors.

The resulting number, commonly referred to as EBITDA, gives us a pretty good approximation of past cash returns, which are the starting point for predicting future cash returns or free cash flow. But to arrive at free cash flow, adjustments to net income would have to be made to add noncash charges and net changes in long-term debt and to subtract capital expenditures and changes in working capital.

A prospective buyer would also take into account other information regarding the target, the business it is in and the current and expected state of the economy, including information obtained through the prospective buyer's due diligence, to make a judgment as to how the target's future cash returns might vary from its historical returns. First, a prospective buyer would look for information relevant to why the target's net income has been growing at the rate of 10 percent per year. This might indicate that future returns (before other appropriate adjustments) can be expected to exceed the past year's returns, and perhaps that these increases will continue for some period of time. The prospective buyer would, in this connection, wish to analyze information about the target's lines of business and its competitive position to judge how much room there may be for future growth. Second, consideration would be given to whether, because of the family's ownership, the target has been paying management more than it should. An appropriate adjustment might be to add back to historical returns the compensation paid to the family, and then to subtract projected management compensation expense for new managers who may be needed. In addition, personal expenses for lavish entertainment and items such as airplanes and boats would be adjusted. A third potential adjustment involves the plant. It may be that the appraised value of the plant significantly exceeds the present value of rental expense that would be required to lease comparable space. If so, a prospective buyer might add the appraised value of the plant (less projected expenses of sale) to the value of the target as a going concern, subtracting rental expense from projected cash returns to replace the plant.

These and other adjustments to past returns may be appropriate to project future cash inflows from the business. But it would be a mistake to ignore future cash outflows. If the projections of the target's future cash inflows depend on the maintenance of the target's competitive position by investment in the replacement of existing machinery and equipment, the outflow of cash required for such investment is just as relevant to the value of the target as are the projected cash inflows.

Once projected cash inflows and outflows are determined, the next step is to discount to present value the target's projected cash inflows, and then subtract from that number the present value of its projected cash outflows. Alternatively, we could determine net cash flows (inflows minus outflows) for each year separately and discount those to present value. In general, a five-year time horizon is used with a terminal value at the end of that period. The terminal value is often determined by estimating a stabilized return at the end of the period capitalized into perpetuity. To determine the present value, we need to determine the appropriate discount rate, just as we did in valuing the bond.

Although it is possible to infer the discount rate that the market currently applies to a publicly traded bond from information regarding the bond's maturity, interest rate and current market price, this cannot be done with common stock or other equity securities. The reason is that in buying and selling equity securities, investors take into account not only the current returns, but also growth expectations. Thus, one cannot infer the discount rate that the market uses in valuing a common stock from that stock's price-earnings ratio, or from the ratio of the company's stock price to its current dividend. A common stock with current earnings of $2 per share and a current dividend of $1 that is trading at $50 per share has a price-earnings ratio of 25-to-1 and a price to dividends ratio of 50-to-1, but that does not mean that buyers and sellers are using a 4 percent rate in discounting the earnings or a 2 percent rate in discounting dividends. It is much more likely that investors are projecting increasing earnings and dividends, discounted at a much higher rate.[93]

Determining the appropriate discount rate to use in valuing equity securities requires experience and good judgment. In recent years, financial analysts have frequently used the Capital Asset Pricing Model (CAPM) and Arbitrage Pricing Theory (APT) to make determinations regarding appropriate discount rates to use in DCF valuation. The development and use of these theories are topics well beyond the coverage of this chapter. What the beginning M&A lawyer needs to know about CAPM was well stated by Chancellor Allen in his appraisal opinion in *Cede & Co. v. Technicolor*:[94]

> The CAPM is used widely . . . to estimate a firm's cost of equity capital. It does this by attempting to identify a risk-free rate for money and to identify a risk premium that would be demanded for investment in the particular enterprise in issue. In the CAPM model the riskless rate is typically derived from government treasury obligations. For a traded security the market risk premium is derived in two steps. First a market risk premium is calculated. It is the excess of the expected rate of return for a representative stock index (such as the Standard & Poor 500 or all NYSE companies) over the riskless rate. Next the individual company's 'systematic risk' . . . is estimated. This second element of the risk premium is . . . represented by a coefficient (beta) that measures the relative volatility of the subject firm's stock price relative to the movement of the market generally. The higher that coefficient (i.e., the higher the beta) the more volatile or risky the stock . . . is said to be. Of course, the riskier the investment the higher its costs of capital will be. The CAPM is widely used . . . [to estimate] the implicit cost of capital

of a firm whose securities are regularly traded. . . . It cannot, of course, determine a uniquely correct cost of equity. Many judgments go into it.

Whatever the method used to arrive at a discount rate, one needs to keep in mind that the risk associated with the equity of a company is affected not only by the risks of its business, but also by the relative amount of debt in the company's capital structure. The higher the ratio of debt to equity, the greater will be the risk associated with the return on equity, and the higher will be the discount rate used to value that return.

In valuing a publicly held company, the market price of its stock will be the starting point. If there is a sufficient float and adequate public disclosure of material information regarding the company, the price that will be paid in an acquisition of the entire company will usually be higher than the market price of the stock; the difference is commonly referred to as an acquisition or control premium. A variety of theoretical explanations have been offered for the existence of acquisition premiums.[95] However, as a practical matter, the current market price reflects the value of a share under current management. The buyer must offer a higher price to entice the shareholders to sell.

A publicly held company, like a closely held one, can be valued through the DCF approach, but M&A lawyers should leave to investment bankers or other experienced financial analysts the DCF valuation of a publicly held company.

Comparable Companies and Comparable Transactions. There are a number of alternatives to the DCF approach. Two worth considering are the comparable companies method and the comparable transactions method. The opinion of Vice Chancellor Jacobs in *Le Beau v. M.G. Bancorporation, Inc.,*[96] is an interesting review of the use of these methods (as well as the discounted cash flow method) by an expert testifying in an appraisal proceeding involving the stock of a bank holding company. As described in that opinion, one expert used a comparative publicly traded company approach to determine the value to the bank holding company of its bank subsidiaries. That approach involved five steps:

- Identifying an appropriate set of comparable companies
- Identifying the multiples of earnings and book value at which the comparable companies traded
- Comparing certain of the company's financial fundamentals (*e.g.,* return on assets and return on equity) to those of the comparable companies
- Making certain adjustments to those financial fundamentals
- Adding an appropriate control premium

This approach involves the use of information about comparable publicly held banks to value a bank that was not publicly held, but was instead the wholly owned subsidiary of a publicly held bank holding company. If one assumes that the publicly held banks are truly comparable to the bank being valued (presumably meaning that the risk faced by the equity, and the growth rates for return on equity, at a minimum, are both comparable), one might assume that if the bank being valued were publicly traded, the market price for its stock would reflect multiples of earnings and book value comparable to those of the publicly held banks. Note that this does not involve the mistake, discussed above, of using a price earnings ratio to determine a discount rate, as no discount rate is used in this method. Rather than projecting future returns and discounting them, as in the DCF method, this method involves an assumption that comparable companies will trade at comparable multiples of assets and equity. The expert in *LeBeau* added a control premium to the value based on the market prices of the comparable banks because the shares that are publicly traded are typically not control shares, so that the value of all of the shares of the subsidiary bank would exceed, by the amount of a control premium, the hypothetical market value as determined by reference to the price at which non-control shares of the comparable banks traded in the market.

Whereas the comparative company approach looks to information regarding the market prices of the stock of comparable companies and then adds a control premium, the comparable transaction approach, as described in *LeBeau*, looks to information regarding the prices at which the stock of comparable companies have been sold in transactions involving the sale of control. This method determines the extent to which those prices are multiples of earnings and book value, and having determined those multiples, applies them to the earnings and book value of the company being valued. Since the information is based on transactions in which the value of control was presumably included in the negotiated price, there is no need to add a control premium.

In both of these approaches, as with the DCF approach, many judgments are required. What is a comparable company? Presumably it should be in the same line of business as the company being valued. If the company being valued is in more than one line of business, a significant problem is presented. Is it permissible to use a company in a different geographical region? How does one determine whether the risks and growth rates associated with the companies' equity are comparable? If the companies have significantly different debt-equity ratios, what adjustments would be required? In assessing the relationship of the comparable company's market price to its financial data, what financial data should be used? Over what period of time? And as of what date should the stock's market price be assessed? Or should it be assessed in terms of the average price over a period of time? How does one determine the amount of the control premium to be included?

Similar questions arise in the use of the comparable transactions method. What is a comparable transaction? How can one be confident that the deal price negotiated in the comparable transaction reflected only a control premium, as opposed to overpayment by an over-eager buyer? How does one know the extent to which the comparable transaction involved an allocation of synergies that the parties believed to be obtainable? If an allocation of synergistic benefits was involved, inclusion of that part of the comparable transaction price in the analysis would be questionable, because the objective is to value a company, which presumably involves a question to be answered without reference to the identity of the buyer. To put the point in a different way, it is a mistake to assume that the entire acquisition premium paid in the comparable transaction is attributable to the value of the target, and very difficult to tell how much of the premium involves instead a division of synergistic benefits or the benefits of replacing management, or perhaps overpayment by the buyer.

Regardless of whether the financial analyst is using a combination of DCF, comparable companies, comparable transactions or some other approaches to valuation, it will necessarily involve many judgments. And each of those judgments has the potential to have a dramatic effect on the valuation reached. Lawyers are not, and should not attempt to be, valuation experts. But with effort and preparation, a lawyer can do a good job of assessing what judgments go into a valuation and challenging (or defending) the judgments that have been made.

Valuation in the Appraisal Rights Context

Appraisal rights in corporate statutes originated when the requirement that corporate mergers be approved by a unanimous vote of the shareholders was removed from the statutes. At that time, consideration in a merger was paid in the form of stock, and appraisal rights were seen as a way of permitting a shareholder who did not want to hold stock in the merged enterprise to cash out of his investment at the appraised fair value of the stock of the corporation being merged out of existence. Appraisal rights were given to shareholders in exchange for the veto over corporate mergers that they previously held.[97] Numerous issues are involved in the exercise of appraisal rights under modern corporate statutes, but for present purposes we are interested only in how fair value is determined.[98]

For many years, the Delaware courts (and courts in many other jurisdictions) used a method known as the Delaware block to determine the fair value of shares as to which appraisal rights were exercised. This method required that the court determine the net asset value, the earnings value, and the market value of the stock, and then determine a weighted average of these three components of value to arrive at fair value.[99]

The Delaware block method has been criticized as illogical and as tending to undervalue the stock being appraised.[100] The net asset value has sometimes been determined by reference to the book value of the assets, which is not likely to be indicative of the value of the assets. But even if a court uses the appraised value of the assets less the corporation's liabilities in determining net asset value, this approach will lead to undervaluation of the net asset value component in the vast majority of cases, because the corporation is being valued as a going concern, and the appraised value of the assets is a liquidation value measure. Conversely, since a corporation's value is the greater of its going concern or its liquidation value, in any instance in which the liquidation value exceeds the going concern value, inclusion of the earnings value component, which is a going concern measure, will lead to undervaluation. Moreover, the earnings value component has usually been determined by reference to an average of the earnings during the past five years, regardless of the trend during that period, because the courts were generally uncomfortable about projecting future earnings. Again, this typically resulted in a built-in bias toward a lower valuation. The courts would sometimes use the price-earnings ratios of comparable companies as a capitalization, or discount, rate, without considering whether these comparable companies had growth expectations comparable with those of the company being valued. In any event, the question arises as to whether the courts should have been using cash flows, rather than accounting earnings, in the going concern valuation.

In *Weinberger v. UOP, Inc.,*[101] the Delaware Supreme Court held that the Delaware block method of valuation would no longer exclusively control stock appraisal and other valuation proceedings. The court adopted what it termed a more liberal approach, permitting proof of value by any techniques or methods generally considered acceptable in the financial community and otherwise admissible in court. The drafters of the Model Business Corporation Act adopted a similar approach.[102] Delaware does not prohibit the Delaware block approach, and it continues in use in a number of other jurisdictions.[103] But in many cases, such as *LeBeau,* the court has admitted the testimony of competing experts as to DCF, comparative companies or comparable transactions valuation, as well as other methods of valuation generally considered acceptable in the financial community.

The Delaware block method of valuation does offer one apparent advantage over valuation methods commonly used by financial analysts, namely that each of the three components of the valuation can be based on objectively verifiable information, particularly if book value of the assets is used for the net asset value component. Financial statement earnings will be used for the earnings component, and information regarding the prices at which the stock traded is available to determine the market value component. Even if the net asset value component is based on asset appraisals, the issue in any dispute regarding this component involves only the market value of the assets. Thus, the Delaware block method may appear more objective and precise because it involves fewer judgments than DCF, comparative companies, comparable transactions or other valuation methods typically used by financial analysts. But despite the apparent objectivity, it is generally agreed that use of the Delaware block method results in undervaluation in appraisal proceedings. In this connection, it is appropriate to reflect on Keynes' remark, quoted by Warren Buffet in a similar context: "I would rather be vaguely right than precisely wrong."[104]

Its bias toward undervaluation would appear to be a good argument against use of the Delaware block method in appraisal proceedings. It is worth asking, however, whether the only alternative to the Delaware block is a proceeding in which the court must base its decision as to the fair value of the stock on the testimony of competing experts regarding valuation methods in common use in the financial community. In this connection, consider the observations of Chancellor Allen regarding DCF: "The DCF model typically can generate a wide range of estimates. In the world of real transactions . . . the hypothetical, future-oriented, nature of the model is not thought fatal to the DCF technique because those employing it typically have an intense personal interest in having the best estimates and assumptions used as inputs. In the litigation context use of the model does not have that built-in protection. On the contrary, . . . the incentive of the contending parties is to arrive at estimates of value that are at the outer margins of plausibility. . . ."[105]

Appendix 7-A
Litigation and Other Contingencies

Excerpt from Note 4 of Notes to Financial Statements in Quarterly Report on Form 10-Q of Exxon Mobil Corporation for the quarter ended September 30, 2004

4.   Litigation and Other Contingencies

Litigation

A variety of claims have been made against ExxonMobil and certain of its consolidated subsidiaries in a number of pending lawsuits and tax disputes. *The corporation accrues an undiscounted liability for those contingencies where the incurrence of a loss is probable and the amount can be reasonably estimated. The corporation does not record liabilities when the likelihood that the liability has been incurred is probable, but the amount cannot be reasonably estimated, or when the liability is believed to be only reasonably possible or remote.* ExxonMobil will continue to defend itself vigorously in these matters. Based on a consideration of all relevant facts and circumstances, the corporation does not believe the ultimate outcome of any currently pending lawsuit against ExxonMobil will have a materially adverse effect upon the corporation's operations or financial condition.

A number of lawsuits, including class actions, were brought in various courts against Exxon Mobil Corporation and certain of its subsidiaries relating to the accidental release of crude oil from the tanker Exxon Valdez in 1989. The vast majority of the compensatory claims have been resolved. All of the punitive damage claims were consolidated in the civil trial that began in May 1994.

In that trial, on September 24, 1996, the United States District Court for the District of Alaska entered a judgment in the amount of $5 billion in punitive damages to a class composed of all persons and entities who asserted claims for punitive damages from the corporation as a result of the Exxon Valdez grounding. ExxonMobil appealed the judgment. On November 7, 2001, the United States Court of Appeals for the Ninth Circuit vacated the punitive damage award as being excessive under the Constitution and remanded the case to the District Court for it to determine the amount of the punitive damage award consistent with the Ninth Circuit's holding. The Ninth Circuit upheld the compensatory damage award that has been paid. On December 6, 2002, the District Court reduced the punitive damage award from $5 billion to $4 billion. Both the plaintiffs and ExxonMobil appealed that decision to the Ninth Circuit. The Ninth Circuit panel vacated the District Court's $4 billion punitive damage award without argument and sent the case back for the District Court to reconsider in light of the recent U.S. Supreme Court decision in *Campbell v. State Farm.* On January 28, 2004, the District Court reinstated the punitive damage award at $4.5 billion plus interest. ExxonMobil and the plaintiffs have appealed the decision to the Ninth Circuit. The corporation has posted a $5.4 billion letter of credit.

On January 29, 1997, a settlement agreement was concluded resolving all remaining matters between the corporation and various insurers arising from the Valdez accident. Under terms of this settlement, ExxonMobil received $480 million. Final income statement recognition of this settlement continues to be deferred in view of uncertainty regarding the ultimate cost to the corporation of the Valdez accident.

Management believes that the likelihood of the judgment being upheld is remote. While it is reasonably possible that a liability may have been incurred arising from the Exxon Valdez grounding, it is not possible to predict the ultimate outcome or to reasonably estimate any such potential liability.

∗   ∗   ∗

(Emphasis added.)

CHAPTER 8

Negotiating the Deal

After a potential buyer and seller in each other have expressed an interest, the process moves into a mating dance phase, in which negotiation permeates every stage. From establishing confidentiality ground rules, reaching agreement on the price and setting the structure, to preparing the acquisition agreement and related documents, closing the deal and resolving post-closing tiffs, representatives of the buyer and seller (quite often the lawyers) and the clients themselves are involved in negotiations at some level. This chapter deals with setting the basic terms, including price and structure, and the documentation of the deal in its preliminary stages.

> **Know yourself***
> (the needs of your client)
> **Know your enemy**
> (the needs of your adversary's client)
> **Fight a thousand battles**
> (negotiations)
> **Win a thousand victories**
> (agreements acceptable to both parties)
> * with apologies to *Sun Tzu*

Acquiring Background Information

Before becoming involved in direct negotiations, counsel should at the outset either have or gather background information that might be helpful in effectively representing the client, including information regarding the business and industry of the buyer and the target, the level of experience and sophistication of the parties, their competitive positions, the comparative leverage of each party vis-à-vis the other, and the business goals and objectives of each. This fact gathering may be particularly important in representing a new client.

Here are some examples of information that counsel might well try to obtain.

- What is the business case for the buyer's acquisition, and how does it fit within the buyer's current and long-term strategies?
- What is the industry in which the buyer and target operate? Is it growing? Is it contracting? Are the industry dynamics changing? Are there strong concentration trends in the industry or among the customers? Is the industry regulated? Are those regulations changing?

- How is the business of each of the parties performing compared with past performance, with the other party, and with its peers?
- What aspects of the target's business are of highest interest to the buyer? Is it the ongoing business, its trade name, its market position, a new product line, its intellectual property, its financial performance, its management, or something else?
- What does the buyer want to do with the target post-closing? Continue to operate the target as is? Use it as a platform for expansion or further acquisitions? Move and consolidate its operations with another facility of the buyer? Simply close it down and eliminate a competitor?
- How important to the buyer is financial performance of the target both before and after the closing? A publicly owned buyer will be more concerned about the accretive or dilutive effect of the acquisition on its earnings.
- Are the parties direct competitors? Will the due diligence process yield information that the other party could use to its advantage if the transaction fails to close? Should the client establish an information wall between its operating team and its due diligence team to lessen its exposure to charges of unfair use of proprietary information? Will the transaction attract the attention of antitrust regulators or other governmental agencies?
- What are the seller's objectives? Maximize current cash payout? Receive an equity stake in the buyer, an attractive investment that it believes has strong growth possibilities? Eliminate any worry over post-closing indemnification claims or an earnout, even if it means accepting a lower purchase price? Ensure that the employees continue to have jobs? Ensure that the operations remain in the current community? Obtain capital sufficient to achieve the potential of the business?
- Is the client experienced in M&A transactions? Does it understand the process? Is it sophisticated? Is the client well organized? Does the client have the expertise to evaluate what the target business is worth?
- Does the client need the assistance of other advisors, such as accountants, investment bankers, appraisers, risk managers, or technology evaluators? Can the client be expected to read with care and understand due diligence reports and the acquisition documentation? Will the client go off on its own and make commitments to the other party without consulting or advising counsel?
- How much experience and comfort does counsel have working with this particular client?

These are but a few examples of the types of information that counsel may ideally gather. These questions will not only frame the legal issues to address in the context of negotiating and closing the transaction but will also shape the role that counsel will play and affect the manner in which he interacts with the client.

Negotiating the Price

In the acquisition process, no deal can be done without an agreed-upon price. In many respects, the subject of price negotiation is sprinkled throughout the text of this Guide, as virtually every aspect of the acquisition process can influence price. From the initial decision to sell a business to the exclusion of an unwanted asset, price is influenced. In all business transactions, price receives continuing scrutiny by the parties. Accordingly, price negotiation (usually downwards) is a fluid concept that runs through the whole process.

Usually transactions begin with a stated purchase price. It may appear in a letter of intent or term sheet, or it may merely be raised in conversation between the parties. Rarely is that stated purchase price the same number that appears on the closing statement. Buyers will sometimes suggest a purchase price higher than they ultimately are willing to pay in order to attract the attention of an otherwise complacent seller, assuming that once hooked, the seller will negotiate further on the price. In such instances, the buyer often uses the due diligence process to justify price reductions. Just as often, the buyer tests the waters with a low price, after which the seller, if interested, counters with a higher price. Sometimes an investment bank will be able to push the price higher.

Issues such as consulting agreements, covenants not to compete and the sale of ancillary assets that are owned by affiliates of the target may affect the price negotiations. Sometimes tax advisors will drive the economics of these agreements causing tradeoffs that are truly a price adjustment.

Usually discussions regarding pricing occur before the earliest agreements are negotiated or the structure set, with the parties trying to get a sense from each other as to the general purchase price or range required to make the transaction a reality. Depending upon the parties involved and whether or not brokers, investment banks, or other representatives are participating in the marketing of the acquisition, issues relating to pricing may be in play at very early stages.

The price negotiation process can be highly emotional and clients are well served to understand that "it ain't over 'til it's over."

The Parties and Their Representatives

Once the parties have decided to pursue a transaction, both the buyer and seller should consider the appropriate persons to negotiate price on their behalf. The principals themselves may decide that they are best suited to conduct the price negotiations. Negotiation between principals allows for direct communication and often an expedited pricing process. Direct communications between principals may also help to minimize the spin that may be placed upon offers presented by third parties. On the other hand, direct communications between principals may also inflame the negotiation process. Where the target is a private company, and especially in instances in which the seller has built the business and feels the entrepreneurial pride of having nurtured the enterprise, suggestions of a price below the seller's expectations are likely to result in emotional reactions.

Because direct negotiations between principals often lead to grandstanding and the introduction of emotions in ways that become nonproductive, often third party negotiators are involved. Among these third parties may be attorneys, consultants, brokers, and investment bankers. Attorneys are often placed in the role of negotiating price and serving as the spokesman for the client. The attorney can sterilize the discussions and can often present the position of the buyer or seller in a fashion that is purely business. The attorney may also be able to provide color and insight into the price being offered or demanded when presenting offers and counteroffers. As a non-principal, you may be able to move the process along more rapidly and smoothly.

The prospective seller should have done, or have had done, the analyses and models that support its position on price long before negotiations begin. While attorneys may be helpful, often they do not have the financial or business background necessary to fully appreciate the pricing of a transaction. While much information is available regarding pricing methodologies, valuation techniques, and industry information (such as appropriate industry multiples at any given time), most attorneys would admit that they are not financial analysts. When the attorney is acting as the price negotiator or facilitator, it is imperative that he not get in over his head and always recognize when the price negotiations have passed beyond his comfort zone. For this reason, consultants, business brokers, and investment banks can play a very valuable role in the price negotiation process. Even so, the attorney in the middle of price negotiations should have at least a rudimentary understanding of how value is assessed from a financial standpoint, which is discussed in Chapter 7.

Where specific issues relevant to the transaction are presented, engaging a consultant who is expert in those areas may well enable the parties to quantify a particular risk or value. For instance, in the event of an environmental concern, engaging an environmental consultant who can quantify the extent of the environment remediation risk may enable a party to place a price tag on that aspect of a transaction, allowing the parties to move ahead to an agreement on price.

Business brokers and transaction consultants can often provide information relating to the relevant markets, similar transactions and valuation models that can be applied to the business opportunity in assisting a buyer, a seller, or both parties in recognizing and establishing an appropriate value range for the transaction.

In larger, more sophisticated transactions, investment banks are often engaged, either to market the transaction or to seek business opportunities for clients. Investment bankers are able to provide not only expertise relating to the marketplace and relevant valuation techniques, but are also often able to assist in developing possible purchase price structures. The knowledgeable investment bank is privy to the capital markets and has substantial experience relating to the cost of capital that may need to be developed in an acquisition transaction. Further, when the investment bank possesses significant industry-specific knowledge and knows the likely interested financial and strategic buyer candidates, it can add even more value for a seller.

The particular facts and circumstances, as well as the various personalities involved, will often dictate who and how many persons will make up the negotiating team. As relationships between the parties are developed, the roles of individuals may change, with certain parties taking the lead at certain times, while finding themselves in only ancillary and supporting roles at other stages of the transaction. In any circumstance, however, it is extremely important that all persons participating in the price negotiation process, whether for the buyer or for the seller, are working in a coordinated fashion to achieve the client's goals.

When a buyer or seller has multiple persons involved in the price negotiation on its behalf, it is imperative that the flow of information be unobstructed. The whole team must understand who the point person for price negotiation will be. Multiple lines of communication will invariably lead to inconsistent information being conveyed, issues being conceded without the full understanding of the parties, and in some instances, a need to retract or clarify information. This type of confusion over mixed messages can slow down, if not frustrate or kill, the price negotiation process, and also lead to mistrust.

Personalities

In selecting a price negotiator, do not underestimate the dynamics of personalities. A strong, entrepreneurial, dynamic principal may often serve as a great price negotiator. Such a person may be able to instill great confidence and may be able to tell the story of the business opportunity better than anyone. On the other hand, having a client with a very strong personality lead the price negotiation may cause concern if that person cannot accept the buyer's criticism of the business (which will invariably be raised to decrease or otherwise test the purchase price being sought by the seller). Consideration of who is negotiating on behalf of the other side and the chemistry of the two negotiators is likewise important.

The use of third parties or multiple parties may also serve to allow the parties to obtain two bites at the apple. Where an advisor is used to convey a message relating to pricing and price negotiation, if that message is not well received or otherwise rejected, it still allows the principal to step in and continue to discuss the issue at hand. The use of an advisor also allows the other party to quiz the advisor on how the principal is likely to react to a suggested deal term without necessarily making a formal offer. Similarly, the person receiving the information in a discussion among advisors can reserve making any decisions regarding the pricing issue, on the grounds that the advisor is without authority to make a decision. This indirect negotiation will necessarily prolong the negotiation process, but will often result in more reasoned, less emotional counter-offers and enable the sort of horse-trading often essential to reaching a deal.

Client Priorities

Another issue to be considered by the attorney when participating as a price negotiator is to fully appreciate and understand the priorities of the client. Obtaining the optimum price is not necessarily the highest priority of every seller. Many times, the comfort of limiting representations or avoiding significant indemnification obligations may be more important than additional dollars in the pricing of the transaction. Similarly, a seller's ability to wash its hands of certain business conditions or to know that the duration of representations will be significantly curtailed may cause it to be willing to accept less consideration. Similarly, the ability to continue to have an opportunity to consult and or to earn additional payments after the closing may cause a seller to accept a lower price.

From a buyer's perspective, the converse may be true. A buyer may be willing to pay more for a business opportunity if it is assured of a creditworthy and collectible guarantor of the indemnity obligations, or perhaps if an exclusive supply agreement for the buyer is included. Each of these issues should be fully discussed with the client before the price negotiation process begins. These very same issues must also remain at the forefront of an attorney's thoughts when multiple clients are represented to make certain that these various tradeoffs do not disparately impact the client group.

That Last Dollar Is Often Expensive

A savvy, experienced investment banker friend, when faced with near fatal deal drift in a fully priced deal, observed that over his career whenever a seller (or an auction) pushed a buyer to a price beyond that with which the buyer was comfortable, the deal was inevitably far more difficult to bring together and close.

Internal Factors Affecting Price

Because every business acquisition is unique, it is difficult to discuss meaningfully how a particular pricing model should apply in the abstract. However, regardless of what pricing technique is to be employed, there are various issues to consider in all transactions. Many of these are internal to particular sellers or the business enterprise itself, while many forces will be external and applicable to the marketplace.

Internal forces may motivate the seller to dispose of the business enterprise. In a closely held business, this may include a variety of personal issues. The following are typical of drivers in many deals:

Age of seller. Whether a single or multiple seller is involved, the age of the seller may well impact the motivation to sell the business. Where the seller is approaching or past retirement age, especially when there is no second generation involved in the business, the prospect of selling the business will become more dominant.

Health of seller. The significance of the health of the seller cannot be underestimated. In most closely held businesses, there is a sense of ownership of not only the business itself, but of all its activities and the employees and other people affected by any sale. Where a seller's health is deteriorating or in question, the perception of the ability to continue to keep the business enterprise will serve to motivate the seller and often cause the seller to accept a lower purchase price.

Number of sellers. Where there are multiple sellers, disputes can cause the group to become dysfunctional or otherwise fractious. This tension may lead to some being more motivated to dispose of the business enterprise. This observation is especially true in instances in which minority shareholders are threatening the majority shareholders with claims of oppression or other inappropriate conduct, which can frequently arise when ownership of a family business moves to the second and third generations.

Restrictive agreements. Where the sellers are parties to restrictive agreements or other contractual obligations, the ability to adequately market the business enterprise may be affected. For instance, where shareholders have a right of first refusal, this may chill the marketplace and depress the purchase price offered by a third party, recognizing that it may simply be serving as a stalking horse.

Uncertain management. Where the seller's management team is uncertain, either because of age, health, mobility, non-ownership, or lack of commitment to the enterprise, the ability to deliver a functioning, turn-key operation will be in question. If a buyer perceives that an attractive management team is not likely to remain in place, the risks associated with obtaining the business enterprise will increase, thereby causing the price to decrease.

Expiration issues. Where some of the significant assets of the seller are likely to expire or otherwise cease to have the market advantage that the business presently enjoys, the buyer will be less likely to pay top dollar. For example, where a seller has developed certain intellectual property that has not been protected and is likely to be replicated in time, the window of opportunity will be seen as closing. Similarly, where patents or other protected intellectual property are among the assets of the business enterprise, the duration remaining on the protection will directly influence the purchase price. Other examples where the timing of the business cycle or opportunity will significantly depress the purchase price include disappearing contracts with major customers and market opportunities that will be of a specific duration.

Financial condition. Many businesses enjoy favorable financial relations through leases or other business settings, including the use of fully depreciated equipment. As these favorable financial circumstances expire and additional capital is required by the business enterprise, the owners often determine that it is an appropriate time to sell the business. These potential expenditures may have a significant impact on the value to outsiders, and may strongly motivate the seller.

External Factors Affecting Price

In addition to various internal forces, the marketplace itself will dictate many pricing issues, including the following:

Number of interested buyers. The number of prospective buyers in the marketplace will greatly affect the purchase price. Where the business attracts a number of suitors, the seller is in an enviable position and can often play them off against one another to obtain the most favorable price. On the other hand, especially in specialized industries, there may be very few prospective buyers. In those instances, especially where it understands the marketplace, it is the prospective buyer who may have the upper hand. The purchase price will also be influenced by whether the prospective buyers are financial or strategic buyers, and whether one or more of them are competitors.

Cost of money. The purchase price will necessarily be influenced by the cost of money that the buyer will have to pay to consummate the transaction. Where third-party funds are being sought, the interest rates and terms of borrowings will become a part of the economics of the transaction. In instances in which the buyer intends to use its own funds, the lost opportunity cost of the inability to deploy these funds in other investment opportunities will influence the price. Even in instances in which the seller is willing to finance some or all of the purchase price, the prevailing interest rates will necessarily influence the price negotiation and ultimate purchase price.

Form of payment. The form of payment the buyer desires and the seller is willing to accept will influence the price negotiation. Where the seller is willing to consider alternatives to an all cash purchase price, there will be greater flexibility in the price negotiations. Whether a seller is prepared to accept stock or other equity in the buyer (or in an affiliate of buyer), to accept notes or other subordinated debt instruments, to include an earn-out or other post-closing payments, or to lend a portion of the purchase price (through seller financing), will all influence the price negotiation as these elements will be taken into account in developing the "true price" in the eyes of the parties.

Similar opportunities. If other similar opportunities exist in the marketplace, the opportunity offered by the sale of the target will necessarily be affected. As with virtually any good, as the supply of businesses in the marketplace increases, the price is generally depressed. A sophisticated buyer should be aware of alternative business opportunities and will pursue the most favorable one. Conversely, where the supply of businesses is limited (especially in settings in which the number of prospective buyers is greater), economic forces will increase the ultimate purchase price.

Synergies. Many prospective buyers will see synergies that can be developed between the target business and other businesses already operated by the prospective buyer. Where the business can be a supplier or a customer of other related business enterprises, the value to the particular buyer will be enhanced. While the prospective buyer may not acknowledge this increased benefit, the seller needs to consider this issue so that it can better understand a buyer's motivation, perspective and likely willingness to meet its pricing demands.

Complementary companies. A buyer and seller must be cognizant of not only competitive businesses, but also the effect the transaction will have on the complementary businesses relied upon by the target, such as suppliers, vendors, and customers. A sophisticated buyer will factor all of these issues into its assessment of value.

Sale of a subsidiary or division. Where the target is a subsidiary or division of a much larger company, often the seller will have many priorities unrelated to price, such as the certainty of closing within a targeted year or quarter, the placement of key management people, or the desire for a continuing market for product lines retained by the seller. Any or all of these objectives may cause a seller to consider a much lower price from a buyer that can address these issues than from a competing buyer who cannot.

Closing Price Adjustments or True-Ups

While most acquisitions are priced off a multiple of the earnings stream or cash flow, implicit in the price is a certain level of assets (particularly current assets) to support the business. Therefore, most buyers want assurance as to the value of the balance sheet of the acquired business at the time of closing. The acquisition agreement will usually contain a representation about the status of a current balance sheet (typically unaudited). Parties frequently negotiate a purchase price adjustment (often referred to as a true-up) by which a cash payment is made to the buyer if there is a deficiency from an agreed-to amount of net current assets, net worth or other measure (often determined by reference to the latest balance sheet upon which a representation has been made).[106]

Method of measurement. While two frequent methods of measurement are net worth or net current assets (working capital), the precise formulation could be anything agreed to by the parties. Often it is argued that net worth is not the appropriate standard because in setting the purchase price the parties have already agreed that the target is to be valued by some other means. Net current assets are relevant to most buyers because a certain level of working capital is required to operate the business in the ordinary course.

Setting the target. The target figure is determined by what is shown as net assets or net current assets, usually expressed as a dollar amount. While the latest balance sheet usually provides an appropriate reference point, in some instances the parties may negotiate a normalized figure. For example, for a cyclical business such as a retail, where inventories vary substantially, a snapshot taken at the end of October may not be appropriate when the closing is expected at the end of January. When the most current balance sheet does not represent the business being purchased (e.g., a subsidiary that will be stripped of cash or the purchase of less than all assets), the measurement method and target amount will need to be adjusted.

Settling up. If on the closing date, determined by a closing date balance sheet, the net worth, working capital, or other measurement is less than the target amount, the seller would be required to make up the difference. Most sellers argue that, as a matter of comity, the converse ought to work as well—if there is an excess, the sellers should get the benefit. Arguably the true-up should be coordinated with indemnification. For example, many acquisition agreements contain representations with respect to the accounts receivable and inventories. If the values of those are adjusted in the closing date balance sheet and the purchase price is adjusted, does the buyer get a second bite at the apple (presumably for the same damages) through indemnification?

Whose perspective? From whose perspective is the calculation made? Buyers may have a new basis in the assets of the business through a purchase of assets, a deemed purchase of assets, or push down accounting. While it would be possible to measure the value of assets from the buyer's perspective (that is, a new basis), it would be unusual to do so. Both the seller and buyer know the seller's basis in the assets. How the buyer will account for the assets in the purchase is not known to the seller and may not be known to the buyer for a substantial period of time after the closing. Therefore, the seller's accounting is what is normally used for the true-up calculation.

Who prepares? Who prepares the closing balance sheet, the seller or the buyer? The preparer of the closing date balance sheet has a distinct advantage. The buyer will argue that it needs to have the information for purposes of setting up its own accounts, and in fact it may need to involve its auditors in preparing its own opening balance sheet. The seller will argue that it understands how the historical financial statements have been prepared and the methodology that needs to be applied. It is usually the same accounting personnel (now employees of the buyer) doing the accounting, so that may not be persuasive. When the target being sold is a business unit and the seller keeps the books centrally, the case may be more persuasive.

Security. Sometimes the payment of the true-up is secured in some way. As between a corporate buyer and a corporate seller in a divestiture situation, the obligation may be unsecured. Normally, however, the buyer will withhold a portion of the purchase price or will put a portion of the purchase price in escrow solely for purposes of securing the true-up. Other arrangements are possible, such as the ability to reduce the principal amount of a note given by the buyer in the event of any deficiency.

How is the measurement made? The methodology applied pursuant to the acquisition agreement in preparing the closing balance sheet is variable. Often the agreement will specify that it is to be prepared in accordance with generally accepted accounting principles consistently applied or as applied by the target. The problem with the standard is that the results produced by GAAP are generally imprecise. That may be particularly true in the sale of a business unit where non-GAAP measures may have been historically used and either adjusted at an intermediate subsidiary level or otherwise regarded as immaterial. If there is concentration on a few assets, such as inventory, the methodology in determining the value becomes much more critical and historic practices may or may not represent GAAP. There is also tension between GAAP and consistent application. Assume that the buyer understands the principles by which the latest balance sheet was prepared, but it is not GAAP. Assume that the seller failed to include an accrual for vacations on the latest balance sheet. Consistency would require that accrued vacations also be ignored on the closing date balance sheet; GAAP requires that they be accrued. Most practitioners believe that GAAP trumps consistency.

Certain classes of assets pose problems. For example, in the sale of assets certain prepaids may disappear (insurance normally is not assignable) and the unamortized amount of premiums paid would be shown as a prepaid. The value of inventories is fluid—how are manufacturing variances handled? Are reserves properly established? For example, in a business involving many items of inventory, how can one know what is slow moving or obsolete? The auditors may not have historically questioned accounting methodology used by the target, but in the acquisition of a business it becomes very important.

Sometimes instead of using imprecise measures such as GAAP, the parties actually agree to a methodology for valuation of particular assets. A listing could go on for several pages describing how particular classes of assets are to be valued for purposes of the computation. This often is a description of the target's historical practices, but it could also involve a negotiated formulation of how a particular class of assets is to be valued, such as inventories.

Estimate. Often the net worth, working capital or other target amount is estimated at closing and the payment made at closing is adjusted based on that amount. The purpose of doing so is to reduce swing in the amount of the purchase price adjustment. The seller normally bases the estimate upon a good faith estimate, although it may be required to present supporting documentation.

Reviewing the closing date balance sheet. While the preparer of the closing date balance sheet has a leg up, most agreements do not provide that the closing balance sheet as prepared is final. Buyers preparing it may attempt to achieve such a position by providing that the seller cannot object except for arithmetical or manifest error. Usually the agreement provides, however, that the preparer provides the balance sheet and associated workpapers and the recipient is given a specified amount of time to object. The recipient is normally provided access to the books and records. It is usually required to object with some specificity.

Disappearing assets. One consistent problem is assets that disappear with the deal. For example, in the sale of a subsidiary, cash will usually not go with the sale because most consolidated enterprises manage cash out of a central location. Therefore, in determining net current assets, the balance sheet needs to be normalized to reflect what will be eliminated in the transaction (typically cash and intercompany payables). One particular asset that would be eliminated in many acquisitions is a deferred tax asset held on the books of a subsidiary where the buyer is taking a new basis in the assets. Immediately prior to the sale those assets exist; immediately after the sale they do not. Therefore, what appears on the closing balance sheet? This illustrates the need for specificity in determining how a closing balance sheet will be prepared.

"Is You Is or Is You Ain't My Asset?"*

Seller agreed to sell several of its subsidiaries pursuant to an acquisition agreement. One of the subsidiaries carried on its books a "deferred tax asset" in the amount of $9 million. The acquisition agreement provided for an audit, as of the closing date, and a post-closing adjustment based on the difference between the net book value of the subsidiary entities determined in accordance with GAAP (with certain specified adjustments) as of the closing date, and the preliminary net book value taken from the preliminary financial statements which seller furnished to buyer shortly before the closing. Seller's auditors certified that the $9 million deferred tax asset was appropriately accounted for on the books of the subsidiary as of the closing date. However, the buyer invoked the dispute resolution provisions relating to post-closing adjustments when it realized, some months after the closing, that the deferred tax asset had "disappeared" once the target's subsidiary was no longer a part of the seller's consolidated group. An arbitrator ruled that the closing financial statements fairly presented the financial condition of the subsidiaries as of the closing date and refused to allow an adjustment. The buyer's internal financial due-diligence team, its lawyers and its outside auditing firm may have wished their diligence was more diligent and that the specific exceptions to GAAP described in the stock purchase agreement had included a carve-out relating to the deferred tax asset.

---

*With apologies to Billy Austin-Louis Jordan ("Is You Is or Is You Ain't My Baby")

A discussion of the actual operation of true-up provisions post-closing is contained in Chapter 15.

Resolving differences. If there is an objection, the agreement normally requires that the parties negotiate their differences in good faith for some period of time or it may have an internal mediation procedure, such as kicking it up to the CEOs of the two entities. While the agreement could be silent, leaving the ultimate remedy to litigation, the parties typically select a form of arbitration (although rarely labeled as such)—usually formulated in different ways, the agreement normally provides that the parties will have a recognized accountant determine the accuracy of the closing balance sheet. Sometimes the accountant is actually designated in the agreement while at other times it requires mutual agreement after the fact. Courts have held that the proceeding is in the nature of arbitration and that judgment can be entered on the award.[107]

Earnouts

Although it can take as many forms as there are varieties of transactions, an earnout is essentially a form of deferred purchase price payment tied to post-closing performance indicators. The amount (and sometimes the obligation to pay at all) is related to the success of the business sold measured against milestones that can range from one big financial factor to a laundry list of items.[108]

Earnouts lend themselves to creative thinking and can be tailored to a particular transactional hurdle or type of business. In many M&A transactions, the buyer and seller are simply unable to agree upon what both believe to be an appropriate purchase price, often as a result of differing views on valuation of the target business or its significant assets. Earnouts can be an effective tool to bridge that gap. For example, in many service business acquisitions, the assets that are being purchased are comprised of client or customer lists or goodwill; items that do not necessarily command a high value due to the speculative nature of continued revenue or even any revenue. Sellers can simply be unrealistic in their expectations, and earnouts can be a "middle ground" approach to get a deal done.

For the financial buyer, earnouts are often also used as a means of providing incentive to individual owners to increase the profitability of the acquired business. For the strategic buyer (as well as the financial buyer), the earnout is also an effective tool to ensuring a successful transition of ownership. Tying up a part of the consideration for the business typically proves to be an effective motivator. In addition to the acquisition of service businesses, earnout structures are also sometimes used in transactions involving the acquisition of new products or product lines—assets whose value is wholly dependent upon the future sales or performance of the new product. Acquisitions of troubled companies may also include earnout provisions, as both buyers and sellers would like to base a portion of their valuations on the future performance of the once-troubled company, since historical financial performance is necessarily not a good indicator of value. In a sense, the earnout is a variation of the post-closing purchase price adjustment that lets the seller "put its money where its mouth is" in that continued positive results will result in a higher purchase price.

The drafting of an earnout is fraught with issues. To highlight just a few—what measurement standard ought to be used—gross revenues, net income, EBITDA? What business unit should be evaluated for purposes of calculating the earnout payment—the entire business or just a specific product or division? Over what period of time should the earnout measurement apply? What calculation would be the best method to use—a percentage of gross revenue, a multiple of net income, or some combination? Finally, how should the parties deal with differences in accounting approaches used by the buyer and the target?

Standards of measurement. Gross revenues or sales, although easily measured, are not really a measure of profitability or value. For example, significantly increased gross revenues post-closing may have been generated as a result of management significantly increasing expenses to generate that kind of revenue. That having been said, it is probably the most objective measurement standard available. EBITDA (or some variation) is a seller-favorable standard of measurement, as it will permit the seller to realize an earnout payment based upon an earnings measure that does not reflect any post-closing changes to the capital structure of the acquired unit or any increased interest expense associated with post-closing working capital that varies from what was assumed by the buyer in its valuation modeling. It is an often used standard of measurement, as it is generally thought of as a good indicator of true post-closing financial success of an acquired unit.

A standard of measurement that is anything other than EBITDA will require that the agreement specifically address how the parties will treat items such as the capitalization of transaction-related charges by the buyer, amortization of goodwill and increased depreciation charges or changes in depreciation by the buyer as a result of any step-up in basis. Fees and expenses associated with acquisition indebtedness should also be addressed in the acquisition agreement and, from the seller's perspective, excluded from any calculation.

Generally speaking, the seller should also be very cautious about expense treatment by the buyer post-closing. Overhead, compensation (including employee benefits), insurance premiums and any other costs that might be charged by the buyer against earnings should be specifically identified and appropriately treated in the earnout provisions so that it is clear which expenses affect the earnout calculation and which do not. A seller will want extraordinary one-time transaction expenses to be excluded as income deductions for purposes of calculating the earnout.

While this discussion highlights the most common financial measurement approaches, a variety of other measuring sticks (including non-financial, such as a product in development actually coming to market) will be used, from time to time, as circumstances dictate and as the parties negotiate. If an earnout is being used to bridge a gap in purchase price expectations between the parties, it is important to customize the earnout to address the root cause of those divergent perspectives. Therefore, while certain traditional standards can be pointed out, no exclusive, dispositive list of approaches exists, nor should it.

What business unit? Having agreed as to the standard of measurement, the next critical issue is to what that standard of measurement will be tied. For example, where the strategic buyer has purchased a target in order to acquire a specific product or product line, a standard tied specifically to that product or segment is the appropriate business unit to measure. Sometimes the measurement standard of the entire target that has been acquired is the most appropriate unit; particularly where the earnout has been suggested to reconcile significant valuation disparity between the buyer and the seller. In addition, where the seller's management team will remain employed by the buyer post-closing, utilizing the entire target as the business unit is a way of further motivating the management team to perform.

In many acquisitions, the operations of the acquired business will be integrated with the buyer's existing business. Because of this significant overlap in products or business segments, it is important to carefully establish what the buyer can and cannot do to ensure that sales, for example, are not moved away from the acquired business to an affiliated entity and therefore reduce the standard of measurement for purposes of calculating the earnout payment.

Determining the measurement period. Another critical issue involves establishing when or for what period the standard of measurement generated by the business unit is to be determined. Is the earnout to be calculated and paid on a periodic basis over a period of time, or will it be calculated and paid on a one-time basis? Often a buyer and seller agree upon a specific period of time over which to measure performance. This period of time is often subject to acceleration or termination upon the occurrence of certain specific events, or even sometimes at the option of the buyer (subject, usually, to some sort of buyout provision). For example, the termination by the buyer of the employment of an owner employed post-closing can trigger an earnout calculation, payment and termination. The sale by the buyer of the business or product line that it acquired from the seller could also serve as an earnout payment event. Many times, where the buyer contemplates a future disposition of the assets or business acquired from the seller, it will negotiate an election to terminate the earnout provision in order to facilitate the disposition of that asset; typically the seller will then ask for a make-whole provision that represents an early buyout of the now-shortened earnout period. Sometimes these negotiations result in affording the parties various puts and calls that can be exercised under specified circumstances. The seller might even receive some sort of consideration based upon the value realized by the seller in its disposition of the acquired assets or business.

Calculating the payment. The acquisition agreement should address the method of calculation and payment of the earnout. With respect to the method of calculation, there are a few options. Many buyers and sellers will agree upon either a percentage of value or a multiple of value, depending upon what standard of measurement they have already agreed to use. In other words, where the parties have agreed upon the use of an EBITDA standard of measurement, the earnout amount is likely to be some multiple of EBITDA for a specified period. Often, logic dictates that this multiple correspond to that used by a buyer in valuing the target company.

Conversely, percentages of gross revenue might be used in the product acquisition situation where a gross revenue standard has been chosen as the standard of measurement. Another issue to consider is whether the earnout provisions will include payments triggered by the acquired entity or the product meeting certain performance or financial benchmarks—and whether an earnout payment will nevertheless be made where performance falls just short of the benchmark.

Specific issues for the seller. It goes without saying that the seller's interest is to structure the earnout to maximize the amount it will be paid for the business. Of course, underlying that goal should be the concern that the seller not realize less than what it ought to because of the structure of the earnout. Since the buyer will usually be in full control of the business it has purchased, as well as the accounting for revenue associated with the business, proper planning against intended or unintended effects of the buyer's post-closing actions is necessary to protect the seller's interests.

The most important issue from the seller's perspective is avoiding or obviating the buyer's ability to reduce the amount of the earnout through its control of the acquired unit or product. The tension here is that while sellers, particularly those that remain as members of the management team post-closing, would like to be able to directly impact the amount of their future compensation, the buyer is likely not willing to cede control of its newly acquired asset. Although a buyer and seller might try to address this tension with a contractual covenant requiring the buyer to operate the acquired unit in a manner consistent with the seller's conduct of the unit prior to closing and to adequately promote the products of the acquired business through appropriate (perhaps objective) marketing efforts and expenditures, these kinds of provisions are fraught with ambiguity. Closely tied to this issue is that of the buyer sufficiently capitalizing the acquired unit on a post-closing basis, as this is another area of potential intended or unintended effects on an earnout calculation resulting from actions of the buyer. Other items that the seller should concern itself with are situations where the buyer makes a subsequent disposition of some or all of the acquired assets or business, extraordinary items such as a casualty loss or substantial increases in capital expenditures.

As a final note, if the buyer's venture post-closing is highly leveraged, a seller may discover that the earnout payment that was bargained for is deeply subordinated to the lender.

Consistent accounting methodology. An important step in negotiating an earnout is to require consistent accounting methodology, both pre- and post-closing. If the buyer applies an accounting methodology that is not consistent with what the seller employed, the parties' earnout calculations will differ. Simply requiring application of GAAP accomplishes nothing. A specific covenant is often included in the acquisition agreement regarding accounting methodologies to be used by the buyer post-closing. Some particular areas of concern are LIFO versus FIFO inventory methodology, depreciation schedules, and bad debt allowances. In addition, post-closing changes in GAAP probably ought not affect the accounting treatment and methodology for purposes of calculating earnout payments and the parties may wish to so agree.

As a means to determine compliance, sellers should consider including a contractual right to examine the appropriate books and records of the buyer, particularly if the seller will not have any direct involvement with the business post-closing. Where an examination right is granted, it is not unusual to complement this provision with an obligation of the buyer to bear the costs (along with interest or some other penalty) if the examination should reveal that the results on which the earnout is to be based have been misstated.

Avoid hamstringing the acquired unit. As already discussed above, the buyer should consider the need to negotiate a contractual right to terminate the earnout mechanism, whether through a buyout or otherwise, if the continued existence of the structure would prove to be an impediment to the buyer's subsequent ability to deal with the purchased business. A buyer should also be concerned with, and guard against, hamstringing the acquired unit by agreeing to so many limitations or conditions upon operation of the unit post-closing that it stunts the growth or success of the business.

Exercise of Control over an Acquired Unit

The case of *Horizon Holdings, L.L.C. v. Genmar Holdings, Inc.*[109] illustrates the risk in not addressing in the acquisition agreement the manner in which an acquired unit will be operated after the closing. This case involved the acquisition by Genmar Manufacturing of the aluminum boat manufacturing business of Horizon Marine, in which Horizon and its founder had an opportunity to realize up to $5.2 million additional consideration in an earnout. It appears that a number of issues relating to the earnout had been discussed by the parties, but were not covered in the acquisition agreement.

The operations did not produce the earnings to support an earnout payment, and Horizon and its founder sued, claiming that the defendants breached both the express provisions of the acquisition agreement and the implied duty of good faith and fair dealing. A jury returned a verdict awarding the plaintiffs $2.5 million in damages on the breach of contract claim. The jury was instructed that under Delaware law they should consider "whether it is clear from what was expressly agreed upon by the parties that the parties would have agreed to prohibit the conduct complained of as a breach of the agreement had they thought to negotiate with respect to that matter." The court heard several post-trial motions, and denied a motion for new trial. The court stated that because the acquisition agreement was silent as to most of the issues discussed by the parties prior to its execution, evidence as to those discussions was appropriate to provide context for the good faith and fair dealing claim. It concluded the jury could have determined that the defendants engaged in conduct inconsistent with the spirit of the agreement, namely undermining the founder's authority to run the operation after the closing, abandoning the Horizon brand, mandating the production of other boats at the facility and reimbursing only for standard cost for the production of the other boats.

While most buyers will assume that, at least as to significant business decisions, they will be entitled to operate the business that has been acquired, those decisions (such as, in this case, using the acquired facility to produce several lines of boats and thus achieve some synergistic benefits) may be directly counter to a seller's interest in achieving payment under the earnout.

Unanticipated benefits to the seller. While it might be going too far to say that the buyer's goal is to minimize the amount to be paid through the earnout, there are ways to effectively control the amount of the earnout—not to minimize what should rightfully be paid to a seller, but rather to prevent overpayment to a seller based upon the buyer's efforts post-closing or sheer good fortune.

A buyer will want to avoid paying for an increase in the performance of the acquired unit post-closing that has nothing to do with the acquired business itself. For instance, these increases are sometimes directly the result of the buyer's more effective skills or even perhaps simply a result of increased efficiencies resulting from the combination of product lines. The buyer does not want these events to inure to the benefit of the seller through the earnout. If the purpose of the earnout is to more realistically reflect the true value of the transaction, the buyer would want to exclude these kinds of growth items. The practical problem is that it is very difficult to draft around these kinds of unanticipated events. The buyer should consider and identify any items that it can address in advance and exclude them from the earnout, such as expense reductions achieved by the buyer's management.

Disputes. As should be evident, disputes can (and often do) arise when actual numbers and results are determined and the earnout calculations are made. Parties to an earnout may therefore want to carefully consider whether these disputes should be dealt with in the same way as any other contract interpretation dispute (whether by litigation, arbitration, or some other dispute resolution mechanism) or whether they want to include a specific dispute resolution mechanism to deal with the earnout. For instance, the parties may choose not to deal with earnout disputes using the same alternative dispute resolution mechanism that is used for other disputes in the acquisition agreement. They could, for example, provide a mechanism where the earnout dispute is resolved by discussions between the accountants for both the buyer and seller, with a third accounting firm designated to finally resolve the matter in the event that the buyer's and seller's accountants are unable to do so. That having been said, parties who provide that disputes will be resolved by accountants should understand that they will, in all likelihood, approach any dispute as a number crunching exercise and will not consider the equities among the parties. Therefore, an arbitration panel consisting of those with legal, business, or other backgrounds may be preferable.

Negotiating the Structure

Structuring the transaction is one of the most challenging aspects of M&A practice. The goal is to find the optimal structure given different, often conflicting, considerations and desires of the parties.

Negotiation of the structure is largely a function of first considering all of the issues that may influence the structure. Once all of the relevant issues are assessed, the parties should be able to determine which structure or structures will be acceptable and should be in a position to assess and weigh the economic, tax and other consequences of alternate structures. The costs and benefits to each party should be considered.

After determining which alternative structures are possible and the likely economic consequences of each, negotiation of the structure, hand in hand with negotiation of the price, can proceed rationally. While negotiation of the structure is distinct from price negotiation, it often involves many of the same issues and there is frequently an interplay as structural changes impact the economics of the deal. Counsel usually takes the lead in these negotiations because the structure will more often revolve around legal considerations and the transaction documents.

It is critical to have a clear understanding at the earliest point possible regarding the form of the transaction, as this decision influences the purchase price. In general, where the acquisition is for stock, all of the liabilities and assets of the business enterprise will be acquired as a result of the acquisition. The owner of the assets will not change, but rather only the ultimate owner of the enterprise. Conversely, in an asset transaction, only those assets that are expressly included in the transaction will be transferred, and in general only those liabilities that are agreed to be assumed by the buyer will pass.

A buyer will want to pay less for an acquisition of stock (in which it assumes all known and unknown liabilities of the business enterprise) than it will be willing to pay to acquire the assets and assume only specified liabilities of the target company. The form of the transaction will substantially influence the ultimate value as perceived by the buyer and seller. The tax considerations of the transaction, including the tax effects on the seller and the buyer, as well as the ongoing tax consequences resulting from the form of the transaction and allocation of the purchase price, must be considered and given due attention to avoid unintended consequences. In an asset sale, whether the selling entity is a C corporation or an S corporation will have a material effect on the ultimate amount to be received by the shareholders of the target. Similarly, where portions of the purchase price are attributable to capital assets and other portions are attributable to items that must be treated by the seller as ordinary income (such as consulting agreements and covenants not to compete), the amount of the purchase price is likely to be affected. These same issues must be considered by the buyer from a standpoint of the basis, deductibility, depreciation, and other tax consequences that it will experience.

Many of the structuring issues will be transaction specific, while others will reflect general market conditions. Some of the more important issues are discussed below.

Substance of the Transaction

The structure often follows logically once certain agreed upon aspects of the transaction are known. For example, once it is determined whether the transaction is a true acquisition or business combination, decisions as to whether to pursue a statutory merger or stock acquisition as opposed to an asset transaction will become more apparent. Similarly, when a division of a company is being acquired, the fact that only a portion of the company is involved will result in the transaction being structured as an asset sale. These examples point out the importance of considering the economic and strategic substance of the transaction before proposing a structure.

Stock vs. Assets

Most acquisitions can be consummated either as an asset or a stock transaction.[110] Where an asset transaction is favored, a variety of issues must be considered as the transaction is truly one of the sale of each of the individual assets and an assumption of agreed upon liabilities.

Conversely, where the transaction is structured as a stock acquisition, by its very nature the acquisition results in a transfer of the ownership of the business entity itself, but the entity continues to own the same assets and have the same liabilities.

Whether to Structure as a Stock or Asset Purchase

Tax issues are not always the most important factor in determining whether to structure a transaction as a stock or asset purchase. When taxes are a consideration, the parties generally consider the amount of the shareholders' net after-tax proceeds; the buyer's desire to assign a high basis to the assets for depreciation purposes; and any gain recognition by the corporation.

An important non-tax reason why parties choose an asset purchase is the buyer's desire to avoid responsibility for the seller's liabilities.

The seller sold the assets of its business to a newly incorporated buyer. The trade name of the seller was well-known and protected by a registered trademark. As part of the transaction, the seller sold its trademark to the buyer, which chose to use the trademark as its name.

The parties included a provision in the acquisition agreement that the buyer "shall not, either directly or indirectly, assume any of seller's liabilities or obligations of any kind whatsoever, absolute or contingent, whether or not accrued, determined or determinable." The seller also agreed to indemnify and hold the buyer harmless from any of these excluded liabilities.

A year after the closing, the buyer was served in an action for breach of contract. The claim arose in the year prior to the sale of the business and was based on an alleged breach of contract between the seller and one of its customers. The buyer was not in existence at the time the claim arose and claimed it was improperly named as a party. The plaintiff responded that it had named the buyer appropriately as a defendant, since it bore the name of the company that breached the contract with the plaintiff.

The general rule is that a corporation purchasing the assets of another corporation is not liable for the debts and liabilities of the selling corporation. This general rule is based on the premise that a sale of corporate assets transfers an interest separable from the corporate entity, but is subject to certain exceptions discussed in this chapter.

Even before discovery could begin, the buyer was dismissed as a party to the lawsuit. If the transaction were structured as a stock purchase, rather than an asset purchase, the buyer would not have been dismissed.

Where the transaction is structured as an asset purchase, a variety of other factors must be considered in defining and refining the structure. First and foremost is a clear definition of the scope of the assets to be sold. As a general premise, most asset transactions contemplate a sale of all of the operating assets of the seller. However, this basic definition is hardly unambiguous.

It is imperative that the parties understand precisely which assets are to be sold. In instances in which the operating assets will not include accounts receivable, cash, or cash equivalents, the buyer will need to make certain that it has access to capital sufficient to operate the business until it is able to generate its own receivables and turn those receivables into operating capital.

It is also important to fully determine which assets of the operating business the target owns and to address fully any liens that may encumber the assets. In many businesses, certain of the operating assets are not owned by the enterprise, but rather are licensed, leased, or being purchased on time. In such instances, it is necessary to fully appreciate and understand the relationships that the target has with third parties that supply those operating assets.

In almost all asset transactions, there are certain excluded assets. These too must be well defined. It is not uncommon for a transaction to exclude cash and cash equivalents. Similarly, in instances in which the buyer is attempting to minimize the purchase price, the accounts receivable can be excluded from the assets to be sold.

The parties may also agree to exclude a significant asset from the transaction, where that asset presents difficulties for the buyer. This observation is particularly applicable to instances where real estate is involved. Issues involving environmental contamination or past use of the property may create concern, or the parties may be unable to agree upon the fair value for the particular asset. In such instances, the structure of the transaction may be modified by the use of a lease or license to address these concerns and allow the deal to proceed.

When determining which assets are to be included or excluded from the transaction, it is critical to the buyer that the assets that allow the target to enjoy success be included. Where assets such as intellectual property are necessary to the target's operations, a buyer will only be interested in the transaction if it can continue to make use of the intellectual property. In most instances, the buyer and seller will understand this to be the case; however, where a seller does not wish to part with ownership of the intellectual property, or otherwise is only a licensee of the intellectual property, the structure of the transaction must address these issues.

In an asset transaction, each of the assets must be transferred from the seller to the buyer. Title to the assets must be the subject of an appropriate deed (for real property) or bill of sale or assignment (for personal property and contracts). Further, assets that are the subject of public filings or registration (such as patents) will require assignments and filings with appropriate governmental entities to ensure that the buyer can enjoy the assets. This aspect of an asset transaction causes it to be significantly more cumbersome. Where the assets to be conveyed are incapable of being assigned or transferred because of restrictions, required third party or governmental consents, security interests or other reasons, the transaction may have to be structured to avoid a transfer of assets. In such instances, the use of long-term paid-up licenses may be a tool to avoid the prohibition on transfer while still allowing the buyer to enjoy the benefits of the assets.

One of the most difficult features of an asset sale is the need to obtain consents to assign material contracts of the seller as well as the transfer or reissuance of various governmental permits and other rights to do business held by the seller. This issue is addressed in more detail later in this chapter. From this standpoint, a stock sale or merger (and especially a reverse merger) presents fewer impediments.

An asset transaction also raises challenges (and opportunities) in the treatment of employees of the target. They are generally under no obligation to join the buyer nor do they automatically have the same right to a position with the buyer that may be provided in an existing employment arrangement with the target. Stock sales and mergers pose fewer issues in this regard, but also afford the buyer less flexibility to pick and choose whom it wants to employ.

Nature of the Buyer

The structure of the transaction will often be affected by the nature of the buyer.[111] A strategic buyer (an entity that plans to actively run the company), will likely have certain goals and plans for the target. These plans may include dismantling the target, selling off certain assets or folding certain of the business functions into an existing business owned or operated by the buyer. On the other hand, a financial buyer (an entity that does not intend to actively run the target with its own management), may leave the business enterprise intact with essentially the same management, with the buyer causing the target to improve its financial performance and enhance its return on investment.

Legal Form of the Target

The form of the business being acquired must be considered in assessing the appropriate structure for the proposed transaction. Whether the target is a subsidiary, a division, a corporation (S corporation or C corporation), a limited liability company, or other business enterprise, must be addressed to make certain the structure will achieve the intended results for the parties, from a business, tax, economic, and contractual viewpoint.

Form of Consideration

The form of consideration the buyer intends to use will affect the structure. Where seller financing is involved, the seller will demand that certain aspects of the business remain in place and will often place other restrictions on the buyer's ability to change business operations, dispose of assets, or otherwise impair the security that supports the seller financing. In this instance, additional issues regarding the buyer's principal commercial lenders and competing security interests must be addressed.

How will the price for the target be paid? The subject of how the price for the target will be paid should be explored and considered early in the transaction. Even if cash is going to be the medium of payment, a seller should determine if the buyer has the cash resources available or if the buyer will be required to finance the purchase price.

If the buyer plans to finance the purchase of the target, will arranging for the financing be a condition of the buyer's obligation to close? Should the seller insist that condition be satisfied or waived a significant amount of time before the closing date? Should the seller negotiate for a break-up fee if the buyer does not close because of a financing condition? A seller might also consider having the right to walk if the buyer has not waived or confirmed satisfaction of its financing condition by a certain date. The seller may insist on the right to continue marketing the target until the condition is satisfied. A good deal depends on how long the seller will be comfortable keeping the business off the market and how confident it is in the ability of the buyer to obtain its financing. This suggests that these issues should be considered for inclusion in some fashion in the letter of intent or term sheet.

Seller financing. Sometimes a buyer will propose that the seller finance some portion of the purchase price. This is not a financing approach adopted in most M&A deals, but is sometimes encountered in connection with the purchase of small or family-owned businesses.

Accepting the buyer's promissory note has some appeal: It has the effect of deferring the payment of part of the purchase price and, therefore, deferral of a part of the taxable gain that may have to be recognized in connection with the sale. The deferred balance bears interest, typically at a rate higher than what a seller can obtain from its bank or on its other investments, which may seem attractive. Because part of the price is to be deferred, a seller or target may be able to negotiate a higher price for the target if it is deferred rather than paid all in cash at closing.

There are usually a number of considerations that militate against a seller's willingness to accept the promissory note or deferred payment. The seller becomes a lender to the buyer in this situation. Most of us remember what our bank or other lender requires of us in buying a car or home. Is the buyer creditworthy? Who on the seller's team is qualified to evaluate this? Is there to be security? If so, what is the collateral? Is there to be a guaranty of the obligation? If so, from whom? Is the guarantor creditworthy? Will the security interest and/or guaranty be subordinated to the obligations owed by the buyer to others? Will the security interest be capable of a speedy foreclosure if there is a default? What if the business files for bankruptcy? Or the guarantor or buyer? The questions go on and on and pose a real challenge in advising the client. Needless to say, if a significant part of the purchase price is to be deferred and there is a default, the seller is likely to lose and never see most of the price for which it bargained, and the business recovered via foreclosure of security interests will likely barely resemble the business that changed hands at the closing.

Given the number of considerations and issues, this again, is an area worth considering for detailed coverage in the letter of intent or term sheet.

What about the buyer's stock? Because a seller is interested in liquidity, stock used to pay the purchase price in a transaction is usually only acceptable if it is publicly traded and marketable.

Stock transactions can be very appealing because they may permit the sale to be treated as a tax-free reorganization. That means the taxable gain the shareholders of the target would recognize will be deferred until they sell shares of the buyer's stock received in the reorganization.

An initial question if stock is to be the medium of payment is whether the seller would invest an amount equal to the purchase price in the buyer's stock in the first place. Thus, this becomes a very significant investment decision for the seller in which the help of an experienced professional financial advisor or investment bank may be appropriate. Counsel should consider making that recommendation in those circumstances.

Keep in mind that there are numerous varieties of stock: common, preferred and different series and classes of each. Common voting shares are usually required as the consideration to be exchanged in a tax-free reorganization.

If the buyer's common stock has performed well in the market, accepting its stock may be worth considering. What are the issues: What kind of stock? Will there be voting restrictions on the stock? Will it be marketable and when? When can the client sell or borrow against it? Stock may not be freely marketable unless procedural steps (such as registration under the Securities Act) have been taken to make it marketable. Post-closing registration is often problematic in that a buyer may lose its ability to register. Post-closing disputes between the parties may cause the buyer to use registration as leverage in the dispute. Events affecting the buyer may require that it defer or delay registration efforts temporarily. If the market price of the shares to be registered is falling, the target or its owners bear the decline in value and will be pretty unhappy.

Again, these issues are worth discussing early and dealing with in reasonable detail in the letter of intent or term sheet.

Another stock-related issue is: how many shares will be issued at the closing? Public company stock prices obviously fluctuate. The number of shares to be issued may be determined by dividing the price for the target by the price of a share of the stock to be received at closing as of some date. But what date?

The buyer may want to price the deal by fixing the value of its traded stock and the exchange ratio with the target's stock at the time of signing the acquisition agreement or the announcement of the deal. The seller will be concerned that the buyer's stock will decline and may want a formula that sets the value of buyer's stock and adjusts the exchange ratio at a date close to the closing (or through an average price over a defined period prior to closing.) The buyer may be worried about a precipitous drop under such a formula that results in too much dilution for buyer's shareholders, although if there is a steep increase, this formula would protect against a windfall for the target's shareholders. There are a variety of mechanisms (such as price collars and walk rights) to address some of these concerns over extreme price moves. These issues are often negotiated in some detail early in the deal process.

Pricing Risk in Taking Publicly Traded Stock

The manner in which stock of a buyer is valued for purposes of an acquisition can have a significant impact on the seller and the buyer.

Let's say that the parties agree to a price of $10 million for the target, payable in shares of the buyer's publicly traded stock. At signing of the acquisition agreement, the market price of the stock is $100 per share and the agreement provides that the seller is entitled to receive 100,000 shares ($10 million divided by $100). At closing, the market price of the buyer's stock is $150 per share so the 100,000 shares are now valued at $15 million. The share price can drop up to $50 after closing, and the seller will still have $10 million in the buyer's stock.

What if the parties agree to a price of $10 million for the target, but the market price of the buyer's stock is to be determined at closing. Since the market price of the stock is $150 at closing, the seller will receive 66,667 shares, which still have a market value of $10 million. If the stock declines to $100 shortly after closing, the stock received by the seller would be valued at $6,666,700.

The effect of significant fluctuations can be ameliorated by collars on the upside, downside, or both. Of course the market value in these examples is only on paper, and the real value will not be realized until the stock is ultimately sold.

Because the market price of stock may fluctuate widely over time, parties often seek to ameliorate the effect of the fluctuations in several ways: (i) using averages of market prices of the stock over a period of consecutive trading days, for example, 10 days or 30 days; and (ii) using ranges or collars such that if pricing occurs close to closing and the value of the stock has drastically fallen or has significantly increased with a commensurate reduced number of shares, then the adjustment may be modified or the seller may walk. Conversely, if the pricing occurs early on when the letter of intent is signed and then the market price of the shares rises dramatically over the price used to determine the number of shares, the buyer has the right to limit the number of shares or walk owing to a now significantly over-valued purchase, excessive dilution, or both.

The Speed of the Transaction

Depending upon the sensitivity of the parties to the timing of the transaction, and if the size does not require governmental clearances, some structures may proceed more swiftly than others. For example, acquiring the assets of a corporation, without assuming the liabilities, may be perceived as a more expeditious way to acquire the business than to acquire the stock, as the buyer will likely perceive a need to conduct a more detailed and extended due diligence where it is becoming liable for all of the obligations of the enterprise. On the other hand, obtaining clear title to each of the assets and rights to be acquired in an asset transaction may cause substantial delay. Where a swift conclusion of the transaction is important, achieving this goal may be assisted by negotiating alternative structures.

Psychology of the Transaction

In many instances, a transaction takes on a life of its own. The personalities involved will develop a psychology that may influence the structure. Where there is a sense that the transaction is becoming too complex or convoluted, attempts to streamline the structure may allow the transaction to move forward. Conversely, where a party expresses very specific concerns, the anxiety expressed may be alleviated by the addition of certain terms tailored to the transaction.[112] The psychology of the transaction may also dictate a need to give and take in the negotiation process, including negotiation of the structure. It is human nature to expect something in return when being asked for a concession. While this reaction may seem obvious, it should not be overlooked. When seeking a concession from the other party, you should expect to be asked to provide a *quid pro quo* for that concession. By the same token, where the requested concession makes sense and will allow the transaction to proceed, it may be counterproductive to demand a concession simply for the sake of saving face or winning the last point.

In many instances, the structure and the concessions requested are intended to benefit the transaction, and address one or more series of concerns, rather than to renegotiate the deal. The handling of how these requests are presented and, just as importantly, how they are responded to, can be as significant as the substance of the request itself. Once the deal terms or the structure have been determined, attempts to change these points will often be perceived negatively and adversely affect the relationship of the parties and the psychology of the transaction. Whether expressed or not, most parties will keep a mental scorecard regarding issues addressed, and how each is resolved. One should not lose sight of the importance of how issues are presented in addition to what issues are presented.

Existing Impressions

If there is a letter of intent, or if there have been discussions among the principals or their advisors before any definitive agreement has been prepared, these early documents and discussions will likely influence the expectations of the parties. Information included in the letter of intent and discussion points between the parties may establish a preliminary expectation regarding the structure. For example, where a letter of intent expresses plans to enter into an asset acquisition, this preliminary statement will likely serve as an impediment to any change in the absence of compelling justification.

Liabilities of the Target

Whether the transaction is asset-based or stock-based, the intended and unintended assumption of liabilities will influence the structure and the negotiation. While an asset acquisition allows the parties to specifically address liabilities intended to be assumed by the buyer, various liabilities may, by statute or common law, still become the buyer's obligation. Environmental, employee benefit, employment, tax, and products liability matters, can all become obligations of a buyer depending upon the structure of the transaction and the provisions of the documents. Where liabilities are intended to be assumed, one expects the price of the transaction and the structure to overtly address this condition. Balance sheet adjustments are often used to address liabilities for which the buyer will be responsible. In most transactions, some liabilities will be unknown, contingent, or otherwise uncertain. In these instances, indemnification provisions will often allow the parties to proceed while acknowledging the uncertainty of these issues. The use of certain thresholds and limitations (baskets and caps) can effectively quantify a range of acceptable risk.

Ownership of Assets

When a party acquires the stock of a corporation, all of the target's assets remain owned by the corporation, together with the leases, licenses, and other contracts to which the target is a party, thereby delivering to the buyer all of the benefits of the property and contract rights. Generally, the acquisition of all of the stock of the target will also allow the buyer to make use of all of its operating assets, whether or not they are owned by the target or are the subject of leases or licenses, but even here, limitations on assignment may create impediments to a buyer.

In the asset sale, the bill of sale conveying ownership of the target's assets, and assignments of the contractual rights of the target under contracts to which it is a party, are intended to deliver to the buyer the ability to operate and make use of all of its operating assets. However, where non-assignment or "change in control" provisions are included in contracts, they must be carefully reviewed to determine whether the form of the transaction can avoid triggering such provisions or, if they are triggered, to properly address the need to obtain consents of third parties. Regardless of the structure, the parties must negotiate and address the issues that affect the ability to continue to use those assets of the target and of third parties that are necessary to the continued operation and success of the business.

Financing

The buyer of a business enterprise will in many instances seek financing for the transaction from a new lending source. In such instances, it is generally required that the assets of the target be sold free and clear of encumbrances. Where a buyer (or its lender) is willing to acquire assets that are and remain encumbered, the purchase price will be significantly affected and the structure of the transaction may be modified to appropriately address these consequences.

Guaranties

In closely held businesses, one or more of the principals often guarantees the obligations of the target. Similarly, in many acquisitions, the obligations of the parties are guaranteed. Structuring issues in a transaction can be significantly simplified where a principal is willing to guarantee the obligations of the entity. Where a creditworthy guarantor is present, many concerns of the parties may be alleviated, allowing the structure of the transaction to be less cumbersome. On the other hand, the refusal to grant a guaranty may result in the need for the structure of the transaction to include a variety of characteristics to ensure that further or continuing claims can be addressed and remedies obtained. From a seller's standpoint, the challenge may be to remove shareholders from guaranties to which they are subject.

Existing Agreements

It is important that all of the agreements to which the company is a party be carefully reviewed to make certain the proposed transaction will not violate existing duties or obligations. For example, where "change in control" provisions exist in agreements to which the seller is a party, these agreements should be closely scrutinized.[113] The structure of the transaction may avoid triggering certain "change in control" provisions. Similarly, where rights of first refusal are triggered only by a sale of stock, rather than by a sale of assets, the parties may structure the transaction to avoid having to address this issue.

Every business is party to a host of contracts that affect its operations. From machinery and equipment leases to supply agreements, companies obligate themselves to continuing relationships with third parties. In the context of an acquisition, these contractual relationships must be addressed to ensure the benefits of these contracts are not lost, or that the target is not otherwise in breach as a result of the transaction. In most instances, the third party will be willing to consider an assignment to the prospective buyer. This is especially true when the prospective buyer will continue the business and may enhance the business opportunity for the third party. However, as with most other business situations, where a third party perceives it has greater leverage, it may make demands as a trade-off for permitting or consenting to an assignment. All of these issues can influence the structure of the transaction.

Issues Specific to Stock Transactions

A stock acquisition has several issues that are unique, each of which may influence the structure. Some of these are internal to the corporation while others are statutory or market driven. In contemplating a stock transaction, each of the following issues should be considered.

Securities law issues. In a stock transaction, the conveyance of the capital stock is the sale of a security. As such, federal securities laws as well as applicable state laws must be reviewed to make certain that the transaction comports with these laws. In many instances, certain notices and other disclosures will be required.

Shareholder matters. Participation by all of the shareholders is required to deliver all of the shares of the target to the buyer. In some instances, shareholder agreements will exist which include drag-along rights that require a minority shareholder to agree to sell its shares when holders of a majority (or supermajority) of the stock are selling their shares. In the absence of drag-along rights or unanimous consent, it may be necessary to engage in a statutory merger or other transaction to permit all of the shares to be acquired.[114] Short of unanimity, the buyer may face having to deal with minority shareholders and this possibility will likely affect the structure of the transaction.

Many shareholders in closely held corporations enter into shareholder restrictive agreements that grant various rights and place various restrictions on each shareholder's ability to transfer stock. These documents must be considered in structuring the transaction. Only after a thorough review of all applicable shareholder agreements can counsel intelligently discuss and negotiate the structure. Tag-along rights, drag-along rights, supermajority requirements, rights of first refusal, dissenters' rights, and other provisions may all significantly influence how a transaction must be structured.

Substantive Law Issues

There are many substantive law issues, the resolution of which may impact the structure of the transaction. Some are:

Environmental. Of significant concern to buyers in today's business world is the avoidance of environmental exposure and liability. Federal and state statutes address responsibilities for environmental contamination. The quantification and assessment of these risks and the likelihood of exposure will often influence the structure of the transaction, the exclusion of certain assets, or the indemnification obligations of the parties.

Employees and employee benefits. Where the company provides pensions and other employee benefits, the effect of the transaction upon these obligations must be considered. ERISA includes various requirements and may cause the buyer to become liable for certain obligations. Assessing and quantifying these obligations is a necessary part of developing the structure. In addition to pension and employee benefit matters, issues relating to union contracts, unemployment compensation, workers' compensation, and other employee matters must also be addressed. If the buyer intends to employ the entire workforce, and continue the same working conditions (and union contracts, if applicable), the structure may not need to substantively address displacement of the workforce. On the other hand, where the buyer is interested only in the assets of the target and is not interested in acquiring the human capital associated with the business, a variety of issues may become not only relevant but paramount.

In most businesses today, absent a union or other contractual arrangement, the workforce is employed on an at-will basis. In the at-will setting, the acquirer is generally free to offer employment to those employees it desires, but is not under an obligation to do so. However, certain federal statutes, such as the WARN Act, and some state statutes, place requirements upon a business where there will be a substantial displacement of workers as a result of the transaction.

Where union labor is present, the union contract (collective bargaining agreement) must be addressed. Certain collective bargaining agreements will prohibit transactions without consent being obtained or concessions being made. Often, the form of the transaction will be negotiated to permit the buyer to address the employment issues in the most favorable manner. Even where the employees are not unionized, issues relating to successor liability as an employer are relevant and must be considered. Where employment agreements with certain key employees are desired, the parties may choose to structure the transaction in a manner that does not trigger the right of an employee to terminate the agreement and obtain severance or other benefits.

Taxation. Various tax issues must be considered in determining how to structure an acquisition. Issues relating to the tax consequences of the transaction itself, as well as the allocation of assets, depreciation and basis issues, must be considered. Shifting various portions of the purchase price from a recognition of capital to ordinary income can produce adverse tax results and cause the effective value of the transaction to vary significantly. Attention to these issues will avoid unintended consequences and disappointment. The importance of addressing the tax consequences of an acquisition cannot be overstated. What may appear as an equivalent transaction can produce extremely disparate tax results to the parties depending upon the characteristics of the entities and the structure of the transaction. The characteristics of the selling entity, whether a pass through entity for tax purposes or a tax paying entity, will influence decisions regarding structure. The characteristics of the assets being sold will influence the structure. The ability to cause the transaction to be "tax deferred" and the allocation of the purchase price among various assets or contractual obligations will influence the structure.

Intellectual property. The ability to acquire the benefits of patents, copyrights, trademarks, and licenses may be critical to the success of the enterprise. The transaction must be structured to avoid the termination of rights or otherwise adversely affect licenses and claims to intellectual property. Where the intellectual property is owned by parties other than the target (and is licensed to the company), the structure of the transaction will have to address these tangential relationships to make certain the buyer obtains the right to continue to utilize the intellectual property.

Other Regulatory Issues

Depending upon the business of the target, and upon its capital structure and size, a variety of regulatory issues may influence the structure. Any acquisition in a regulated industry (such as in the banking, insurance, television and radio or healthcare industries) may require governmental filings or approvals.

Moreover, the HSR Act, if applicable, will require a statutory notice and clearance of the transaction by the Federal Trade Commission or the Department of Justice. The size of the transaction and the parties participating in the transaction will influence whether or not this statutory requirement is relevant. When applicable, the necessary HSR filing will influence the timing of the transaction and may influence negotiation regarding certain aspects of the structure.

Successor Liability

Every buyer's nightmare is that, after closing, an unknown and costly liability presents itself and attaches to the target business. Successor liability is not an inevitable consequence of buying a business—it can be planned against and addressed in a pro-active fashion.

Although there are nuances from jurisdiction to jurisdiction, there are some fundamental successor liability principles. If an entity acquires the capital stock of another, the transaction results only in a change of ownership of the acquired entity and all obligations in existence prior to the transaction remain those of the acquired entity. The buyer only becomes obligated for those liabilities to the extent of its ownership of the target company. A merger transaction is no different. Acquisitions by merger result in the surviving entity succeeding to all of the rights and obligations of the acquired entity. Consequently, these transactions start with a baseline assumption of obligations by the buyer and, while efforts can be made to push back this baseline by contractually excluding certain obligations, bolstering representations and indemnification provisions, or providing for an escrow, the fundamental risks remain—absent a favorable contract provision after applicable indemnification periods have run or when no sell-side party remains to recover against, the buyer remains holding the bag. As a result, stock purchases and mergers can often leave attorneys little room to maneuver.

Asset purchases, on the other hand, may avoid these problems, subject to legal limitations. Asset purchases do not, as a general proposition, result in the buyer assuming any of the obligations of the target outside of those expressly assumed by contract in the acquisition agreement. As with most rules, certain exceptions apply by virtue of federal and state statutes and judicial decisions.[115] The principal recognized exceptions developed by the courts to the standard proposition that buyers in asset deals are not subject to successor liability (significant distinctions exist within this general framework from jurisdiction to jurisdiction) are as follows:

- *Express or implied assumption.* The buyer expressly or impliedly agrees to assume the liability.
- *Liability imposed by law.* Failure to comply with bulk sales laws, fraudulent transfer, and tax laws may be subject a successor to liability.
- *De facto merger.* The transaction amounts to *de facto* consolidation or merger, whereby the seller is effectively absorbed into the buyer. The elements required for a *de facto* merger generally are that there be a continuation of the seller's enterprise, a continuity of shareholders (e.g., the selling shareholders are given a stake in the continuing business), a cessation of business and liquidation, and an assumption of those liabilities necessary for the uninterrupted continuation of normal business operations.
- *Mere continuation.* There is a continuity of the corporate identity, as distinguished from the continuation of the business or operations. This continuity can be evidenced by the common identity of the officers, directors and shareholders, and the existence of only one corporation on completion of the transfer.
- *Continuity of enterprise.* There is a continuity of the business operations, as distinguished from the corporate structure. This can be evidenced by the same employees, supervisors, production facilities, products and name, together with a continuity of assets and general business operations.
- *Product line.* The transaction involves the acquisition of a manufacturing company and continuation of manufacture of the products. The other elements are the virtual destruction of the plaintiff's remedies against the original manufacturer, the buyer's ability to spread the risk and the fairness of requiring the buyer to assume the burden of being responsible for defective products which attach to the predecessor's goodwill.
- *Fraud.* The transaction is entered into fraudulently for the purpose of escaping the liability.

In order to isolate any known or unknown liabilities, buyers often form an acquisition entity to acquire assets and avoid merging the target into buyer when the buyer is acquiring stock—at least until unforeseen liabilities have had a chance to surface. Conspicuous concerns known prior to closing can be dealt with in any number of specifically tailored ways, including reference in the representations, the escrow of funds, set-off rights, etc. Those concerns that spring up after closing are often understood too late to be addressed adequately. Consequently, the key to reducing successor liability risks is getting out in front of the issues as soon as possible. There is no substitute for thorough and thoughtful due diligence.

What to Avoid

Given the nature of the successor liability inquiry, the laundry list of do's and don'ts for asset transactions is constantly changing as new fact patterns and policy concerns present themselves to the courts. None of the factors included in the following list is dispositive; although as indicated, some are viewed as more determinative than others.

- *Inadequate consideration:* The failure to provide a fair price for the assets purchased is a common problem. The policy concern rests in providing adequate consideration for the seller to meet the claims of its creditors.
- *Stock as consideration:* If stock of the buyer is a significant portion of the purchase price paid to the seller (and then distributed to its shareholders), it can result in a continuity of ownership between the buyer and seller that is problematic.
- *Dissolution of seller:* A highly damaging fact is any contractual obligation for the seller to cease business and to liquidate soon after closing. Also, rendering the seller incapable of meeting its obligations by the immediate distribution of the purchase price or the payment

  of part or all of the purchase price directly to the shareholders will leave the seller incapable of meeting its obligations.
- *Continuity of management:* Retaining the officers, directors, and senior employees of the seller to operate the post-closing business creates operational continuity and continuity from the perspective of the public.
- *Continuity of employees:* Contractual provisions requiring the buyer to hire the seller's employees should be avoided.
- *Same facility:* Operating at the same facility and using the same telephone number as the seller can be pointed to as an indicator of continuity in the operations.
- *Same products/services:* Performing the same services or producing/selling the same product as the acquired company can be a factor.
- *Using the seller's trademarks/trade names:* This factor reflects a concern that the public would not appreciate a difference between the buyer and seller given that the public face of the operations remains unchanged. Adopting a similar corporate name is a corollary to this indicator.
- *Holding buyer out as a continuation:* A buyer holding itself out as being the same or a continuation of the seller, including by claiming that the business has been in existence since the date the seller commenced business, can be a problem.
- *Assuming critical obligations:* Assuming obligations that are necessary for the uninterrupted operation of the purchased business, such as real property leases, purchase orders and employee benefits, are indicative of a desire to preserve the business in its pre-transaction state.

Certainly, some of these factors simply cannot be avoided if a buyer intends to gain the full benefits of its acquisition. In most acquisitions the entire purpose is to produce or sell the same product or service; therefore, trying to avoid this indicator is nearly impossible. Moreover, a number of these factors being present in any given transaction is not necessarily problematic. The troubling part is that, without any bright-line rule or a set number of factors that trigger successor liability, a buyer can never be absolutely certain that successor liability can be avoided. Consequently, the key is to avoid as many of the factors as possible, while still achieving the objectives of the acquisition. Or make sure there is adequate indemnification supported by a third-party credit.

Letters of Intent

At some point during the process, one or both of the parties will want a more concrete understanding of the terms of the transaction that is being discussed. A seller will want to know whether the buyer has in mind a price and structure of a deal that will be acceptable, will be reluctant to continue to disclose its business secrets and will want to know whether it should look for other buyers or simply go back to business as usual. Similarly, a buyer will eventually want to know whether there is a possibility of a deal acceptable to the seller before it continues to invest time and expense in the due diligence investigation and further negotiations.

Whenever negotiations result in a sufficient outline of terms to encourage the parties to move toward a binding acquisition agreement, the question will likely arise as to how to document the understanding that has been reached. A common suggestion is a letter of intent (sometimes called a memorandum of understanding or an agreement in principle) or term sheet setting forth the preliminary understandings such as they are. The letter of intent is generally a more formal document that is signed by the parties, whereas a term sheet is often simply an outline of the terms that may be signed or initialed by the parties. The businesspeople doing the negotiations quite often push for some document of this sort, for a variety of reasons, including just wanting to see in print what they think they have accomplished to date.

Experienced M&A counsel will have a variety of reactions to this suggestion. Many lawyers and commentators will counsel strenuously that a letter of intent can only create exposure, is the "handiwork of the devil" and should be avoided at any cost, urging their clients to proceed to a full-blown acquisition agreement. Other equally experienced counsel, either out of resignation to their client's desires or confidence in their own ability to craft a letter of intent with sufficient clarity to protect against the risks, will view the benefits and reasons for the letter of intent sufficient to justify its use.

The Gentleman's Agreement*

There is an oft quoted characterization of a gentleman's agreement that captures some of the concerns of counsel cautioning against letters of intent:

A gentleman's agreement is an agreement which is not an agreement, made between two persons neither of whom is a gentleman, whereby each expects the other to be strictly bound without himself being bound at all.

*Attributed to Justice Vaisey, *Chemco Leasing SPA v. Rediffusion P.L.C.,* 1 F.T.L.R. 201, Q.B. Div'l Ct. (Transcript: Association, 1985).

Deciding Whether to Use a Letter of Intent

There are a number of reasons cited for using a letter of intent.

- It is quicker and easier to prepare and therefore easier to read and more readily understood by the clients, and can assist the parties and counsel in avoiding misunderstandings at an early stage.

- It sets forth the major terms to be reflected in an acquisition agreement and can therefore facilitate the preparation of the agreement.
- The buyer may need a letter of intent to pursue financing as banks, equity investors, and other financial institutions sometimes will not proceed with an investigation and the desired commitment letter until a letter of intent has been signed.
- In certain transactions, a letter of intent allows the process of obtaining government approvals or clearances to begin. For example, a letter of intent, even one devoid of substantive terms, will permit Hart-Scott-Rodino filings to be made so that the time period starts running.
- Often buyers are reluctant to commit to substantial expenses for due diligence, environmental consultants, accountants, or financing commitment fees without having a signed letter of intent. Businesspeople believe that sellers and buyers, even though they may not be legally bound, feel a great moral obligation to observe the terms and conditions set forth in a letter of intent at later stages in the acquisition process.

The buyer and seller may have different objectives and interests in deciding whether to use a letter of intent. Note the relative bargaining strength and position of the parties at this stage. The buyer will want to pin down the seller on price as a starting point and then negotiate binding terms that attempt to lock up the target, such as no-shop or exclusivity clauses, breakup fees, and expense allocations. The seller, on the other hand, will likely never have more leverage than it has at this stage of the courtship. This is clearly the case if there are a number of interested buyers. Once the seller says yes to the price, its leverage will in all likelihood only go down as the process plays out. No buyer is going to volunteer a higher price upon gaining a better impression of the target after due diligence. Now is the time for the seller to use this leverage to negotiate for as many favorable deal points and address as many potential skeletons as it can before it signs onto the price. On the other hand, the buyer may attempt to defer decisions on difficult issues because it will generally be in a stronger position once the seller signs a letter of intent. After the letter is signed, the seller may mentally consider that the deal is done and be more amenable to compromise. This result may be particularly likely if there is a no-shop provision in the letter of intent so the seller is unable to explore other opportunities.

There are issues particular to a public company seller or buyer after signing a letter of intent. The letter may increase the pressure to make a public disclosure regarding the potential transaction if it would be material to the public company. Often, a seller will be concerned about the damage to its business by a premature disclosure as there will be concern by the seller's employees, suppliers and customers.

Terms to Include in a Letter of Intent

The common practice is that the business terms included in a letter of intent are not binding on either party. Accordingly, caution should be taken to make certain that a letter of intent is written in such a way as to be absolutely clear which terms are not to be binding.[116] Most often the non-binding sections describe the business points of a deal and include a description of the assets or stock to be sold, the liabilities to be assumed in an asset deal, and the purchase price and payment terms. They often include certain conditions to closing, provisions pertaining to employees and benefits, and the timing of the process. Sometimes they also include an outline of the indemnification rights and limitations, including caps, baskets, deductibles, and survival periods and a provision with regard to escrowing part of the consideration.

The binding provisions of a letter of intent often provide for the following:

- the confidentiality of the proposed transaction and any information that is turned over by the seller to the buyer, unless already covered in a confidentiality agreement;
- the right of the buyer to have access to the target, and its personnel, properties and records;
- a no-shop or exclusivity provision, which provides a period of time in which the buyer has the exclusive right to negotiate with the seller;
- a break-up or termination fee should the business ultimately be sold to a different buyer;
- the responsibility of the parties for certain costs and expenses; and
- the non-binding nature of all the other provisions.

While there are certain common themes and practices in the process, every deal is different and specific to the parties involved. Virtually every letter of intent is subject to variation depending upon the facts and circumstances of the proposed acquisition and the parties involved and there is no such thing as a standard letter of intent applicable to all proposed acquisitions.

With these apparent benefits to letters of intent, why do so many attorneys caution clients about their dangers and some adamantly urge avoidance? There is a legion of cases where a letter ostensibly believed by at least one of the parties to be non-binding resulted in significant exposure and damages. Accordingly, it is extremely important to be careful and precise in the drafting of a letter of intent. Even where the letter is carefully crafted, the parties' course of conduct and the "done deal syndrome" can overcome the caveats of the letter and convince a judge or jury that there was a meeting of the minds.

The $10 Billion Letter of Intent

The poster child for caution in letters of intent remains *Texaco, Inc. v. Pennzoil Co.,*[117] involving Pennzoil's and Texaco's fight over the acquisition of Getty Oil Company and its valuable oil reserves. Pennzoil had negotiated with the Getty family and the Getty Trust, the controlling shareholders of Getty Oil, to buy a controlling interest in Getty Oil. Representatives of the Getty shareholders entered into a Memorandum of Agreement and issued a press release that stated that a definitive agreement was contemplated. Neither document contained a disclaimer of a binding agreement or legal obligation. There was also considerable done deal talk and conduct. The next day Getty announced an agreement to sell to Texaco at a higher price, which indemnified Getty against liability to Pennzoil. A Texas jury rendered a verdict of $7.53 billion in contract damages and $3 billion in punitive damages in favor of Pennzoil against Texaco at a time when Texaco's entire net worth was only $9.5 billion. While the punitive damage award was lowered, the case remains the most noted letter of intent case and features many of the issues found in such cases:

- binding effect of preliminary documents;
- reference to later definitive agreement;
- done deal syndrome; and
- parallel negotiations and abrupt termination.

CHAPTER 9

Pacing the Deal and Negotiation Impediments

The length of time from initiation to completion of an M&A transaction may range from a few months to over a year. There are many reasons why the timing may become more prolonged in the normal course of a transaction, such as a buyer having to arrange financing or a need to seek regulatory approvals. When the human element is introduced, the timing becomes even more unpredictable. Timing is greatly influenced by the players, including the M&A lawyers, and sometimes impediments are encountered that affect the negotiations and moving toward closing at the pace initially anticipated.

The Pace of the Deal

Deals have their own unique life cycles. Most will have phases where the pace will change dramatically. There are many factors that can influence the pace and the savvy M&A deal lawyer will sense when either quickening or slowing the process will favor the client.

Counsel can do everyone on his side (himself, the team, and the client) a significant service by having a candid discussion with the client at the outset about the expected time schedule (what to really expect, not what the investment bank circulated as aspirational) and what could or is likely to get the schedule off track. Some of the reasons or excuses for delays may be unacceptable to the client (e.g., your vacation or the absence of support), but it is usually better to deal with these issues up front than after the fact.

It is not always in the client's interest that deals proceed at a full-speed, pedal-to-the metal pace. Emotional cooling-off periods, delays to allow better clarity of a situation impacting an issue, a step back from a thorny issue to reflect on the full picture and gain perspective can postpone bringing a deal to a closing or breakdown, but may well contribute mightily to getting the deal done.

Conversely, there will also be deals where the client's interests are best served by pushing ahead to closing as quickly as possible. Giving a key decision maker more time to think and reconsider, closing windows of financing availability and other dynamics may dictate a need to force the teams on each side to resolve all issues immediately, expedite the documentation and get to a closing if a deal is to be done at all.

To the extent counsel can influence the pace of a deal, there are often times where the client's interests and the ultimate ability to reach a deal and closing may be best served by coasting, flooring the accelerator, taking a detour or even turning off the engine for a time. The trick is knowing which course to pursue. There will be points in a deal when delaying resolution of seeming deal-breaking issues, rather than wrestling them to the ground at the time they arise, will be a better course. Similarly, there are other times where an all night effort to turn around a draft or obtain a consent is critical to keeping the deal in play. Some issues are soluble only when packaged with the right mix of other issues to enable horse trading on all of them.

A variety of factors influence the pace of a deal at any given time:

- the desire of one or both parties to meet some real or perceived deadline (e.g., the end of a fiscal period or change in tax treatment);
- the unavailability or distraction of key decision makers;
- a weak link at a key point in the process;
- the inability to get a decision out of the client or the other side on critical issues;
- the failure or inability to staff the project properly;
- the discovery of troubling facts about the target;
- an inability to obtain governmental approvals or key third-party consents;
- an inability to obtain financing or to speed up the process of the financing source;
- indecision of a party as to the desirability of the deal, due to industry or other changes in the business environment; and
- the loss to the team of a key player through leaving the firm, health problems, petulance, or other unanticipated causes.

One of the challenges to M&A counsel is recognizing just what is the true cause of a delay and what is an excuse. Any of the above factors could be either the true culprit or a convenient excuse offered to cover the real roadblock. Many times the ostensible excuses have to be peeled away before the real reason for a stalled deal is appreciated. On some deals, one will never know.

Negotiating Impediments and the Human Element

At exasperating moments, many an M&A lawyer will mutter, "if only we didn't have clients to deal with." On other deals, substitute "counsel for the other side," "the turkeys on my team," "investment banks," or various other players for "client."

However, remember that no one is perfect, including your own team, and accommodations often have to be made for personality quirks, the schedules of other players and the unexpected to achieve a successful and smooth deal. Deal stress can bring out both the best and worst in people.

Here are some suggestions on overcoming the impediments of personalities and conflicts arising out of deal pressure and stress.

- E-mails and letters are not always best as a means of communication; pick up the telephone or propose a face-to-face negotiating session.
- Set a realistic timetable for exchanging drafts and for closing. Notwithstanding unrealistic timetables set by clients or the other side, talk to the other counsel and put together a joint timetable and revise it periodically after discussion. This will avoid finger pointing by one side against counsel on the other side. Also, experienced counsel will instinctively know issues that can cause delays and be willing to build slippage into the timetable.

- Identify who will be responsible for which documents and which tasks. As early as possible, put together a time and responsibility schedule or a closing agenda delegating responsibility. Also, list the people who need to see, and sign off on, various draft documents.
- Obtain client buy-in to both the timetable and the time and responsibility schedule. In many cases, clients are genuinely surprised by the length and scope of getting the deal to closing when they see a time and responsibility schedule or closing agenda. Also, keep the client fully informed as to changes in the timetable whether the change is good or bad—avoiding surprises for the client is the rule.
- Set, at a minimum, weekly (or more frequent) status conference calls, first with the client to define and discuss issues and settle strategy, then with opposing counsel. Report back to the client.
- Sometimes cutting the lawyers on the other side some slack can pay off later in the deal when you need a break. Sometimes does not mean always.
- Try hard to stay on schedule. The client will appreciate that, but, again, if it appears that the transaction will be off schedule, tell the client immediately and explain the reason for the delay.
- Not only Scouts should "Be Prepared." On virtually every deal there are hitches and surprises, so do not be surprised, offended, or take things personally. Counsel's role is to get the job done successfully as long as that is what the client wants.

This said, consider some of the recurring tensions that can impede a deal.

Your Team

Communication is of paramount importance among members of your legal team and in dealing with your client's deal team.

Within your own firm, clearly delineate areas and limits of responsibility. Ensure scheduled meetings do in fact take place. Those who cannot attend in person should do so by conference call. Otherwise, they should send a delegate from whom they can receive a report as soon as possible after the meeting. Prepare an agenda for each meeting, even if it is repetitive, and leave a spot for general discussion or questions that do not fit under a specific agenda item. Many times one-hour meetings are more than enough if run properly and tightly, unless there are major items to discuss requiring more time. Also, make sure your team knows the proper communication channels with the client, and discourage team members from discussing matters with the client unless cleared to do so.

Difficult Counsel on the Other Side

Looking back on an acquisition that has just closed or doing the same after years of engaging in M&A work, one thing stands out as a constant: every deal has a unique twist and flavor because of the interplay of the human beings involved, usually driven by the role played by the lawyers on the other side of the table.

How smooth and efficient a deal goes depends enormously on the roles played by counsel for the buyer and seller. Out of such interplay often emerge career-long friendship and mutual respect between the counsels involved. Less frequently, this interplay can produce feelings of enmity toward, disrespect of and impatience with one's counterpart in a deal. Sometimes, the feelings are mutual and not always unjustified.

This observation is not intended as a cry for M&A lawyers to attend charm school or to suggest for a moment that a client's legitimate interests be abandoned or subordinated so lawyers can become chums to their counterparts across the table. What is intended is to point out some of the typical situations that produce the enmity, and to suggest how to address and deal with them and how to avoid creating the situation yourself.[118]

Consider some of the kinds of situations one may encounter and what might be done to head off the tension in the first place or deal with it when it arises.

The failure to introduce yourself. This seems simple. You are going to spend a lot of time dealing with the other lawyer by telephone, e-mail, fax, and mail. It makes sense to call him at the outset and introduce yourself. While this seems obvious, it is often not done: you are too busy or disinterested, it does not really matter or the attorney or firm is a major M&A player and you are embarrassed or too intimidated to call.

Nonsense! None of these is a reason not to call. Experience teaches that the introductory call not only is uniformly well received and appreciated, but typically elevates the caller instantly to a peer status with the call recipient. The call will certainly not hurt the process. If you remain too intimidated to call and introduce yourself, how hard will it be to call to raise some important, tough or sticky deal points later? Look up biographies on the opposing firm's website or Martindale and find something to talk about. Above all, make the call.

The failure to meet with the other side. There is a tendency today to rely heavily on e-mail, fax, and other rapid forms for the transmission of data, drafts, comments, and revised documents so that, in the effort to save money, the parties and counsel avoid meeting, thereby saving airfare, out-of-town lodging and similar trip expenses. The trade off is a protracted exchange of revisions, telephone conferences and seemingly endless negotiations in written form conducted at a distance.

Until the advent of e-mail and facsimile transmission, parties usually met at least once to resolve issues, instruct counsel, and conclude negotiations on all but very incidental points. There is little doubt that face-to-face discussions usually lead to a resolution of issues much quicker than trying to deal with them or even deflect them impersonally in writing or over the telephone.

Since getting a deal done quickly is usually the universal goal, serious consideration should be given to having face-to-face meetings. Often, the out-of-pocket cost is a pittance and huge savings compared to the potentially extended, inconclusive nature of negotiations conducted electronically or in another fashion.

Dealing with the other side. Like most human endeavors, negotiating, documenting, and closing a deal are affected by the experience (or sometimes, lack of experience) of the people involved—particularly those on the other side. When asked by a client about the timing or cost at the outset of a transaction, experienced counsel will factor into his answer who is on the other side, both the party and its counsel.

Fairly often, one runs into behavior, examples of which follow, which need to be faced without seeing the deal sidetracked by protracted argument, impasse and ego, usually having little to do with the deal itself but rather the players involved.

How are some examples and ways of seeking to overcome them:

Unreasonable diligence requests. Opening with a grossly over expansive due diligence request can set the wrong tone for the whole process.

Sending the Wrong Message

You represent a client selling a product line (a group of assets and the related contracts with few employees involved) for cash. Relatively speaking, it's a small deal. The principals have agreed on basic terms. The seller is a substantial company and is willing to stand behind meaningful indemnities protecting the buyer's title to the assets to be acquired and against liabilities the buyer does not intend or agree to assume.

The buyer's lawyer, who is inexperienced, begins asking for copies of minutes of your client's board and shareholders' meetings, letters from counsel to your client's auditors, press releases and strategic planning and marketing plans. The buyer's lawyer also presents a very comprehensive due diligence questionnaire for a transaction involving a sale of all or substantially all of the assets of a company. Most of the information requested is way beyond the reasonable scope of inquiry required for the deal. Much of the information requested is privileged and its production would be unusual in most deals.

Why the overkill?

This was not a hypothetical situation! The seller offered the product line for sale because it did not fit its long-term strategy. However, the buyer's lawyer believed that the sale was motivated because the product line was unprofitable. The lawyer was on a hunt to uncover evidence of this fact in his broad ranging due diligence.

The buyer's lawyer practiced with a small general practice firm and had been practicing less than five years. The seller's principals could not get the buyer to rein in its lawyer out of a concern over going against his advice.

The deal collapsed and was never completed.

This scenario sets up a formula for tough sledding in getting the deal done. Maybe the best that can be done with these facts (small deal, a buyer's inexperienced lawyer and a buyer that may not have much experience) is (hopefully) to get involved with your client early, try to assess the experience level of the other party and counsel and assist your client in framing the deal for the other side—define precisely what is being sold, make it clear that the seller will indemnify as to title, require a quick closing, have you prepare the first draft of the agreements and reach an understanding as to reasonable costs and expense your client is willing to bear—and not go beyond—in relation to the price. Often, even with an inexperienced buyer, a prepared seller's "wood shedding" of the buyer by succinctly laying out the ground rules at an early stage may help you avoid having to deal with an overly cautious and suspicious counsel.

The rewriter. If you have engaged in M&A work for a while, it would be very unusual if you have not met the "Rewriter." The Rewriter comes in many forms from "full on" to the "obsessive fine tuner." All forms wind up taxing our patience, driving up the expense of a deal and wasting time.

The classic form of the Rewriter is the one who, after receipt of (usually) the first draft of an agreement, returns the agreement almost 100 percent entirely rewritten—all without notice, discussion, or comment and sometimes not marked to show changes. This is an almost universally unforgivable and unacceptable act. As the Fine Tuner label implies, almost no negotiated and agreed-upon principle can ever be finally set down in words with the Fine Tuner on the job. While no one can argue with the concept of working on provisions to make them as clear and unambiguous as possible, the compulsion of a Fine Tuner usually goes well beyond the goal of achieving clarity.

Usually the complete or almost total rewrite can be dealt with by involving the clients in stopping the practice; similarly, the Fine Tuner can sometimes be controlled, after one or both of the clients becomes tired of the exercise and concerned about the effect he is having on the cost of the deal. Losing one's cool or becoming angry with a Rewriter is almost never effective. The solution usually comes by working on the problem with your client.

Other unpleasant characters. Besides the Rewriter, other unpleasant characters in M&A practice include the Slaggard, the Pit Bull, the Know It All, and the Welcher. There are others, but these are some of the more common characters.

Keeping Your Powder Dry

We were engaged to represent a company in a series of acquisitions in the beer distribution business. One of the transactions was for approximately $20 million, and the seller had retained a very prominent law firm to represent it in the transaction. The partner in charge of the transaction for the seller had an abrasive personality style which started to rub lawyers in my firm the wrong way from the first introductory call. Comments like "my firm views this as a bill of sale transaction and nothing more" were not helpful in keeping tempers in check during the transaction. Towards the end of the transaction, this lawyer wrote a three page letter which included ten points that he said were points in which I was either "out of market" or was somehow unreasonable, and, in all instances, were completely unnegotiable; if I continued to insist on any of the points, the seller would walk and the transaction would disappear. He also sent a copy of the letter to my clients, the investment banks, representatives of the various breweries and other parties involved in the transaction.

We closed the deal a week later with each of the ten points that he mentioned being resolved in our client's favor.

I keep a copy of this letter under my calendar in my office. Each time a lawyer in my firm comes into my office complaining about opposing counsel or discussing how they intend to send drop dead letters or other kinds of inflammatory correspondence, I pull a copy of the letter out from underneath my calendar, make a copy of it, and explain to them what happened. Deals seem to get done much easier, and the clients seem to get much better work product, when unfortunate personality traits driven by ego and arrogance are minimized.

Your client becomes most important in dealing with the situation created when any of these characters appear. Whether the client is buying or selling, it will have a lot of leverage with its counterpart on the other side. However, you cannot expect the client to solve every impediment created in a deal by the lawyer on the other side. What will be necessary, nine times out of ten, are preparation and a close relationship with your client.

Time and again the better prepared lawyer will be able to navigate the minefields laid down by the Slaggard and Pit Bull. The prepared lawyer knows his client's essential goals, knows the opponent's likely goals, weaknesses, and trade offs and can stay focused on achieving maximum benefits for the client. Usually, by definition, the Slaggard, Pit Bull and Welcher figure to use tactics other than preparation (and the confidence and competence it brings) to deflect and wear down the other side.

The Obstreperous Client

One of the most difficult situations to contend with is the obstreperous client—yours or the party represented by the lawyer on the other side.

Taking a careful read of your client early in the process helps the lawyer assess the likelihood of the client becoming difficult. This early recognition enables frank discussions about the track on which the deal may well run, who is to make the calls and what are the client's goals.

Sometimes, however, all the upfront discussions and understandings go for naught. In those circumstances where it is your client who becomes obstreperous, you have to consider whether you are being put in a position that could potentially compromise ethics or your reputation and create a fair chance of a claim against your firm regardless of the outcome of the matter. Withdrawal may be the only answer.

Here are some practical procedures to consider in dealing with a client on the way to a successfully completed transaction.

- Keep the client informed and in the loop regarding the process and schedule of the steps in the process to closing, and even beyond.
- See if it is possible for the client to designate a senior management coordinator to act as a funnel for passing information and questions between the client and your law firm.
- Set up rational and workable procedures for regulating who talks to whom at the lawyer and client level. Rumors and innuendoes can start from needless chatter between the buyer and the seller at the wrong levels and even side deals unknown to the lawyer. Give authorization only to a few who need to deal with the other side. Depending on the sophistication and deal experience of your client, you may want to discourage meetings with the other side without counsel being present.
- Work with your client to set up a process so that copies of correspondence, e-mails, facsimiles, and draft documents reach the appropriate team members.
- Periodically talk to the client and ask: "How is my team doing?" "How can we improve our performance for you?" The client will appreciate the inquiry even if there is nothing to report.

If it is the other lawyer's client that is the problem, the deal may wind up in an impasse. If your client cannot bring the other party around, it is very doubtful you will be able to do so.

Ethical issues. One tactic or style issue worth a brief word is the extent to which an attorney may use a client as the vehicle to bring up and negotiate points with its counterpart without the latter's counsel present.

Consider warning your client that such tactics are not unheard of and to report to you situations where it appears that the other party is talking to your client and seeking resolution of points that the lawyers would normally deal with, i.e., the lawyer on the other side has given his client a shopping list of points to resolve with your client—without you involved. See Chapter 2 for a more detailed discussion of the ethical ramifications.

Final Thoughts on Style

Managing an M&A deal with sophisticated clients and ethical, experienced counsel on the other side can be extremely challenging, exciting and enjoyable. Change the mix and it can be a lot like trying to herd cats. Not only will your professional skills be taxed and put to the test, but so will your abilities to manage and deal civilly with the other participants.

There is no substitute for being well prepared on the deal and establishing a trustful relationship with your client. Those two approaches will see you through some tough going with an opposing side who may be missing these elements, and will make a deal with people having similar capabilities on the other side professionally stimulating and enjoyable.

CHAPTER 10

Conducting Due Diligence

The initial response to the question "Do you have any interest in buying XYZ Widget Co." would almost always be, "Well, tell me about it" (and probably not, "What's the price?"). Due diligence, in simple terms, is an investigation of a business in connection with a transaction or possible transaction. It is usually thought of as being carried out by someone who is considering whether to make a purchase or significant economic investment in the business (buy-side due diligence). However, it is also appropriate for a seller (or its agent) to identify the potential and problems of the business (sell-side due diligence) in connection with its preparation for its sale. Conceptually, the same process would be carried out on each of the sell-side and the buy-side. However, the seller usually has a significant knowledge advantage and may not want to make additional inquiry as to ordinary course of business items, which it presumably knows about. Therefore, buy-side due diligence tends to be much more intensive.

There is much to be learned about a particular business. The legal status and affairs of a business are usually only a minor portion of the inquiry to be made. Most businesses are valued on their potential (which is often measured by their history). Accountants, industry experts, other consultants, and executives of the buyer are often involved in the due diligence process, not just lawyers. Frequently, responsibility for different aspects of the due diligence process will be allocated among the various professionals according to areas of expertise. Because of their familiarity with the process, lawyers may play a far more pervasive role in a transaction than might otherwise be expected, and because of their attention to detail, may be asked to play a more significant role in due diligence. The objective of due diligence nevertheless remains to accumulate sufficient information for business decisions to be made by the client.

There is a common misconception that the sole purpose of the process is to identify problems or risks. Most businesses are purchased because of the upside they might bring to a buyer. For example, a buyer purchasing a bleeding business with unused capacity will want to discover how effectively that capacity can be utilized to produce synergies. A buyer able to identify the potentialities of a business will be more comfortable with its purchase and may be able to outbid rivals (or it may choose not to share the value of synergies). To be sure, an understanding of problems and risks is important, and no one would suggest that such an inquiry should not be launched. But identifying risks may not be the most important function of due diligence.

This chapter does not address;

- the scope of due diligence;
- the depth of due diligence;
- how legal due diligence should be performed or techniques to be utilized; or
- how the results of due diligence are used in a particular transaction.

Instead, it attempts to introduce the facets and the variables of the due diligence inquiry.[119]

Due diligence is usually a continuous process during an acquisition. While often presented as a task to be completed before the drafting of an acquisition agreement begins, in fact, it will customarily continue as the acquisition agreement is negotiated and indeed even after the agreement has been signed. One of the functions of the negotiation of representations is an explanation of the intricacies of a particular business. Preparation of the schedules to be attached to the acquisition agreement will undoubtedly identify information not previously recognized. After the deal is signed, buyers will usually perform confirmatory due diligence as to the continued accuracy of the representations. Buyers will also perform post signature due diligence as they address integration of the business and other operational issues.

General Observations

What is important to a buyer varies from deal to deal and from buyer to buyer. A buyer considering the purchase of a competitor may believe that it knows as much (or more) about the business being sold than does the seller. That notwithstanding, the details are important and even in that scenario a prudent buyer, while having a firm understanding of the seller's business, would undoubtedly attempt to uncover particular risks and problems. At the opposite end of the spectrum, a financial buyer, perhaps not having previously invested in the target's industry, may have only the most cursory knowledge about the business. It will therefore need to learn much more about the target than the competitor. Other potential acquisitions range between these extremes. Even similarly situated buyers may react in an entirely different manner, some being cautious and risk averse (implying extensive due diligence), while others, believing themselves intuitive, may engage in only the most basic due diligence.

The due diligence process continues to evolve. Today it is almost always performed by a team, comprised of both employees of a buyer and outside consultants and professionals. How well it is done varies considerably. A few highly experienced buyers may have honed due diligence to a science. But the process is not usually as finely tuned for most buyers or sellers who participate in acquisitions only occasionally. The objectives and process of a hastily pulled together team may not be understood. Even the most experienced business person may have difficulty in organizing a team whose members may come from various parts of an organization and from various outside advisers. A team leader may be working with borrowed personnel from other divisions and functions, may be shuffling a variety of schedules, may have an opposing party who is implicitly attempting to limit access, and may have less than a clear objective (is the process merely window dressing for a decision that has already been made?).

One traditional process was for the buyer to prepare a list of requested documents. Often it was the lawyers who put together the list and the scope often extended beyond legal due diligence. The list was then presented to the other side, which may or may not have negotiated the scope of the list. In a relatively short period of time, the seller would assemble the documents, after which the buyer's team would pore through them. Historically, confidentiality concerns and more limited copying capabilities required that the buyer travel to the seller's place of business for purposes of reviewing documents. The due diligence team might spend a few days or longer poring over the documents, after which the team members would provide an assessment of what they had seen. This traditional process continues to evolve and in many cases has been replaced with document replication and "online" data rooms sponsored by sophisticated service providers.

The Objective of Due Diligence

Lawyers often express the objective of due diligence in narrow terms such as identifying legal risks or verifying the accuracy of representations. From a business perspective, due diligence is far more fundamental. For most buyers, an acquisition is not just a financial exercise. Most buyers buy businesses not as an investment but to enhance their own business strategy. Due diligence will allow them to answer questions such as the following.

- Can I effectively integrate the newly acquired business?
- Are there synergies available in this acquisition?
- Are there risks involved in this acquisition?
- What is the value of this business (the inherent value, the value to a buyer because of synergies involved and the discipline in retaining the synergistic value)?

Each participant in the acquisition team will see that objective through the prism of his or her own experience. Lawyers may focus on the risks and uncertainty, accountants on the numbers and the champion of the acquisition on its benefits. Nevertheless, all participants need to understand both the business objectives and those objectively identifiable risks or potential problems of a particular deal that are peculiar to their area of expertise.

Due diligence is largely a document production process—it is easy to crank up a copy machine and it may be dangerous to let a buyer speak to too many employees. Oral interviews and presentations are also limited in their effectiveness—bland assurances and lack of problems. Arguably, the best type of due diligence is analysis (usually numerical analysis) prepared by a seller in response to a buyer's request. A seller may shy away if that analysis is time consuming, delays the process or leads to more questions. Often the written documents are unimportant, being repetitive, routine, and uninformative. Sellers often make up in quantity what they miss in quality.

There is usually far more information about a target discovered in due diligence than ultimately appears in an acquisition agreement. The usual details of why a business makes sense in a basic form (financial statements) are usually too summary and too qualified for a buyer's analytical purposes. What is most important about financial statements, which are themselves qualified by materiality, is the build-up of those financial statements, division by division, and the concurrent operating data used to analyze the business for comparable periods. That is to say, representations in an acquisition agreement are not likely to address much of what a business is about.

Technology Advances: Virtual Data and Deal E-Rooms

As the auction process has become more prevalent in selling companies (in which an investment bank uses a confidential offering memorandum, management presentation, and data room to attract buyers), the data room has become a customary feature of many M&A transactions. The information assembled may often be responsive to a checklist provided by investment banks, with or without internal and external legal review. Sometimes data rooms are presented as a fait accompli rather than being responsive to requests made by other lawyers.

The modern age has many conveniences that have improved the deal process. One such area is the e-room, sometimes referred to as the virtual data room. This is a tool that not only is used by our litigation colleagues to manage document review and production but also is used in private and public M&A transactions for due diligence and disclosure of information.

Investment bankers and some attorneys set up virtual data rooms early in the process to facilitate communication with potential buyers and to provide access to documents without having to set up a physical location. The use of a virtual data room has many potential benefits for a seller.

- The seller saves the costs of setting up and staffing physical data rooms (some times in multiple locations), which are typically off-site, staffed by a paralegal or junior associate, and staged over long periods of time.
- When updating information in the data room, it can be disseminated by computer-generated notices that information has been added. This allows for greater assurance that all parties are making their offers based on the same information. In addition, if a bidder requests additional information, it is much easier with this approach to update all bidders by posting the information or document in an e-room. All persons with access then receive an e-mail, notifying them of the new information.
- The virtual data room can significantly decrease the time needed to get to a final offer when there are multiple bidders involved. With a virtual data room, the seller does not have to stage access by interested bidders into a physical room or rooms, which can often take weeks as one uses the room while others wait. Multiple bidders can access documents in a virtual data room at the same time.
- The virtual data room is generally set up with tracking abilities to enable the seller to view exactly which documents or areas of the e-room were accessed (down to the page level), by whom and for how long. This feature helps a seller to identify whether a prospective bidder is serious. It may also identify what their concerns are, based on the nature of the documents reviewed and the time spent reviewing them.
- These sites are encrypted and password protected so that documents retain their confidentiality. An e-room can also prevent printing or copying of certain documents.
- The seller can establish different levels of access to permit only certain persons or groups to access specific information. Each person, depending on his level of access, will see different information, and the rooms are sophisticated enough not to highlight or indicate missing or restricted data. This feature is particularly useful when dealing with sensitive competitive information when there are strategic, as well as financial, buyers participating in the process.

The convenience afforded by virtual data rooms is offset to some extent by some downside. Sellers are increasingly concerned that wide-spread dissemination (despite the existence of confidentiality agreements) may risk inappropriate disclosure of information about the target.

Sophisticated buyers expect and appreciate the virtual data room, especially in larger M&A transactions. Potential buyers benefit from the following.

- Significant cost savings in travel expenses and time by avoiding the need to fly business and legal teams from all over the country (and sometimes the world) since information can be accessed through the web 24/7.
- Many larger documents challenge a recipient's e-mail system. Frequently, multiple documents including pdf files cannot get through firewalls at some organizations that restrict the size of incoming files and require large documents to be broken up. This is not an issue when accessing an e-room.

- Documents can be posted in e-rooms in many different formats, e.g., TIFF, MS Word, Acrobat, PowerPoint, or Excel. Buyers can access sophisticated search capabilities in the e-room that can facilitate document review and identification of potential issues early in the process.
- In a physical data room, access needs to be staged since only one bidder can be in the room at any given time. This obviously means that each bidder is given only a short window of time within which to review everything in the data room. Since multiple bidders can access documents in a virtual data room at the same time, potential buyers are able to take as much time as they need to properly review documents in the virtual data room. They can also leave and return to the virtual data room any time to further check a document or a particular point.

A potential downside for a buyer conducting due diligence via a virtual data room is that reviewing documents from the comfort of one's own office by individual team members compounds the problems of lack of communication and lack of urgency. In an onsite visit efforts are more focused, team members consult with each other and share observations much more candidly and in real time; to the extent that the requirements of the deal allow only two days to conduct due diligence, the job gets done within two days.

In addition to due diligence and document review, e-rooms can be used for the review and exchange of comments on current drafts of deal documents, both internally and externally. Updated drafts (including redlines) can be posted on and accessed from the website. E-mail links for working group members, typical contact information, and a calendar function to establish deadlines and arrange working group meetings or conference calls on the deal are also often features in these rooms.

The advantages outlined above, especially when considering a fairly large M&A transaction, quickly justify the additional cost of setting up a virtual data room. Documents can be scanned and an e-room can be up and running within 24 to 72 hours.

An attorney's knowledge and familiarity with time and cost saving tools like the virtual data room may determine whether that attorney's firm is retained for a particular deal.

Due Diligence in a Nutshell

Theoretically, the seller should know everything about the business being sold. A potential buyer may know nothing or a lot about the business, but presumably not as much as the seller. In practice, those distinctions might not exist. One can envision a corporation selling off a neglected subsidiary (perhaps with the recent departure or turnover of key managers): the seller may know virtually nothing about the business or competition, while a buyer in the industry may know the seller's business as well as it knows its own. But in general, the consequence of the due diligence process will be to bring the buyer up to speed. Indeed, it is possible that, based upon its due diligence review, a buyer may become more knowledgeable about a particular business than the seller.

A business inquiry has potentially broad breadth and depth. Where does one begin? How does one determine the existence of something that presumably the other side does not want to have disclosed or may not itself know?

The beginning point must always be common experiences. The most valuable due diligence expert is one whose experience enables him to readily identify problems and risks that may pertain to a particular business. Although due diligence request lists attempt to collect and characterize meaningful information about businesses, they unfortunately are not nuanced and quickly become out of date. Those lists do, however, begin to formulate the scope of the investigation. The investigation itself increasingly focuses on a review of written documents, and includes a repetitive element as information ferreted out begets a request for more information.

Coordination among team members is important. Relevant information originating from one member of the team needs to be communicated and acted on by other members of the team. For example, the existence of litigation may require an insurance expert to determine whether adequate insurance exists.

The results of the inquiry need to be effectively communicated to a user of the information. Is the communication made orally or in writing? Is it short and to the point or thorough? Will it be appreciated and acted on or will a report be tossed into the file?

Factors Affecting the Extent of Due Diligence

One may consider due diligence as ultimately an exercise in risk allocation, in the context of negotiation of terms, price adjustment, or indemnification. Seller and buyer must each assess the respective risks they are willing to take, given the nature of the transaction and the respective obligations they negotiate to bind the parties at any particular juncture of the process. The due diligence process will usually be affected by the nature of the transaction in question: a private share or asset transaction, a joint venture, a combination, merger, or other hybrid form of equity or asset transaction, a public company deal, an international transaction, an auction, or a variation on or combination of any of the foregoing.

The nature and extent of due diligence will vary depending on whether the deal is:

- a simultaneous sign-and-close transaction following a completed due diligence process;
- signing with a deferred closing with continuing due diligence designed to verify the accuracy of representations and the satisfaction of conditions to closing; or
- the less common transaction involving signing with the closing subject to satisfactory due diligence, known as a "due diligence out," effectively amounting to an option to purchase during a specified period of time at a fixed price, typically in favor of the buyer.

Superior knowledge about the target remains the key to being in a position to negotiate the shifting of risks as between the seller and buyer. Each of the seller and buyer will establish their respective objectives in the due diligence process and their respective strategies based on their evolving, comparative knowledge. The party with superior knowledge regarding the target will normally achieve a negotiating advantage resulting from its ability to:

- better quantify the probable cost of each risk;
- determine more intelligently the risks it is willing to assume;
- magnify or understate in negotiations the perceived costs of the risks;
- bargain for more favorable terms by assuming a particular risk in return for a concession that exceeds its real cost; or
- shift to the other party the most costly of the risks in question.

The nature of the target or the buyer can greatly affect the scope and depth of the due diligence examination, as well as the process. For example, Sarbanes-Oxley and related rules of the SEC brought about changes in due diligence for acquisitions involving public companies.

Public buyers will typically conduct more intensive and comprehensive reviews of a target's financial reporting and internal controls, as well as examining its disclosure controls and procedures and loans to officers and directors, even if the target is a small private company. Noncompliance by a target with these requirements can result in liability to the buyer, affect its financial statements, cause the certifications of its officers to be inaccurate in filings with the SEC, or simply be an embarrassment to the buyer or its management on an ongoing basis. These changes in due diligence have had an impact on these types of transactions, causing delays in the time it takes to close.

Game Theory and Due Diligence

Preventing a buyer from discovering all of the business' warts would appear to be in the best interests of the seller. There is, however, a caveat. Most bad information eventually comes to the surface. Perhaps a target employee, attempting to ingratiate himself with a potential new employer, brings the information forward. Perhaps it is contained in a due diligence document. Perhaps there is scuttlebutt in the industry. The usual result is that the parties deal with the revelation in some way—perhaps a reduction in purchase price, expanding the scope of indemnification, terminating the deal in egregious circumstances, or leaving behind the problem. The seller will argue that while it may appear to be disadvantaged by the late revelation of information, it is usually no worse off than it would have been had the information been properly disclosed in the first place. However, a buyer may react badly to later disclosure because the buyer has revealed information only after some work. Are there more problems lurking? Is the seller being less than honest? The reaction may range from a termination of the deal to slowing it down as a buyer examines and reexamines the business and takes a more tenacious approach to the acquisition agreement. These are consequences usually not benefiting the seller. That is, the seller may be worse off because of the buyer's reaction.

A seller, normally having a superior informational advantage with respect to the target, will desire to maintain that advantage. It knows that it will begin to lose that advantage through the buyer's due diligence. It may adopt strategies to slow down or minimize the loss of its advantage, but it must also bear the risk that the tactics chosen may adversely affect its credibility and negotiating posture with the buyer.

Professional Risks in the Due Diligence Process

Participation in the due diligence process involves rendering professional services with concomitant liability risks. While lawyers are a natural and indispensable part of a due diligence team, their responsibility should be limited to legal due diligence. It is normally not advisable for the lawyer to be the team leader, a position that is better filled by a business person. Because of prior experience, lawyers may be more familiar with the due diligence process than other team members. They may be asked to assist in the due diligence planning and to pull together and edit due diligence request lists. But lawyers should resist actually taking charge of or leading the due diligence process, which will involve a business review far beyond their legal expertise. The consequences of a problem or risk not identified are obvious.

Sell-Side Due Diligence

Risks to a Seller

The sale process itself can have an adverse effect on the business being sold, regardless of whether the sale is completed or not. If the sale process is unsuccessful, the seller will have to continue to operate a diminished business. Even if a sale is completed, the price and terms received may be adversely affected by the effects the sale process may have on the business. Elements of this risk faced by a seller include:

- general disruption to the business and operations;
- premature disclosure of sensitive information if the deal does not close;
- resources necessary to close in light of the scale or magnitude of the transaction;
- disclosure of information which compromises key assets or relationships of the target, whether or not the deal closes, including:
  - pricing
  - shipping
  - market share
  - personnel (employees, agents, pension plans, etc.)
  - suppliers
  - customers and accounts receivable
  - production/distribution network
  - investments (including value of inventory, plant, equipment, etc.)
  - third parties/creditors/liens and related consents which may be required to close
  - regulatory notices and/or approvals
  - compliance programs
  - leases (real and personal property)
  - information technology (hardware, software, MIS infrastructure)
  - product liability/litigation or other investigations
  - tax returns/financial information
  - other proprietary/sensitive information
- peculiar sets of distinct disclosure and approval requirements for a regulated industry;
- other regulatory considerations, including antitrust, foreign investment and related or analogous pre-notifications and/or consents; and
- securities commission and stock exchange requirements applicable to a public company.

Particular legal risks of the due diligence process include loss of the attorney-client privilege through disclosure, possible breach of applicable right-to-privacy legislation and breach of contract in respect of information disclosed during the due diligence process (e.g., information that is the subject matter of a confidentiality agreement).

Objectives and Strategies of a Seller

While the role of a seller in the due diligence process is thought to be passive, well-advised sellers will consider their own objectives. A seller will attempt to stay in control of its initial (but inevitably diminishing) superior knowledge about the target, both before and throughout due diligence, and will attempt to identify the target's existing and potential problems before the buyer does so through its due diligence. To do this, a seller needs to put into place its own team to conduct due diligence of its business, as well as to enable it to respond to a buyer's due diligence requests. The seller's team may include:

- a team leader
- in-house personnel (operations and data management team)
- accountants, actuaries, investment bankers, etc.
- risk managers and various other consultants and advisors
- external lawyers
- miscellaneous experts such as evaluators, environmental consultants and surveyors

Sellers should always consider their procedures for controlling the disclosure process. As discussed below, there are varying practices and different concerns with each. Sellers will want to consider:

- making available both electronic and hardcopy documentation and information
- collating, vetting, and indexing of documents
- logging and storing
- retrieval and distribution
- analysis and reporting of each phase of due diligence
- special issues of access (who, when, how, etc.)
- particular problems regarding the security of electronic information (intranet, web sites, servers, e-mail, listserves, virtual data room, etc.)
- locale/situs of buyer's due diligence (seller's premises, lawyers' offices, etc.)

Due diligence is perhaps too narrowly considered the formal process of reviewing written records. In fact, the process of information transfer begins far sooner than that and continues until signing of an acquisition agreement and beyond. When an investment bank prepares a confidential offering memorandum, or even when a seller begins to interest potential buyers without the involvement of an intermediary, information about the target will be conveyed. More detailed information may be transferred through the due diligence process. The information flow will continue as the acquisition agreement is negotiated—often the best understanding of aspects of a target's business are developed in the discussion of particular representations. Logically then, a seller's objectives in this longitudinal due diligence process would include:

- taking advantage of its greater knowledge to negotiate better terms and less onerous representations and indemnification;
- attempting to minimize adverse effects revealed by buyer's due diligence;
- deciding when to notify, and otherwise controlling and managing the knowledge and reaction of, the marketplace in respect of the transaction prior to an actual closing; and
- positioning itself for appropriate damage control if an announced deal fails to close.

To achieve its objectives, a seller may put in place various strategies to preserve its position vis-a-vis the potential buyer by:

- controlling the disclosure process;
- responding only to written due diligence requests;

- addressing adverse facts and issues discovered through either internal or the buyer's due diligence:
  - remedying defects before closing,
  - disclosing problems with the risk that the buyer may ask for specific indemnification for such problems,
  - ignoring problems in the hope that buyer will not discover them,
- excluding or spinning off specified assets from the transaction; and
- causing the buyer to assume specified liabilities.

Often, disclosure is staggered in order to prevent premature disclosure of sensitive information. Thus, in an auction, one will often see an initial level of disclosure to solicit expressions of interest followed by more detailed disclosure after the list of potential bidders has been narrowed. Additional issues arise if one or more of the potential buyers is a competitor of the seller. A seller will most likely be even more reluctant to make a complete disclosure to a competitor at this stage of the process. Sellers often stage the disclosure to a competitor to give themselves the best protection against unwanted disclosure and competition if the deal craters. Often intermediaries are used to review the competitively sensitive materials such as pricing, margins, or costs, and more care is taken to keep this material out of the hands of operating people. Even beyond the business concerns of the target, freely sharing information with a competitor can trigger antitrust exposure.[120] Staggered disclosure methodologies can also include selective escrows of sensitive data/information, with disclosure linked to specific concessions from the buyer; a critical path regarding disclosure of select categories of data/information leading to disclosure as and when particular milestones are achieved toward closing (for instance, after some preliminary conditions have been satisfied); or a negotiated timetable for access by the buyer and its representatives to management, other personnel and facilities of the seller. To protect itself, a buyer who agrees to staged disclosure may want to provide in the acquisition agreement that such disclosure will reveal some predetermined minimum position or, perhaps better for a buyer but not as good for a seller, an ability to terminate if the buyer is not satisfied with the results of the later disclosure.

Finally, and perhaps the most important of these strategies, negotiating carve-outs from representations either in the text of the representations themselves or by developing detailed disclosure schedules which contain appropriate exceptions to otherwise comprehensive and unqualified representations.

One or another aspect of the due diligence process from initiation to completion will be governed (and the custom in this respect varies with the jurisdiction in question) by one or more of the following types of documents, which the seller needs to prepare or negotiate in its best interest:

- confidential offering memorandum;
- confidentiality agreement (a universal prerequisite);
- standstill agreement (as applicable); or
- termination agreement containing compensatory provisions and specified restrictive covenants (i.e., non-solicitation of employees), as applicable.

The due diligence process itself may include specific rules or agreements as to how the buyer's representatives will be allowed to act. This may include a data room letter or agreement or rules of engagement (if not covered in a comprehensive data room agreement). Matters addressed include rules such as hours of availability, the number of days during which access will be provided, a check-in/check-out system, which documents will be copied, the rules for obtaining copies and similar mechanics.

A seller will be aware that a disappointed buyer may have a securities-law based or tort-based remedy despite the existence of a contract and will take measures to assure that there is no basis for such claims. A seller may put in place the following procedural safeguards:

- exercising caution regarding any loose talk or the provision of other information in pre-contractual negotiations;
- avoiding or monitoring such talk or other information prior to closing that is outside the strict written confines of the acquisition agreement and related documentation;
- establishing clear lines of communication among, and controlling actions of, members of seller's team; and
- setting guidelines for conduct and respective responsibilities and controlling disclosure of all data and documents (both timetable and access):
  - limiting access to data and documentation (check-in/check-out system), and
  - requiring that information requests be in writing.

Seller's Presale Due Diligence

Planning for the sale of a business should begin well in advance. A typical venture capital or private equity investor always considers an exit strategy (and a direct sale of the company is the most prevalent form). Often the entrepreneur only vaguely considers selling the company, but outside advisers (investment banks and business brokers) are sure to suggest that putting business affairs in order and packaging the company achieves a higher value. Advisors may suggest enhancing the bottom line, cleaning up distractions, assuring that audited financial statements are unqualified, clarifying competitive positions and otherwise rationalizing a business. While this may be considered planning and not due diligence, it is conceptually a preliminary due diligence investigation. With many private companies, including private equity fund sponsored entities, this is a useful time to assure that business procedures are appropriate and, in particular, that legal documents are in order. While any lawyer who has done a modest amount of due diligence can confirm that often details are not completed, there is also often a lack of critical detail: customer arrangements are not documented, bonus arrangements are vague, expected employee arrangements (confidentiality agreements and covenants not to compete) do not exist. If these items would be of concern to a potential buyer, it may be worthwhile to try to correct them sooner rather than later (unless the remedy is more costly than the problem) because the fix may take time and may not be possible at the last minute.

While sellers will often heed the general advice of a financial intermediary and will make a few cosmetic changes, few sellers take the next step of advising outside advisors—lawyers, accountants, benefits consultants, and others—of a possible sale and soliciting their input at a point in time when that input could be meaningful.

Too often there is no sell-side due diligence. Instead a lawyer gets a call announcing that a seller is selling the business and that a data room will be prepared and soliciting counsel's involvement (but usually not primary responsibility) setting up the data room. The exercise is identifying contracts, not making sure that they work. Typically, no one goes through the process of looking at the business from the perspective of a buyer to determine what needs to be done to dress it up and correct deficiencies. It might be relatively easy to clean up the corporate minute book to reflect necessary corporate actions rather than to do so in response to a potential buyer's comments, which inefficiently requires one to listen, explain and perhaps overly correct. Perhaps, if the defect had been remedied earlier, the potential buyer would not have even noticed it.

If there are problems that cannot be corrected, it is wise to determine how they will be presented. For example, assume a lawsuit, which, short of settlement, will not go away. When questioned, does the seller simply say that it is not important, it is being handled by counsel, do not worry about it, or would it be better to develop an explanation, with the assistance of counsel working on the matter, to alleviate any concerns that a buyer might have?

That exercise might also produce a better data room or might allow a quicker and better response to a due diligence request. Data rooms are often assembled by junior investment bankers or junior lawyers whose objective often seems to be quantity not quality. Using lists from prior deals, the process involves opening the file cabinets and turning on the copier. There is often a delicate balance between too much and too little, but having the right mix of documents readily available rather than requiring that the buyer engage in an arduous request for relevant documents would enhance the potential buyer's confidence and expedite the process. Too often, sellers never gain the buyer's confidence due to hasty and sloppy development of the data room.

What sellers actually do varies and is not necessarily rational. Those experienced in buying or selling companies know that the sale process is usually not smooth. Concerns develop and responses are formulated, all with a cost. Planning the process of the sale would appear to be a modest investment with potentially great rewards. A seller may determine not to initiate its own extensive seller due diligence program for various business reasons. At least it should think about the implications of not doing so.

Putting Together the Data Room/Responding to a Due Diligence Request

Despite the concerns, strategies and tactics of a particular seller, when it comes to putting together the data room or responding to a written due diligence request, theory may yield to the practicality of getting it done and subtleties may yield to the inexperience of the person doing the heavy lifting. Arguably, responding to the due diligence request is easier—you just follow the road map. Putting together the data room may be responsive to another list (such as an investment bank's general practices or the data room index from the last deal) or may involve judgments as to what is produced. The caveat to assemble enough, but not too much, may not be helpful to the junior banker or junior lawyer recruited for the first time to put together a data room. While a few documents may be in the files of a law firm representing a private company or in the legal department of larger companies, the pertinent information for most targets is scattered and not in a central depository. With smaller private companies, it is often the controller who has a handle on where documents can be found. In larger companies, it requires persistence and asking the right questions to ferret out pertinent documents. In doing the hard work of locating and copying documents, the subtleties of a seller's approach may very well get lost. Time pressures may not allow the documents to be read and understood before being put in the data room.

Various approaches are used with respect to indexing documents, either in response to a due diligence request or for the data room. Sometimes the documents are simply thrown into a box without any indication of the specific inquiry to which they are intended to be responsive. Most sellers will attempt to identify documents as being responsive to a designated portion of the request list and to annotate the request list to indicate responsiveness. At a minimum, a seller should keep a copy of what has been supplied to a buyer. It will facilitate preparation of disclosure schedules in the acquisition agreement, provide ready reference when there is discussion on a particular document and allow a seller to contradict the complaint that "we never got that agreement" (although the preferable practice is to maintain an index and a transmittal showing what items of the index have been supplied, on what date and to whom).

The data room usually includes divisions and categories, and documents are placed in those various categories. Most sellers prepare a listing of the documents provided, although that is not universal and it is certainly not uncommon to find a category on an index with no responsive documents included.

Probably the most frustrating aspect of due diligence is the inevitable follow up. Whether it is in a data room or on a request list, a buyer will often ask, "Have I received everything responsive?" The process of due diligence will also generate requests for additional information involving either subtle variations of what has already been requested, amendments to existing documents or the demand for the documents that should most certainly be there (but do not seem to have been presented). Depending upon the indexing method used, a buyer may get frustrated and confused because it does not know to which requests particular documents are intended to be responsive or it knows that there are other documents not being produced. On the other hand, sellers are frustrated by the incessant demands for documents they believe they have already produced, by round after round of requests for documents when it appears that the buyer has not been able to get itself organized and by requests for documents that are trivial.

The meaning and import of particular documents may not be self-evident. Buyers may seek an explanation of how a document may work, what its implications may be, and so on. These questions pertain not only to legal documents, but to operational reports and other matters as well. Most sellers are not willing to provide unfettered access to their personnel. How interviews are set up, whether a buyer representative is allowed to contact a counterpart with the seller directly and whether a law firm or investment bank participates in all discussions are highly variable. But no buyer should be willing to merely review documents without an opportunity to understand the implications of the most important of those documents by face-to-face discussion. The same goes for lawyers reviewing documents on behalf of the seller.

Running the Data Room

It is customary to provide a set of rules for the data room to facilitate an orderly process and assure that all bidders will have access to all documents (that is, documents are not removed by some bidders). Various investment banks, through their own experience, have developed sets of rules. These may involve:

- a sign-in procedure;
- a check in/check out procedure for documents;
- a mechanism for copying certain (or all) documents, such as a request for copies form, coupled with a statement as to those documents that will not be copied; and
- a procedure for requesting documents not in the room.

An example of rules for a data room is attached as Appendix 10-A.

Coordination of Seller's Due Diligence/Preparation of Schedules

The persons from seller's organization who have responded to the request list or put together the data room are best positioned to put the disclosure schedules together. The exercise of obtaining documents, of responding to additional requests, and having extensive discussions about the subject matter of documents and their responsiveness to requests usually puts them in a position to use that same information to begin to produce schedules.

Buy-Side Due Diligence

How does a buyer deal with the seller's perspective described above? Sellers may regard potential buyers as adversaries. Particular sellers may in fact attempt to hide or brush off problems. But most sellers will know that a potential buyer will uncover any problems and that the consequences of that discovery may be problematic. Perception may be worse than reality. Potential buyers are often spooked by problems found by them but not identified by sellers. They may come to believe that the seller is hiding the ball. They may become skeptical, abandoning deals, or slowing the process down. Delays in providing information may imply a cover-up to a potential buyer. Many sellers will believe that their interests are best served by offering reasonable access to information.

To be sure, there is always a disparity in information. Reducing the disparity will be critical to a decision to enter into or continue negotiations as well as to pricing, risk allocation and other subjects.

Risks to a Potential Buyer

As noted previously, the sale process in general poses risks to the seller in that it will have some effect on the business being sold. The most notable risks to a buyer are obvious: if it buys a lesser business than it expected, the price paid will not be justified, and the work involved in correcting matters can be disruptive and detract from a buyer's other businesses. Legal remedies may not be adequate.

There are risks to the buyer in being involved in an unsuccessful purchase. While the consequences of completing a bad deal almost always outweigh the consequences of not doing a particular deal, the latter consequences are not insignificant. There is usually significant distraction to a potential buyer in doing a deal. Those running the buyer's business on a day-to-day basis may be diverted to work on the deal, perhaps resulting in a decline in the ongoing business. There is the expense of outside advisors. There is the reputational expense of failing to complete a deal, particularly if it is the result of indecision or belated identification of problems. Often these problems relate to an early commitment to an inadequately investigated deal. To avoid or mitigate these risks, a potential buyer may want to ease into a transaction, moving to the next milestone only after there is a thorough discussion of the likely outcome of the process.

Objectives and Strategies

The objectives and strategies of the seller were described previously. In simple terms, a buyer will attempt to counteract many of those objectives. It will be aware that the seller, justifiably concerned about disclosing proprietary information, may not be forthcoming with all of the information. It will also be aware that a seller may, for many reasons such as preserving an informational advantage, laziness, or incompetence, be less than forthcoming on disclosure matters, requiring the buyer to be clever and hardworking. A potential buyer will seek legal assurances (a tough acquisition agreement) and practical assurances (it knows as much or more about the business as the seller) that it has obtained full disclosure about the target.

A potential buyer may develop a number of strategies to achieve its ends, from mobilizing superior resources, to internal discipline, to making sure its team knows how to negotiate. Reliance solely on the acquisition agreement is fraught with peril: it covers only a limited number of items pertinent to the acquisition and, in any event, buying a sound business is much more important than buying a claim. Learning all there is to know about a business should be the primary objective of the due diligence process: all other objectives follow from that.

60 Minutes of Diligence

We had spent weeks getting the purchase agreement in form while my client pursued due diligence on the company. Our due diligence list and the contract contained provisions relating to disclosures of pending or threatened litigation, governmental investigations, etc. On the day of signing we were still working out some final minor points with the intention of funding the purchase the next day. One of the seller's employees approached us and "off the record" informed us that *60 Minutes*, the well known news show, had recently visited the company and was going to feature the company in its show the next week in a less than flattering light. My client took me aside and told me to make up a story about how I had an emergency back home and that I had to leave. I made my excuses and left. Thus, without counsel, my client left. Upon further investigation, we determined that *60 Minutes* was going to feature allegations of fraud and questionable business practices by the seller. Of course, the transaction then collapsed. What this episode taught us to do with future deals was to not only perform the typical lien searches, but also demand to speak with lower level personnel to ask probing questions like, "have you seen any news crews around here lately?" Diligence is cheap, regret is costly.

Initiating the Due Diligence Process

Preliminary discussions about a possible purchase will have already elicited some due diligence materials, such as a confidential offering memorandum, publicly available documents, or other types of internal information, whether a transaction is proceeding by way of an auction process or as a negotiated deal. A confidentiality agreement will likely be in place.

Who takes the next step may depend on the type of selling process.

In an auction, it is customary for a seller to put together a data room that will be made available in connection with a management presentation to potential bidders. However, not every auction will have a data room. A potential buyer may want to put together its own checklist to assist it in determining the adequacy of information in the data room. But it may be presumptuous to actually submit the list to the seller. An alternative is for the seller simply to check the data room index against its own checklist to ensure completeness or to identify holes. There is a wide variance in the types of information that are produced in a data room as previously discussed.

In a negotiated process (and in some auctions), potential buyers may be expected to request documents to be reviewed as well as access to the target's management, independent accountants, and other third parties. Those documents may be copied and sent directly to buyer's representatives or put in a data room, or the original documents may be offered for an in-office review. Sometimes, even in a negotiated deal, a seller may start to put together a data room or send copies of documents without waiting for a buyer's request, particularly where the deal being done represents a failed auction or a remnant of an auction or where the seller is attempting to entice a particular buyer into a deal (the logical strategic buyer, for example).

The Due Diligence Team

Assembling the Team

The due diligence team should consist of persons responsible for at least three main areas: legal, accounting, and business. More than one of these areas may be combined in a single person, so long as each person has a clear understanding of his responsibilities. Depending on the nuances of the seller's business, the buyer's team may contain one or more consultants other than the buyer's legal and accounting advisors to address specific aspects of the business. For instance, it is very common for environmental, health, and safety consultants to assist in reviewing manufacturing facilities and real property. The risks associated with each facet of the seller's business will influence a buyer's allocation of resources needed to provide an adequate investigation. Seasoned buyers tend to overstaff the review because experience has taught them that it is much easier to walk away from a bad deal before, rather than after, the closing.

Some members of the buy-side team may be devoted only to due diligence. Indeed, in the law firm itself, document review may be relegated to associates. Specialty lawyers (such as those in the employee benefits area) may be involved in due diligence and in the negotiation of particular sections of the acquisition agreement. Other lawyers may be involved only in deal negotiation.

Often the team is organized on the fly. Prior involvement with the client or greater expertise may be sacrificed to availability. The client requests to have a due diligence team on the ground the next day, half a day's travel away, comes relatively frequently. Even within the same law firm, team members may not know each other; drawing team members both from within the potential buyer's organization and from outside advisors compounds the problem of working together.

It is not uncommon for a law firm to assign its youngest and least experienced associates to handle legal due diligence. Obviously, a more senior and experienced lawyer should explain the purpose and processes of legal due diligence to the younger lawyer and be available to answer the younger lawyer's questions as due diligence proceeds.

Agreeing on the Objective

The due diligence team viewing material in the data room often has little time to plan who does what. Normally, there is a team leader, usually not the client's lawyer, whose job includes determining priorities, particularly when time does not permit the review of all documents. Whatever background information exists needs to be shared and the potential buyer's objectives need to be communicated. Approaches vary. The problem of communication and allocation of work differs significantly in the three-person team than in the fifty-person team.

If the team must first develop a due diligence list (where there is no data room), it will have a different challenge. Each set of experts will be tempted to contribute its own list, and in order to prove its value, will offer up a list that is dozens of pages long. Put together, the lists are often overlapping and burdensome and, if actually responded to, might produce more chaff than wheat. One person is often allocated the role of rationalizing the list.

Communications

Members of the team need to communicate their findings to each other during the process. Information discovered about one facet of the business will often affect other areas. Each of the persons responsible for the legal and accounting areas might brief the business person, late in the process, about the business questions that have arisen as a result of the due diligence review. By then, it might only be possible to have those questions answered on the fly during a dialogue between the businessperson and a representative of the seller. The earlier questions are answered, the more likely that the issues they represent will be covered in the acquisition agreement.

There are varying techniques to facilitate communications. Often, it is difficult getting team members to share information with other team members rather than with the buyer's senior representative who selected the team in the first place. Even within the buyer's organization, reporting and sharing relationships may be confused. Skillful leadership skills are required to overcome this problem.

The Due Diligence Checklist

The due diligence checklist is the backbone of the due diligence investigation. The checklist is a list of all agreements, documents, and other information requested by a potential buyer to facilitate its investigation of the target. A good checklist will contain all of the information initially requested on behalf of the buyer and should be developed with input from the various members of the due diligence team. The checklist should be the result of the buyer's own pre-investigation into the industry and business of the seller.

The responsibility for customizing the checklist is often delegated to the person who is to head the legal due diligence team. Even though due diligence should be more concerned with business matters than strictly legal, lawyers are often asked to prepare the initial due diligence request list. The tried and true form emanates from word processing. These lists often have an undue emphasis on legal matters and are usually not tailored to the particular business of the target. An experienced buyer having an in-house team often has its own request list that is often peculiar to the industry involved and is tailored to that buyer's concerns. Financial buyers are likely to use an accounting firm to provide due diligence since the firm knows what its client wants to cover.

Thoughtful buyers will seek input, review and comment on the list from all members of the due diligence team. The scope of the request and the depth of the request will depend on many factors, including a buyer's risk profile, its experience in doing deals, its budget for the deal and its comfort with the target.

Properly Tailoring the Due Diligence Checklist

Prior to customizing the checklist, the experienced buyer will gather all information available about the business being sold, including public information and any confidential information previously furnished by or on behalf of the seller. If audited financial statements have been furnished, the notes are often a good place to find the unique features of the seller's business. While a standard form due diligence checklist can be used as a broad net, it may be advisable in certain circumstances to customize it to the seller's business or industry in order to eliminate searches for documents or information that might be deemed nonessential or irrelevant to the primary purpose of buyer's due diligence. The goal should be to develop more knowledge about the material features of the seller's business and how it has been operated in order to draft a comprehensive acquisition agreement that protects the buyer's interests. For instance, if the seller owns a residential construction business, information related to its largest customers may not be very relevant, while information related to its referral sources is relevant. The experienced buyer will have anticipated this nuance and customized its checklist to focus on the source of the seller's future revenues. This also allows the seller to focus its document production efforts and streamlines the investigation process.

A significant problem with all due diligence is doing just enough. For reasons such as wanting to appear to be smart, assuring that one can never be criticized and misunderstanding the process and lack of time, due diligence request lists are often too long. A buyer should consider that a seller's reaction to a particular request list may have implications to the success of the process. The list as presented may suggest to a seller that a buyer is foot dragging, nitpicking to such a degree that it sends a signal that it will never be able to get to a signed deal, that the buyer is naïve or uncertain–all of which may be contrary to a buyer's objective of appearing to be willing to move quickly toward signing. Lists are often internally duplicative and overlapping, suggesting, as is often the case, that they represent an amalgamation of the team members' favorite lists.

Tailoring Due Diligence Requests

In representing a buyer, the last thing you want is to create a bad impression and irritate the seller at the very beginning of the negotiations. But all too often, this initial negative impact can be the result of an extensive due diligence checklist dumped on the seller without much thought. For example, in a deal where the target was a service company, the seller's checklist included a request for a breakdown of inventories and other items that were clearly only applicable to manufacturers. In another, the checklist asked for periodic reports filed with the SEC and reports distributed to shareholders, notwithstanding that the target was owned by a few shareholders.

The seller, in reviewing a checklist that covers soup to nuts without zeroing in on the particular target and its business, will think that the buyer's counsel is just not giving a lot of thought to the transaction and some sellers can be outwardly offended. It would take very little time for someone familiar with the deal to reduce the checklist to those things that are potentially pertinent to the target and its business. Whatever the potential advantages may be of using an exhaustive, standard list of items for every deal should give way to crafting a checklist that is clearly designed to elicit information and documents from the specific target.

Extensive duplication between checklists submitted by various advisors to the buyer can also set the wrong tone. This usually occurs between the checklists used by counsel for the buyer and its accountants. Legal checklists often request a considerable amount of financial and accounting information and documentation, which is probably not even examined by the lawyers. Some coordination in preparing these lists might be helpful in avoiding another chance to irritate the seller.

Pre-Visit Requests Regarding the Data Room

A potential buyer may request that the data room visit be delayed to follow the management presentation by some days. Until the management presentation, the degree of interest in a particular target is difficult to measure, so why waste the time and energy? Further, it is difficult to formulate the team without knowing the pitfalls of the business.

Most sellers are willing to share the data room index and may in fact volunteer it. A buyer can get a feel as to the scope of the review required (and what experts need to attend) as well as the quantity of information available (setting the size of the team and how long the review will take) through a review of the list. Based on that list, some buyers prefer to short circuit the process and ask for copies of all of the data room documents. Some sellers are willing to comply, depending on a number of circumstances, such as the number of bidders and the perceived need to keep a particular buyer happy (because it is the only, the most qualified or the most likely bidder). Some sellers may have contemplated that step by making the documents available in a virtual data room or on a CD-ROM. Some sellers are willing to make copies of some documents but not those that are highly sensitive. Some insist that no documents be copied prior to the data room visit. Still, a potential buyer should not be shy to ask.

The Response to the Due Diligence Request

Particular sellers may be willing to copy documents, while others will expect that documents be reviewed on site. Where the prospects of the transaction are uncertain, a seller may want to avoid the labor involved in copying and actually require that buyer bring a team to review the documents as a measure of its interest.

The response to the request may be handled in different ways. Sometimes a junior banker or junior lawyer is asked to be in charge. The document gathering process may be sloppy. Documents may not be categorized as responsive to the request. Document lists may not be prepared. The documents furnished may be incomplete or not responsive. The inadequacy of response is not necessarily intentional.

The process may be protracted, as documents are supplied in waves. The preferable way to deliver documents is to create an index, and is best when the seller prepares the index and shares it with the buyer. That allows the buyer to check off what has been received and provides a means for the parties to communicate (a buyer seeking missing pages, for example, can refer specifically to the document being discussed). A buyer would want to prepare its own index if seller does not, and may want to prepare its own or an annotated index of what has been received to facilitate handoffs of reviews to various members of the team and to check off affirmatively that the document has been reviewed. A lesson soon learned is that passing off the sole copy of a document often results in missing documents: the coordinator will almost always make copies for further review by members of the team. Even the best practices will still lead to uncertainties and frustrations in determining the status of various reviews.

The Data Room Visit

Elaborate protocol may surround a data room visit in any particular transaction, from extensive sets of rules, to specified visiting hours and other procedures. Sellers and their representatives will want to compress data room visits to hurry the deal along. Space is often limited and hours are long. There may only be a limited opportunity for team members to compare notes. What is found in the data room may not correspond to the data room index. Sometimes there are no responsive documents to particular portions of the data room index, for a variety of reasons, such as just not getting around to it or an intention to furnish highly sensitive documents at a later time. Sellers may not explain why documents were not furnished.

When visiting the data room, a potential buyer may be allocated one or two days. Buyers will be concerned that their review will not be complete. In an auction, it may be appropriate to suggest in the bid letter that further due diligence is required in order to avoid any misunderstanding.

Reviewing Documents (in the Office or the Data Room)

Documents are reviewed not only by lawyers but also by any number of the buyer's team. All reviews should be done with a view to reporting to others within the buyer organization, assuring that the documents reviewed are responsive and determining whether other requests should be made.

To the extent a seller is willing to make its executives available to explain the documents, the review process may be facilitated. There may be site visits for selected personnel (operations, environmental). Accounting experts may be hired to review financial matters. All of this may generate additional requests for information.

Management Presentations and Site Visits

Management presentations and site visits are often the most important parts of the due diligence process. In an auction process, if a potential buyer has been able to negotiate for a management presentation several days prior to the data room visit, it will be much easier to formulate an approach to the document review because the upside and downside of the target's business will be better understood. In a non-auction context, a potential buyer will typically negotiate for interviews with key management to understand the visit better.

A prospective buyer is usually eager to have its acquisition team talk to the target's management and visit the target's facilities. Targets and their investment banks are often likewise eager to have their executives make a presentation to a buyer or to several prospective buyers as part of the effort to sell the business. But unless the target is convinced that a prospective buyer is serious about a transaction, it may be reluctant to expose its facilities and lower level employees to the disruption of site visits from the buyer's diligence team or to devote much management time to the preparation of a presentation about the target's business. Moreover, groups of "suited" strangers trooping through a target's facilities may cause word (or rumors) of an impending sale to spread beyond those management team members at the target who have a need to know about a potential transaction. A loss of confidentiality can wreak havoc with employee morale and lead to defections by employees and customers. For that reason, the timing of management presentations and site visits are often the subject of serious negotiation, as is the subject of who, from the buyer's team, will be permitted to attend the management presentation and site visits.

The target's senior management team generally prepares detailed written information for its presentations, often with the assistance of the target's investment bank, and presents the material to the buyer's acquisition team. Management presentations can also give some of the target's managers an opportunity to impress their prospective new employer.

On some occasions, depending on the sensitivity of the material to be disclosed, the target's outside lawyers may be brought into the preparation process. In rare circumstances, lawyers for the target and the buyer attend management presentations. Certainly an argument in favor of having the lawyers attend is that it can give the lawyers a much better understanding of the business and can help reduce the likelihood of misunderstandings regarding representations as the deal progresses. (Buyer's counsel: "You have to be willing to make that rep in the purchase agreement. Your CFO made it at the management presentation." Target's counsel: "Well, I don't know because I wasn't there but. . . ."). Considerations may vary depending on numerous factors, including the relative sophistication of the buyer and the status of the transaction.

Some practitioners have been known to go so far as to tape-record management presentations. This tactic is most often viewed as somewhat hostile and as evidencing a mistrust of the other side or perhaps anticipating litigation. The target's management certainly needs to be reminded that the Power Point presentations, handouts, and videotapes used at these sessions, and their answers to the buyer's questions, are fair game in the negotiations over representations.

Absent some unusual interest in the arcane art of the target's processes, there is seldom any need for either the buyer's or target's counsel to accompany the buyer's diligence team on visits to the target's facilities. The task of coordinating those visits is generally left to the target's personnel or the investment bankers. On the other hand, the deal lawyers, particularly the target's lawyer, should have some say in (or at least give his management team a heads up to think about) the number and type of personnel from the buyer who should be permitted to visit the target's sites. A swarm of the buyer's technical people, accompanied by a contingent of environmental consultants, may make for a very long day at each of the target's facilities and make it impossible to keep confidential the prospective sale of the target's business. Depending in part on the position the target decides to take with respect to representations regarding the condition of its facilities and its willingness to allow a prospective buyer to conduct, for instance, environmental investigations pre-closing, site visits should be for the purpose of making the buyer's team generally familiar with the location and condition of the target's facilities, not for a detailed analysis of those facilities and their operations.

As the diligence process continues, many buyers will want various team members to be able to speak to their counterparts at the target organization. For example, buyer's environmental consultant, armed with various reports placed in the data room, will want to understand better the risks identified (and other risks not identified). Because most confidentiality agreements prohibit this contact without consent, permission to make contact needs to be negotiated. The seller will want to make sure that there is a small group involved in such discussions, all of whom know about the deal. It may want to limit the amount of discussion and control the flow of information. Sometimes a seller insists that its investment bank be involved in any discussion so as to know what was said and to some extent control what may be revealed.

The Review Process: Next Steps

If a required bid and mark-up of the acquisition agreement is due soon after the due diligence visit, that process begins to drive what happens next. Depending on the message it wishes to send and how disciplined it is, a buyer in negotiated situations will want to request additional information. A data room can never be current and is rarely complete, and the due diligence process itself will always generate the need for additional information. The due diligence process may get out of control. Normally investment bankers want all questions directed through them. But often access to officers and staff of the target is granted to the buyer. Discussions may generate informal requests for documents. Sometimes requests are made orally. Such requests are often handled in an undisciplined manner. A seller may insist that any requests for additional documents or information come through a central person.

The Due Diligence Report

Communications about the results of due diligence are often informal, percolating up to management as the process continues. Decisions are sometimes made before the diligence process is completed. Nevertheless, there frequently is an attempt to formalize the information gathered and conclusions reached in a written report.

During a typical due diligence investigation, thousands of pages of documents and other information will be reviewed and summarized. A summary of the documents reviewed and the information gathered by the due diligence team is often reflected in a written report or memorandum. This summary should be prepared as close in time to the completion of the investigation as possible since it will be used to prepare and negotiate the acquisition agreement. Depending on corporate cultures, the dedication and experience of the team and other factors, the report may represent a data dump or may be a summary. Sometimes a fill-in-the-blanks approach is used. Because particular concerns may indicate a necessary focus on how the acquisition agreement is constructed (firmer representations, special indemnification provisions, etc.), the concerns should be brought to the attention of the negotiating team, but often are not. Reports are often incomplete because the seller has not provided information in a timely manner.

The prompt completion of the report is usually the responsibility of the team leader. One method of preparing this report is to have a computer-friendly format in advance, so that sections of the report may be completed on a laptop at the scene, in the airport or on the plane home. The report should be designed so that it might ultimately be used to double check the information on the seller's schedules during completion of negotiations on the acquisition agreement. Another good practice is to place an executive summary or recommendations section at the front of the report in order to highlight any immediate action that the buyer should consider (e.g., negotiations to extend or renew a material lease that is about to expire shortly after the projected closing date).

However, depending on the buyer's time constraints, comfort level, budget, or other circumstances, there may not be a written report. Often written reports get in the way of conveying information. They take time to prepare, so they may not be timely. Because most reports go into some detail about everything that was reviewed, rather than reporting on problems or exceptions, a written report may bury the issues on which focus is needed. Even if a written report is anticipated, a prompt oral heads-up report is often the most effective.

Because a lawyer is usually only one of many team members, there is sometimes confusion on how information should be reported. The deal itself may be lead by an experienced M&A lawyer not a part of the due diligence team. Sometimes specialty lawyers may have direct internal contacts at the client, either to an in-house lawyer or a businessperson. The issue to be dealt with is assuring that information gets to those who need to know, while being sensitive to political issues.

The Result of the Process

The due diligence process amounts to an evaluation of the business. It has elements of quantification (how much is this business worth) but it also drives a buy/do not buy decision, structural issues, deal terms, and other matters. There is no one process, outcome, work product, or standardized practice that is followed. It is iterative, as additional information produces a need for depth and clarification or suggests other avenues of inquiry. The process can always be improved.

There is some risk of knowing too much. If the buyer knows of the untruthfulness of a particular representation before signing or becomes aware of such untruthfulness after signing but before closing, a buyer's remedy for misrepresentation may be limited under the case law of some states.[121]

What Happens After the Due Diligence Report Is Made?

In many cases, those who have been a part of the due diligence team and contributed to an extensive report may feel that their work is not appreciated—a note of thanks is issued (sometimes not even that) and that is the last the team hears of due diligence. Has the information uncovered been used by a potential buyer to make a buy/do not buy decision or to improve its bargaining position in the process? Information is, of course, used in different ways. If time has permitted the due diligence report to be finished before negotiations are initiated, the information in the report may have been fully utilized in the bargaining process. In other circumstances, whether the information was used is less obvious. If discussions are underway at some level, as they inevitably are, information will have already been conveyed to the negotiating team by certain members of the due diligence team. That information will have been used already at the time the due diligence report comes out, so there may appear to be less of a cause and effect relationship. Sometimes particular revelations may be ignored because they have been determined not to be significant and the fragile state of negotiations simply will not permit the interjection of yet another issue.

So too, it may be that despite the cost and expense of a due diligence report, its function is relegated to the status of identifying deal killers. If the report identifies a multitude of issues to be addressed, but none has independent significance, there may not be effective use of the due diligence report. The report that is not completed until after the acquisition agreement is signed raises the question: Were the road signs along the way communicated?

Whether any particular buyer can use the results of due diligence to its advantage is always a problem. Often quantifiable elements, such as a softness in the income statement or balance sheet, can be used as the basis of price negotiation. Risk concerns may generate a request for indemnification. A buyer may have its greatest strength in understanding the totality of the problems to be negotiated at one time. But without knowing of the identified problems, the negotiating team will be powerless to use the information to its advantage, hence the need for timely and thorough communication.

Continuing Due Diligence

The due diligence report, revelations during the negotiation process and other sources of intelligence will generate a need for continuing due diligence. The process may break down at this point. The due diligence team may have been effectively disbanded, or its leader may be part of the negotiating team and otherwise distracted. The rapidity of the process may cut against the methodical due diligence investigation and reporting techniques. Access to information may have been lost. Despite these hurdles, there is an obvious need to make sure that effective due diligence is continued and utilized.

Review of Disclosure Schedules

As discussed in Chapter 11, while there often is a handoff between those involved in due diligence and those involved in the final negotiations, it is essential that those involved in the due diligence also be involved in reviewing the disclosure schedules. That is particularly true in the circumstance where the acquisition agreement includes a "disclosure for one, disclosure for all" concept (that is, a disclosure in one schedule counts as a disclosure for all schedules) so that the implications of listing a particular document and its effect on many portions of the acquisition agreement are understood. While buyers always hope to have drafts of these schedules early enough to circulate among the various lawyers and other advisors working on the matter, even a deal with the best intentioned seller usually includes some changes in the schedules at the last minute, either due to changes in the representations themselves or a refinement of the drafts of the schedules that have been produced. While the better practice is that those involved in due diligence also remain attuned to document design, negotiation, and drafting, it may at least be advisable for the due diligence team to be brought in to review the draft schedules prior to signing the acquisition agreement.

Post-Signing Due Diligence

While parties often talk about post-signing or pre-closing due diligence, which is assurance that the closing conditions are satisfied, too often this is not done in a vigorous way. Because at that time the buyer and employees of the target may be discussing integration plans and issues, a buyer may rely on the identification of troublesome issues during those discussions. Ironically, once a buyer has gained the contractual right to conduct due diligence (virtually every acquisition agreement will assure that the buyer has access to the target's properties and employees, subject to reasonable controls and ongoing confidentiality obligations), it often fails to exercise its right. Perhaps buyers are distracted by the closing process, or just have deal fatigue.

Buyers bargain hard to assure that the conditions to closing are stringent in order to receive the business for which it bargained. Often, a buyer will rely merely on the bring-down certificate delivered at the closing with little independent investigation, other that what it has learned informally and mechanical aspects that the lawyers can monitor (were the consents received?). While a false seller's certificate may generate a lawsuit, that usually is not a buyer's objective. Hard evidence of the satisfaction of various closing conditions will be put on the table at closing, such as consents. But the truth of three basic conditions is too often provided only by a certificate instead of back-up due diligence: (i) the accuracy of the representations (as made and as brought down), (ii) the fulfillment of post-signing covenants, and (iii) whether a material adverse change has occurred.

Included in post-signing due diligence is post-closing integration planning. Mostly operational in nature, integration planning may involve some members of the due diligence team (but usually not lawyers and accountants) or certain internal staff team members. Some would argue that the ability to integrate two businesses is the mark of a successful deal and, accordingly, the determination of whether they can be integrated is a key buy decision. Consequently, it is important that adequate resources are devoted to assuring that what was possible does in fact occur. The point here is twofold: the lawyers have little to do if the objective of this phase of due diligence is only integration, and the planning for integration during this phase is variable: some buyers do nothing at all, while others are intense in their efforts.

Post-Closing Due Diligence

While usually not thought of as due diligence, buyers may want to affirmatively undertake to determine whether they have received the benefit of the bargain, particularly when the time period for seeking a remedy under the acquisition agreement is about to expire. Remedies are normally sought when a particular purchase has not gone well for a buyer and it then attempts to discover whether a remedy is available or an inquiry may be initiated before the lapse of a claims period. Another possible approach would be to reassemble the due diligence team a reasonable time after closing to determine what has happened and whether the understandings going into the deal have proven to be false.

APPENDIX 10-A
Data Room Procedures

Introduction

- These data room procedures relate to the manner in which potential buyers and their representatives may use the facilities made available to them at the data room located at the offices of [*law firm*] in [*city and state*] (the "Data Room").

Confidentiality

- The documents contained in the Data Room and any other information supplied on request (the "Information") in connection with and relating to the proposed transaction constitute confidential information for the purposes of the Confidentiality Agreement executed with [*investment bank*] on behalf of [*target*]. Accordingly, the Information must be held in complete confidence and subject to the terms of the Confidentiality Agreement.
- The Information is made available subject to, and on the terms contained in, the disclaimer of liability set out in the Confidential Memorandum. No representation or warranty (express or implied) is given and no liability is accepted by [*investment bank*], [*target*], or any of their affiliates, officers, directors, advisers or representatives, as to the accuracy, reliability, completeness or reasonableness of the Information or for any errors, omissions or misstatements, negligent or otherwise, in relation thereto.
- The provision of the Information does not constitute an offer to sell [*target*], and the Information will not form the basis of any such contract.

Upon Arrival

- The hours of the Data Room are from [*time*] to [*time*]. Visitors should ask for [*contact person*] on arrival at [*law firm*] and sign the visitor register provided.
- Access to the Data Room is with the consent of [*target*] and [*investment bank*], acting on behalf of [*target*], and may be withdrawn at any time and without prior notice. Visitors must comply immediately with any request by [*investment bank*] or [*law firm*] relating to the Data Room.
- The size of your data room due diligence team should be limited to those people essential to the due diligence process. Please designate a team leader who will be responsible for liaising with [*law firm*].
- Visitors must comply with any reasonable request from the [*law firm*] representatives and, in particular, with any security regulations and procedures required from time to time by representatives of [*law firm*].
- The receptionist will be notified of the presence of those signing the visitor register and will forward calls and take messages. Special arrangements can be made with [*contact person*] for sending relatively short messages or documents by facsimile, for which you will be billed at $[*amount*] per page.

Documentation

- An index of documents contained in the Data Room will be made available to you prior to your visit to the Data Room (the "Data Room Index"). The Information in the Data

Room has been organized into indexed files and binders as reflected on the Data Room Index.

- Please ensure prior to your departure that the Information in the Data Room is in the same order as when you entered the Data Room.
- You must not remove any Information from the Data Room other than the materials copied for you by [*law firm*].
- You are welcome to bring laptop computers into the Data Room if you wish, but portable copiers, scanners, fax machines, photographic or other electronic equipment will not be permitted.
- You must not mark, alter, modify, vary in any way, damage or destroy any of the Information in the Data Room.
- Further documents may be added to the Data Room from time to time. These will be clearly marked in a separate file and you will be notified as soon as practicable of any additions to the Information in the Data Room.

Copying

- [*Law firm*] will accept reasonable requests for copying, and will endeavor to provide the copied documents prior to your departure or by the close of the following business day. If you wish to have documents copied, you should complete a Copying Request Form and place it in the box marked "Copying." You will be billed for copies at the rate of $[*amount*] per page. [Note that many sellers in large deals will not charge for copying at all, viewing it as a sales expense.]
- Certain Information is designated in the Data Room Index as not copyable.

Lunch

- At the request of the visitors, lunch can be provided in the Data Room.

Questions

- [*Law firm*] has been instructed only to supervise the operation of the Data Room. Visitors should not ask any questions of them as to the Information, other than to ask where certain documents may be found.
- All questions relating to the Information or the Data Room should be reduced to writing and directed by facsimile to: [*names and fax numbers*]. [*Investment bank*] will coordinate the process of providing answers to these questions.

Preparing the Acquisition Agreement and Related Documents

If there is any part of an M&A transaction that is thought to belong to the lawyers, it is the preparation of the acquisition agreement and related documents. Too often that results in a handoff to the lawyer without clear direction. Even among experienced businesspeople, the acquisition agreement and other documents are thought to be fill-in-the-blank type forms—names, economic terms, and boilerplate[122] for the rest. The lawyers, in accepting the handoff, zealously attempt to protect the client's interests, but often lack an appreciation of the fragile nature of the business deal.

The discussion below begins with an understanding of the client's objectives and then deals with the process of preparing and negotiating an acquisition agreement, including some of the recurring issues that might be encountered. This section is followed by a discussion of putting together the schedules to the acquisition agreement and a description of some of the other documents that often find their way into an acquisition.

Understanding the Client's Objectives

Other chapters are replete with the need to understand and respond to the client's objectives. While such an understanding is necessary in any phase of the M&A process, it becomes crucial at the point of drafting and negotiating a letter of intent or the acquisition agreement, which will involve many issues, many subtleties and many approaches. What is important to a particular client will depend on its experiences, risk tolerance, needs (e.g., a retirement-age seller), and numerous other factors. Some clients are risk averse, while others are carefree. Some are experienced and know where the deal is going; others are naïve. Some have an intuitive understanding of these types of agreements; others are clueless. The ultimate objective—of either a buyer or seller—will be to complete the transaction, but on a reasonable basis. Of course, there is a very broad range of what might be reasonable depending to a large extent on which factors are considered important.

An agreement never signed is certain to belong to a transaction not closed. That being said, buyers always have some expectation of protection in entering into a deal and sellers are usually willing to provide some measure of protection—the "as is, where is" deal is rare. The following are some examples of client objectives that might be encountered.

- A buyer, instead of insisting on absolute protection, may be willing to take reasonable risks, particularly in areas it knows well, either by being in the same business or through due diligence.
- Parties may eschew the lengthy negotiation process required to achieve their ends if they can get modest protection and can move quickly to signing.
- Parties (either side may take comfort in this tactic) may settle on ambiguous, open ended language rather than precise, highly negotiated language if it advances the deal, on the basis that the drafting process will have had the cathartic effect of exposing the problem or that ambiguity is in their best interests.
- A buyer, confident of its position, may insist on a gold plated agreement and take the risk that a seller may balk and not move forward.

In most cases, there are numerous trade-offs that a client may be willing to make (or refuse to make) as part of the process, even though the issues may be unrelated and not economically quantifiable—that is to say, the process may be viewed as almost irrational.

Some clients, however, will have certain bedrock principles for every deal. For example, many buyers want solid protection against environmental matters and may set their standards accordingly. Due diligence may have produced some absolutes. Usually any terms negotiated in a letter of intent or term sheet become absolutes unless one party (normally the buyer) forces the other to back down based on newly discovered facts.

Preparing the Agreement

Once the parties have agreed on the basic terms of the transaction, relying on an oral understanding or a letter of intent or term sheet, they will proceed to the preparation and negotiation of the acquisition agreement. Sometimes this stage is delayed until an important condition is satisfied or at least there is some assurance that it can be satisfied, but ordinarily preparation of a draft of the acquisition agreement will commence shortly after an understanding of the parties is reached.

The typical issues in preparing a draft are determining who prepares the first draft, what should be used for precedent, by whom is it to be reviewed, and how is it to be distributed. Another consideration is anticipating and, if possible, influencing the response of opposing counsel. The discussion in this Chapter assumes that the transaction is a negotiated acquisition, rather than an auction, as to which the process and preparation of the acquisition agreement differs as discussed in Chapter 6.

Who Prepares the First Draft?

Counsel for one of the parties will prepare a first draft of the acquisition agreement. While the possibility of a deal counsel acting as scrivener for both sides has been suggested as a possibility, that just does not occur. Like most issues in an acquisition, whether buyer's counsel or seller's counsel prepares the first draft is negotiable. That having been said, buyer's counsel typically prepares it. An exception occurs in the case of an auction, which is discussed in Chapter 6.

Counsel may also want to consider whether there are geographical or cultural differences. Even within the United States, various regions have developed different patterns or customs applicable to acquisitions. This factor may be particularly relevant in cross-border transactions where local or cultural differences are likely to be much more pronounced. In these cases, it may be advisable to retain local counsel to prepare all or portions of the acquisition agreement or at least obtain their input.

Although deal etiquette or custom is often cited as the reason for buyer's counsel to want to prepare the first draft, from the buyer's perspective, there are substantive reasons. Buyer's counsel can ensure that the client's best position is put forward and that the agreement meets the client's objectives by, for instance, fully describing the assets being purchased in an asset transaction, including broad representations to deal with issues particular to the transaction in respect of which the buyer requires protection, providing in detail for the conditions which the buyer requires be satisfied before it will complete the transaction, providing the terms upon which the buyer will be indemnified if there are undisclosed liabilities or seller's representations turn out to be inaccurate (including how long those protections will continue post-closing, whether the buyer will be entitled to set off damages against amounts still owing to the seller, etc.), and so on. Indeed, if counsel for the seller prepares the first draft, experience dictates that the draft agreement will probably contain minimal representations inevitably leading to a longer negotiation process, which of course is not very practical.

It is also easier to negotiate from a position of having included a provision and reacting to opposing counsel who now will want to either remove or modify it, than from having to argue for the inclusion of a provision not already in the document. Indeed, it may be difficult for seller's counsel, even if careful and experienced, to identify certain nuances or biases that are built into the agreement from the beginning. Although one should not count on it, inexperienced counsel may underestimate the value of fighting to advance a new provision or concept or might not even be aware that the issue has not been addressed—out of sight, out of mind. The draftsperson also has the ability to internally structure the document and craft the language in a way that can make revising certain sections more difficult.

Another advantage of drafting the agreement is the ability to set the tone and the basic structure of the deal. For example, a draftsperson can signal an approach by how the representations are presented in the agreement. A draft that includes every representation known to mankind, whether relevant or not, and without any materiality or knowledge qualifiers, will signal something very different to the other side than an agreement that includes only those representations that are relevant to the particular transaction with some fairly typical materiality and knowledge qualifiers.

Establishing the Basic Structure

Can the first draft set the basic structure of the deal? Take for example the acquisition of the assets of a chain of retail stores that include a number of store leases. One approach would be to require that landlord consents be obtained with respect to each of those leases before the transaction can be completed. However, a buyer can establish a very different basic structure for that transaction if the first draft divides the leases into different categories: those leases where consents are required, those where there can be one or two for which consents are not required, and those where there is even more latitude. Obviously, the draft will also have to deal with the consequences if some of the consents are not obtained. This can, for instance, be dealt with in monetary terms without the entire deal collapsing if the seller is unable to obtain some of the less important consents.

Sources of Precedent

Once a decision has been made as to who will prepare the first draft, the draftsperson will be interested in accumulating helpful precedent. Whatever the form and terms of the acquisition, the organization of these agreements and the order in which the provisions appear is usually the same:

- deal provisions, including the structure, price, form of consideration, payment terms, and the time and place of the closing;
- representations of the parties, generally divided into representations of the seller and those of the buyer;
- covenants, including those pertaining to the period before the closing and those pertaining to the period after the closing;
- conditions to closing, consisting of conditions to both parties' obligations to close the transaction and conditions to each party's obligation to close;
- indemnification, allocating risk among the parties in a transaction involving a divestiture or a privately held target;
- termination, setting forth the circumstances in which the agreement may be terminated and the effect of termination; and
- miscellaneous or general provisions, containing terms that are generally applicable to commercial contracts.

While the organization of these agreements may be similar, the format, style, and prose of these and other business contracts varies considerably and, in the view of some, is in need of significant overhaul. At least one recent attempt has been made to aid the draftsperson and bring some consistency in contract drafting.[123]

Precedents for the agreement. While someone at some time must have drafted an acquisition agreement from scratch, every current agreement originates from something that exists, whether it be a standard or model form or an agreement from a prior deal. The draftsperson will consider the objectives to be achieved by the client against the form or agreement selected and begin the drafting process. The problem is that every form represents some bias—actual negotiated deals reflect the relative strengths and weaknesses of the parties and standard forms usually express a point of view on behalf of one of the parties to the transaction. In any event, more than changing the names and filling in the blanks is required.

A number of model or standard forms have been prepared for use by practitioners in M&A transactions. While all acquisition agreements have standard elements, stock purchases, asset purchases, and mergers usually originate from their own set of forms. The leading forms for two of the three transactions, the MSPA and MAPA, were prepared by the Committee on Negotiated Acquisitions of the Business Law Section of the ABA. Both publications are accompanied by a floppy disc. A form of merger agreement for public companies is currently being prepared by the Committee on Negotiated Acquisitions, and the MSPA is currently being revised.

These publications approach the model as a buyer's draft, although they are not totally one-sided. Some practitioners would comment that the forms have idiosyncrasies. Regardless of that, the cardinal rule should be to prepare an initial draft reflecting the client's objectives, so none of these should be used as a fill-in-the-blank type form.

Other publications contain forms of agreements. The last volume of *Mergers, Acquisitions, and Buyouts* includes forms in electronic format representing differing points of view and differing situations. For example, several of the forms include pro-seller, pro-buyer, and neutral versions. While these are helpful in pointing out where differences might lie, one should not take it as gospel that these represent precise lines of demarcation. Certainly other practitioners could have differing perspectives. That publication also contains forms dealing with subsidiary/ divisional divestitures.

Many law firms maintain their own set of standard forms, representing their approach to standard issues. While those forms normally are not published, the first draft received from one of these firms is often a close approximation of its standard form.

Similarly, many acquisitive companies have developed their own forms. A deal for one of these clients would usually begin with that form, unless the type of transaction varies substantially from the standard. The obvious virtue in using a standard form is that it is more likely to be understood by the client's businesspeople. If a client wants to use its own precedent, the lawyer might ask what worked and did not work in the deal involved.

The most common source of forms is one's own experience. Using agreements from one's own files can often be more efficient and produce better results because of the lawyer's familiarity with the transactions and the selection process, which leads to an appreciation of the workings and interrelationships of the various provisions of an agreement. Other lawyers in a firm also should be consulted, and may be able to contribute particularized forms. A search of the firm's file server may produce too many forms of unknown provenance—the lawyer involved in the transaction should be contacted before beginning use of such a form. It is sometimes difficult to adapt these forms to different industries and types of transactions. Whatever the source, too often the draftsperson will start with a signed agreement as the form and not go back to the first draft or otherwise back out the results of the negotiations. This is a good reason for retaining the first drafts of acquisition agreements in the firm database. Particularly embarrassing are the names and other identifiers that do not get changed in the draft.

The SEC's database (EDGAR) should not be overlooked as a source of forms. Since the SEC deals with public companies and only material agreements are required to be filed, it is a less than complete source. Use of the SEC's website usually requires identification of the sought after agreement through another means. Some search providers, such as LIVEDGAR, have put together a searchable M&A library with properly formatted electronic documents. EDGAR is probably more useful as a source of various clauses rather than the beginning point for a complete agreement.

Precedents for particular clauses. While the process of particularizing a document involves modifying existing clauses and approaches, often the representations are particularized by the target's industry, the buyer's concern about the target, and other factors. Even when a satisfactory form of agreement has been identified, the most experienced M&A attorney may still need precedents for particular clauses.

The usual suspects apply. Most lawyers search their own memory banks for applicable clauses or perhaps search the firm's file servers or ask colleagues. A client may have good precedent because the issues are often the same within an industry. Form books and current texts, particularly those used for continuing legal education, should not be overlooked. The CLE texts, if they contain forms, may be more current.

Because representations are a consistent component of many other types of agreements, those agreements may be a source of precedent. Financing agreements, in particular, such as underwriting agreements and loan agreements, may be a rich trove. These types of agreements, as well as acquisition agreements, are readily available through EDGAR, so a skillful search may locate good precedent. Vendor and customer agreements may also be a ready source, where an industry is subject to a broad regulatory scheme.

From time to time, widespread publicity may give rise to approaches to various clauses. For example, the decision in *IBP, Inc. v. Tyson Foods, Inc.*,[124] caused many to reevaluate clauses dealing with material adverse changes (or MAC clauses). Articles in various M&A publications may collect examples or suggest approaches to clauses unique to M&A transactions, such as MAC clauses, collars, walk rights, and other conceptual provisions.

Legal specialists often develop their own sets of representations, although it may be appropriate to assure that they fit the tone of the deal and are applicable to the form of the transaction (e.g., a broad ERISA representation may be condensed and more focused in an asset sale). Employee benefit, environmental, and intellectual property representations are often provided by specialty lawyers, although these will need to be tailored to the deal.

There may be other lawyers not directly involved in M&A deals having substantive knowledge of particular areas, such as litigators. While delegating the drafting of particular representations would not be done, they can often point to applicable laws to be complied with and suggest an approach to the representations.

Preparing the First Draft

Counsel preparing the first draft must make an effort to understand the transaction and any specific issues or concerns of the client. To understand the deal, the attorney should review the letter of intent, if one was created, or otherwise obtain the details from the client where an agreement in principle has been reached based on the parties' conversations. Although a close review of a letter of intent is important (particularly where the attorney was not involved), it is essential to listen closely and critically to the client's description of the terms of the deal and to be particularly attuned to any possible false expectations or misunderstandings by either party. At this early stage, a misunderstanding between the parties or unrealized expectations on the economics or structure can cause significant cost and delay, or even cause the deal to crater.

The attorney should endeavor to gather as much information and client feedback as possible before setting pen to paper. In doing so, the draftsperson should identify the business issues that need to be addressed in the document, whether there are any particular technical issues that need to be specifically addressed (for instance, a target business that is heavily dependent upon proprietary software will require far more detailed representations with respect to attributes of that software than a business that merely relies on "off the shelf" programs), as well as those issues that are particularly sensitive for these particular parties.

In general, a buyer will be focused on return on investment, but the acquisition could also be a strategic move to position the client for future growth or to keep a competitor out of a market. There is often a particular asset, product line or a key employee, customer or supplier that is critical to the client's deal. For the acquisition to be successful, the client may require certain accounting treatment of the deal, the ability to take advantage of the seller's tax attributes, such as net operating losses, or that the deal be completed by a certain date. Perhaps these parties previously dealt with each other in a similar transaction, in which case it might be helpful to see whether particular areas of concern had arisen as a result of those prior dealings. An attempt should be made to identify the relevant "hot buttons" to ensure that they are adequately covered in the draft and that the draft is carefully crafted to address them without triggering unintended reactions from the other side.

Ideally the first draft should not be completed until the buyer has conducted its due diligence. This timetable will enable the draftsperson to reflect the results of that due diligence in the draft agreement. Rather than including standard form representations, those relevant to what was learned in the course of due diligence can be modified to address the facts that actually exist. In addition, specific closing conditions might be introduced to address a state of affairs discovered during the course of due diligence.

As clients tend to be anxious to see progress, it is more often the case that the draftsperson is asked to prepare and deliver the first draft while due diligence is still being conducted or, sometimes, even before due diligence has begun. If counsel has not reviewed or even seen all of the due diligence materials, the client will need to weigh the risks and benefits of expediting the process by delivering to the other side a potentially incomplete draft against slowing the process down to ensure that all of the issues identified in due diligence have been addressed. If the decision is made to proceed with the drafting, the draftsperson will simply have to reflect as much of the results of the due diligence as are known at that time. Under these circumstances, it may be appropriate for the draftsperson to reserve the right to make further changes based on due diligence when the draft is distributed.

Deciding on the Approach

So how aggressive should the attorney be in preparing a first draft? It should come as no surprise that the answer to that question is not always the same. The circumstances of the particular transaction and the prevailing deal climate may assist in answering that question. For instance, if the buyer is the only one on the horizon and the seller has no other realistic choice than to sell the business and, in doing so, to sell to this buyer, the buyer's attorney can be more aggressive in the first draft and, thereafter, in deciding whether to concede some positions in the negotiations. On the other hand, if the client says that this is "the deal of a lifetime," there are several other potential buyers waiting in the wings and it can just as easily sell to someone else, then obviously an overly aggressive first draft runs the risk of sending a message that this buyer is either not really interested in the deal except on its terms, or that it will be exceedingly difficult to deal with, which could result in the seller going elsewhere before even bothering to respond to the draft.

In this context, the suggestion is often made that one should prepare and offer a reasonable first draft. That having been said, what is reasonable in the circumstances is in the eye of the beholder. Some will suggest that the draftsperson should not ask for something from the other party that he would not be prepared to give if asked for the same thing by that other party. That may be an overstatement, since it may be beneficial to include provisions for the purpose of setting up straw men for negotiation. What is important is whether the draft facilitates ultimate tradeoffs or poisons the well.

While a strident position taken in a negotiated deal may adversely affect how a deal goes forward—the contentious deal may not move forward—it may become even deadlier in an auction. The auction process is normally designed to separate the wheat from the chaff. A hard line position in a negotiated transaction may be perceived as grandstanding, but life goes on. A hard line position in an auction may disqualify a bidder in favor of more reasonable buyers. What becomes a driving factor for the seller is the perception of reasonableness.[125]

The buyer's first draft can range from being a middle of the road agreement to an over the top draft. Where a buyer's counsel starts will depend on a number of factors such as knowledge of the industry and business being acquired, relevant bargaining power, need to close quickly, desired reaction from the seller and its counsel, expected horse-trading, and so on. It is of course more time consuming and expensive to produce a thoughtful, narrowly tailored draft than it is to take the broadest, most comprehensive draft off the shelf and change the names, economic terms, and dates. The latter option will also not endear the buyer's counsel to the other side and may end up taking longer by provoking the seller to reject the entire document and demand a more reasonable first draft. This can also be a quick way of communicating to the other side that the buyer and its counsel do not know anything about the seller or its business. Presenting an agreement that attempts to deal with every conceivable concept, without stopping to consider whether they are relevant to the particular deal, will often lead to more protracted and difficult negotiations than might otherwise have occurred if the draftsperson had taken the time and care to craft a document that is specific to the actual transaction.

If a softer approach is taken, it is important to alert opposing counsel to the fact that the first draft may be revised as due diligence proceeds. It will, however, often be difficult to later tighten up a provision unless counsel can point to a material issue raised through due diligence or otherwise. The difficulty of later tightening up a provision may argue in favor of being more comprehensive in the first draft but conveying that the buyer is willing to discuss the provisions as due diligence proceeds.

When drafting the document, the attorney should also consider what on the surface appear to be contradictory approaches. Any negotiation consists of giving up something to get something. Depending on the circumstances (which might include time constraints, other potential buyers waiting in the wings and so on), the draftsperson might consider giving something up in the first draft in order to improve the chances of getting the deal done. At the same time, attorneys will often engage in "loss leader" drafting in which they intentionally include provisions that they are willing and able to compromise and that can later be traded for concessions by the other party.

Against all of that, the draftsperson must consider that it is possible one can go too far in advancing one's own position and prejudice negotiations. As indicated above, there is a risk that a poorly thought out, poorly presented document could result in loss of the deal. Although that is an extreme reaction, a more likely response is that less than reasonable provisions presented in the first draft may result in hardened positions being taken by those responding to the draft that will lead to longer, more difficult, and more expensive negotiations than might otherwise ensue from a more reasonable first draft.

One final point to note is that the approach to the first draft may change when the attorney and the client know with whom they are having the pleasure of dealing. Where parties have previously done deals together, the draft is more likely to reflect what the draftsperson and client know about the other party's predilections and sensitivities.

Arranging for Review Before Distribution

Once counsel is reasonably comfortable with the first draft, a decision must be made as to who should review the draft before it is distributed to the other side. Once again, time pressures may dictate the answer. If a junior member of the counsel's team has created the draft, the entire document probably should be reviewed by an attorney who is familiar with the terms of the deal and preferably also familiar with the client and its business. It is always helpful to have the client review the draft to ensure it reflects the client's wishes and to promote the early adoption of more reasonable positions that will expedite the negotiation process. At the very least, the attorney can sensitize the client to what the other party might be expected to raise in the context of particular provisions in the draft. The client may also choose to have particular sections of the agreement reviewed by employees in the organization who have specific knowledge of areas dealt with in the agreement. For instance, the client's environmental engineers may be asked to review the provisions that are intended to address environmental concerns.

The lead attorney should also consider having legal specialists within the attorney's firm or elsewhere review specific provisions. Depending on the structure and type of business, this might be more important in some areas than others. For example, where the tax treatment of the transaction is critical to the client, tax counsel will be asked to review the relevant provisions. Other areas in which issues often arise requiring a specialist include intellectual property, employee benefits, labor and employment, environmental, and so on.

There may also be other advisors who should review the draft prior to delivery to the other side, such as the client's auditors and investment bankers. The auditors may have useful comments to offer based on a knowledge of the client's business and industry, and of areas of sensitivity or potential exposure from auditing the client's financial statements and preparing its tax returns. The investment bankers can share their insight and make suggestions as to the use of language in the draft for posturing in anticipation of the eventual negotiations.

There is somewhat of a downside to a piecemeal review by specialists or other advisors in that often comments about particular provisions need to be put in perspective and considered in the context of the overall transaction and other provisions of the agreement. Thus, the lead attorney needs to carefully consider any comments to determine whether they are somehow addressed elsewhere in the document or, while of concern to the specialist, are otherwise toward the bottom on the scale of significance to the deal.

Distributing the First Draft

If the draftsperson and client are satisfied, the draft will be delivered to the other side. The easiest approach is to deliver the draft only to opposing counsel, who can then determine who else should review the draft. In many transactions, a distribution list will have been created for this purpose, in which case the draft can be sent directly to those on the list. The distribution list may be more narrow than a working group list, which may include persons or advisors who do not need to receive the first draft. A simultaneous distribution to everyone who needs to review the first draft will obviously speed up the process.

When the draft is actually delivered, it is often helpful to explain some of the draftsperson's or client's thinking in putting the draft together. This explanation may be a discussion of material issues that had not previously been addressed or certain assumptions on which the draft is based. Accompanying the draft with an explanation of the material issues or concerns may be crucial in keeping the tone of the negotiations positive. Often, the draftsperson will include bracketed sections, clauses, or even individual words. By bracketing them, counsel alerts everyone reviewing the draft that whatever is within the brackets is not set in stone and needs to be further reviewed or discussed. Often, bracketed materials are inserted as a place holder, i.e., an indicator that there is something that needs to be dealt with when the parties have more information or an opportunity to discuss the particular item. Sometimes, the draftsperson may also include bracketed or boldface notes or footnotes in the draft. A note or footnote is another way of signaling to anyone reviewing the document that there is something that needs to be further dealt with or may serve as an explanation for why a particular provision has been included.

If the client has not had adequate time to review the agreement prior to delivery to the opposing counsel, it may be appropriate to mention this point and reserve the right to make further changes and comments. Some counsel include that caveat automatically with the delivery of every single draft. While a reservation of rights is probably not critical, it does allow the client to make later revisions in good faith. Another advantage is that it may allow the client to back away from a provision by blaming the draftsperson if the opposing side reacts unfavorably.

The method of delivery is really a matter of convenience. Copies of the draft can be distributed by fax, mail, courier, or e-mail. Considerations such as confidentiality and whether all parties have access to e-mail or fax, timing concerns and the like, will usually dictate which method is used. Ideally, counsel will already have discussed and agreed upon the method to be used for the distribution of all drafts.

It is possible to provide access to draft documents by a centralized, secure website. This approach allows the draftsperson to deposit the draft into the website. All persons to whom the draft is to be distributed would have been registered and would already have their passwords enabling them to access the website. An e-mail alerts the parties when drafts are deposited. Comments and revisions can thereafter be dealt with through that website.

When documents are delivered by e-mail, the draftsperson should consider whether to attach a WordPerfect or Word version or whether to use a pdf version. The principal reason for using a pdf version is to maintain control over the document and force the other side to actually mark it up by handwritten changes and insertions, perhaps stifling comment. The ease of revision may encourage the other party to be overly aggressive in making the revisions. The usual response, however, is to ask for the document in a Word or Word Perfect format so that it can be more easily manipulated. Although many lawyers also assume that pdf versions cannot be further manipulated (which may or may not be a concern in the context of ongoing negotiations), modifications of a pdf document are possible with the more sophisticated programs.

Another advantage of using a pdf version is that when the document is printed, it will appear exactly the same for all recipients (e.g., page set ups will be the same for everyone). The fact that a pdf version will appear the same for every recipient should certainly be considered as the parties further refine the draft document so that when they circulate the version for execution, they are all dealing with a document that looks the same. If the parties are going to sign the document remotely and merely exchange signed counterpart versions, it is helpful if the versions that are exchanged all look the same.

Sometimes overlooked is the fact that the path on the document itself may unintentionally disclose information the draftsperson did not intend to disclose. For instance, a path that indicates that the draft being distributed is the fifth version of the document with a notation that it includes the client's comments (for example, v.05(with client comments).doc) might prove embarrassing to counsel who accompanies that draft with a statement that the client has not yet had an opportunity to review the draft and therefore counsel reserves the right to make further changes. Indeed, there might even be a circumstance where the client on whose behalf the draft has been prepared is prematurely identified by way of the path on the first draft document.

It is also important to consider the use of track changes in Word for redlining before the document is distributed. Because track changes shows various versions of drafts and other information on who is making changes, it can provide a window for the other side into the changes that went into a particular draft and the original precedent for a document. In addition to avoiding track changes, many lawyers use special software to remove so-called metadata from their Word documents. Metadata are invisible data embedded in a computer file that contain information about the file, including when the document was created, who created it, and when it was last modified. It also can reveal text and comments that have been deleted and the different versions of the document. In lieu of stripping out the metadata, it can be saved in a Rich Text Format, or rtf, or sent as a pdf file.

Reviewing and Responding to the First Draft

The first draft will represent a point of view and presumably is designed to achieve a client's ultimate objectives. Accordingly, the language in the draft will overstate the client's position to set up the negotiations. At this point, the draft will be reviewed by counsel on the other side and distributed for comment to the client, specialists and other advisors, much like the initial review of the first draft before it is distributed.

In reviewing the draft with the client, it is particularly helpful to be able to measure the client's objectives against particular provisions, rather than relying on the lawyer's own experience of what is customary. That form of review requires that the client understand the implications of the various provisions and that the lawyer understand the client's position. Too often that chasm is never bridged. Clients are often their own worst enemies, insisting that things be done much sooner than would permit a mutual understanding of objectives, having fallen under the influence of others who emphasize speed over protection. The lawyer may be able to comprehensively explain the operation of an indemnification clause, but if the client desires (or assumes) a risk-free deal, that may do little to advance understanding. Too often the lawyer will assume that an acquisition agreement is understood simply because it has been read by the client. Reading does not necessarily result in comprehension.

It may be tempting to go through the draft page by page, but by the third page, one is likely to have a bored and inattentive client. The most effective way of assuring there is an understanding is through a written outline of terms, or a written summary of what has been received, thoroughly discussed with the client, but that takes time. For the unsophisticated client, a more basic approach to the intricacies of how the agreement works is probably best. For the more experienced client, it may be only necessary to highlight unique points. Even if there is no detailed review, there should be a general understanding of how the agreement will be approached.

After this review and consultation, counsel usually will revise or mark-up the document to reflect the client's position on the various provisions. There then follows a discussion of the mark-up. Sometimes buyer's counsel will make requested changes that it believes are acceptable before the first negotiation occurs; in other instances, buyer's counsel, while readily willing to make the requested changes, will retain them as trade bait.

If it appears from a review that the first draft from the buyer is over the top or the parties are too far apart, a seller and its counsel might want to chose a different tactic. Marking up the agreement may imply concession to the process. Instead, the seller may want to vigorously contest some of the concepts in the agreement. This tactic can be accomplished by seller's counsel preparing an issues list with a statement of the client's position and rationale, and circulating it to the buyer's team. The hoped for result, from the seller's perspective, is that the fundamental issues are negotiated before the agreement is turned to, since resolution may have a ripple effect on the draft agreement. Another tactic, whether in combination or separate from presentation of an issues list, is to arrange a meeting of the parties to discuss their respective positions without the intervening mark-up. A meeting may be a somewhat inefficient way to negotiate because there are issues that the buyer might otherwise have readily conceded without sitting down and posturing.

Not unlike the thought process that went into preparation of a first draft, counsel must determine how aggressive to be in the mark-up. Will the response to the first draft be counsel's in-house form of the opposite persuasion (i.e., the first draft that seller's counsel would have prepared), or should there be an element of compromise? Or is an objectively reasonable first draft (to be sure all presenters of first drafts describe them as reasonable, even when they are blatantly not) taken as a sign of weakness and met with an unreasonable response? While it is probably demonstrable that an unreasonable first draft is likely to be met with an unreasonable response, will a reasonable first draft result in the return of a thoughtful and nuanced response? The proposition is difficult to prove, but desirable in terms of representing the interests of the parties.

In any event, the mark-up usually will also be an overstatement of the client's position— again a point of view designed to achieve the client's ultimate objectives and establishing the bid and asked for the eventual negotiations. Seller's counsel may also take a negotiating posture on its own by raising issues that it does not hope to ultimately win as trade bait for other issues it feels strongly about. Ultimately, this tactic may not prevail and by trying to inject needless issues, negotiations may be prolonged, increasing the risk that a deal will not be signed. But the tactic works frequently enough that it is a well-developed arrow in the quiver.

Determining what position to take in a mark-up may be particularly difficult where a potential bidder is asked to mark up a form agreement presented by the seller's counsel as part of an auction process. Depending on the strength of the price bid, a bidder may be reluctant to substitute a buyer-friendly form for what was offered, out of fear of being disqualified as a bidder. There is always a need to balance absolute legal protection with the need to continue in the process.

Again like the preparation of the first draft, counsel will probably want to compare various forms or precedents of agreements from other acquisitions and consult with the client, specialists and other advisors. In an acquisition by a publicly held company, it is often helpful to compare agreements that the acquiror had used in other acquisitions and filed with the Securities and Exchange Commission. Similarly, it can be helpful to review agreements that have been drafted by the law firm that is representing the other party. These might be available from colleagues in the law firm or listed in a transaction database.

Blacklining and Other Customs and Courtesies

It is customary for counsel presenting revisions of an agreement to present both a clean version and a blackline showing changes made. Blacklining typically shows both deletions and additions. Where automatic blacklining programs are used, what gets shown and how it is shown is simply a matter of the parameters selected by the draftsperson. In some cases, blacklines are offered in which additions are somehow marked (often by bolding or underlining) and deletions are merely marked by indicating where words or a clause have been deleted. This obviously requires the reviewer to compare this draft to the earlier draft in order to see exactly what has been deleted. Most of these programs also allow deletions to be shown by strikethrough or by showing the words deleted separately at the end of the document. Depending on the number of deletions within the document, strikethrough can be very cumbersome and make the document difficult to read.

Where revised versions are submitted by e-mail and in Word or WordPerfect format, the recipient can obviously make its own comparison and select whatever parameters it desires. It is also possible for a recipient to request that the draftsperson use the parameters that are best for that particular recipient. For instance, one attorney can ask for deletions shown by strikethrough in a document while another asks merely that deletions be shown without including the deleted words.

Where blacklines are prepared by automatic programs, one can also determine whether the current draft should be blacklined against the most recent draft, or whether it should be blacklined against a much earlier draft. Depending on who is receiving the revisions, it will be of assistance to determine the starting point for the blackline comparison. It is helpful for this reason alone to imprint as a header the date of the draft. Again, however, it is important that everyone know which blackline they are working with so that, if they are going to discuss specific provisions, they are all working with the same document. The need to prepare blacklines, and to sometimes prepare them against even earlier drafts for certain recipients, should make it evident that the draftsperson should retain separate versions of every single draft, even where blacklining against earlier drafts is not foreseen.

Whether counsel should rely on the blackline to show all the changes will to some extent depend on the degree of confidence in the person who prepared the blackline and the technology of the program. However, it is clear that in the fast pace of the M&A practice, parties are relying on these blacklines.

Finally, occasionally you will come across revisions marked manually the old-fashioned way, creating concerns for the reader that a change or deletion may have been missed, through human error or worse.

Negotiating the Agreement

As might be expected, many of the elements and techniques of negotiating an acquisition agreement are not unlike those involved in negotiating the price, basic terms, and structure of an acquisition as discussed in Chapter 8. Nevertheless, it is well worth covering some of this ground again and relating it to the acquisition agreement.

Obtaining client direction for the negotiations over the acquisition agreement may not be easy. Even if the objectives are clear (which rarely is the case since there are always tradeoffs), the tactics are variable. Even if the tactics are clear, who is to implement the tactics? It may be the principal or one of a number of advisors. Nevertheless, prioritizing concerns, understanding whether the client wants to take a particular approach and understanding the absolutes are essential before the negotiation process is begun.

There is no good way to handle this issue. Lawyers struggle to do the best they can under the circumstances. Sometimes lawyers will simply stake out a position in the first draft or mark-up utilizing an understanding of acceptable practices. That may produce a resolution. If buyer's counsel prepares the first draft and it remains unchanged, there is nothing to discuss. Once the issues are framed, it becomes much easier to counsel the client on the implications of the opposing positions. How this gets sorted out is highly variable, depending on the working relationship between client and lawyer, whether legal or business issues are being negotiated, the relative bargaining strengths and risk tolerance of the parties and other factors.

Who Will Negotiate the Terms?

Who will be negotiating what issues depends on numerous factors, such as the stage of negotiations, whether other professionals are involved, the experience of the principals and what is being negotiated. The most important term, being the price, will probably have been negotiated by the principals or their advisors at the outset. Other substantive terms may or may not have been negotiated or included in a letter of intent. The question then becomes who will handle those negotiations.

As a matter of negotiating strategy, it is often thought best not to involve the ultimate decision maker for the client. In that way, a negotiator backed into a corner can always escape a concession by deferring to an absent decision maker or can make a concession, dependant upon the decision maker's agreement. Further, upon reflection, if a position was erroneously conceded during negotiations, it may cost less to renegotiate the point on the basis that an absent decision maker countermanded the decision rather than the negotiator had second thoughts. It may be that for certain issues (such as price), the decision maker is simply the most forceful negotiator. However, the client may want the lawyer or another advisor to lead the negotiations so that the client can make appropriate concessions or perhaps signal intransigence on a particular point important to the client.

The question of who negotiates the agreement usually gets sorted out quite easily. It is largely a matter of style, experience, and practice. If the client has a corporate development group, it might be expected to assume responsibility for not only price but also significant terms of the acquisition agreement. Clients and investment banks may feel quite strongly about being involved in the negotiation of the economic and business terms, and less inclined to insert themselves in the more legalistic portions of the document. While it is tempting to divide the acquisition agreement between legal and economic or business points, there is no clear division. Often many of the details of the acquisition agreement are thought to be legal in nature and are negotiated by the lawyers. But anything smacking of business may be fair game for either lawyers or businesspeople to negotiate.

Is it a Business, Legal, Economic, or Deal Issue and Who Cares?

There is no clear demarcation among these issues. When the lawyer is the negotiator for a deal, the legal issues are likely those that his principal is willing to leave to the lawyer and not necessarily those requiring a law degree and lawyering experience to address.

Often a non-lawyer client with considerable experience in buying and selling businesses will have strong views on components of the acquisition agreement (e.g., the basket, survival period, termination clauses). Inexperienced participants in an M&A deal may not even anticipate these are issues and will look to the lawyer to decide or require a tutorial to understand.

The seller of a manufacturing unit in a management buyout was represented in the negotiations by one of its in-house counsel. He would dig in his heels on every issue that was raised each week by the buyer, the management team and the lenders until Friday afternoon when the lawyers and principals would have a conference call to break the logjam. One week the group plowed through an agenda of 47 issues, 43 of which the seller CEO resolved against his lawyer. After the principals disconnected from the call, the seller's attorney commented, "That went fairly well, the CEO usually cuts my legs out from under me." The other lawyers on the deal later grumbled that the process would move more quickly if the

> seller's counsel had a better sense of his client's objectives or was replaced at the table by someone with greater authority to resolve issues.

It is not unusual for negotiation of particular portions of an acquisition agreement to be relegated to legal specialists. This is particularly the case when covenants relate to post-closing activities or elections. If, for example, a Section 338(h)(10) election is to be made (treating a stock sale as an asset sale), the implications of that election are usually worked out by tax lawyers.[126] Matters with respect to benefit plans are usually worked out by ERISA lawyers.

A fundamental problem with this delegation is that these specialty lawyers may not be aware of a client's overall objectives and may negotiate within their own spheres of truth rather than the give-and-take of most transactional practice. Most experienced transaction lawyers develop a sense of how these provisions should be negotiated even though they may not be experts in the particular field and will provide guidance and supervision to their specialist peers. The best practice is usually to make sure that the specialists understand the overall objectives and avoid getting too far out on a limb.

Coordinating the Negotiations

Lawyers will almost always be involved to some extent in the negotiations, and where the client or other advisors are also playing a role, the lawyers can participate by strategizing and co-ordinating the negotiations. The lawyer's approach may depend on whether those who can make decisions are sitting at the negotiating table or participating in the conference call.

If the decision maker is not present, it is expected that the lawyers or others doing the negotiating will have some authority over the issues that are being negotiated—that is, the purpose of the negotiation is not to assemble a list of issues to send back to the principals, but to try to resolve issues, utilizing the list for those issues on which resolution cannot be reached. There are some issues for which they would not expect to have authorization (e.g., price), while with other issues there may be little doubt (e.g., legal language, the wording of legal opinions or the scope of title representations). Accordingly, they would be expected to commit on some issues and reserve on other issues, subject to client direction.

To be sure, even a negotiator with authority may not want to make a commitment on behalf of a principal, instead seeking clarification of the issue so that it can be presented to the principal. Even concessions made by the negotiator can be countermanded by the principal—one of the primary reasons not to have principals involved in negotiations. In general, there is no binding agreement until there is final agreement on all points and the parties have executed the written agreement.[127] While it may be possible to backtrack, this is not a good negotiating philosophy when done in excess, but it sometimes happens. There may be a tremendous cost in doing so because ultimately it means that the negotiator cannot be trusted and that may encourage the other side not to candidly concede its position to reach a compromise.

If the principals are present, negotiations become trickier. Even with the decision maker present, others (such as the lawyers or investment banks) may be the primary negotiators. Nevertheless, principals often join in to move things along. The problem is that they may suggest compromises without fully understanding the implications. Even when a principal is participating only to resolve issues, communications are awkward. Counsel might ask to confer with the principal separately, but frequent conferences disrupt the flow of negotiations and perhaps signal too much about particular types of concerns. Sometimes counsel must boldly interrupt and caution the client against making a particular concession.

How and Where Negotiations Occur

There is no standard practice for how and where to conduct the negotiations. There are a variety of formats that are in common use today, all of which may be used at various times in a particular transaction:

- face-to-face meetings;
- conference telephone calls (occasionally videoconferences);
- e-mail exchanges (with or without attachments); and
- trading of revisions and mark-ups.

Before conference telephone capabilities, faxes, overnight couriers, and e-mail, virtually all negotiations were face-to-face as a matter of necessity. There are often compelling reasons for meeting face-to-face, at least once, but there are also reasons for not doing so. Travel remains expensive and tends to slow down the process. Today, unless a buyer and seller are in the same general area, face-to-face negotiation of the business terms will be somewhat limited. Usually, there are a series of calls and drafts of letters of intent exchanged by some electronic means. But these techniques may or may not lend themselves to negotiation of a much longer acquisition agreement. Certainly when it comes to final details, conference calls, and e-mail exchanges may be far more efficient.

When there is a revision of the agreement or a mark-up (most often when the comments are minor) they are usually sent by scanning the document as a pdf file and then e-mailing it (less frequently, by faxing it). Copying the document and sending it by overnight courier only rarely occurs today and only by counsel that is technologically challenged. Proposed inserts can be included in an e-mail or as an attachment or can be sent by fax.

It seems that it has become an accepted practice to negotiate commercial agreements by an interminable interchange of e-mails. Whatever the wisdom of this practice, it is not something usually done in an M&A context—the documents are too long, there are too many tradeoffs and the issues are far too complex. The technique might be used, however, in negotiating a particular clause.

Resolving Issues

If the mark-up approach to negotiation is used, there is a clear bid and asked on particular points throughout the document. The totality of the respective positions is known. Having identified the issues, there are probably two ways to resolve them, to take the document from the first page to the last or to attempt to hit the major issues first. While it may be desirable to hit the major issues while everyone is fresh with lots of energy, far more often the acquisition agreement is discussed page by page and the issues one by one. Sometimes there is a ready concession (such as to correct an error) or where the point is trivial. For something more material, the parties might mockingly keep score of the concessions (although they probably really mean it). Certain issues are inevitably reserved as being too important to be conceded or on the basis that one side wants to understand the totality of the sticking points before coming to an agreement.

While it is customary to resolve issues one by one, that is not necessarily logically appropriate or desirable from a negotiating perspective. Group dynamics, bargaining power or other factors may mean that one side may loose a series of one-by-one points, receiving no credit at all for its position. On the other hand, attempting to reserve all points for some future tradeoff is just not practical. Negotiators attempt to reserve certain issues for this very purpose, arranging tradeoffs of groups of issues for one or a group of another issues. Sometimes it is not necessary to explicitly reserve issues when there are tradeoffs within provisions related in concept and proximity ("We will agree to the $10,000,000 cap if you agree to the $100,000 basket"). Issues are also reserved for resolution by decision-makers, usually because of their magnitude or simply to avoid conceding them at the time.

A skillful negotiator only concedes important issues in return for something. There may be an appropriate time to concede. Often several sets of issues are being reserved, some more important than others. Some issues may be conceded periodically, such as when all of the representations have been discussed. Other issues, such as business issues, may be reserved until after the meeting or for the end of the meeting. It is not unusual at the end of the day or the end of negotiations for one party to put a proposition on the table, offering to compromise a series of positions, by retaining the initial position on some, conceding the point on others, and suggesting an intermediate ground on yet others. Often it is the primary business negotiator or the lawyer on behalf of the client who offers these points.

Sometimes there is the hopeful theory that business issues will be negotiated in plenary session, while the lawyers will then negotiate legal issues separately. Often that does not work. It is difficult to isolate the business and legal issues. Even when some artificial demarcation is made, the lawyers may not be able to successfully reach a resolution. Sometimes, without the bargaining chip of business issues, it is difficult to resolve legal issues; and lawyers, reluctant to make concessions, do not.

Isolated provisions need to be looked at in the context of the agreement. In an agreement in which the basket would appear to cover a multitude of sins and the conditions of closing are loose, the tightness of a particular representation may be of less concern to a seller. It is important to step back and determine what is significant, not just to take the position that material must be inserted at least 50 places for seller's counsel to be effective.

While raising issues to gain leverage has some risk, depending on the sophistication of the other side, there may be a large cost when the issues raised are only many nits divorced from business reality. There is often enormous cost involved in dealing with the inexperienced deal counsel (often representing a seller) who under the guise of protecting the client objects to virtually every provision of the agreement.

Negotiating Tactics

Numerous books and seminars emphasize reaching agreement in negotiations.[128] Often lawyers are viewed as deal killers by the positions they take in negotiations. What position should lawyers take and how should they go about it? Above all, lawyers should represent their clients' interests. Presuming to understand what clients would like to accomplish is always dangerous. But it may be that clients do not understand either the positions they are too willing to concede or that tactics are necessary to end up in a superior position.

Above all else, the lawyer must comport with professional ethics and should demonstrate professionalism. That means that outright lying is unacceptable, but that hyperbole is not. Adequately representing a client means more than "Getting to No." It is important to be able to articulate reasons, not just positions. Explanations may help suggest solutions or, when said, demonstrate that the position is unsound or overstated. A skillful negotiator realizes that a seller is not at the bargaining table *not* to sell a business. Instead, the negotiator attempts to find a position for completing the sale and protecting the client's position.

Usually theatrics, such as the threat of walking, should be avoided. Often they are not credible, particularly when used repeatedly. Displays of emotion usually should be avoided as well. A principled, rational articulation of positions, even when the response appears to evince a misunderstanding, is almost always better. That is not to say that an occasional dramatic statement or even a slight display of frustration would be inappropriate, and it simply may happen.

A skillful negotiator will quickly identify particular concerns that are more important to the other side than others and what pressure points may be brought to bear in the negotiations.

Iterative Process

The usual process of negotiating an acquisition agreement is iterative. Redrafts are prepared in response to the first series of negotiations. There is a discussion of the redraft. The resolution of some issues is discussed. What did the parties really agree to? Does the language reflect that agreement? One side or the other will have control over the draft of the document. Lawyers often trust the ultimate drafter of a document to reflect in a revision the negotiated concept. It usually does not happen that way. In preparing the revisions, even a lawyer trying to be objective will usually reflect the client's perspective. New issues may have developed, either because one party thought the better of some provision (or just thought about it), or due diligence has revealed the issue, or because the party has rethought an earlier concession. Issues that had been reserved may be discussed again, or issues decided by someone outside the negotiating group may be discussed (what did they really decide?). Another draft is called for.

And so the process goes. Ideally each round reduces the gap between the parties. A relapse may occur. The process can go on for numerous rounds. There is a downside to shuffling drafts back and forth. It often becomes a battle of the forms—my form versus your form—and bulk replaces discourse and thought. To be sure, in negotiating, parties can always suggest alternative language, perhaps by providing the other side a draft of acceptable language. That is often far preferable to endless discussion about concepts or nuances, with the person in control of the document left to work out the language, perhaps imperfectly, engendering another round of discussions. Often the recipient of a rider is quite willing, having looked at the proposed language, to just accept the wording or concept.

Electronically revising the document is the equivalent of providing riders. All too often, however, those providing an electronic revision are undisciplined in their approach. The changes become so overwhelming that they distract from the true issues. A younger lawyer, charged with reviewing the document and attempting to demonstrate prowess, might go overboard with changes that could not possibly matter or reflect a particular style or approach used by that firm over the equivalent presented (this also happens in the word processing or secretarial level where stylistic changes are made to reflect the practices of the firm marking up the document). These changes may have the effect of inhibiting discussions. The receiving lawyer may be angered by an attempt to substitute one style for another or may just decide that sorting out what is a meritorious change from the garbage is just too hard.

In sending out an electronic revision of an agreement, thought needs to be given to the impression that the recipient might gain and what might be done to better inform the recipient of the nature of the changes. For example, a cover e-mail provides an opportunity to explain larger issues (or at least through bullet points identify the overarching concerns). Sometimes revisions are sent out without all of the issues addressed by a change to the language. Rather than allowing the other side to draw the worst inferences when a section that has been discussed remains unchanged, bracketed language might be included to indicate that a particular issue is under review, perhaps outlining a possible compromise or approach. In that way, there is communication about a compromise, and a knee-jerk reaction—to offer up the same language apparently rejected by the lack of change—can be avoided. The same technique may be used to convey other information. For example if some language has been left intact but moved to another place in the document, standard blacklining programs make it appear that the language has been deleted. Adding a bracketed explanation that the language has simply been moved may be helpful to the recipient.

Regardless of whether the positions of the parties may be unreasonable, many deal counsel believe that their job is to attempt to reach a negotiated position through the education of both their clients and the opposing side about various concerns rather than by table pounding. Face-to-face meetings provide the greatest opportunity to do so—raw responsive language usually does not tell a story.

It is possible to work around the need for the continual circulation of drafts. In situations where face-to-face meetings have been eschewed, the telephone remains an instrument of moderation. Even one-on-one e-mails (that is without cc's to the entire working group), while less desirable, also remain a possibility.

How Negotiations Are Broken Off

Frequently the parties simply drift apart. The responses become slower, diminishing to non-existent. A party may say that it has its position under advisement. Sometimes the breakup will be more dramatic—the summit meeting in which one party summarizes its major issues with the expectation that they be conceded. When they are not, the breakdown is inevitable. Sometimes the breakup is sharp and one party may simply advise the other party that the negotiations are over. Negotiations may have been broken off for dramatic effect—to get the other side to understand the depth of feeling associated with the party's position. In that case, there is always the hope that reality will set in and the negotiations can be rekindled with a fresh start.

Even when the break off is serious, it may not stop a party from attempting to restart the negotiations, particularly if alternatives (such as a sale to others) have been pursued unsuccessfully. Of course, it usually results in a substantial change in the economic terms.

How Negotiations Are Successfully Concluded

The objective of negotiations is a signed acquisition agreement. At some point in time, the parties realize that they are separated only by a few details—perhaps a few provisions in the agreement, the negotiation of ancillary documents or the preparation of schedules. There may be a final push to have everything concluded, including working long into the night as information is exchanged, negotiated, tweaked. Often a signature page may be lodged with counsel, to be faxed off once agreement is reached, with the understanding that the signature page is meant to be attached to the finally negotiated agreement. It is becoming unusual for the parties to meet in a signing ceremony to finalize an acquisition agreement, although some clients will prefer the ceremonial nature of this process or simply view it as an opportunity to again meet face-to-face.

Recurring Issues in an Agreement

In negotiating an acquisition agreement, practitioners find there are recurring issues that are present in almost every deal and relate to many portions of the document. Because, at least historically, a buyer prepares the first draft, negotiators, not entirely able to reject the draft, have developed ways to limit or qualify what a buyer requires, in order to provide, at least from the seller's perspective, a more balanced document. The purpose of the discussion below is not to suggest the substance of what should be negotiated, or to suggest how or what to negotiate. Instead, it is to identify some of the issues, words and concepts that lawyers use in negotiating acquisition agreements and some points of contention frequently faced.[129] It is not preordained that deals have to be negotiated or documented in certain ways, so there are certainly many other issues that need to be negotiated and many variations in what is discussed.

The Parties

Necessary parties. Who are the parties to the acquisition agreement and what are their respective responsibilities? In private deals, particularly when there are a limited number of sellers who are all active in the business, a buyer would like all the sellers to stand behind the contract. If it is a stock acquisition, that happens by virtue of the structure of the transaction because they are the sellers of the stock. Even though the target is not a necessary party to an agreement for a stock acquisition, the buyer may want to add it as a party because it believes it can more directly bind the pre-closing activities of the target. The shareholders also may feel more comfortable in having the target make representations (about which they have no knowledge), even though they will stand behind those representations. This approach requires some careful drafting. The agreement should be clear that the target's liability to the buyer disappears at closing, that the buyer may look to the shareholders directly and that the shareholders agree not to make any claim against the target for any false representations it may have made.

In some deals the prospective buyer which has been negotiating with the seller may be a substantial business with significant assets but structures the deal so that the actual buyer party to the acquisition agreement is a shell subsidiary with no significant assets. In these circumstances the seller may well want to seek to have the parent company join in the agreement or guarantee the obligations of its subsidiary under the agreement.

In an asset acquisition or a merger, in which the target itself is a party, the shareholders are not necessary parties but they may nevertheless be asked to stand behind the target's representations and obligations. This can be accomplished by making them parties to the acquisition agreement or binding them through a separate joinder agreement, whereby they are bound without executing the acquisition agreement through enabling language in the acquisition agreement.

Joint and several. A buyer would like the liability of the responsible parties, either as a direct seller (in a stock purchase) or as a shareholder (in a merger or asset purchase), to be joint and several, so that it may pursue one or a small number of parties to get complete relief, rather than suing a number of parties over whom it may have some difficulty in gaining jurisdiction. Shareholders will assert that any liability should be proportionate to their holdings. In situations where shareholders are active in the business, buyers usually prevail. Where shareholders include both active and passive investors (particularly when holdings are modest), some of them may not face joint and several liability, although the buyer would hope to retain this right over a few major players.

Conventions

Defined terms. The use of defined terms has become accepted practice in contract drafting. To make it clear that a word or phrase has been defined, it normally appears in initial caps (*e.g.*, Net Worth). Historically, terms that are used again would be defined within the sentence in which they were first used ("THIS STOCK ACQUISITION AGREEMENT (the "Agreement") is made by . . ."). As acquisition agreements became longer, it became customary to include as the first or second article (or in a separate appendix) the definitions of terms that are used frequently throughout the document. However, it is still customary to define certain terms in context, in which case the usual practice is for a listing of defined terms to refer to that definition ("'Agreement' has the meaning set forth in the preamble").

The defined terms applied to the parties in any agreement varies. Further, if the target is being acquired in a merger or is the subject of a stock acquisition, it may be referred to as the "Company" (and sometimes that convention carries over to an asset acquisition agreement where the target is actually the seller). Sometimes it is "Buyer" (not preceded by the) while others specify the "Buyer" (with a concomitant application to the seller). Sometimes, to make it clear when there is a defined term, the defined term is italicized, boldfaced or underscored, (e.g., "THIS STOCK ACQUISITION AGREEMENT (the '*Agreement*')"). The convention also is that the defined term does not include the article "the" within the quotation, even when "the" would always precede the defined term in usage (*e.g.*, such as use of "Company"). Sometimes, a defined term is merely included parenthetically without the quotes (e.g., "THIS STOCK ACQUISITION AGREEMENT (Agreement) is made by . . .").

Subdivisions. It is customary to divide an acquisition agreement into major divisions, united in theme, typically at most a dozen, rather than to have sections run concurrently, as one might see in a commercial agreement. For example, the seller's representations might all be found in the same division, with the buyer's representations found in a separate division. It is not important what the division is called. Some drafters refer to "articles" (with subdivisions being "sections") while others refer to "sections" (with subdivisions being "subsections" although frequently referred to as "sections"). Thus Article 4 might have as its first division Section 4.1, while Section 4 might have as its first division Section 4.1. Often the specific designation is not included before the numeration (just 4.1, not Section 4.1). Many different numbering schemes are used.

Schedules. Because an acquisition agreement is about buying a business, it needs to contain information about the business being purchased. While it would be possible to include that information in the body of the agreement (and that is sometimes done), generally factual information is developed by others in a different timeframe from the drafting of the main agreement and is included in schedules. The information may be presented affirmatively (listing schedules, such as "All material Contracts are listed on Schedule 3.10") or negatively (exception schedules, such as "Except as set forth on schedule 3.14, no litigation is pending against the Company"). As a consequence, it is customary to include factual information on separate schedules and to refer to those schedules in the agreement. Schedules are also typically used to set forth exceptions to the representations. A discussion of the use and preparation of schedules appears later in this chapter.

Exhibits. Exhibits are often used to attach to the acquisition agreement other ancillary agreements to be entered into at or prior to the closing, such as leases or employment agreements. A discussion of some of these ancillary agreements appears later in this chapter.

Captions, tables of contents and key lists. Because of their length, acquisition agreements almost always use captions for various divisions (articles, sections or others) and include a table of contents. It is becoming increasingly common for the table of contents to be followed by a list of exhibits, a list of schedules and a list of (and cross reference to) defined terms.

Exceptions and Qualifiers

There are recurring exceptions and qualifications to representations and covenants, and common concepts used throughout an acquisition agreement. Some of these will be discussed below. At some point in time the use of qualifiers to representations and covenants comes quite naturally. The buyer who wants the representation that seller is "in compliance with" may be countered with a representation that seller is "in material compliance with." Some of these qualifiers may be defined, while others are not.

Use of qualifiers. Buyers customarily receive representations that allow exceptions for trivialities. No target is perfect and no buyer would expect that to be the case. Buyers for the most part are expecting only something reasonably close to perfect. Anything else would probably not be truthful or require niggling detail in the schedules. However, broad exceptions to some representations are often perceived as the exception that swallowed the whole and raise hackles with buyers.

Knowledge. When only third parties may know the truth of a particular representation, a seller will often seek a knowledge exception. It may insist that to the extent third parties know such information but not by the seller, it is unfair to impose that knowledge on the seller. A buyer may insist that the seller be responsible for what employees know or that in any event, as a matter of risk allocation, the risk should be that of the seller, which is in a superior position to know the truth of the representation and in any event should be responsible if the representation is not true. To the extent third parties would know such information, a buyer may still insist that as a matter of risk allocation the risk should be that of the seller. There is no way to predict how the negotiation of any particular exception will come out, but suffice to say that it is customary to see several knowledge exceptions in even the most tightly crafted agreement.

Sellers will insist that knowledge needs to be precisely defined. It should not be anyone's knowledge, but only the knowledge of a select group of responsible individuals (e.g., officers and senior managers). Buyers may insist on some level of diligence (e.g., after reasonable investigation) if they will accept such a limitation. Other formulations and negotiations are possible. The end of this process is a definition of knowledge.

Material. A typical agreement finds the material exception sprinkled throughout ("The Company is in compliance with all material Contracts"). What exactly does that mean? What is an immaterial Contract? Why not a flat representation to compliance with all agreements without this limitation? How does material relate to in all material respects?

Despite the inherent ambiguity of the word material, it is an expression with which lawyers are comfortable. Nevertheless, at least in private deals, lawyers often do not rely on the fact that there is a common understanding (or that the ambiguity will always induce a seller to err on the side of caution) and provide a determinable standard when there is any possibility that something may be material. It has been more common to particularize some classes of documents or litigation to assure that disclosure is made. A buyer may insist that, rather than a listing of all material contracts, that there be a listing of all contracts not cancelable within a specified period, of a certain dollar amount or of a particular type (such as financings). Rather than a listing of material litigation, a buyer may require a listing of litigation where the claim exceeds a specified dollar amount.

In all material respects. The phrase "in all material respects" usually applies to actions taken or omitted, while material usually refers to a thing, such as a statute or property. Its use peppers most acquisition agreements ("The Company has complied in all material respects with all applicable laws"). As a practical matter, buyers understand that there will always be immaterial breaches of law and of contract. Those misdeeds may not even be actionable.

There typically is no formulation of what in all material respects means. Buyers may have a higher degree of concern over some matters than others, and may not permit an exception where the matter is important and wholly within the control of the seller. For example, a representation with respect to compliance with a target's charter documents would usually be unqualified.

MAC/MAE clauses. The concept of a MAC clause is essential to M&A practice because of the broadness of the exception it creates. The concept is not regularly used in agreements for other types of transactions. Sometimes a MAE clause is used. MAC stands for material adverse change, while MAE stands for material adverse effect.

This clause has a number of functions. It is usually first encountered (at least in public company deals) as an exception to a representation. A buyer may request a representation that a target company is qualified to do business in every jurisdiction where it is required to be so qualified. Because of the relative unimportance of this representation, a target may request some wiggle room with respect to the absolute nature of the representation, because, in practice, many corporations (and in particular insignificant subsidiaries) may not comply literally with this requirement. The target may therefore request that the representation be modified to say that it is qualified to do business "except where the failure to so qualify, individually or in the aggregate, would not have a Material Adverse Effect on the Company."

The clause also has use as a measure of conduct, not merely an exception to a representation. A buyer would commonly ask for a seller to represent that "The Company has not suffered any Material Adverse Change since December 31, _____ [often the date of the most recent audited balance sheet]." Another use is as a condition ("The Company shall not have suffered any Material Adverse Change since the date of this Agreement").

The complete meaning of a MAC clause and how it is negotiated are far beyond this discussion. A typical beginning point would be to define a MAC as "a material adverse change in the Company's assets, financial condition, operations, results of operations or prospects." A seller would object to this formulation, insisting that prospects is too indefinite and too forward looking. It may also suggest certain developments that will be defined *not* to constitute a MAC (such as changes in general economic conditions or conditions within a particular industry).

Best efforts. Most acquisition agreements contemplate some lapse of time between signing and the actual closing, normally to permit certain conditions to be satisfied, some of which require third party action. Most buyers and sellers will want to increase the probability that these conditions will be satisfied. A flat agreement to cause a condition to be satisfied would subject the contracting party to liability if the condition were not satisfied. Most parties will not want to take the risk when the ultimate action is beyond their control. But they will agree to take some quantum of action toward assuring that the condition will be satisfied, normally referred to as the best efforts obligation, such as "The Company will use its best efforts to obtain the Consents listed on Schedule 7.1."

An agreement to use one's best efforts is a high standard, but its parameters are somewhat fuzzy. Often there are attempts to limit both ends of the spectrum, particularly in the antitrust area. For example, a buyer may propose that in using its own best efforts it is not required to dispose of any of its remaining businesses. Or a seller could impose an affirmative requirement that the buyer agree to resell a certain portion of the acquired business in order to obtain antitrust approvals. Another example relates to obtaining consents: a seller might negotiate a provision that it not be required to pay any money, while a buyer might seek a clause that requires the seller to pay money (up to a cap), particularly when it is known that fees must be paid to software licensors.

The historic best efforts is often supplanted by another formulation such as reasonable efforts. Great angst has arisen because of the apparent urban myth that best efforts gives rise to an obligation to spend the agreeing party into bankruptcy to achieve a given result. Because most practitioners always believed that best efforts had a rule of reason associated with it, often the concession to include a phrase with reasonable in it is made without much protest.

Attempts to define best efforts may not be successful because they often use similarly vague language, although it may help to alleviate concern about the extreme views of what might be required. The use of different formulations of the standard in the same document (such as best efforts and commercially reasonable efforts) without definition may be unwise, because a court may infer a greater difference in the standards than otherwise would have been expected.

Ordinary course of business. There are a number of places throughout an acquisition agreement where the term "ordinary course of business" is used in an attempt to distinguish between major and routine matters affecting the business. For example, the consent of the buyer may be needed for certain actions of the target other than in the ordinary course of business. In some agreements, an attempt is made to provide greater specificity for this term.[130]

Representations

The concern about the representations is essentially two fold: that they may create liability if they are incorrect when made, and that, because a usual closing condition is that the representations be true as though made as of the closing date, a closing condition will not be satisfied.

A seller might express concern with respect to litigation, that, if a schedule is required to list litigation and an immaterial piece of litigation arises after signing but before closing, the condition of closing would not be satisfied because there would be pending litigation not on the schedule. It may therefore propose that the representation be limited to litigation pending "as of the date of this Agreement." Such a representation would not pose an obstacle to a seller in the face of subsequent litigation because it will remain true at closing. But that is of little comfort to the buyer if the subsequent litigation is of the bet-the-company variety. The seller's request is not unreasonable, but the buyer's concern is also legitimate. It probably means that another condition will need to be included dealing with material but undisclosed litigation that exists at closing. A more flexible standard to accommodate both buyer and seller concerns may be appropriate.

Pre-Closing Covenants

Pre-closing covenants are designed primarily to assure that the conditions of closing are satisfied and that the status quo is preserved in the interim.

There are a surprising number of variations in limiting pre-closing operations of the target. Some covenants are brief, some are detailed. There usually are affirmative covenants, negative covenants and notification requirements. The affirmative covenants usually provide for operation in the ordinary course and compliance with law and contractual obligations. The negative covenants often go on indefinitely with a list of things the target may not do. Sometimes a qualification is offered up ("without the consent of Buyer" or "without the consent of Buyer, which shall not be unreasonably withheld").

The general best efforts clause (to cause the conditions to be satisfied) is usually supplemented with a series of more nuanced requirements pertaining to particular areas. Thus there may be a flat requirement to call a shareholders' meeting and to make HSR filings within a specified time period. The best efforts clause with respect to certain activities may specify the minimum and maximum to be done, particularly in the antitrust area, as discussed above.

Post-Closing Covenants

Post-closing agreements are expected except in public company deals (where the target becomes a part of buyer and the shareholders are the public at large). Such agreements range from the modest (further assurances as to property transferred) to the essentials of protecting the goodwill of the business purchased (non-competes).

A well-meaning seller may attempt to contractually protect various constituencies (such as employees) by purporting to require the buyer to do (or refrain from doing) certain things. Despite the clear attempt to protect third parties, even if they agree to the covenant, most buyers will insist that the contract specifically provide that no third-party rights are being created. Occasionally a seller will prevail in getting specific recognition of third-party rights (in that instance, the question of how those rights can be modified short of consent of every employee may be relevant). If explicit third-party rights are not created, it is not clear how a seller would enforce the covenants (or indeed would really have any interest in doing so). There nevertheless is some power to these provisions, at least a moral obligation and probably a recognition that a failure to honor the agreement would result in employee mutiny.[131]

Almost every acquisition agreement will address employees and their benefits in some fashion, even if negatively ("Buyer has no obligation to hire any employee of Seller"). The most common forms are a no-layoff policy (for some period of time) and a no-reduction in pay (for some period of time). Exceptions would include termination for cause or based on a downturn in the financial performance of the business. A seller may try to impose its benefit program on the buyer; a buyer (particularly a strategic buyer) will always resist because it will want to substitute its own programs. Sometimes a buyer will agree to provide benefits "substantially similar in the aggregate" to those provided by a seller, but usually only because it is in its best interest to do so in approaching integration issues.

Covenants related specifically to the scope of the acquisition agreement typically are found in the agreement itself. For example, post-closing access, assurances, and cooperation would typically be part of the main agreement. Covenants not to compete might be included in both a seller of assets in the main agreement, its shareholders in separate agreements. But other types of agreements might be signed separately at closing because it is customary (such as employment agreements), because they may look more like a commercial contract (such as a supply agreement, with unique remedies, a term lasting far beyond the acquisition agreement and anticipating future amendments) or because they do not exist at the time the main agreement is signed (transition services agreements are a good example—they are often negotiated as the closing approaches when the buyer really knows better what types of transition services will be required).

Conditions

A simultaneous signing and closing will occasionally occur. In that case, there is no need for conditions and the representations are simply used as a basis for future indemnification claims. But agreements usually contain conditions to closing, most being designed for the benefit of the buyer. The main conditions (active conditions) go to whether there can be a closing at all (e.g., governmental approvals and financing). Others will be status conditions, designed to provide some assurance to the buyer that it will receive the business it bargained for when the deal does close.

Bringdown. The most heavily negotiated of the conditions is normally the bringdown, the requirement that if the representations had been repeated as of the closing date, they would be true. It should be noted that this is a theoretical concern; the representations are not literally repeated at the closing. The tension from the seller's viewpoint is that, if there is a lapse of time between signing and closing, there will always be a change in the business, some for the better, some for the worse. But the seller will get no credit for the improvements, and the buyer may use the adverse developments to take a second bite at the apple. How does a seller try to cope with the situation? It is, of course, possible to eliminate the bringdown entirely, but that is rarely done.

The seller may assert that, because of the risk of change between signing and closing, the requirement that the representations be true at closing is unrealistic. Even the qualification that they be true and correct as though made at the closing in all material respects is often unsatisfactory, because of the perceived close tolerances of that clause. A seller may propose that instead the representations be true and correct except "for such changes that in the aggregate would not have a Material Adverse Effect." Undoubtedly, the formulation of "Material Adverse Effect" would have been negotiated.

A buyer may raise concerns with any of these formulations on the basis that many representations already contain some form of materiality qualifier. For example, a bringdown of the representation that "The Company is in compliance with laws in all material respects" would be doubly qualified. This approach may result in a formulation that says representations qualified by some form of materiality must be true in all respects, while flat representations must be true in all material respects.

A buyer normally requires that an officer's certificate be delivered by the seller as to the accuracy of the representations at closing. To counter the concern that a seller, in order to move toward closing, may have little incentive to assure the accuracy of the certificate, a buyer may require the delivery of updated schedules in order to determine for itself the details on which it can conclude that the officer's certificate is correct.

Consents and approvals. In larger public deals, particularly involving regulated companies, the required governmental approvals are known. In smaller transactions, governmental approvals are less common, but could become an issue in some situations. For example, in some states, a change in control of an entity or the sale of its assets may require an agency approval of a transfer of an environmental permit.

For most private transactions, the action involves obtaining consents under contracts, either because assignment is prohibited or the transaction in question would trigger a change in control clause. Without the required consents, the target may be in breach of contract or in an asset deal the buyer may not have received effective assignments of important contracts. It normally is up to the seller to procure the consents, which is appropriate, since the seller has the relationship with the counterparty to any contract. Parties frequently underestimate how difficult it is to obtain the consents. The counterparties normally have no incentive to consent—usually there is no additional fee received. Businesspeople have a reason to be concerned that relationships will be jeopardized. It is usually impossible to overplay the strategy for obtaining consents.

Termination

Termination clauses have received increasing visibility in M&A agreements, undoubtedly stemming from public company deals where a right to terminate in certain circumstances may be mandated by fiduciary duties. While that may not be a compelling reason for private companies, the parties will always want the right to terminate their agreement in certain circumstances. At such time it becomes clear that one side or the other is unable to perform its bargain, the other side would want the right to walk from the deal. For example, assume a buyer that has put a credit line in place for purposes of consummating a deal. It may be obligated by the implied covenant of good faith, by best efforts or by a cooperation clause to maintain that facility in place even when the seller is unable to close. The buyer would want to be in a position to terminate the agreement and get on with its life. The fail safe is to allow a party to terminate on a certain date (the "drop dead date") if the closing has not occurred by then. This is usually some period beyond the designated closing date.

A buyer may be able to negotiate other termination rights to its benefit, such as the ability to terminate if it is unsatisfied with its due diligence or it is unable to obtain financing (there may be a more objective formulation of the standard for termination). These types of provisions may turn a firm agreement, even though subject to conditions, into an option.

Remedies

While our thoughts are drawn initially to the elaborate protocol for indemnification in the event a deal closes, thoughtful lawyers will step back and also consider what happens if the deal does not close (justifiably) or if one party wrongly refuses to close.[132] Most agreements do not specify what happens in those instances. A termination provision usually specifies that all rights are reserved. The attempt to make termination an exclusive remedy (that it is without right to seek damages) is normally not acceptable, but the payment of a termination fee may be.

In the event that one party wishes to go forward but the other party unjustifiably refuses to close, equitable relief may be available to the non-defending party. In the event of a closing, indemnification is usually stated to be the sole remedy, except for fraud or other willful misconduct. That provision may not be sufficient to limit various other theories of relief, but probably would work to confine contract claims. Indemnification supplants the contract claim and adds to it. For example, indemnification usually protects third parties not a party to the contract. That goes beyond the contract relief that would otherwise be available.

However, elaborate limitations and extensions of contract rights are woven into the indemnification procedure. For example, the litany of what constitutes a loss, such as "diminution of value," may contain a measure of damages not contemplated in contract law. On the other hand, formidable procedural and substantive limitations are also imposed. Indemnification may extend beyond instances that might be available for a breach of representations or covenants—the parties may agree that seller will be responsible for certain matters, such as business activities prior to the time the buyer purchased the business (our watch/your watch) or items of particular concern (such as pending litigation).

As a matter of private ordering, buyers normally agree to a shorter period to bring claims than would be available as a matter of the statute of limitations for enforcement of contracts. How short is a matter of negotiation. Regardless of the general standard, there is usually a carve-out for certain legal areas where a problem may not be promptly discovered, such as tax and environmental matters. To avoid any doubt, acquisition agreements specifically provide that the representations survive the closing.

Sellers are usually successful in negotiating a limit on their liability. There is no theoretical reason for this. If a buyer is damaged, it is damaged—the environmental claim that exceeds the purchase price is easy to theorize. Sellers may take their cue from public deals, where because of the public nature of the shareholder base there is effectively no survival of any claims. Some sellers, particularly in heady times for M&A, have been able to negotiate a small cap (or maximum exposure) on their liability. Perhaps buyers simply realize that it is unlikely that any claim would arise to anything very substantial and easily concede the issue.

Sellers are usually successful in negotiating a provision that any claim must achieve some degree of magnitude before a seller will be responsible. This basket will be negotiated and no rule of thumb as to its amount can be given, although it is usually modest. Sellers will argue that precise representations about what are essentially business matters are difficult and that it needs some latitude before it has any liability. Some baskets are set up as a true deductible, so that the first dollars of any loss are for the account of the buyer. At other times, the basket becomes a threshold, after which the buyer gets to collect from dollar one. Sometimes sellers will be successful in arguing that each claim should have its own minibasket so that the buyer is not incentivized to aggregate many trivial claims together.

Buyers will counter with the argument that, while it is true that representations about businesses of necessity are somewhat imprecise, the seller already has sufficient wiggle room through the various materiality and other qualifiers sprinkled throughout the representations. Accordingly, a buyer may insist that, while it will agree to the basket, for purposes of making a claim all materiality standards must be read out of the acquisition agreement.

Miscellaneous Provisions

Acquisition agreements and ancillary agreements contain a number of provisions, usually at the end under a "miscellaneous" or "general" heading. These provisions often are pulled from form files and in rote fashion inserted in the draft without much thought. In many deals the standardized clauses survive the negotiation process under the radar with little reaction.[133]

The lawyer drafting his first acquisition agreement should resist the temptation to drop in these provisions without first gaining an understanding of whether they fit the deal, serve the client's interest, add anything to the agreement and what they mean. Similarly, the lawyer commenting upon the other side's first draft should pay close attention to these provisions to be sure they will not operate to the disadvantage of the client. Finally, after the definitive agreement is fully negotiated, counsel is well advised to take yet another close read of the general provisions to assure that the off-the-shelf language does not undercut or trump some carefully crafted language in the main body of the agreement over which the parties have agonized for hours.

Some general provisions can be a trap for the unwary. For example, a standard integration or merger provision ("This Agreement contains the entire understanding among the parties hereto with respect to the subject matter of this Agreement and supersedes all prior and contemporaneous agreements. . .") may vitiate a confidentiality agreement between the parties or a side letter bearing on a critical point of interpretation or substance that the parties intended to survive and have independent significance.

Some provisions attract more attention than others. Those dealing with the governing law, jurisdiction, and service of process can have real significance and are the subject of extensive substantive learning. Notice provisions should be clear as to the recipients, the means of communication, the permissible time deadline, and the procedure for changing the recipients or their contact information. Prohibitions on assignment, third party beneficiary clauses, amendment and modification and similar clauses can have real economic significance in particular deals.

Provisions designating which party bears which expenses, if not considered carefully, can result in unintended consequences, when, for example, after a statutory merger a buyer discovers that it has assumed by operation of law obligations for expenses of the deal that it thought were being absorbed by the target's shareholders under a typical provision that each party bear its own expenses. Expense allocation clauses should address which expense should be borne by which party, which should be shared and on what basis, and what happens in the event that a party terminates the agreement due to a breach.

The canon of construction that ambiguities be resolved against the drafter of the document may not make sense where both parties have heavily negotiated the document. An innocent appearing *force majeure* clause can undercut the otherwise intended meaning and structure of the covenants, conditions to closing and indemnities.

A severability clause (i.e., providing that if a particular provision is found by a court to be unenforceable, the remaining agreement remains enforceable) may not be desirable if certain components of the agreement are true core issues.

Schedules to the Agreement

Acquisition agreements will almost always contain references to a disclosure letter, disclosure schedules or sometimes just schedules.[134] Schedules are a means by which a party can list items that are required by an acquisition agreement. If an agreement requires that the seller list contracts to which the target is a party or is otherwise bound or the assets being sold within various categories, these lists would be included in the schedules. Schedules are also used to disclose exceptions to a party's representations in order to make them accurate. A seller might represent that the target is duly qualified to do business in all jurisdictions in which qualification is required. If this is not accurate, reference would be made to a schedule that discloses the jurisdictions in which the target is not, but should be, qualified. This method is in lieu of including the exceptions in the representations themselves.[135] The seller most often provides schedules, but the same considerations will apply to any schedules provided by a buyer.

The importance of the schedules should not be underestimated.[136] A misrepresentation or omission by a seller caused by an inaccurate or incomplete schedule might provide the basis for a buyer to terminate the acquisition agreement or to close the transaction and recover losses or damages under the indemnification provisions of the agreement. That is not to say, however, that the schedules are not important to a buyer. One reason for a buyer to pay particular attention to the seller's schedules is that they can shift the risk from the seller to the buyer. For example, disclosure of litigation as an exception to a representation that there is no pending or threatened litigation will make that representation accurate. If the litigation is at all material, the buyer may want to back out of the acquisition, attempt to renegotiate the price or demand that the seller remain responsible for the defense, cost and outcome of the litigation. Similarly, a lack of care by a buyer in reviewing the schedules or permitting overly broad exceptions when the acquisition agreement is signed may seriously impair its ability to terminate the agreement or later recover for losses or damages.

The schedules can also serve as a valuable tool in completing the buyer's due diligence. Whether they contain lists or more complete descriptions of contracts, litigation or other items, they can be used as a checklist to make sure that all the contracts, pleadings and other source documents have been reviewed.

Exceptions to the Representations

Most buyer's first drafts of acquisition agreements will not include language allowing for exceptions to the representations, either because of a lack of knowledge on the part of the buyer's counsel as to which representations might have exceptions or more likely a desire to simply put the burden on the seller to provide the necessary exceptions. It will therefore be up to counsel for the seller to propose that clauses be added to the representations that would allow exceptions on the schedules or, in some cases, to add exceptions to the text of the representations.

The manner in which exceptions to the representations are to be disclosed will vary depending on the structure of the acquisition agreement. Sometimes there will be a general statement at the beginning of the representations to the effect that they are true and correct except as otherwise set forth in a single disclosure letter or schedule. This approach greatly favors a seller, because any such disclosure will be an exception to all the representations, and the buyer may have some difficulty in determining which representations are affected by the disclosure.

More often, separate schedules will be used to disclose exceptions to specific representations, and will be numbered to correspond to the sections of the agreement to which they pertain. For example, Schedule 3.5 will contain an exception to certain of the representations made in Section 3.5, and a clause such as "Except as disclosed on Schedule 3.5" would be added to that representation where appropriate. MAPA provides for a single disclosure letter, but it is to be broken down into parts, and the exceptions to the representations are referred to by numbers corresponding to the sections in which the representations appear (e.g., "Except as set forth in Part 3.14").

The approach of having the schedules correspond to specific representations makes it more important that counsel identify all the representations to which a particular exception might apply so that disclosure of that exception can be included (either directly or by cross reference) on all the appropriate schedules. For example, the occurrence of an event causing an undisclosed liability of the target might be an exception to the target's representation concerning its financial statements, as well as to its representation as to the absence of liabilities. It may not be enough to simply disclose the liability on one schedule. The safest approach would be to disclose the liability on each schedule where necessary to insure that the corresponding representation is accurate.

Tying Exceptions to Particular Representations

IBP, Inc. v. Tyson Foods, Inc.[137] demonstrates how a failure to tie exceptions to all the appropriate representations can become an issue in a dispute. In this case, the Delaware Court of Chancery granted the target's (IBP) demand for specific performance of a merger agreement with Tyson Foods. The Court considered, among other matters, whether the disclosure of a particular risk on one schedule precluded Tyson Foods from using IBP's failure to disclose that risk on other schedules as a basis on which it could terminate the agreement.

In Section 5.11 of the merger agreement, IBP represented that there were no undisclosed material liabilities other than as set forth on Schedule 5.11. That Schedule disclosed liabilities associated with certain improper accounting practices of DFG, a subsidiary of IBP. Tyson Foods contended that disclosure on Schedule 5.11 had no effect on the representations in Sections 5.07 (SEC filings), 5.08 (financial statements) and 5.09 (disclosure documents), which were unqualified. It pointed out that IBP had made cross references among other Schedules, but there were no cross references to Schedule 5.11. The Court determined that Tyson Food's reading was not the only one, and permitted the introduction of parole evidence. It appeared from the evidence that the DFG disclosure in Schedule 5.11 had been prepared by IBP's general counsel and had been specifically discussed with the negotiators, including counsel, for Tyson Foods. The Court referred to Tyson Food's argument as a "hairsplitting interpretation," and concluded that it had accepted the risk of the DFG-related problems through IBP's disclosure.

While IBP was successful in its argument that disclosure of the DFG-related problems on only the one schedule shifted the risk to Tyson Foods, this was not an easy decision for the Court and the result should not be read any broader than the particular facts.

Approaches to Schedule Preparation

There are many approaches used by attorneys in putting together schedules. For example, in listing contracts that may require a third party's consent for an acquisition, some attorneys will simply include the title, the date, and the parties for each contract on the theory that this identifies them sufficiently so that counsel to the other party can then review them and determine how the provisions requiring consent operate given the structure of the particular acquisition. Others will, in addition to identifying the contracts, add references to the specific provisions requiring consent and perhaps describe whose consent is required and how the provisions might operate.

Another example in which practice varies is the disclosure of litigation. The litigation might be identified by the case name, court, and docket number, again on the theory that counsel to the other party can review the pleadings as part of due diligence. Sometimes, however, a description of the litigation and status is added to the schedule.

While expanding the description of contracts and litigation certainly makes the disclosure more complete, the risk is that the other party will not review the contracts or the pleadings, but rather rely on a description that turns out to be inaccurate in some respect. This circumstance may be particularly true if a schedule describing pending litigation includes a comment on the expected outcome that does not ultimately materialize. Without a statement to the contrary, such a comment might be deemed to be a representation for which the seller would be responsible.

Preparing the Schedules

It is always in the best interests of the party making the representations that its counsel prepare the related schedules. In most cases, this will be the seller since it will be making more extensive representations. However, as a result of due diligence and familiarity with the form of acquisition agreement, the buyer and its counsel might be in a better position to prepare these schedules, and are sometimes asked to do so in the interest of saving time. The temptation to assist in this manner should be avoided for fear that the buyer will be taking on responsibility for the completeness and accuracy of the schedules in the event a dispute later arises. Commenting on the schedules or suggesting additions based on due diligence is different from actually preparing the schedules for a seller.

It is customary for schedules to be prepared by junior attorneys, often toward the end of the negotiations and in an expedited fashion due to time constraints. Ideally, these junior attorneys have had some M&A training and are receiving close supervision, but unfortunately that is not always the case.

Your First Assignment: Preparing Schedules

You're the new kid on the block, having just joined a firm fresh out of law school. After completing your first research project, a senior partner asks you to help with a matter that the firm is handling—the sale of the outstanding stock in a private company. You'd heard that "M&A" was a hot area, and so you're anxious to get involved. When you look up the partner, he gruffly hands you a copy of the current draft of the acquisition agreement and a box of documents, and says somewhat matter-of-factly that you need to prepare some schedules for the acquisition agreement—just follow the rules of the road—list all of the documents that are in the box that would constitute an exception or are required to be affirmatively disclosed. Simple. Upon asking, you are told that the box contains copies of the documents that the target provided the buyer for its due diligence. What do you do?

This is not an easy assignment. Here are some of the problems you face:

- You probably do not understand the full implications of the acquisition agreement. Do you even understand what the representations mean?
- You can probably figure out that if financial statements are to be attached as schedule 3.5 how to do that. But what about the schedules constituting exceptions to the representations? The acquisition agreement has lead-ins that qualify various representations by "except as otherwise disclosed." How do you figure out whether exceptions are necessary?
- How do the documents in the box tie to the acquisition agreement?
- What does a disclosure schedule even look like?

At the outset, you need to make sure that you understand the meaning of the representations being made. For example, there is a representation that: "The Company is not subject to any liabilities or obligations other than those shown on the Latest Balance Sheet." Will there be exceptions to be listed? Many lawyers will view "liabilities and obligations" to include not only liabilities recorded on the balance sheet in accordance with generally accepted accounting principles, but also any contingent liabilities and contractual obligations of the target. Since only in rare circumstances would contingent liabilities and contractual obligations be shown on the balance sheet, the schedule literally would require a listing of each contingent liability, contract (material and immaterial) and perhaps a variety of other matters. So if this representation remains unchanged, you may have your work cut out for you.

You will also need the name of someone at the target who can work through the representations with you and locate any responsive documents and discuss with you the exceptions that may be required.

Here might be a work plan for this task:

- Find a mentor to help you understand what the representations are all about—a senior associate or young partner—and/or check out one of the treatises or the commentary to the model agreements that discuss the standard representations in some depth.
- Organize the documents in the box in some thematic way, perhaps as crudely as corporate documents, employee benefits, intellectual property, leases, contracts, etc.
- Once you have an understanding of the meaning of the representations, call your contact at the target for the purpose of discussing each of the representations in some detail and determining the exceptions that would be appropriate. Some of the documents from the box will probably be responsive, but there undoubtedly will be a host of additional documents to be identified and listed.
- Get some sample disclosure schedules from other deals and begin to outline what the disclosure schedule should look like, probably using one of the folders in the box such as that for employee benefits.
- Make sure you understand the timetable for delivery of a first draft.

These steps might get you started, but you will probably need a lot of support to get through this first deal. Understanding the implications of the representations and trying to identify responsive documents and appropriate disclosures takes a lot of time and effort, not to mention the time involved in making use of the experience of those more familiar with the process.

After the schedules are drafted, representatives of the client normally review them before they are delivered to the other side. It is often helpful at this stage to convene a meeting of counsel, both the junior and more senior attorneys, and those within the client's organization most knowledgeable about the business, to review in detail all the representations and related schedules.

Once the schedules are presented to the other side, they should be examined by counsel to determine whether any of the disclosures are material and, if so, the client should be made aware of those disclosures and their potential impact. Not only can the disclosures on the schedules shift the risk to a buyer by disclosing exceptions to the representations, but sometimes they will in effect negate the representations. An extreme example might be where the seller lists or references on a schedule all the target's accounts receivable as an exception to a representation that all target's accounts receivable are collectible.

Establishing General Principles

It has become increasingly common for the parties to establish some general principles that will apply to construction of the schedules and the interpretation of the disclosures made on the schedules. These might be included in the acquisition agreement, in the disclosure letter or in an introduction or cover sheet to the schedules.[138] A seller often will suggest language in an effort to have more flexibility, avoid misinterpretations and, in particular, protect itself against failing to key a schedule to all the representations to which it might be deemed to be an exception. The proposed language is often presented just prior to signing the acquisition agreement, which may be concurrently with delivery of the draft schedules to the other party or sometime after delivery. Because this typically comes so late in the process, it might not receive the amount of attention that would otherwise be appropriate, since the principles can significantly affect the internal structure of the agreement, the intention of the parties and the allocation of risk.

One of the issues that is often covered is that the inclusion of items on a schedule will not imply that they are material or that their inclusion establishes a standard of materiality or any other standards for purposes of other disclosures. Parties should be encouraged to over include exceptions rather than to exclude them on the basis of immateriality, which is, of course, based on a subjective judgment as to which opinions might differ. Sometimes the general principles will include a provision to the effect that statements in the schedules are not intended to constitute representations, which might give a party more latitude in describing the various exceptions. It is also helpful to expressly permit use of the same defined terms in the schedules as in the acquisition agreement and to include headings describing the schedules or subparts of the schedules for ease of reference. In addition, the general principles will often allow incorporation by reference from one schedule to another. This avoids having to repeat lengthy lists or disclosures.

Most of the negotiation is over establishing whether the disclosure of an exception to one representation will also serve as an exception to other representations. The buyer will want each exception to be related to a specific representation, so it can fully determine the effect.[139] For example, a buyer would not want the mere identification of numerous contracts in a list of contracts to be considered an exception to a representation as to the absence of defaults. However, the seller will argue that it should not be deemed to have made a misrepresentation simply because its disclosure of an exception in one schedule was not also made on a schedule to another representation.[140] A compromise might be to provide that disclosure of information on a schedule with respect to one representation shall be deemed to be disclosed with respect to each other representation, but only to the extent it is reasonably apparent that such disclosure is applicable to such other representation.[141] Of course this is a subjective test and raises a question of "reasonably apparent" to whom. Another alternative would substitute at the end "only to the extent that the relevance to such other representation is manifest on the face of the schedule."

Examples of General Principles

The following is an example of what might be agreed upon by the parties as an introduction or cover sheet to the schedules:

The following schedules accompany the acquisition agreement dated [date] (the "Agreement") by among [parties], as contemplated by the Agreement.

In some respects, these schedules may provide more information than is strictly required by the Agreement. No implication should be drawn that such information is necessarily material or otherwise required to be disclosed or that the inclusion of such information establishes or implies a standard of materiality, a standard for what may be in the ordinary course of business or any other standard set forth in or for purposes of the Agreement.

These schedules are qualified in their entirety by reference to the Agreement and no statement made in these schedules is intended to constitute representations, warranties, or covenants, except to the extent expressly provided otherwise in the Agreement.

Capitalized terms used in these schedules shall, unless the context indicates otherwise, have the same meanings as in the Agreement. The headings or subheadings of the schedules are for convenience only and shall not control or affect the meaning or construction of that schedule or any portion thereof. Reference in any schedule to another schedule shall be deemed to incorporate the schedule or matters so referenced.

Information disclosed on any schedule with respect to one representation shall be deemed to be disclosed with respect to each other representation, but only to the extent it is reasonably apparent that such disclosure is applicable to such other representation and warranty.

Delivering the Schedules

The common practice is for the schedules to be completed and delivered by the time the acquisition agreement is signed. Unfortunately, it is often at the last minute that changes are made and the final schedules are approved and accepted by the parties. Because the schedules may be in the form of separate pages keyed to particular representations, there can be a last minute shuffling and substitution of pages. This can present a potential problem in being able to identify the final schedules if a dispute should later arise. For this reason, some require that the schedules be initialed so as to avoid later questions about which pages were included in the final schedules. Putting the acquisition agreement and schedules on a CD-ROM at the time of signing might also avoid later disputes.

Whose Schedule Is It Anyway?

The following is one example of the type of controversy that might arise in electronic or mail closings. Prior to closing the purchase of a specialized flooring business, seller's counsel furnished, in narrative form, a summary of what the schedules would contain as exceptions to the representations. Buyer's counsel requested that the exceptions be set forth on separate pages corresponding to the separate sections of the representations. Buyer's counsel also requested that the description in one schedule be updated since it referred to proposed job completion dates that were already past when the narrative form was received. Subsequently, seller's counsel sent separate pages for the exceptions as buyer's counsel had requested. There was no updated description for the stale schedule, but seller's counsel had requested, and buyer's counsel agreed, that a letter be attached to that schedule. Some months after the closing a controversy arose concerning several problem jobs that had been referred to in the stale summary, but were not mentioned in the letter attached to the final schedule. In a protracted and expensive arbitration involving the problem jobs, seller took the position that the problem jobs had been disclosed in the narrative summary and should have been added to the final schedule by buyer's counsel. The matter was settled before the arbitrator rendered a decision.

Sometimes there is pressure to sign an acquisition agreement before all the schedules are completed. While it may be best to hold off the signing, this might not be acceptable to the parties for a variety of reasons. If delivery of some of the schedules is delayed until after signing, the buyer must have some control over what is later disclosed. The usual approach is to require delivery of the missing schedules within a specified number of days, with the buyer having the right to approve or disapprove them within a given period after delivery or, alternatively, providing that the additional schedules are deemed accepted unless disapproved by the buyer within a specified period after delivery. If the additional schedules are disapproved, this will ordinarily result in the acquisition agreement being terminated.

Supplementing the Schedules

Representations are usually made as of the date of signing, and therefore the schedules must be accurate and complete as of that same date. If events occur after signing that affect the representations, or any inaccuracies or omissions in the schedules are discovered after signing, the seller will want to supplement the schedules or otherwise disclose the event, inaccuracy or omission to the buyer.

Acquisition agreements often require that the seller notify the buyer of any fact or condition that causes or constitutes, or the occurrence of any fact or condition that would or would be reasonably likely to cause or constitute, a misrepresentation or omission, and that if the fact or condition requires any change to the schedules, the seller will deliver a supplement.[142] Usually, these agreements further provide that delivery of a supplemental schedule will not affect any rights of the buyer under the termination or indemnification provisions[143] and that a supplement will have no effect on a condition to closing that the representations be accurate at that time.[144] In practice, these supplemental schedules and other proposed changes often come to the attention of counsel for the other party shortly before or even at the closing and leave little time to digest their import. In some cases, this might be intentional but usually it is simply through lack of attention to updating the schedule disclosures with the client until the last minute.

Depending on the seriousness of the matter, the buyer may decide to terminate the acquisition agreement, to attempt renegotiation of the price or to close and recover from the seller under the indemnification provisions or otherwise. However, if the buyer closes with knowledge of a misrepresentation or omission and without amending the acquisition agreement, its remedies for recovery from the seller may be affected.[145] Consequently, a buyer might proffer a provision that expressly permits it to close the transaction and seek indemnification for something that has been disclosed by the seller in a supplement. A seller may object to such a provision and would generally prefer to provide that the buyer's recourse under these circumstances is limited to terminating the agreement. Some acquisition agreements provide that the buyer can object to any supplemental disclosure for a specified time period. If it objects within that period, it can only terminate the agreement. If it fails to object, it is deemed to have accepted the supplemental disclosure, thereby giving up its right to terminate the agreement or to close and recover losses or damages based on that disclosure.

Related Documents

In addition to the acquisition agreement, a number of other documents will be required in any acquisition. Some of these documents may be delivered in the early stages of the negotiations, such as confidentiality agreements described in Chapter 6. Others may be delivered concurrently with execution of the acquisition agreement or after execution and prior to or at the closing. The purpose of these documents may be to evidence consents or approvals of third parties, to amend or clarify the agreement, to reflect ongoing arrangements with third parties or among the parties to the acquisition or to satisfy closing conditions.

There is no standard practice as to who should prepare these documents, although closing documents and the buyer's counsel usually prepares most ancillary agreements because they are primarily for the benefit of the buyer.

Third Party Consents or Approvals

In most acquisitions, various consents or approvals of third parties will be required. These typically are included as conditions to the buyer's obligation to close the transaction.[146]

In an asset sale, many of the seller's material agreements with its suppliers, customers and landlords will require consent to assign those agreements to the buyer.[147] This may also be true in a stock sale or a merger in which control shifts to new ownership. Standard forms for assignment and attornment are often prepared for this purpose. If the buyer is assuming indebtedness of the target, arrangements need to be made with the lender and assurances given as to the principal amount outstanding and terms of the indebtedness. If the buyer obtains new financing, it is not unusual for lenders to require that lessors subordinate and execute non-disturbance agreements. If indebtedness is being retired, releases of encumbrances of the assets and reconveyances may be required.

The permits and licenses under which the target has previously operated may need to be transferred or reissued, which can require approvals of governmental agencies.[148]

Side Letters

The parties to an acquisition will sometimes enter into so-called side letters. Side letters usually address matters that the parties want to make legally binding, but do not want included as a part of the acquisition agreement for confidentiality reasons or because of the inconvenience of having to revise the agreement before it is executed or to amend it after it has been executed. Sometimes these letters are used to provide an expression of the parties' understanding or interpretation of a specific provision in the agreement in an effort to avoid later disputes. They can also provide illustrations of complex earnout formulas or other computations required by the agreement, although illustrations of this nature are often attached as schedules or in some other fashion to the acquisition agreement. Side letters are sometimes used at closing as a means by which the parties can disclose, and if necessary come to agreement with respect to, inaccuracies in the representations or other matters that have come up since the acquisition agreement was signed. The closing or flow of funds statement discussed in Chapter 14 can also be in the form of a side letter.[149]

Care should be taken that the commitments contained in a side letter are not abrogated by the integration or merger provision of the acquisition agreement that was discussed earlier in this chapter. If a side letter is entered into prior to or concurrently with the execution of the acquisition agreement, it can be identified as part of the agreement between the parties in the integration clause. If a side letter is entered into after execution of the acquisition agreement, it might specify that it constitutes an amendment to the agreement. This concern is sometimes dealt with by adding a clause in the side letter to the effect that it is intended to constitute an agreement of the parties notwithstanding the integration provision of the acquisition agreement. On the chance that this language will not trump the integration provision, it might be safer to follow one of the approaches set forth above.

Side Letter*

The following letter was acquired from the confidential files of Karl Holtzschue, a colleague in the American College of Real Estate Attorneys. We have reviewed it and edited it, but have assumed and relied on its completeness as to matters of fact and law. We have not made any independent investigation of it, and we make no representation as to the sufficiency of our investigation for your purposes.

It is not intended to be relied upon by any individual or entity.

_____

To: Messrs. _____

Re: Contract of Even Date

Sirs:

   In reference to the Contract of Even Date (hereinafter called the "Apparent Deal"), this letter sets forth the further understanding of the parties (hereinafter called the "Real Deal"). This Real Deal is, of course, sincerely meant by the parties, but shall be enforceable in the manner indicated below (check one):

Not at all.
By the same legal means as the Apparent Deal.

By the withholding of future business.
By strong, swarthy youths with sticks.
By notification to defaulting party's spouse of events occurring after signing ceremony.
By unspecified means too hideous to mention.

Considering that the parties have entered into the Apparent Deal without realizing the implications of the Worst Case, the parties now declare the Real Deal as follows (check one or more, as appropriate):

The Apparent Deal is off.
Only the Apparent Deal will be publicly disclosed.
All monetary amounts express in the Apparent Deal hereby are increased/decreased by a factor of _____.
Expressions of mandatory commitments in the Apparent Deal hereby are declared to be only Best Efforts.
Clauses ____ through ____ of the Apparent Deal are in there only to show the Board of Directors of the parties, but form no part of the Real Deal.
Undisclosed personal fees and commissions are payable to negotiators of the Apparent Deal as follows: _____.
Only the seller in the Apparent Deal shall be bound.
Only the buyer in the Apparent Deal shall be bound.
The terms "Buyer" and "Seller" in the apparent Deal hereby are reversed.

Very truly yours,

Firm:
By:
Title"

(Check one)

Agreed and accepted
Read but not understood
Yes, but if asked will deny
Signed under duress

Firm:
By:
By:
Title:
Title:

*Reprinted with permission of the Pennsylvania Bar Institute and Harris Ominsky, Esq.

Any material matters covered by side letters should of course be disclosed to lenders and possibly other third parties. When a side letter is being used to avoid disclosure to taxing authorities, regulators, or public bodies, consideration should be given to whether this might constitute a violation of requirements mandating filing or disclosure, and whether it is proper to withhold delivery of the side letter when production of copies of the acquisition agreement or documents pertaining to the acquisition are requested or required.

Ancillary Agreements

The acquisition may require certain ancillary agreements, which can be among parties to the acquisition agreement or with third parties whose commitments will be critical to the consummation of the transaction. Because many of these agreements reflect customary business arrangements, standard client forms may be used or in-house lawyers may prepare them or lawyers specializing in the relevant practice area. Otherwise, counsel for the buyer will usually be responsible for drafting the ancillary agreements, since most of them are intended to protect the interests of the buyer.

If the ancillary agreements involve only parties to the acquisition agreement, the issue is more one of timing and presumably the terms and form can be agreed upon before the acquisition agreement is executed. If third parties are involved, it may not be practical to negotiate the terms and form prior to execution of the acquisition agreement, in which case the parties to the acquisition will be at risk with respect to reaching a meeting of the minds with the third parties. It is not unusual for negotiation of the terms of certain of the ancillary agreements to be more difficult and contentious than negotiation of the acquisition agreement, many times resulting in the termination of discussions over the proposed acquisition.

Ancillary agreements usually are attached in draft form as exhibits to the acquisition agreement with the expectation that the final forms will be executed at or prior to the closing. Most often, the execution and delivery of ancillary agreements are conditions to the obligation of a party (or parties) to close the transaction.[150] That being the case, the draft should be in final form or nearly in final form so as to avoid later disagreements over changes. As a precaution, references to the ancillary agreements as a condition to closing sometimes include the words "substantially in the form of . . ." to allow minor but appropriate changes. If negotiations have not been completed, the parties might attach a term sheet to the acquisition agreement that outlines those terms that have been agreed upon by the parties. Sometimes, a covenant will also commit a party to the acquisition agreement to use best efforts (or some other standard of commitment) to cause the appropriate persons or entities to execute and deliver the ancillary agreements.[151] This approach might provide some recourse to another party in the event the condition is not fulfilled.

Because parties to the acquisition agreement or their affiliates may also be parties to the ancillary agreements, a buyer will often seek a right of set off against payments required to be made pursuant to these ancillary agreements for indemnification claims or simply claims for contract damages. If the agreements are silent on this point, there may be a common law right of set off depending on the applicable law. If the intention is otherwise, a party might insist on adding a provision to the acquisition agreement or ancillary agreements expressly denying the right of set off.

The ancillary agreements that are most often encountered in acquisitions are described below.

Employment agreements. In order to maintain the continuity of business operations, a buyer will often want to retain the services of those primarily responsible for the management and success of the business. In a closely held business, these persons are commonly the sellers who have a financial interest in the transaction, or they may be certain key employees who have no financial interest. In a publicly held company, they often are key members of management who may or may not have a financial interest in the transaction.

The desire to retain the services of sellers, managers or other key employees will to some extent depend on the type of buyer. A strategic buyer may have its own management personnel that it can inject into the acquired business, whereas a financial buyer often will be dependent on current management to continue running the business.

If it is expected that the sellers or managers will be involved in day-to-day operations after the acquisition, this can be accomplished with employment agreements that set forth, among other things, compensation and benefits, a minimum term of employment and the conditions under which the employee can be terminated. Of course, if the execution and delivery of employment agreements are a condition to the buyer's obligation to close, the parties should have some confidence that the employees will be willing to agree to the terms. At a minimum, the terms should be discussed with the employees and their intentions determined in advance. For added assurance, it is not unusual for employment agreements to be executed concurrently or in advance of the acquisition agreement to become effective on the closing.

It should be kept in mind that employment agreements are one sided, in that they commit a buyer to continue the employment relationship (subject to the negotiated termination provisions), but cannot prevent an employee from voluntarily leaving. For this reason, many companies as a general rule avoid employment agreements, but may make an exception in the case of an acquisition. Occasionally, sellers will insist that the buyer offer employment agreements to particular employees. A seller could be motivated by a paternalistic protection of long-time employees, the shifting of severance liability for employees no longer needed or the perceived protection of an earnout or other continuing interest in the business after sale. From an employee's standpoint, it might be important that the term of the employment agreement coincide with the term of a covenant not to compete that the buyer is requiring, so that the employee at least has some assurance of being employed while being unable to compete.

Consulting agreements. If, following the acquisition, the seller or managers will not be involved in day-to-day operations, the buyer may still want to retain their services using a consulting agreement. This arrangement might involve, for example, general business consultation, consultation on technical matters, or assisting in maintaining important business relationships. Many of these agreements require that the consultant review materials provided by the buyer and remain available to consult at the request of the buyer, with limitations as to the term, subject matter, location, duration, etc.

Sometimes a consulting agreement can be motivated by the desire of a buyer to apportion part of the purchase price directly to the sellers for tax or other reasons. This can create a natural tension between a buyer and the consultant, who views the consulting payments as an entitlement. For this reason, the consultant will want the agreement to contain minimal obligations and performance to be objective and easily measured (e.g., availability for a specified maximum number of hours per month at an agreeable location or only by telephone or e-mail).

For tax purposes, the buyer will expect to deduct the consulting payments, but the payments will be taxed at ordinary income rates to the consultant. However, deductibility by the buyer will depend on the reasonableness of the compensation and other terms in relation to the services to be rendered. If the buyer does not really desire to utilize the consulting services, at some point the consulting agreement may become so watered down that the taxing authorities could regard it as a sham and treat payments as disguised purchase price.

Covenants not to compete. Most buyers will want to obtain covenants from the sellers or key members of management restricting their right to compete following the acquisition. These covenants not to compete (sometimes called non-competition covenants or agreements) are often heavily negotiated because they can effectively preclude sellers and managers from engaging in the only business they know. Depending on the parties involved and the structure of the acquisition, a covenant not to compete might be the subject of a separate agreement or contained in the acquisition agreement or an employment agreement.[152]

The enforceability of these covenants is a matter of state law, so that the laws of those states where the issue is most likely to be litigated should be reviewed in fashioning the terms and scope.[153] Some states will disregard the governing law of an acquisition agreement, taking the position that strong public policy considerations will prevail to protect those who reside in their states against unreasonable restraints on competition.

Generally, covenants not to compete must be of reasonable duration and scope. Courts will more likely enforce covenants in connection with an acquisition for a longer period than a post-employment covenant in an employment agreement. In addition, the restrictions must be limited to the geographic areas where the business is conducted. If a key manager who has no financial interest in the transaction is giving a covenant, thought should be given to whether it is supported by sufficient consideration to be enforceable. These covenants are often expanded to include restrictions on soliciting or hiring employees of the business being sold and confidentiality provisions.

Buyers often sought to have a large portion of the purchase price allocated to the covenant not to compete in an effort to obtain a deduction for the amount allocated. Similar to a consulting agreement, this allocation created a tension because that amount would also be taxed as ordinary income to the person subject to the covenant. However, this tension has been reduced by a change in the tax law permitting amortization of goodwill over a 15 year period. One other tax issue can arise from efforts of buyers to provide in an earnout that a breach of a covenant not to compete or voluntary termination of employment will cancel any entitlement to future earnout payments. This can create a risk that the earnout payments will be considered compensatory and therefore will be taxed at ordinary income rates.

Leases. When the facilities of the acquired company are owned separately (by shareholders or others) and are not transferred with the rest of the business, it may be necessary to negotiate a lease between the property owner and the buyer. If there is a lease already in effect, the parties may have to negotiate changes in the rental rate or other terms to satisfy a buyer. Sometimes, the term of the lease has to be extended or shortened, or provisions may be added to extend the lease term at the option of the buyer. In some asset sales, real property might be retained and distributed to shareholders. This also may require negotiating a new lease with the buyer.

Escrow agreements. A buyer may negotiate an arrangement whereby a portion of the purchase price is withheld and deposited in an escrow account for the purpose of satisfying claims the buyer may have after the closing.[154] This structure will give the buyer some assurance that the funds or securities held in escrow will be available to it regardless of the solvency of the seller. It is also a useful device where the buyer may otherwise have to look to multiple parties for recovery. Negotiation of the terms of the escrow agreement is not unlike negotiating limitations to the indemnification provisions because they are so closely related. Included are terms dealing with exclusivity, duration, and conditions for release.

Escrow agreements are also sometimes used as a means of withholding payment of part of the consideration pending satisfaction of an important post-closing condition or event.

Transition agreements. Acquisitions of a division or subsidiary present a number of unique issues, particularly when they are part of a highly integrated enterprise. In most cases, the division or subsidiary will have intercorporate or other relationships that the parties will want to continue after the closing. These relationships, which can be with the seller or with various of its operating units, might continue for a number of years or, in most cases, only for a short period of time until other arrangements can be made.

An acquired division or subsidiary may also purchase some of its raw materials or components from the seller or its affiliates. The buyer might insist on getting the benefit of long-term purchase contracts that are very favorable due to volume purchases. It is also possible that the seller or its affiliates are customers of the acquired division or subsidiary. If they are the sole or primary suppliers or customers, the continuation of this arrangement on a long-term basis might be documented in a supply agreement with established volumes and a pricing mechanism. This can often be an essential element in justifying the acquisition from an economic standpoint.

Another situation often encountered is where an acquired division or subsidiary continues to utilize facilities of, or share facilities with, the seller or its affiliates. Again, this can be a long-term or short-term arrangement. It can be documented in the covenants portion of the acquisition agreement, or by a separate lease, sublease, or license of space, depending upon the seller's interest in the property. The same situation can arise with the joint use of equipment, such as a machine shop, or intangible property, such as software or tradenames. These arrangements can present insurance, liability, intellectual property and other issues.

A seller typically will be providing various support and administrative services to its divisions and subsidiaries.[155] These services often include information systems, human resources and employee benefits, accounting and tax, sales support and marketing, and insurance and risk management. The type and level of services needed after the closing will depend to some extent on the type of buyer. A strategic buyer may be able to perform all these services immediately following the closing, whereas a financial buyer most likely will have only limited resources available and will need the cooperation of the seller until the division or subsidiary can outsource the services or develop its own support staff. If the seller is downsizing, it may want to eliminate some of these functions and personnel so it may not have the resources to provide these services.

It is often difficult to come to agreement on pricing the services to be continued. The seller may charge its operating units based on direct cost burdened with an allocation of overhead. Because of the difficulty of determining an appropriate overhead burden, many sellers simply charge a buyer on a fixed-price or direct-cost basis because of the short term of the arrangement. Another method of evaluating the appropriateness of the charges is by comparing them with the cost of the services if they were to be outsourced to third parties.

Contribution agreements. Contribution agreements are a means whereby those who may be responsible for the representations in an acquisition agreement can agree among themselves on the manner in which they will bear a share of liabilities in the event that claims are made for indemnification.[156] For example, sometimes the controlling (and often the active) shareholders of a seller in an asset transaction might be willing to be jointly and severally liable to the buyer. They could agree to a right of contribution against one another so that the ultimate liability will be borne proportionately to their respective shareholdings. It is also not unusual for the shareholders who have been managing the business to take on greater responsibility for claims under certain of the representations than those who are merely passive investors, although the active shareholders may object on the basis that the risk of indemnification liability is a price element to be shared equally. The legal representation of parties to these agreements can raise ethical issues that are discussed in Chapter 2.

Satisfaction of Additional Obligations

Acquisition agreements often specify certain documents, certificates, or opinions, in addition to the ancillary agreements, that are required to be delivered by a party. These could be listed toward the front of the agreement in connection with the closing, or toward the back as part of the conditions to closing.[157] The following are examples[158]:

- bills of sale, assignments, and assumption agreements in asset acquisitions;
- assignments and assumptions of leases, together with estoppel certificates;
- assignments of intellectual property registrations and rights;
- certificates of officers bringing down the representations to the date of the closing (so-called bring-down certificates);
- certificates of officers as to the requisite corporate approvals and the forms of the charter and bylaws; and
- certificates as to the incumbency and signatures of officers and opinions of counsel (corporate and, if appropriate, tax).

In addition, certain certificates may not be specified but nevertheless are expected to be delivered by custom. Examples are copies of charters of the parties certified by the secretaries of state or comparable officials and good standing certificates from the states in which the target is incorporated or qualified to conduct business (both from the secretary of state or comparable official and possibly tax authorities).

Execution of Documents

In recent years, acquisition agreements and other related documents are often executed long distance. The parties and their lawyers exchange faxed signature pages or e-mail pdf files or attachments bearing the required signatures, often with the promise that the original signatures will follow by overnight delivery.

How comfortable should deal lawyers and their clients be with representative or facsimile signatures—whether faxed or pdf'd or generated through some other electronic means? The history and, in many states, the erosion or abrogation of the best evidence rule and other rules relating to the authentication of documents is beyond the scope of this chapter. Suffice it to say, many states have done away with the old rules that would have required the introduction of an original document to prove a writing.[159]

It may be one thing for a lawyer to feel comfortable relying on a photocopy or a faxed version of an original signature. Even though all these versions are electronically generated, it may be quite another thing for lawyers to become comfortable with e-mails or pdf'd documents.[160] But should there be any difference?[161] During the past six years, there has been a flurry of legislation concerning the reliability of electronic signatures. Forty-five states have now passed some version of The Uniform Electronic Transactions Act (UETA)[162] promulgated by the National Conference of Commissioners on Uniform State Laws (NCCUSL) in 1999, while the federal Electronic Signatures in Global and National Commerce Act (E-Sign) became effective on October 1, 2000 in an effort by Congress to make uniform the electronic signature legislation among the states.[163] Both laws provide for the validity of electronic signatures.[164] Deal lawyers should read both laws because they are limited in scope as to the type of transactions to which they apply, and the parties may be required to expressly opt in to the law's coverage.[165]

One must still be wary when determining which law (or laws) applies to an electronic signature issue. Generally, E-Sign preempts state UETA provisions that are not identical to the UETA provisions approved by the NCCUSL.[166] If a state has passed a version of UETA and E-Sign preemption does not apply, then the state UETA normally will control over E-Sign.[167] New York has its own unique electronic signature legislation[168] that makes both New York law and E-Sign rules applicable to an interstate e-signature issue.[169] As can be seen, there are many issues to consider before relying on electronic signatures.[170]

That's Not What I Signed!

In addition to anecdotal accounts of mass confusion, reported cases are appearing involving disputes over what version of an agreement was signed by the parties and whether the pre-signed signature pages were affixed to the right version.

In *Midwest Mfg. Holding, LLC v. Donnelly Corp.*,[171] a United States District Court for the Northern District of Illinois, grappled with a number of issues involving a suit by a potential buyer against a seller who backed out of a heavily negotiated deal. The defendant alleged that the signature pages its officer had signed and were exhibits to the complaint had actually been attached to earlier drafts of the agreement and not the agreement referred to in the complaint. The court was left with factual issues as to which version of various drafts of the agreement the signature pages applied to and whether the signor knew that the signature page he was signing related to the deal being litigated.

The SDNY district court opinion in *AIH Acquisition Corp., LLC v. Alaska Industrial Hard-ware, Inc.*,[172] got the attention of many deal lawyers, as the court held that the fact that a fully negotiated stock purchase agreement was not signed by the parties would not neces-sarily preclude the court from finding it enforceable, having concluded that "the mere lack of signatures is but a ministerial formality." On appeal, the Second Circuit vacated and remanded the lower court order, based in part because of factual disputes over which draft version of the stock purchase agreement the defendants had agreed to.[173]

Of course, these issues also arise in connection with the closing documents as discussed in Chapter 14.

CHAPTER **12**

Getting from Agreement to Closing

Given practical considerations, a simultaneous execution of the acquisition agreement and closing of the deal is often not possible or desirable. The period between signing and closing may require substantial time when regulatory approvals, such as SEC clearances or antitrust clearances under the HSR Act, are needed. Even in smaller or private deals the process of obtaining needed consents may take an extensive amount of time. Some acquisition agreements are executed and delivered as part of the closing, but this chapter does not cover those.

Avoiding the Post-Signing Let Down

Once the acquisition agreement has been signed, a major attitudinal shift often occurs among the participants. Prior to signing, nearly everyone involved viewed each other as being on opposing sides of a zero-sum negotiation, but upon signing everyone will normally take a deep breath, calm down (at least a bit) and begin working more cooperatively toward the next stage—the closing. The deep breath is probably natural (and to a large extent may even be unavoidable), depending on the effort and stress that went into getting the agreement signed. The relaxation of the adversarial status of the opposing parties is also natural, in that the primary task of each side is now the same—to get the transaction closed (although that is not to say that there still will not be negotiations from that point forward). How deep a breath everyone gets to take will usually depend on the length of time anticipated to satisfy various closing conditions, coordinating the transfer of employees, obtaining financing, obtaining shareholder approval, and negotiating to obtain third-party consents.

While everyone, especially in a deal where extraordinary effort was undertaken to produce the signed agreement, would like to take a break (or, in the lawyers' case, at least remind their other clients that they still exist), deals tend to flow upon streams of momentum, and allowing a deal to lose its momentum makes it more likely that it will not close as soon as it otherwise could and increases the risk that it will not close at all.

While every participant may be tempted to put the file aside, failing to proceed promptly should be considered in light of two factors. While the negotiation process dealt with legal requirements and numerous theoretical contingencies, with the signing, the actual transfer of the business must be planned for—a task that may require the marshaling of huge resources in a finite time and in a way not totally disruptive to the business being purchased.

The first factor is the ubiquitous best efforts clause that is found in acquisition agreements requiring that parties use their best efforts to take all actions necessary and appropriate to effect a closing.[174] The client risks contractual liability if it does not fulfill this requirement. A client could be found to have violated such a provision when its lawyers have failed to pay attention to the matter.

The second factor is the practical risk that allowing a deal to lose the momentum that it had developed prior to the signing makes it harder to regain that momentum to move toward closing.

One practice that directly inhibits momentum is the substitution of an entirely different team of lawyers for those lawyers who had been working on the transaction until the signing of the agreement. Whether this substitution is a result of a team of legal specialists being moved in because the transaction has now shifted from the negotiation of an acquisition agreement to the negotiation of financing documents (or the preparation of a proxy statement or of an HSR Act filing), or because the partner who had been in charge of the negotiations has left control of the transaction to one or more associates to get the deal closed while he moves on to the next deal, or for what appears to the clients to be no good reason at all, such a substitution can make it both more time consuming and more expensive to get the transaction closed.

Contemplating the Closing

Three principal factors drive conduct between signing the agreement and closing:

- the parties' desires to complete the transaction to satisfy their business objectives;
- the need for third-party consents and approvals required to achieve the fruits of the bargain; and
- the covenants in the agreement (probably the least important).

Given the almost natural inclination for a deal to slow down upon signing the agreement, it is important to understand the timeframe in which a deal is really expected to close. Sometimes drop-dead dates in the agreement are established without any understanding of what it will take to get the deal done on time. With an understanding of the expected timetable and what needs to be accomplished, a plan can be put in place to reach the goal line. Ideally, this plan is formulated early while the negotiations on the agreement are beginning.

The list of consents and approvals will have already been developed through the negotiation of closing conditions. As those provisions have been negotiated, a general understanding of what is needed to be accomplished would have been formulated. But in many cases the full game plan will not have been developed. Conditions may have been specified to assure that the buyer will purchase the business it intended to buy, such as a condition that it would have been able to hire a base of employees. Is there a plan to assure that such a contingency will be satisfied? While some things can be left to happenstance or are so uncontrollable that there is little point in worrying about them, the conditions need to be understood and a plan developed to assure that they are satisfied within the timeframe anticipated.

Acquisition agreements customarily contain covenants requiring the parties to take, or refrain from taking, certain actions during the pre-closing period. Because parties want assurance that the deal will close, instead of merely relying on the parties' desire to consummate the transaction, they usually bargain for a best efforts covenant to move the deal toward closing and better assure that the conditions of closing are satisfied.

Practical Issues Not Covered by the Acquisition Agreement

The acquisition agreement often in only an incidental way deals with fundamental issues of closing—how to assure that the buyer receives the business for which it has bargained. For example, assume a purchase of assets where the buyer intends to hire the seller's employees. Employees are not sold—they need to be hired. That process needs to begin long before, not at, closing. Many employers require that each new employee sign an employment application and protective agreements (invention assignment and confidentiality) and perhaps undergo testing. Getting the payroll records set up and time recorders in place may take several weeks. Without employees, the buyer will not be able to operate the business—but these requirements are rarely the subject of a separate condition in the acquisition agreement.

Employee benefit plans also require planning and coordination. If retirement plans maintained by the seller are to be assumed by or transferred to the buyer, both significant practical and legal steps need to be considered by ERISA professionals. Customers may be offended to read about a deal for the first time in a newspaper. Such things as announcements about the deal and access to information are dealt with in the agreement, but often in a negative way (neither party may issue an announcement without the consent of the other). Premature announcements are probably not in the interest of either party. The practical need to explain the deal appropriately to various constituencies must be dealt with in light of the restrictions imposed by the agreement.

Some practical concerns may be an express condition to closing, such as financing. But even if the parties had failed to make the financing an express condition, there still may be the need for cash to complete the acquisition. A buyer will usually have begun exploration for financing before a deal is signed—it would not be interested in expending considerable time and effort if financing did not at least appear to be available. A prudent seller would have demanded some assurance of the availability of financing prior to signing. To be sure, buyers resist obtaining commitments (and sellers can often be persuaded that getting a commitment is not particularly useful) because they require the payment of a commitment fee.

Counsel's role is not necessarily to perform these tasks but to monitor the requirements and assist as necessary. The lawyers also provide practical help to clients who may not think ahead by putting various tasks on a closing agenda. For example, if the signage of the seller is supposed to be moved promptly after closing, a rigger might be lined up before closing, and if business cards with the newly acquired logo are to be available at the time of closing, the order needs to be placed.

Organizing for the Closing

Some practitioners use the last hours in the negotiation of an agreement—when the proposed agreement has been presented to the other side but it has not responded—to put together a basic outline of what needs to be done after the deal is signed. Others prefer to focus on getting the agreement signed, taking a day or so for some "R&R" and then promptly turning to the issues. In any case, review both the closing conditions and the pre-closing covenants. It is possible to have a condition not supported by a covenant—but letting it just happen may not be wise. We are told that there is a covenant of good faith and fair dealing in every contract. While the parameters of that doctrine vary with state law, it is possible that sitting on one's hands and not taking any action to achieve a closing condition is a violation of this duty. In addition, regardless of whether a party is required to take action designed to achieve a closing, most, having signed a deal, intend to close and might be surprised that necessary actions are not being taken because they are not required by the agreement. Pre-closing covenants need to be observed, particularly the negative covenants.

It has been suggested that the best way to explain a deal to a client is to prepare the closing agenda. If you took that advice, you may already have a substantial leg up on a "to do" list. This may have been contemplated by a detailed Time and Responsibility Schedule (see Appendix 3-A) circulated early in the negotiations, as discussed in Chapter 3. Or perhaps the other side has put together a closing agenda before the deal was signed. One good way to keep the momentum going, as well as to make sure that all required actions are taken prior to the closing, is to prepare and circulate a closing agenda as soon as possible after the signing that lists all actions that need to be taken between the signing of the agreement and the closing, as well as all documents that will need to be prepared in order that they can be executed and delivered at the closing. It is probably not wise to merely show up at closing with a list of what you thought you would receive—instead, the closing agenda should drive the preparation of all necessary documents and deliverables, such as third party consents.

Depending on the size and complexity of the transaction, the team leader may turn to the who, what, how, and why of making a deal come together. It is often appropriate to develop various teams to do major tasks. Preparation of the filings required in the HSR and SEC processes is time consuming and difficult, and requires special expertise, so assembling special teams for each of those tasks is quite common. Any other specialized regulatory approvals may require another team. Financing might also be shunted off to a team.

But other responsibilities may be corporate in nature, such as obtaining necessary consents, and therefore be more in the province of the deal lawyer to complete. Depending upon the number of consents identified, the mechanism used to determine which consents will be obtained (e.g., all required consents, all material consents, all Required Consents (defined by reference to a list)), the form of the transaction (asset deals usually require more consents than stock deals), and other factors, the job may be big or small. The team approach may be appropriate, or it may turn out to simply be incidental to the job being performed by someone else working on the matter.

The general point is that the broad tasks need to be identified, an approach taken as to how they should be accomplished, a team assembled and the details worked out.

Conferring with the Client

Too often there seems to be an assumption that everyone understands how to get from signing to closing. That may be true with the major tasks, such as getting a proxy statement cleared with the SEC, but even then the process needs to be discussed. As with all portions of an M&A deal, a lawyer should not assume what the client wants or how it proposes to handle things. It should also not be assumed that the client understands the implications of its representations or covenants. For example, a seller may have agreed to a covenant that it will not amend any

Material Contract (assumed to be defined in the acquisition agreement). It may be that the sale has not yet been announced to the seller's employees, but that sales contracts are routinely amended by the sales organization without much input from senior management. If the seller puts in place restrictions on amending contracts, it may have inadvertently announced that the company is being sold. If it does not, it may face breach of a covenant. It probably is not sufficient to hope for the best.

There are other practical reasons to involve the client: many of the consents required for closing need to come through assurances provided by the buyer and seller. For example, a key customer having an agreement for which consent is needed may need to be handled more delicately than mailing out letters seeking consents. How and when various constituencies may be contacted needs to be worked out. In deals where the transaction is not publicly announced, contacting employees, customers, and others may be at best awkward and perhaps in breach of the acquisition agreement.

Covenants

There are several essential purposes for pre-closing covenants.

- Covenants may assign to the parties the responsibility for carrying out specific tasks that are required to effect the acquisition, such as obtaining third party consents and regulatory clearances.
- The buyer will want to assure that the business it has agreed to buy will not differ substantially at closing from what it thought it was buying. Covenants may impose restrictions on operation of the business by the seller prior to closing.
- Covenants may require the seller to provide access to the business and communicate developments. These covenants are intended to identify potential problems early, particularly those that relate to a closing condition.
- There may be deal protection measures designed to protect the transaction by limiting the ability of the seller to solicit or entertain offers from third parties.
- Covenants may impose requirements, such as who will be offered employment, the level of benefits or adjustments to the corporate structure.

Either party typically has the right to refuse to close the transaction if the other party fails to perform its covenants in all material respects. More importantly, there may be an inability to close—most buyers would not close in the face of a required HSR filing not being made— or a practical limitation—the failure to obtain the consent of a customer that was the basis of buying the business in the first place.

Bridging the Gap—Best Efforts

It is altogether reasonable that a buyer would insist on certain conditions to closing. Usually the conditions relate to assurances that the buyer must have before it is willing to put its money up for the purchase of the business. The parties will usually want to assure that the conditions will occur and will not be left to happenstance. For example, assume that receipt of noncompetition agreements from the sellers is a condition to closing of a stock purchase. Since all sellers are probably signing the acquisition agreement, it would be easy to add a clause that the sellers agree to execute and deliver a noncompetition agreement at closing. In that case, the condition is supported by an absolute obligation to fulfill it. At the other extreme, assume that the buyer imposes a condition that no material adverse change will have occurred to the business being purchased. Most sellers are unwilling to provide any present assurance with respect to an event not within their control, and so there may be nothing in the agreement that relates explicitly to the seller's obligation to satisfy this condition. A covenant to operate the business in the ordinary course relates to this covenant in only the most general way.

The usual way to bridge this gap between providing no assurance and providing absolute assurance as to satisfaction of a condition is through a best efforts clause, explained to some extent in Chapter 11. This may be in the form of a general covenant, such as best efforts to satisfy all conditions, or may be nuanced, such as best efforts to obtain early termination of an HSR filing.

Best Efforts

Case law does not present a consistent interpretation of provisions that require a party to an agreement to use its "best efforts" to achieve an end. Some courts have held that such a provision adds little or nothing to the basic requirement of good faith. Other courts have held that a best efforts provision demands more than good faith, but does not prevent the promisor from giving consideration to its own interests. Still other courts have held that a best efforts provision denotes efforts beyond what is merely reasonable, or that such a provision is akin to a guarantee of performance, notwithstanding financial difficulties even to the extent of insolvency. The meaning of the best efforts standard is generally dependent on the circumstances of the agreement and the facts of the parties' situations.

Some practitioners seek to avoid the potential harshness that can result from the uncertain meaning of best efforts by using instead a term such as commercially reasonable efforts that is thought to be less stringent. Whether referring to best efforts or commercially reasonable efforts, the parties may wish to consider defining those terms in the agreement, specifying exactly what measures the promisor is required or not required to take. If the parties do not intend the provision to represent a guarantee of performance without regard to financial difficulty, they could, for example, include in the definition of the term a proviso establishing that the promisor is not thereby required to take actions that would impose a material burden, or is not required to make any payments in excess of normal and usual filing fees, or other such limitation as may be agreed to be appropriate. Qualifications of this sort, by not insisting on financial hardship, result in a limitation of the promisor's obligation to what is commercially reasonable.

Access and Due Diligence

Most acquisition agreements provide an access covenant, giving the buyer access to the seller's business and employees, customers and suppliers prior to the closing. Most acquisition agreements contain as a condition to closing the accuracy of the representations and compliance with the covenants. As an outsider looking in, a buyer will not know whether, in fact, there has been compliance with this condition. Buyers often demand that an additional condition of closing be the delivery of a certificate to the effect that the representations are true and the covenants have been complied with. But that's just another piece of paper. If a representation was inaccurate in the first place, will the paper delivered at closing make it accurate? Buyers demand the right of access to engage in confirmatory due diligence—to better assure that the representations were (and continue to be) true.

Often, once the agreement has been signed, buyers do not fully use their access rights. Perhaps their pre-signing due diligence has given them comfort of the truth of the representations. Perhaps the reality of the need for integration has hit, and other matters distract them. Perhaps they are just tired. This is an opportune time to remind buyers that their work may not be complete.

The access covenant also supports a buyer's efforts to begin the work that will be necessary to integrate the two organizations with a minimum of disruption. There are significant administrative challenges to integrating the businesses of two substantial organizations, including employee relations and communications, computer systems and software and data processing. In addition, in the case of a public buyer, given the certifications that will be required of the buyer's chief executive officer and chief financial officer under Sarbanes-Oxley, it will undoubtedly seek to use the pre-closing period to review the adequacy of the target's internal and disclosure controls, particularly if a closing is scheduled to occur near or at the end of a fiscal quarter.

In some instances, the access covenant is reciprocal, usually in cases where the seller will receive securities of the buyer. Except in a merger of equals, the seller's rights are significantly more limited and are generally focused on information necessary for the seller to assess whether there are developments involving the buyer that could impair the value of the securities that the seller has agreed to receive in the transaction.

Although the parties have agreed to the acquisition, antitrust laws may continue to regulate the parties' competitive activities until the closing. Care must be taken to assure that the parties do not prematurely exchange competitively sensitive information or take other prohibited actions. Caution should be exercised with respect to any exchange of information regarding open contract bids, bidding practices, pricing, specific marketing information, and other comparable information prior to closing.

Confidentiality

Confidentiality obligations are sometimes neglected in the drafting process. They should remain in place for the buyer until closing. Too often the acquisition agreement fails to mention an existing confidentiality agreement at all, leaving the parties to wonder whether confidentiality obligations have been integrated into the acquisition agreement. If nothing is said in the acquisition agreement, is there a confidentiality obligation? Sometimes the acquisition agreement contains its own confidentiality provision, which differs from the previously executed confidentiality agreement. Counsel will need to sort out how all of this works and to make sure that the confidentiality obligations are properly adjusted once the closing occurs.

Buyers will sometimes require that sellers attempt to recover confidential information distributed to other potential buyers. If the confidentiality agreements have not been entered into directly by the target company (as when a corporation is selling a subsidiary), the buyer may want those agreements assigned to the buyer.

Adjusting the Business Being Purchased

One or the other of the parties to an acquisition agreement may insist on some adjustment to the business being purchased before the transaction is closed. For example, if a subsidiary is being purchased, a buyer might insist that the intellectual property being used by the subsidiary be contributed to it by the seller. Or a buyer might require (or a seller insist) that another business included within an entity being sold be extracted from it before the closing.

While these requirements seem to be more prevalent in the sale of a subsidiary, it is not unusual in the purchase of a privately owned business. The shareholders may own the operating facilities of a business individually—a buyer may insist that the property be contributed to the target. Another common requirement in the purchase of a private business is the repayment of borrowings by individual shareholders or their relatives.

These mechanics are contained in either of two places. Because they go to the structure of a transaction, they may appear in the portion of the agreement dealing with the actual sale and purchase, whatever the form. Alternatively, they may appear in the portion containing the pre-closing covenants. These are usually absolute, not best efforts covenants, because they are usually within the control of the seller.

Complying with these covenants can be surprisingly complex, particularly in the sale of a subsidiary where the covenant requires freeing all entanglements among the parent and other subsidiaries built over the years. Attention must be paid to the details when there is a commingling of cash between parent and subsidiaries because it is centrally managed. Getting started early to identify what needs to be done and then doing it is always wise.

Operational Covenants

Any buyer has a strong interest in assuring that the business it is agreeing to buy will be substantially the same on the closing date as it was on the date the acquisition agreement was signed. To do so, it will try to negotiate strong covenants to maintain the status quo. It will use covenants because reliance on the representations, as they are brought down to closing, to satisfy a condition of closing that the representations remain true and correct on the closing date will not be adequate. There are three primary reasons why representations are insufficient. First, to the extent the representations deal with only certain aspects of the business, even if they remain true at closing, they will be insufficient to assure a steady hand on operational matters. Second, the condition that the representations be true at closing as though made at closing typically is qualified by some form of materiality exception, often by the MAC exception for public deals, meaning that this qualification would remove much of the sting from the bring-down. A MAC exception would mean that the representations could be untrue at closing and the closing condition would still be satisfied so long as they did not have a material adverse effect on the target. Third, reliance on a condition assumes that the target is appropriately motivated to close; failure to comply with a condition, without more, does not provide a buyer with a claim for damages.

While most sellers would attempt to limit these covenants, they might look at this in another way. When negotiating representations on matters that are outside their control, they may desire some latitude, represented by various materiality exceptions, so that they will be comfortable that the representations as brought down to closing will be true. A seller may be less concerned about strict covenants where it is in control of its own destiny, particularly with respect to covenants that merely prohibit certain types of actions.

While there may be arguments that the best efforts clause and implied covenants of good faith and fair dealing would compel a target to assure that conditions are met, including the operation of the business in the ordinary course, most buyers would want explicit agreement on these operational points from a seller. These usually involve:

- affirmative covenants, although often using vague concepts (e.g., "ordinary course of business");
- negative covenants—some explicit in nature, some vague; and
- notifications by the target to the buyer of certain events related to the closing, such as regulatory clearances and receipt of consents.

These pre-closing operating covenants are highly negotiated. They will be tailored to the business being purchased and will take into consideration the confidence that the buyer has in the management team, the length of time expected to elapse between signing and closing, the relative bargaining strength of the parties, the relative size of the parties, the level of detail and tightness with which other provisions (particularly the representations) have been negotiated, and the particular circumstances of the seller. Usually sellers desire to assure operational latitude, but not in all situations. In a particular transaction having a high degree of probability of closing, a seller may be receptive to whatever is proposed.

There are business and legal limitations and risks associated with these covenants. Boards of directors of sellers will typically resist any attempt to allow a buyer to run the business of the seller. Until the transaction is closed, that remains the responsibility of the seller's board of directors and management. There can be no assurance that a particular sale will be completed, so the board needs to assure that the target remains viable. Some buyers, in particular, may want a target to operate the business in a manner to best assure coordination with the buyer's business upon closing. Any significant control over a target by the buyer may give rise to legal concerns, among them antitrust, regulated industry restrictions (such as banking), controlling person liability under the securities laws and perhaps something akin to lender liability. A transaction subject to the HSR Act may not be closed until the waiting period has expired or been terminated, and actions by a buyer to run a target's business prior to that time (gun jumping) may be treated as tantamount to closing and therefore prohibited. Antitrust counsel should be consulted to determine whether these pre-closing covenants might constitute prohibited gun-jumping or might otherwise violate applicable antitrust laws.

Affirmative covenants. Affirmative covenants vary, although a covenant to operate the business in the ordinary course is universal, even though its formulation may vary. A typical covenant would require the seller to assure that the target conduct its business and operations in the ordinary course of business consistent with past practice and in compliance with all applicable legal requirements and all material contracts.

A second affirmative covenant would require a seller to use its best efforts to assure that the target preserves its business organization, keeps available the services of its current officers and employees and maintains its relations and goodwill with all suppliers, customers, landlords, creditors, licensors, licensees, and employees. There are three general themes in this process: preservation of the business organization, retaining the services of various constituencies, and maintaining the goodwill of another class of constituencies.

Some buyers may suggest additional affirmative covenants based on their practices, customary practice in certain industries or various legal requirements, such as to make certain SEC and tax filings.

Negative covenants. In an attempt to preserve the status quo, acquisition agreements will usually contain a series of prohibitions on the target between signing and the closing of the deal, referred to as negative covenants (sometimes forebearances). In contrast to the affirmative covenants, which tend to be general in nature, the negative covenants pinpoint specific activities, such as the payment of dividends. Specific negative covenants often deal with concerns in a particular industry or the circumstances of a particular target. It is always appropriate to adjust negative covenants to fit the target. Negative covenants are expected in a public deal, but can become a problem as they shade into the ordinary operations of the target, particularly if the time between signing and closing is significant, as would be the case of a target in a regulated industry or where other regulatory clearances are expected to take considerable time.

Notifications. A covenant usually requires that the seller notify the buyer about certain events relating to the conditions to closing, such as:

- the discovery of a material inaccuracy in any representation;
- any material breach of any covenant;
- any legal proceeding pending against or with respect to the target; and
- any event that could be expected to have a material adverse effect on the target.

Notifications usually tie to the closing conditions. It is worthwhile to seek reciprocal rights and responsibilities in this area; however, buyers typically try to impose these obligations solely on sellers.

Satisfying Closing Conditions

For most acquisition agreements, there are a number of conditions to be satisfied before closing, which take time and effort. Most major conditions are supported by their own set of covenants. For example, for a public target there would be a requirement to call a meeting of shareholders and to file and attempt to have cleared by the SEC a proxy statement (usually supported by a best efforts obligation). Other conditions may be less specific, but ultimately supported by a best efforts obligation. The interrelationship between some of these conditions and the covenants is discussed below.

Consents

What are consents? Often the legal and practical aspects of obtaining consents are not well articulated in acquisition agreements. Narrowly, consents may be required for the assignment of a contract, but the phrase also relates to relief against change in control clauses, automatic defaults, an adverse change in contract terms (an increased interest rate, for example), or other relief where necessary for the buyer to fully enjoy the business purchased. A broader reading may include governmental consents for the assignment of government licenses and permits. The definition may refer to new governmental authorizations under circumstances where licenses and permits are not assignable.

Do we need all consents? Sometimes a required consent just is not worth the effort. So what if the copy machine lease requires consent—is there any practical risk if such consent were not obtained? One way to work out what consents will be required before the deal is signed is to develop a list of "Required Consents." The list then becomes a work plan for getting to closing. Without such a list, the seller may have to engage in the process of obtaining all consents because of uncertainty whether certain unobtained consents might be deemed material. Often seeking some consents is just a waste of precious time.

Who must obtain consents? Normally one thinks of being responsible for obtaining the consents of contracting parties with which one is in privity or from one's own regulator. Thus, if a buyer needs a waiver under a credit agreement to which it is a party, it is up to the buyer to obtain it. This means that the bulk of the consents in any deal—those to be obtained from contracting parties with the seller or target—are obtained by the seller, although this is often a cooperative effort.

Often there is a best efforts obligation to satisfy the conditions that apply to one's own performance—that is, a buyer would agree to use its best efforts to satisfy the conditions to its performance. That may not work appropriately in the case of consents. Both the buyer and the seller may have agreed to use their best efforts to obtain these consents. So whose responsibility is it? Let's assume that the buyer expects the seller to get the necessary consents since they involve the seller's customers. The consents are not obtained and the deal does not close. The buyer sues on the basis that seller breached the best efforts covenant. The seller defends and counterclaims on the basis that the buyer did nothing at all and therefore in fact violated its best efforts obligations. As a matter of drafting, responsibility is best allocated to one party, with the other party required only to cooperate. In the face of less than precise language, the parties may want to amend the agreement or arrive at a plan acknowledged by both parties on how consents will be obtained.

Practical aspects of obtaining consents. There are two recurring scenarios that are troublesome. In the first, little attention is paid to the closing until a week or so prior to the scheduled date, when the process of drafting the documents to be delivered at closing begins. At that point someone notices that no effort has been made in obtaining consents. A mad scramble begins, but with no hope of actually getting any substantial portion of the consents in time for closing. In the second, laudable in its objective but naïve in its approach, the seller's law firm is asked to obtain consents. A letter is skillfully prepared, having very precise language. An associate is tasked with obtaining the consents. The names, addresses, and contact parties are obtained and the letter goes out on law firm stationary, asking parties to contact the associate involved. Nothing other than the name of the buyer is mentioned. What is the likely reaction to this request? Since little is said about the buyer or its creditworthiness, the person that this goes to may be reluctant to do anything. The benefit to the contracting party has not been explained. Or the reaction is that, since a law firm is making a request, the letter is immediately sent to the other party's law department, with attendant delays. The result in either case is that many consents are not received and the buyer is faced with the prospect of waiving the condition and closing.

Contrast either of these two scenarios to this one: prior to signing, the parties have worked out a process for obtaining consents. The number of consents has been limited to those that are truly material. An approach has been agreed to in which the buyer can explain itself and the strategic reason for the deal in written materials (and, in some cases, plans are made for telephone conferences or visits). The obligation and creditworthiness of the buyer is clearly explained, and the consent form itself is in "plain English," not legalese. The materials go out soon after signing (and after a public press release). The buyer and seller have agreed to a timetable for seeking consents, involving action items and weekly status reports. It is agreed that after some period of time, follow-up action will be taken. A proven team leader from the business side is assigned to obtain these consents.

The SEC Process

The task of getting materials cleared under the securities laws can be so Herculean and the timeline so long that it often becomes the overriding issue in the drive to closing. In fact, most acquisitions of public companies are timed so that the approval by shareholders in the morning is followed by an immediate closing. But the condition is shareholder approval, not SEC clearance of materials. To be sure, in some forms of private transactions (a merger or the purchase of all or substantially all of the assets of a corporation) a similar condition is necessary. If shareholder approval is a condition, it will usually be necessary to have a meeting.

Getting materials through the SEC will be required when the approval of the company's shareholders is necessary (requiring a proxy or information statement) or when a company is offering its own securities in a deal and no exemption from registration is available.

Buyer securities would normally be registered on Form S-4, unless the buyer is relying on an exemption from registration. The registration statement must be declared effective before there is a shareholder solicitation on the deal. The prospectus contained as a part of the registration statement becomes a proxy statement for the target's shareholder meeting (and is usually called a Proxy Statement/Prospectus). When the buyer's shareholders must approve the transaction (usually because of stock listing requirements based upon the number of shares being issued in the deal), the same document may also be used as a proxy statement for the buyer's shareholder meeting.

When buyer securities are not being issued and the target is a public company, it must still comply with the proxy statement requirements applicable to it. The information required to be disclosed is voluminous and the proxy statement will be subject to SEC review.

Sometimes when buyer securities are being used, an exemption from registration can be found when a public body is authorized to determine the fairness of the transaction. Several jurisdictions, including California, have statutes that explicitly authorize "fairness" hearings. The required disclosure is typically not as extensive as that required under the federal securities laws, and the process can be much faster than SEC registration.

The usual covenant supporting the shareholder approval condition has elements of both an absolute covenant and a best efforts covenant. There is usually an absolute obligation to call the shareholder meeting (and for states having force-the-vote statutes submit to shareholders the approval of the transaction), sometimes by a time certain and in other cases as soon as practicable. A similar obligation might be imposed on submitting materials to the SEC. On the other hand, since SEC clearance and shareholder approval are subject to the actions of a third party, there typically is only a best efforts obligation to obtain SEC clearances and shareholder approvals. The obligation to obtain shareholder approval is usually subject to some fiduciary standard.

The problems in moving toward closing discussed at the beginning of this chapter are particularly applicable to this covenant. The task is so large that the breathing room between signing and turning to this task is often long. This task is often turned over to another group, perhaps the target's regular SEC counsel. The problem with delaying the start of this task is that it is already on the critical path and deferral only lengthens that path. The best efforts obligation, as applied to this covenant, could have some sting. Some buyers may insist that in the acquisition of a public company preparation of SEC materials actually begin while negotiations are still under way.

Possible Failure of Best Efforts

Buyer, a private equity fund sponsored manufacturer, signed up a complex agreement to combine its operations with two other entities, one of which was publicly held while the other was a subsidiary of another corporation. It was contemplated that the manufacturer would issue its stock in exchange for the stock in the public company and the private company. Since stock was being offered, it was necessary to register the stock with the Securities and Exchange Commission (no exemption was available). In essence, this would have been an initial public offering by the manufacturer. A reasonable time for completing this task is probably six months at best. In order to register stock, a registration statement is prepared and filed with the SEC, reviewed by the SEC staff, comments issued and a response to the comments filed by means of amendment. The process may be repeated several times.

The acquisition agreement had a 60-day drop dead date. It would have been virtually impossible to get through the SEC and close in 60 days. The manufacturer terminated the agreement when the transaction was not closed within 60 days, as it was permitted to do. The publicly held entity then sued the manufacturer on the basis that it had violated its best efforts obligation and an implied duty of good faith and fair dealing. The motion for summary judgment was denied on the basis that there were genuine issues of fact to be decided. The manufacturer, rather than risk going to trial, settled for a tidy sum and bore the costs of defense until settlement.

The manufacturer may have avoided being backed into a corner if the drop dead date had been longer or if best efforts had been defined to include or exclude conduct that would not have tripped the clause.

HSR Filings

If an HSR filing is required, it is always a gating item, since the failure to comply with the statutory procedures would be a violation of law. The related covenant is typically a combination of an absolute and a best efforts covenant. There is usually an absolute covenant to make the filing (often by a date certain) and a best efforts obligation to get the clearance. It is probably in the area of antitrust clearances that the best efforts covenant has become most nuanced. Often, the HSR clearance is routine. The filing is made, no questions are asked and early termination is granted. But the best efforts covenant may address what happens when clearance is not prompt.

What does best efforts mean in this context? Often antitrust officials will not object to a merger only if there are assurances that undue concentration in a particular market will be avoided. That might be accomplished if the seller were to sell only a portion of the bargained-for business or if the buyer were to dispose of an existing business (or agree to dispose of a portion of the business acquired). If nothing is said, does the best efforts obligation require these set asides, even when complying with such an obligation might deprive a party of the benefit of the bargain? Often the parties will negotiate a provision in the best efforts clause providing for what they do not have to do, that is sell or set aside a portion of the business being acquired or another business.

Example of Carveout to Best Efforts Clause

In the AT&T Wireless/Cingular agreement by which Cingular, owned by Bell South and SBC (the buyer entities), would acquire AT&T Wireless, there was an obligation on the buyer entities to use their reasonable best efforts to obtain all necessary governmental clearances. There was concern that, because of concentration, there would be antitrust objections to the acquisition. Presumably to address this concern, the best efforts obligation was qualified with respect to any required divestiture that the buyer entities might have to make in order to obtain governmental clearances. The net economic effects on the value of the business of any actions were compared to a defined material adverse condition. If the value of the effects exceeded the material adverse condition, the action was not required to be taken. Here's the actual language:

Nothing in this Agreement shall require, or be construed to require, [buyer entities] to take any action or enter into any agreement with respect to any of its assets, business or operations (the sum of the aggregate positive and negative economic effects of all such actions and agreements on the value of the assets, business or operations of the combined [entities] (excluding synergies anticipated to be realized by [the buyer entities]) and on the value of the assets, business or operations of [the parent entities], as of the date of any determination being referred to herein as the "Net Effects"), that would, individually or in the aggregate, reasonably be expected to result in the aggregate negative Net Effects being more than the Material Adverse Amount (as defined in . . . (a "Material Adverse Condition")). For purposes of calculating Net Effects with respect to the sale of a market or spectrum it is agreed that (i) the Net Effects of the sale of a market owned by any of the Company, Cingular or Cingular Wireless will be an amount equal to the Per Subscriber Amount (as defined in . . .) multiplied by the number of subscribers in the system and operations in such market proposed by Cingular, in good faith, to be sold, and (ii) the Net Effects of the sale of spectrum-only shall be $0.50 per MHz POP.

On the other hand, one of the parties may be reluctant to go forward with a deal unless the other party is willing to agree affirmatively to some accommodation to antitrust regulation in order to get the deal done. This always poses the specter of the self-fulfilling prophecy— that the antitrust regulators will always require what has been volunteered.

Even aside from anticipating how to deal with requested regulatory relief, the parties will need to anticipate the interplay between regulatory objections and the best efforts clause. Will there be a full and complete response to a second request? Will the parties be required to litigate until there is a final order?

Shareholder Approvals

Approval of target shareholders and sometimes shareholders of the buyer may be required. Approval of target shareholders may be required as part of a statutory merger and in some states sale of all or substantially all of the assets. Approval of the buyer's shareholders may be required as a deal structured as a merger or because of stock listing requirements (the use of a significant amount of stock of buyer).

Real Estate Matters

In circumstances where real estate is important or the buyer has otherwise negotiated satisfactory real estate title as a condition to closing, attention usually must be devoted to assuring that the condition is satisfied. The closing of an M&A deal is not necessarily conditioned on title. Many businesses merely lease their properties. Even when property is owned, a seller will argue that in a practical sense title is not important—it is the overall operation of the business, which the seller has operated without problems for some time. A buyer may argue that its ability to resell certain assets may be imperiled unless title matters are taken care of by the closing.

Title insurance seems to have almost universally supplanted title opinions as the best evidence of ownership. Because it is subject to matters that a land survey might show, getting a surveyor involved is also necessary. Any required condition to closing would be an assurance of ownership of title and absence of encumbrances. Even when stock is being purchased, a buyer may insist that the seller's existing title policies be updated and coverages increased. What needs to be done depends on the specifics of the agreement.

Even if the status of title is not a closing condition, it is often wise to address title in connection with the closing. It may be easier to find old title policies and surveys. In an asset deal, it will be necessary to record a deed to transfer title to the real estate, so legal descriptions will still need to be correct. The parties should also consider the handling of expenses often unique to real estate: rent, utilities, real estate taxes, and how to allocate or prorate them among the parties. Real estate usually raises significant environmental law concerns resulting, often, in the need for environmental surveys and significant time haggling over post-closing indemnification responsibilities among the parties.

Financing Contingencies and Dealing with Third Party Funding Sources

Buyers of businesses must sometimes secure debt financing to close the transaction. By bringing a lender into the deal, the buyer introduces a third party player with its own unique business perspectives, legal requirements and timing issues. Negotiating with and ultimately satisfying a lender, while at the same time not re-opening the business terms of the acquisition or delaying its closing, can be like walking a tightrope. The buyer and its counsel must develop a comprehensive strategy for concluding this piece of the deal.

Before the process of negotiating and dealing with a funding source can begin, the buyer must first find that funding source. Different lenders focus on different industries, transactions, geographic locations, types of collateral, and credit quality. A buyer needs to understand which lending sources have the interest, expertise, and appetite for providing the required debt financing. Even within a banking institution, it is important to identify the optimum entry point. A buyer might contact a particular loan officer within a bank and be rebuffed, unaware that a call to a specialized group on another floor would have generated a high level of interest. Some bankers are so focused on their own areas of specialty that they do a lackluster job of referring prospective borrowers to others within their organization who might provide a better fit.

Quotes from multiple lending sources should be obtained. The terms offered by various lenders will vary, and playing one off against the others may achieve the optimum financing package. An important goal is to secure as firm a commitment as possible from a lender, particularly if the acquisition documents do not contain a financing contingency. Lender proposals that are soft and subject to various conditions such as due diligence and syndication of the credit facility (that is, assembling a bank group) can put the buyer at risk. Similarly, the lender's commitment should be as detailed as possible, particularly on pricing, financial covenants, and negative covenants relating to issues such as permitted future acquisitions and investments as well as permitted dividends and distributions. If the buyer fails to settle fundamental terms in the commitment letter, it will be at a disadvantage in trying to raise and negotiate those points down the road when the acquisition is on the line. The usual convention is for the borrower to pay the lender's legal fees and so it is appropriate for the borrower at any early stage to request an estimate or even a cap on those fees. The borrower may request the bank to propose two or three alternative law firms to serve as counsel to the lender, with the ultimate choice left to the borrower.

In speaking with lenders, it is important to understand their approval processes and identify the real decision makers. If a committee that meets infrequently or a senior bank officer with a heavy travel schedule must approve the loan, timing can become an acute problem. In large lending institutions, the initial point of contact will likely be a person with little ultimate decision-making authority and no responsibility for closing or subsequently administering the loan and the relationship. The buyer should meet and become comfortable with the individuals who will be playing those roles.

Buyers must also understand that lenders have their own due diligence requirements. Lenders take some care (and time) in qualifying their borrowers. If the buyer does not already have a business relationship with the lender or has not previously introduced itself, the approval process can get bogged down while the lender makes itself comfortable with the buyer, its business, and its management. As for the target, the lender will want to see any offering materials circulated in connection with the sale as well as annual and interim financial statements and receivables and payables reports. The lender will also want to review and even require the buyer to prepare pro forma financial statements. A lender seeking a blanket lien on all the target's assets will want to understand the nature and value of the those assets, including intellectual property. Finally, it will want to understand the terms of the acquisition and ultimately have its lawyers review the acquisition documents. Of particular importance to the lender will be the strength of the target's representations and allocation of risk with respect to potentially high liability issues, such as environmental compliance and product liability. The lender typically will require the buyer to conditionally assign to the lender its rights, but not its obligations, under the acquisition agreement as further security for its loan. The buyer should provide for this in the typical "anti-assignment" provision in the acquisition agreement.[175] The more quickly the buyer can package and deliver these materials to the lender, the more quickly the lender can approve the financing and the firmer its commitment is likely to be. Even better, consider asking the lender to review these terms prior to signing.

In order to secure financing adequate to close a transaction, a buyer may need different layers of funding (e.g., senior debt, mezzanine or subordinated debt, and equity). Each source of funding will have its own conditions and requirements. A senior lender will typically seek a blanket lien on all assets. Since mezzanine lenders are subordinated to senior lenders and are therefore at higher risk, they will usually demand a higher interest rate and perhaps warrants to give them some share in the upside. Equity investors will usually require securities with a preferential return in addition to warrants or securities convertible into underlying equity on favorable terms.

Coordinating all these players, keeping them informed of changes to the acquisition terms and to each of their deals and prodding them in order to meet the closing schedule can be a challenge. For example, the buyer may want to end up with a set of representations that is common to the acquisition agreement and the documents for the various layers of financing. (The buyer does not want to breach a lending representation, but then lack any recourse against the seller because its representation is slightly different). Likewise, disparities in the covenants made to the various lenders can often cause confusion and should be avoided. Usually, each lender will have its own peculiar requirements, whether with regard to representations, covenants, or legal opinions. At the same time, each lender will also want the benefit of any concessions given to another funding source. Keeping each of them reasonably satisfied, but knowing when to say "no more" can be tricky.

Subordination terms between the senior lender and the mezzanine lender can sometimes become intricate and involved. Since subordination largely involves the relative rights of the lenders, it is for the most part an issue among the lenders. However, the buyer and its counsel cannot afford to just sit back and allow the lenders to fight it out among themselves. They need to understand how the subordination terms may affect the buyer. Sometimes, the buyer's counsel needs to intervene in order to resolve an impasse so as not to delay the closing.

In reviewing loan documents, the buyer's counsel must assure that they are faithful to the lender's proposed terms or commitment letter. Loan agreements tend to be highly stylized documents replete with pages of boilerplate. Typically, the businesspeople at the borrower will not be well equipped to distinguish what is truly important or worthy of negotiation. Buyer's counsel should identify the genuine business issues for the buyer. The buyer should focus on the financial covenants and satisfy itself that there is ample cushion on a post-closing basis to satisfy these covenants even if difficulties are encountered. If the buyer anticipates the need to take certain post-closing business actions, such as pursuing acquisitions, sufficient latitude to undertake those activities should be hard-wired into the loan agreement. The buyer should avoid having to run to the lender for a waiver or consent soon after the loan closing. Doing so does not inspire confidence in the management, and lenders may charge a fee for such items.

A productive negotiating path is to have the buyer discuss the business issues directly with the loan officer rather than going through bank counsel. Similarly, counsel to the buyer should make its client aware that the seemingly draconian and outrageous boilerplate in the security documents is indeed market and not worth fighting over.

Lenders like predictability and generally abhor surprises. What they dislike above all else is being blindsided. Borrowers should keep lenders informed on a reasonably current basis of changes to the acquisition deal and, on a post-closing basis, of changes in the business and its performance. Generally only bad things happen when unwelcome news is withheld and communicated to a lender at the last moment.

A seller should be concerned if a buyer needs financing to do the deal, because that usually means financing availability on acceptable terms to the buyer will be a contingency of the deal. A seller could incur a huge expense pursuing the deal only to find it cratered because the buyer cannot get financing. Sometimes the seller or its counsel will consider requiring the deposit or a breakup fee to cover such a contingency or an early waiver of the contingency by the buyer. Sellers also should be aware that with a lender involved, the seller's representations, covenants, and indemnities will be more inflexible, unqualified and onerous than if a lender were not involved. The lender will insist on protection and the buyer will smile slightly, sigh and say, "I really tried to resist these requirements but could not convince my lender to forego them. You know how lenders are." The involvement of a lender will almost always extend the time needed to negotiate documents and close the transaction.

CHAPTER **13**

Coping with the Troubled Deal

A funny thing happened on the way to the closing. Sometimes deals just do not close. Occasionally parties realize that the marriage made in heaven is just not meant to be and sever their relationship (even though legally binding) without acrimony. On some occasions, a regulator, contracting party, or other third party may prevent a matter from going forward, and the parties need to know how to behave in that instance. While it does not happen very often, one party or the other may, justifiably or not, get cold feet and want to end matters. Sometimes a party will use a problem (or the pretense of a problem) to gain a price concession, using the threat to walk from a deal as leverage.

Too often practitioners look too hard at the carefully crafted language and do not spend enough time understanding the judicial limitations on remedies or the panoply of legal remedies that might be available. The exercise of a termination right may not be a get-out-of-jail-free card.

Walk (Termination) Rights and Limitations

A party (typically a buyer) may want to walk away from a deal for a variety of reasons. It might discover material misstatements in the seller's representations. Events might occur, such as the filing of litigation, which could result in a material liability. There might be developments that could seriously affect the target's future prospects, such as a significant downturn in its revenues or the adoption of governmental regulations. The buyer might have concluded that a condition to closing, such as obtaining a material consent, cannot be satisfied. Or the buyer might simply have soured on the deal (and that is often the rub). At that point, the buyer may ask its attorney whether sufficient grounds exist for walking away, which may also extend to an analysis of remedies available against the other party and how damages would be calculated.

While most of the discussion below relates to the buyer's walk rights, the same principles are generally applicable to a termination by a seller.

Negotiated Termination Rights

Under basic principles of contract law, a party would have the right to suspend or terminate its performance under an agreement in the event of a material breach by the other party or the non-fulfillment of a condition precedent to the party's obligation to perform.[176] Most acquisition agreements, however, specify the circumstances in which they can be terminated (walk rights). An agreement typically can be terminated:

- by mutual consent of the parties;
- by a party, if a material breach of the agreement has been committed by the other party;
- by a party, if certain conditions for its benefit have not been satisfied by the date specified for the closing or the satisfaction of a condition becomes impossible (other than through the failure of that party to comply with its obligations); or
- by either party, if the closing has not occurred by a specified date, or such later date as may be agreed to, unless the party seeking to terminate is in material breach of the agreement.[177]

The first basis for termination—mutual consent of the parties—is straightforward and makes it clear that the parties to the acquisition agreement do not need the consent of anyone else (e.g., shareholders or third-party beneficiaries) to terminate the transaction.

The right of a non-defaulting party to walk away from the acquisition if the other party has committed a material breach counters any ambiguity in the law of contracts that might require that the parties consummate the acquisition and litigate over damages. Breach ordinarily will include an inaccurate representation or a failure to perform a covenant. These provisions sometimes permit a party to cure a breach within a specified period before it will become a basis for termination. As discussed below, if a breach is discovered, extensive analysis may be required to frame a cause of action.

Where conditions to a party's obligation to close are not satisfied or become impossible to satisfy, unless caused by the failure of such terminating party to comply with its obligations, the party for whose benefit the condition was included in the agreement would typically have the right to terminate its obligations. Termination provisions may overlap in that a misrepresentation or breach of covenant will often result in the failure of a condition.

The final typical basis for termination is often referred to as the drop-dead date. An agreement will generally provide that the closing will take place on a specified date or a specified number of days after some event has occurred, such as the expiration of the HSR Act waiting period. Most agreements will also provide that failure to close on the designated closing date will not, by itself, constitute a termination of the obligations of the parties. This then enables the parties to choose a date beyond which either party may call off the deal simply because it has taken too long to get it done. If there is fault, the rights of the party not at fault to sue for breach will generally be preserved. Even if no one is at fault, however, either party would be entitled to call a halt to the acquisition on or after the specified date.

Many other events or situations that permit one or more of the parties to terminate the agreement typically are negotiated. These may be the same events or situations that are the conditions to closing (more accurately the absence of such event or situation), but are of sufficient importance to a party that it does not want to wait until the closing date to determine whether the condition has occurred, thus avoiding additional effort and expense. Sometimes the walk right is just simply an independent right. These kinds of events and situations might include the buyer's inability to conclude an employment arrangement with one or more key persons, its dissatisfaction with something revealed in the due diligence investigation or material damage to or destruction of a significant asset or portion of the assets. A seller might have the right to terminate due to the buyer's inability to deliver a signed commitment letter for acquisition financing within a specified period of time. If a buyer uses seller financing or the buyer's stock to pay part of the purchase price, the seller would likely have many of the same issues leading up to closing and consequently negotiate many of the same walk rights.

The terms of the agreement may determine the liability, if any, of the non-terminating party and may allow either party to walk away without any further liability. The only limit is the creativity and negotiating strength (or ability) of the lawyers and their clients.

Liability Claims Limited by Contract

Whether termination is an election of remedies depends upon the drafting of the agreement and any limitations imposed by law. Careful review of the agreement is in order. Because in negotiating the agreement parties are usually focused on how to get the deal done rather than how to avoid a deal, the precise operation of the termination provisions may not be carefully examined until the issue of termination arises. Sometimes termination is expressed as the sole remedy (that is the terminating party may not sue for damages). Sometimes the right to sue for willful breach is preserved. Sometimes there is a liquidated damages provision, which has a variety of formulations, including a break up fee. As discussed below, particularly in the case of a misrepresentation, the alternative of not exercising a termination right and suing for damages may not be available. Buyers who terminate may simply feel themselves lucky and be wary of the cost of pursuing a legal claim, especially if there is a need to prove willful action by the seller.

Any limitation imposed by the agreement must be understood. For example, do the indemnification provisions, in addition to providing a post closing claim, provide an exclusive remedy upon termination? Provisions may limit the compensatory rights of the parties in an acquisition agreement. For example, the contract may provide for a cap (or upper limit) or basket (or lower limit) on any claims by one or both of the parties. While usually a limitation in the remedy of indemnification, the cap or basket could be a more general limitation.

A substantial deposit may have been paid to evidence the buyer's good faith in negotiating the agreement. Is a claim by seller limited to the amount of the deposit paid?

Does the agreement require any issues to be mediated or arbitrated?

Resisting the Assertion of Termination Rights

A party receiving a threat of termination or a termination notice may accept its fate or may decide to fight. A seller with a favorable deal faced with the prospect of selling the target again against the specter of a failed deal may be particularly motivated. How a party might respond will depend upon the purported basis of termination and the availability of judicial remedies to halt a termination. Governing state law will always need to be examined on the point. A party may want to seek equitable relief in order to prevent the operation of the termination provision and preserve the status quo or a final decree ordering specific performance.

Judicial Limitations on Contract Remedies

One case illustrating a judicial reluctance to enforce express language is *IBP, Inc. v. Tyson Foods, Inc.*,[178] in which the Delaware Chancery Court ruled that the buyer did not have a valid basis to terminate an acquisition agreement and ordered that the merger be consummated. Various representations of the seller were analyzed to determine whether a breach had occurred that would have entitled the buyer to terminate. The court took a pragmatic approach in determining whether certain developments had a durationally significant material adverse effect on the target, which would have constituted a breach. This case illustrates that the reasons initially given by a party for termination should be consistent with the position that party may ultimately want to take in any litigation that questions its right to terminate. While this case involved a merger of two publicly held corporations, the same considerations should apply to closely held businesses.

In the situation where both parties are aware of an inaccuracy prior to closing that would trigger one party's walk rights, the other party may try to force an election of remedies by the innocent party. Under common law principles, a buyer may not accept substitute performance (in this case closing when a closing condition has not been satisfied) and sue under the terms of the original contract. The buyer must elect to close or sue—it cannot close and sue, at least under common law, even with an express reservation of rights.

Cases have held that the application of common law principles is not necessarily dispositive. *Ziff-Davis*[179] held that a buyer was entitled to close and sue, because it was entitled to rely on an express (but inaccurate) warranty made by the seller. *Galli*[180] distinguished *Ziff-Davis* on the grounds that the seller in that case had vigorously denied the existence of any misstatement or omission and each party has expressly reserved the rights prior to closing. Consequently, *Ziff-Davis* application was limited to situations where the buyer alleged, and the seller contested, the existence of certain inaccuracies, and it did not apply where the parties essentially agreed on the existence of a misrepresentation prior to closing. The *Galli* court refused to allow the buyer to close with knowledge of facts that ordinarily would constitute grounds for termination and sue afterwards for the breach (although it indicated that if the buyer had expressly reserved its rights, it might have ruled differently). Since the *Ziff-Davis* and *Galli* decisions, the trend seems to be in the direction of honoring the negotiated terms of the contract provided there is explicit language to the effect that the buyer can close and sue even with prior knowledge of the inaccuracy. At least one court has indicated otherwise.[181] In those jurisdictions that have not yet ruled on this issue, the parties are left with some uncertainty as to how to handle an acknowledged inaccuracy that comes to light pre-closing. The buyer can negotiate for a provision that permits the buyer to close and sue even with prior knowledge, but some pushback should be expected from the seller.

Recourse of the Terminated Party

Even if there is justifiable termination, it does not follow that the terminated party has no judicial recourse. For example, a party may terminate because the drop-dead date has passed. Because the termination right is absolute, there may be no basis for asserting that the agreement should not be terminated. But assume that the terminating party has been foot dragging and did not satisfy a well-drafted best efforts clause or breached the implied covenant of good faith and fair dealing. The termination of the agreement by one party may not avoid the other party's right to assert breach of the agreement. Sometimes by its terms a termination right may not be utilized by a party itself in material breach of an agreement. Whether there in fact is an implied covenant of good faith and fair dealing under the laws of a particular state and how a best efforts clause will be interpreted would need to be examined. Most litigators will need to be guided through the intricacies and interplays of the agreement by the deal lawyer as recourse is being explored.

Assessing Alternatives When a Deal Is Faltering

Usually one is not surprised by a termination notice and does not show up for the closing to find an empty room. It may be because a necessary governmental approval is not forthcoming, or a consent will only be given in circumstances costly to the parties. Or perhaps the buyer is delaying, and the tea leaves indicate something is amiss.

The frequency with which parties walk away from deals seems to have increased in recent years. A decision to terminate should be undertaken only after careful consideration of one's legal position and potential consequences. For example, is the non-terminating party likely to seek damages or specific performance? Terminating also has to be weighed against the alternative of proceeding to close the transaction. If the closing occurs, can the buyer be exposed to loss, and, if so, what is the likelihood of recovering any resulting damages from the seller? What effect will closing the transaction with knowledge of a breach have on the possibility of recovering damages for that breach?[182]

Neither party may be at fault. For example, a transaction may not close due to *force majeure* (where the agreement permits the other party to terminate the transaction in such circumstances). But the refusal of a governmental agency to grant its approval is not necessarily innocent where a party violated its best efforts obligation to obtain approval.

Formulating Strategy—The Not Yet Failed Deal

A party willing to move forward in the face of reluctance on the other side needs to explore its options. Does the agreement contain a termination provision that will allow the non-defaulting party to give notice terminating the agreement and to maintain its rights against the defaulting party? Does a formal notice of breach have to be delivered to the other party? If so, when should that notice be given and what should the notice contain?

Where the actions of the other party are fundamentally at odds with the completion of the transaction and the client is willing to perform (to the extent possible at the time of the other party's actions), even where the agreement does not contain a specific termination right in those circumstances, an anticipatory repudiation of the agreement by the other party has likely occurred.[183] A party will probably not wish to continue to work towards the closing of a transaction that is being repudiated by the other party. If the repudiation is clear and a party does not wish to proceed further, it may want to give the breaching party notice of the anticipatory repudiation and advise that it is proceeding on the basis that the other party has terminated the agreement. Giving notice of termination will permit the party to avoid additional time and expense in futilely pursuing a transaction that will not happen. However, the party will be obliged to substantiate its damages as well as its attempts to mitigate its damages in pursuing a claim against the defaulting party. The manner in which mitigation is to occur may be difficult to ascertain. For example, is the seller obliged to again offer its business for sale and conclude a sale so as to establish the damages as being the difference between the price received and that offered under the original agreement?

To preserve its rights, a non-defaulting party may want to tender performance to the defaulting party by presenting all of the documents, materials, and funds required to be provided at closing at the selected place and time. A failure to accept the tender and close the transaction by the other party will provide evidence of the non-defaulting party's readiness to carry out the transaction and the other party's failure to proceed. If the other party breaches the agreement or otherwise causes the transaction to fail at a time before the closing, a determination has to be made whether this constitutes an anticipatory repudiation of the agreement by the other party. If there has been an anticipatory breach, then no purpose is served in establishing the client's readiness to complete the transaction and a tender is not required. In some circumstances, the parties may agree in writing to waive any necessity to tender.

Specific performance may be sought. Specific performance will only be mandated where the client cannot be compensated adequately in monetary damages for the breach and only if the client will suffer irreparable harm that can only be assuaged by the contract's performance. If this cannot be substantiated, the claim will lie in damages.

Mutual Fault

The issue of breach becomes more complex where there are breaches of the agreement by both parties. The relative fault of the parties will be explored. A party may take the position that its breaches were insubstantial while the breaches by the other party were basic to the transaction and frustrated the intent of the agreement. These so-called minor breaches are likely to be uncovered in the course of litigation.

Preparing for Litigation

Regardless of fault, a paper trail of the events leading up to the termination of the transaction should be prepared. Each letter, document, and note and the recollections of each of the parties involved in discussions and negotiations should be reviewed and, subject to the usual caution in the preparation for litigation, a full record made of the events to the date of the termination. These would include evidence of any steps taken by the client to deal with any events that might have caused difficulty in concluding the transaction to bolster the lack of fault while demonstrating any wrongful course of action by the other party.

All information concerning the termination of the transaction should be sifted carefully to determine whether any third party has induced a breach of the agreement by the other party that might render the third party liable for its actions or if it has otherwise wrongfully interfered with the transaction for its own purposes.

Pre-Closing Discovery of A Breach

In the event of a pre-closing discovery by any party of a breach (or anticipated breach) of its representations or covenants, the primary issue that arises is whether the discovering party will disclose the breach to the counterparty, which involves a number of competing interests and considerations. While the agreement would normally address the discovering party's contractual obligations and the impact of any resulting disclosure, the agreement is only the beginning of an analysis of how the discovering party should proceed, which would include an examination of the facts and circumstances and applicable law.

Discovery by the Breaching Party

The requirements of the agreement. Upon the seller's discovery of a breach, the requirements of the agreement with respect to disclosing the breach and the potential consequences of disclosure need to be examined. Five provisions will need to be given particular consideration: (i) a covenant requiring the seller to promptly disclose any breach; (ii) conditions to the buyer's closing obligations; (iii) the seller's obligation to deliver a closing certificate as to the accuracy of its representations and the performance of its covenants; (iv) the buyer's termination rights; and (v) the right of the seller to cure any breach.

The closing conditions and certificate will normally be qualified as to materiality, e.g., that each of the representations be true and correct "in all material respects." A right to terminate the agreement as a result of a breach also may be limited to material breaches or some other subset of breaches that rise to a certain level.

The breaching party may, as a business decision, ignore its contractual obligations and not disclose the breach. Any such course of action by the seller would usually entail additional and intentional breaches of the agreement. On the other hand, regardless of the obligation to disclose, a seller may opt to disclose. The buyer's perceived response and whether the truth of the disclosure would provide an immediate termination right or merely provide a reason not to close may influence the timing of any disclosure.

Additional considerations. The facts and circumstances of the breach, the transaction and any other relevant non-contractual factors should be considered:

- *Magnitude of the breach.* Is the breach significant enough that it would permit the other side to terminate the agreement or result in the failure of its closing conditions? If so, is the breach nevertheless of a character that it would not cause the other side to walk away from the transaction?
- *Potential to cure.* If there is a right to cure, is the breach one that is capable of being cured in the necessary time frame and at what cost?
- *Overall tenor of transaction.* Has the transaction gone smoothly to date? Have the parties built a solid working relationship and rapport, or is there acrimony? Is this a transaction on which the other side clearly places a high value? Were there additional suitors? Is it realistic to believe that after a busted deal the target could be sold at the same price?
- *Governing law.* Does the law of the governing jurisdiction permit a buyer with knowledge of a breach that proceeds to closing to sue for the breach?

Risks and benefits of disclosure or nondisclosure. In the final analysis, the breaching party will need to balance the risks and potential benefits of each of disclosure and nondisclosure, and then plot a course of action.

Among the risks and benefits to a breaching seller of nondisclosure are the following:

- *Potential benefit: preservation of the transaction or price.* A decision not to disclose a breach results from the fear that upon learning of the breach the buyer will exercise a walk right or will use the threat of termination to negotiate a significant reduction in the purchase price. Nondisclosure, to the extent the buyer does not otherwise learn of the breach, alleviates that concern.
- *Risk: increased liability for intentional breach.* An intentional breach of the agreement through the failure to disclose a breach and a subsequent misstatement in a closing certificate can ratchet up the seller's liability for the breach: (i) intentional breaches may

form the basis for common law claims for fraud, claims for punitive damages and statutory claims of securities fraud in certain acquisitions; and (ii) limitations on the seller's liability for damages may not be applicable to intentional breaches under the terms of the agreement.

- *Risk: personal liability for executive officers and shareholders.* A person signing a closing certificate may be exposed to personal liability for common law fraud, negligent misrepresentation, statutory securities fraud, or contractual breach of representations.
- *Risk: buyer otherwise discovers breach.* A buyer may discover the breach on its own, and then the seller will have lost the ability to be proactive and attack the issue head-on. Additionally, if the buyer discovers the breach in a manner in which it suspects or knows that the seller knew of the breach, an otherwise salvageable transaction may be relegated to certain failure.

Among the risks and benefits to a breaching seller of disclosure are the following:

- *Risk: buyer exercises right to terminate the agreement.* The primary risk of disclosure is that the breach causes the transaction to fail or the price to be renegotiated, perhaps at a deeper discount than otherwise indicated because the buyer will take advantage of the seller's reluctance to have the transaction terminate with the specter of damaged goods.
- *Benefit: maintain integrity; build credibility.* By disclosing the breach, the seller will have maintained its integrity and built credibility, perhaps avoiding a massive buyer overreaction if disclosure is not made until closing.
- *Potential benefit: ability to insist on waiver of breach on closing.* Depending on the law of the governing jurisdiction, the buyer's decision to close despite the breach may preclude the buyer from making a post-closing claim based upon the breach. Notwithstanding the law, the target or seller can always seek a contractual waiver of that right. A waiver of rights may not work.

The calculus in which these factors are applied is complex. The factors listed are not weighted equally. To the listing of benefits and risks must be added the probable buyer response. A seller usually does not come at this disclosure from a position of strength. The disclosure of a breach (as contrasted to the probable inability to satisfy a closing condition) means that a seller is admitting fault. Many buyers will not attempt to be "fair" in this situation and will seek a concession in excess of the amount of the damage. On the other hand, if it is inevitable that the buyer will discover the problem prior to closing, absolutely nothing is lost (and there is something to be gained) by early disclosure of the breach.

Discovery by the Non-Breaching Party

A buyer's decision to disclose a discovered pre-closing breach by the seller is probably less complex than the seller's decision. In the end, the buyer knows what the breach is and knows that it can waive the breach if it would prefer to consummate the transaction. If the breach is such that the buyer no longer wishes to proceed with the transaction on any terms, then it would review its termination rights and proceed accordingly.

If the buyer wishes to proceed with the transaction despite the breach, it needs to determine a course of action.

While paying money and suing for a return of a portion is hardly appealing, additionally the buyer will need to consider whether it will lose its right to bring a claim based on the breach if it closes the transaction. As discussed in more detail above, the law with respect to a buyer's right to bring a claim after closing with respect to a breach of representation known to it is uncertain. If the controlling law precludes a buyer from suing on a known breach, disclosure of the breach is the only way for the buyer to protect itself. Furthermore, if the agreement contains provisions requiring a buyer to represent that it knows of no misrepresentations, the buyer may need to disclose the breach to avoid a defense to the action.

Even when the controlling law permits a buyer to close and sue and the acquisition agreement does not deal with the issue, the buyer may want to give consideration to disclosing the breach and negotiating concessions or protections because the buyer likely will have more control over and certainty with respect to the terms of any such negotiated concessions than it would with respect to the outcome of any future lawsuit or demand for indemnification.

Among the negotiated concessions that a buyer may seek are a reduction of the purchase price (often disproportionate to the economic effect of the breach), a special indemnification and escrow of funds in respect of the potential consequences of the breach, and the elimination or loosening of any baskets, caps, and sunset provisions on the seller's indemnification.

Failed Deal Clean-Up

When a transaction falls apart, in addition to remedies, a variety of other issues must be addressed.

Communications

Each side would identify notices and/or press releases to be given or issued. If a party is a public company and the transaction has been disclosed, a press release of the termination would normally be issued. Generally the agreement will require cooperation and coordination of press releases. If press releases have been issued for a private company deal, disclosure should be considered to put the proper spin on the failed deal for employees, customers, and others. Advising governmental agencies that have been approached for their approval or for transfers or issuances of licenses of the termination of the transaction may be appropriate. Even if not required, advising any governmental agencies with which the client has ongoing contact of the termination should be considered to maintain goodwill.

Advising employees of the failed transaction, if its existence is widely known, helps preserve employee relations. The target may need to contact suppliers, customers, landlords, bankers, and other financing entities to explain the circumstances involving the termination of the transaction.

What Happens to the Deposit?

If a buyer has paid a deposit, it typically will have been deposited with an escrow agent. That agreement will generally provide for all of the optional circumstances that may occur and how the deposit together with any interest earned on it is to be dealt with in each event and who is to be responsible for the stakeholder's fees and expenses. If the transaction does not close, the agreement will usually provide for the return of the deposit and accrued interest to the buyer. If it is the buyer who is at fault, some or all of the deposit will be paid to the seller. Where the parties are at odds over the reason for the breach of the agreement, the agreement will normally provide that the stakeholder is to continue to hold the deposit and accrued interest until a final award is obtained by one of the parties which includes a direction as to the disposition of the deposit. When termination occurs, the innocent party will wish to exercise its rights as soon as possible to lay claim to the deposit.

Return or Destruction of Documents

The seller will want to consider the involvement, if any, that the buyer has had with the seller's business. Where, during the course of the transaction, one party has provided documents to the other, steps should be taken as soon as it is clear that the agreement has been terminated to seek their return. Are there financial statements and other documents that have been delivered to the buyer under a confidentiality agreement that need to be recovered or directed to be destroyed by the buyer? If the buyer is in a similar line of business, and if any of the buyer's employees have been actively involved in the seller's business as part of the buyer's due diligence, an assessment should be made of their level of information and steps must then be taken to advise the buyer and its employees of their obligations under any confidentiality and/or non-solicitation covenants. Depending upon the circumstances, injunctive relief may have to be sought to ensure compliance by the buyer and its representatives with their confidentiality obligations.

Break Up Fees

In the purchase of a public company, a potential buyer will frequently negotiate for the seller to agree to pay the buyer a fee in a negotiated amount, commonly referred to as a break up fee or break fee, if the transaction is not concluded with the buyer and certain triggers (such as the sale of the target to another party) are met. The negotiation and drafting of break up fee triggers other than sale can be complex. The break fee compensates the potential buyer for its time, effort, and out of pocket costs in negotiating the transaction and performing its due diligence and is intended to inhibit the seller from using the buyer as a stalking horse to obtain a better offer from someone else. For the seller, attracting a potential buyer by offering a break fee may be advisable if the interest of that potential buyer also attracts other potential bidders who might not otherwise be prepared to seriously explore the purchase. If the transaction terminates, both parties will examine the terms of the break fee agreement carefully to understand their rights. While generally the courts have been prepared to enforce break fees, the bankruptcy courts have been reluctant to approve break fees where the fee inhibits bids for the target rather than promoting them.

CHAPTER **14**

Closing the Deal

Consider the admonition from a senior partner to a junior associate as they enter the closing room: "Closings would be great if it weren't for the people." The closing itself involves a curious mixture of science and art—science in the careful drafting and execution of documents that reflect the terms of the acquisition transaction, and art in the constant interplay of personalities that determines whether these magnificently drafted documents will ever be executed. As with every other aspect of the practice of law, preparation for this important event is critical, and more is better (and safer) than less in addressing details.

Failure to resolve any one of the many legal and business issues in any deal may result in failure. Closing conditions beyond the control of either party may kill the deal, the most prominent being consents or actions needed from third parties (including antitrust and other regulators) over whom neither the buyer nor the seller has any control. Bankers lurking in the shadows may or may not provide funds for the deal to go forward. Time, the constantly nagging element, in and of itself (through missed deadlines, flagging interest, lost business opportunities, or changing markets) can result in the parties giving up and moving elsewhere.

The typical closing structure is the two-step deferred closing with the closing following the execution of the agreement by a period ranging from a few days to months. This phasing is more typical and usually is the product of practical and legal requirements presented by the transaction itself—completion of due diligence, seeking and obtaining important third party and regulatory consents and approvals, the HSR waiting period, possible SEC and state securities administrator reviews and shareholder approvals just to name a few. Many of these cannot practically be sought or occur until there is a signed acquisition agreement (although the HSR process can be initiated on the basis of a non-binding letter of intent), and, indeed, the occurrence of these kinds of events and completion of these kinds of tasks become express conditions to the closing.

The one-step simultaneous sign and close represents the situation where the acquisition agreement and related agreements will be signed and the conditions to the closing satisfied in a single event. This single event may extend over a day or two and usually occurs after the buyer has completed whatever due diligence it feels is sufficient. The technique is often used where the parties are in a hurry to sign (aren't they always?) and complete the transaction, and the closing conditions are few in number or have been satisfied during the negotiation and drafting process. Even very complex deals can involve a sign and close. One thing is sure— the tasks and timeframes become compressed, and plenty of midnight oil is usually burned to accomplish a one-step simultaneous sign and close.

Planning the Closing Process

Get Ready for Some Fun

It is fair to say that preparation for closing has been ongoing since the first meeting of the parties, for the occurrence of a complete and successful closing is the point of every event in the acquisition process. Developing relationships, negotiating the deal and due diligence all have the sole purpose of making a closing possible. The focus must be maintained throughout on planning for the closing itself—those (hopefully) few hours in a conference room or rooms in which documents are signed and the parties reach the point where the deal is finally done.

Preparation for Closing—The Client

Before meeting with the opposing party and counsel, the first task to be addressed is the client and its needs in the closing process. This warrants an extended phone call or a visit with the client and usually its other advisors. Throughout the entire process it is important for the lawyers and clients to keep in mind any unusual issues that might add extra time to the process or that might be stumbling blocks. Particular attention should be focused on points in the transaction that are not yet settled, such as an employment contract or benefits issues. The essence of closing is the completion of every necessary point of the deal, and every unresolved point should be viewed as a potential impediment. Ideally, there should be no issues to be resolved. The forms of agreements to be entered into at closing might have been attached to the acquisition agreement as exhibits, rather than relying on the parties to negotiate in good faith. Similarly, the exact forms of opinions (including all of the qualifications and limitations) might have been attached. But in these situations and particularly when third parties are involved, it is often the case that the exact form is left to another day (the employment agreement "in form and substance satisfactory to Buyer"). These remaining issues will eventually be incorporated into one or more of the closing documents including the inevitable side letter, which should be highlighted for particular scrutiny as the process continues. This early meeting should also include a discussion of the procedural aspects of closing (when and where it is best to close).

Identifying the remaining issues results in a sorting process. Some will be factual issues on which the client will have clear positions. Other issues will be more legal in nature (wording of instruments of conveyance or provisions of ancillary documents). An occasional crisis can be caused when an early factual assumption by the businesspeople turns out to be incorrect. You should be prepared to deal with all of these. While remaining issues can be a problem for every transaction, surprise issues are far worse and far more likely to get a transaction off track. A lawyer can add value to the deal with his ability to solve those problems that first emerge during the pre-closing process.

Preparation for Closing—The Other Side

Are we enemies or friends? Any young lawyer will quickly tell you that the other side is the enemy and that the objective in closing and in every other aspect of the transaction is to get the better of the other side through brute force and intimidation. Under this theory, every phone call or conference should be an opportunity to force our will on the other side—more often than not, it is an overabundance of hostility that threatens the transaction. If you as counsel have managed during the course of events leading up to the closing to develop an antagonistic relationship with the other side, that relationship will color all that goes on at closing. Every document will be more difficult to draft and every issue more difficult to resolve. If such a relationship exists, it might be worth the effort to patch it up in time for closing or, at minimum, explain the difficulties to your client so that there will be no surprises when sparks fly in preparing for the closing.

Are we neither enemies nor friends? With the proliferation of e-mail, it is entirely possible to approach closing without any in person relationship at all with opposing counsel. E-mail is a great advancement in that it lets us communicate more quickly and with greater ease than has ever been possible before. But communication by computer fails to develop relationships between counsel that could make the difference in getting a deal closed. If to this point you find that you barely recognize the voice of the lawyer on the other side, you have been making excessive use of impersonal communication devices, such as e-mail, facsimile, or courier. The weeks leading up to closing would be a good time to get over this addiction. Pick up the phone and call opposing counsel rather than using the computer. Hearing the sound of each other's voices develops a sense of expectation on the part of each of you that can make communicating in person easier when the actual closing occurs.

Do we all really want this deal to go forward? If one side or the other does not want the deal to go forward, particularly if it is your client, your strategy will be radically different. Your focus should be not only on the client's interest in walking from the transaction but also in advising your client as to the potential legal liability from failing to live up to its commitments. Careful attention should be paid to case law on the obligation to deal with the other side in good faith and the inevitable "best efforts" obligation to which your client may be subject.

The Closing Agenda

Where's My List?

Well in advance of closing, someone should have prepared and updated as the deal develops a comprehensive closing agenda. If you find yourself asking whom that someone might be, then it probably is you. Once prepared in draft form by either the seller's or buyer's counsel (buyer's counsel more often takes this role), the agenda will have a life of its own and will be added to or commented upon by all the parties to the transaction. It will be a central link between all the parties involved and the elements that must be brought together for the closing to occur.

> **What Do You Call It?**
>
> The closing agenda is the phrase used in this chapter, but you may have run across references to a closing checklist or closing memorandum. What is meant by those terms? They may

refer to the same thing: a document used by the parties to a transaction to facilitate progress toward the closing. Sometimes it lists only the documents to be delivered at the closing. Sometimes it lists all actions to be accomplished and all documents to be delivered before the closing, as well as the formal documents to be delivered at the closing and actions to be taken after the closing. Sometimes it lists items that are prerequisites to the actions being taken, such as letters of intent and acquisition agreements.

A closing checklist may refer to an internal document used by one side to internally allocate responsibilities leading to closing. It might go beyond the closing agenda, because it might cover items unique to one side, such as the myriad of considerations in closing the financing portion of the deal, information not necessary to share with the seller.

A closing memorandum may refer to a more robust document that purports to narrate the details of the closing such as who attended. While prepared in advance as a guide to closing, it reads as though it had been prepared after the closing. Because portions are narrative in form, it often recites actions leading up to the closing. It may contain what would otherwise be in the closing statement. Sometimes the parties sign it. Even if it is not signed, because it is a mutual contemporaneous document reciting what purported to happen, it may be given some weight by a court if a dispute later arises. The closing memorandum is most often seen in the closing of an underwritten public offering, where the procedures are much more standardized than in an acquisition.

A critical feature of the agenda is a listing of the persons responsible for the preparation of the various documents or the taking of various actions. The closing agenda serves multiple purposes.

- It is a means of communicating to the various parties who is responsible for what and measuring progress towards closing.
- It is a constant status report on whether the closing is ready to occur.
- It is an essential tool for the attorney in the execution of the post-closing process.

A sample agenda with closing notes is included as Appendix 14-A. The goal in preparing the agenda is to create a universal listing of documents to be prepared and signed at closing and a listing of actions that must be taken to complete the transaction.

The best closing agendas include as much information as possible about where the deal stands. Not only are documents and the responsible party listed, but also a running commentary of where the process stands with each item (such as "drafted and sent to seller's counsel for review"). The agenda is also a place to visit when a deal veers off track and questions must be asked about who is slowing things down. For some parties, the agenda may need to be prepared in multiple parts. For example, the buyer might not warm to the idea of disclosing to the seller that the financing commitment letter has not even been signed or that a new appraisal is needed before funding is secured. In some cases, the agenda would have subparts, such as a deal involving significant real property matters with a separate real estate team handling those matters.

In complicated transactions, there may be a series of checklists that guide one side of a transaction toward closing. For example in a multistate asset purchase of an operating business, the buyer may have to gear up for licensing requirements, tax filings, employee issues (such as withholding and unemployment), and transfer of real and personal property. Each deal will present unique circumstances.

Either in the agenda or in a separate document, a closing timetable should be set out. The timetable establishes expectations from all parties, counsel, and other advisors as to the pace at which the closing is to occur. Many M&A attorneys prepare closing agendas well before closing as a mechanism to facilitate an underlying path to closing. Closing timetables are different in that as the closing approaches, they become much more definitive and act as a key barometer of the status of the transaction.

When Should It Close? The Closing Date and the Timetable

Are You Ready?

The date of the closing is determined by the acquisition agreement. It may be a specified time or follow an event (e.g., five days after HSR clearance). Sometimes when there are no material third party actions that would prevent the closing, the parties may just set a date certain, or a date a specified number of days after signing the agreement.

When asked "When should this deal close?" the answer from most clients will be "As soon as possible." As this date is being discussed, you should bear in mind that many clients have no feel for the magnitude of work that must be done to complete the closing and are anxious to have the transaction close quickly no matter what. The answer to the question depends more on what has to be done prior to closing than on the desires of the parties, and each client should be fully informed that trying to rush a closing before its time is stressful and overly expensive, may in fact delay the closing and can result in a breakdown in relations between the parties that causes the deal to fail altogether. Imposing an unrealistic closing date may delay closing in this sense: many participants in a transaction (especially when they are already tired from the demands in getting the acquisition agreement signed) will simply ignore what is impossible, meaning essentially that no deadline has been established. Once the impossible deadline has come and gone, the parties will then turn to addressing what is possible, but in the meantime time has been lost. It is far better to set a stretch deadline that is possible and then figure out how it can be achieved.

The closing date often depends on the extent to which there are third parties involved whose conduct cannot be controlled or the extent to which conditions beyond the parties will determine when the transaction can be closed. Once a realistic closing date is set, the remainder of the closing timetable can be filled in. This will require input from all the parties to the deal, but the drafter must use his best efforts to be realistic. An unrealistic closing timetable can create the same sort of stress and friction as an unrealistic closing date. While there are no statistics that have been found on the subject, many experienced lawyers would probably endorse an assertion that the duration of a middle market deal in the United States (with no second request under HSR) from letter of intent to closing of 90 days is reasonable and 60 days is a forced march.

Place and Time of Closing

My Place or Yours?

The place of closing is usually governed by the acquisition agreement. In specifying the place of closing, the parties may have heeded the discussion in this chapter. The physical character- istics of the closing place may have a role in its success or speed. Parties who are in comfortable surroundings may be more inclined to take the time to consider various issues and to respond favorably to points of compromise than would parties in an un-air-conditioned warehouse or at the local motel. More important than physical comfort is the ability to communicate. The place of closing should have adequate photocopying, facsimile, computer, and telephone access and a staff to operate them. The party whose counsel is responsible for drafting the closing documents may insist that it will facilitate closing to use that lawyer's office. It is generally best to close in a lawyer's office, preferably outside counsel. Law firms are uniquely set up to handle the demands of a closing, including late night or around-the-clock document prepa- ration, copying, secretarial support, and conference rooms.

Many factors may play a role in the geographical location. Convenience of the parties is typically foremost, but the location of the business being acquired or the need to be near third parties (such as suppliers, recording offices, or capital markets) may also be important. Finally, the negotiating strength and availability of persons associated with the seller or the buyer (or buyer's lender) may be a factor. As you advise your client in selection of location, two con- trasting schools of thought are worth considering. The first is that your client may be more comfortable and at ease in familiar surroundings. The second is that the other side may be more comfortable in familiar surroundings. Most attorneys would jump to the conclusion that your client's favored location should be the objective, but it is equally valid to point out that if you are trying to obtain last minute concessions from the other side, you are better off with a relaxed person with access to his colleagues and superiors on the other side of the table and you may well be willing to travel to increase the comfort level of your opponent. It may be less awkward to storm out of a failed closing if your client is the visitor rather than the host.

May I Come to Your Party?

The traditional practice was to expect that the persons attending the closing would be those whose signatures were necessary or were needed to furnish information necessary to close. In this latter group would be company accountants, outside CPAs, and other advisors. Others considered were counsel, both principal counsel and local counsel, investment bankers, and other central characters whose roles are vital to the closing.

The fewer people in attendance at closing, the more likely it is to progress smoothly. It is not advisable to have very busy and important clients sitting around while the lawyers appear to be just shuffling papers. Unless a person's role is vital, his very presence adds an additional dynamic to the discussions. Every person in attendance will naturally seek a role for himself, be it interjecting comments on various topics or complicating the stream of advice going to one side or the other. None of this is helpful to the closing objective. With the widespread acceptance of fax signatures, it is no longer necessary to have all of those bodies present. The ultimate role of the attorney in influencing who should attend is to take the role of Goldilocks and select the size and mix that is neither too hot nor too cold but "just right." If the clients are to attend in person, it may be advisable for them to be the last to arrive after the lawyering is completed, just in time to sign the closing documents. As with many other aspects of the closing process, there is nothing scientific about this decision. It is all art.

Have the Details Been Arranged?

This question refers directly to the closing agenda and the myriad list of closing conditions that are found there. You should be particularly sensitive to obtaining the consents of third parties who will not be at closing and who may not be so quick to sign papers that are essential to the transaction going forward. Original documents are another issue. Although courts accept photocopies and facsimiles for most purposes, you should pay special attention to originals, such as minute books and stock certificates, which are required at closing. Certificates of good standing, certified copies of patents, business licenses, insurance certificates, and other originals should be in folders and ready for delivery well in advance of closing. You should also be mindful of the need to form new entities in connection with the transaction. It may be relatively fast to form a new Delaware subsidiary, but qualifying it for business in another state may take weeks, and the transaction may require certificates of good standing in both jurisdictions.

In timing the closing, counsel should also attend to non-execution issues, such as the need to move funds to the seller. Wiring and payment instructions will be needed both for the seller and for any other third parties involved in the transaction, as well as for the myriad of service-providers that may be involved (such as, environmental engineers, lenders, and appraisers). Wiring deadlines should also be noted. In some cases a delay of two days between pre-closing and funding can be a good idea when a third-party lender is involved and conditions to the loan transaction must be met. Overseas funds should be wired in advance and parked in a domestic account.

Other last-minute bring down issues should also be considered in advance of closing. The client must attend to any special requirements, such as last minute inspections, physical inventories, updated UCC searches, payoff letters, and third-party estoppel certificates from certain tenants, landlords, franchisors, licensors, and other persons with whom the target deals.

The Pre-Closing

The Cure for the Chaotic Closing

In all but the simplest of closings, it is wise to have a pre-closing session one or two days in advance of the closing. In fact, many lawyers have ceased calling this a pre-closing in order to avoid the sense that it is not important and refer to the pre-closing as the closing and the day on which the deal is actually deemed closed as the funding date. In either event, it is important to have a session, beginning ideally with lawyers only, in which all documents are placed in folders and finalized and made ready for signature. Documents should be prepared with an awareness not only of the words of agreement but also with sensitivity to the fact that document schedules can be equally important and, because of the needed input from others (e.g., accountants, business persons), schedules, and exhibits can take longer to finalize. By the time of pre-closing, all legal opinions should be finalized, and, depending on the comfort level of counsel, signed and placed in folders pending the closing of the transaction.

Can We Spend All Week Doing This?

Depending on the availability of the parties, it might be advisable to schedule a series of days in which the parties can execute documents. The process is simple enough. The attorney coordinating the closing sets aside a conference room in which to place the documents and the various parties arrive at their convenience to execute them. This procedure provides the maximum flexibility and convenience and avoids the opportunity, always present where a formal closing is held, for the parties to engage in discussions that raise new issues. A variation is a FedEx closing, in which the documents are never isolated in a single location but are sent by courier to the various signatories and returned when fully executed (the functional equivalent is the fax closing, with originals sometimes substituted for the faxes). It is fair to say, however, that the closing process itself is tiring, and causing the execution of documents to drag over a long period of time can create its own sort of stress for the parties.

In any event, whether accomplishing the execution of documents through a formal closing, long distance or some combination, it is important for counsel to manage carefully the expectations of the parties. While it is impossible to predict with any degree of certainty how long a particular closing will take, more than one closing has gotten out of hand when a client's patience has worn thin. It is important to create realistic expectations of what time and effort it will take a client to get through the deal, and those expectations should include some idea of unforeseen events that may complicate things. A patient and understanding client will make the lawyer's job easier than one who expected a six-hour closing to take ten minutes.

Do We Really Have to Close?

Virtually every acquisition agreement has a termination right for either side if a closing has not occurred by some agreed date (the drop dead or upset date). The date need not be the same for buyer or seller. Once the date has arrived, failure of the parties to close might give either side (assuming no breach of the agreement) the option to walk from the transaction. The ability to walk away or close provides leverage to renegotiate the agreement. The parties who have traveled the farthest distance or who have made the greatest number of assumptions regarding closing or who are most dependent on the transaction going forward are at a negotiating disadvantage. Signing an extension before the termination right arises is an easy enough task and may be easier to do than waiting until the right has matured.

But There Are Still Issues Out There! The Messy Closing

Pre-closing is a nice idea, documents should be finalized in advance and the signing process should be a snap, but this is the real world. What happens when things are not quite so nice?

There are events that can be planned and those that cannot. If going into a closing, you are aware of 10 separate issues (such as ancillary agreements not fully negotiated when the acquisition agreement was signed) that remain unresolved, each of which could potentially blow the deal, you ought to plan for resolving those issues. Planning might include encouraging discussion and a resolution of the issues in advance, or even delaying the closing until the issues are resolved. If this fails, the closing becomes both a negotiating session and a closing. It goes without saying that if the objective is to get the deal closed, the issues should be resolved first. They should be resolved in a room with the decision-makers present (and as few other people as possible), and they probably should be resolved all at one time, rather than on an issue-by-issue basis. Sometimes it just comes down to horse trading. Once the issues are resolved, corresponding changes to the documents can be made or a side letter put together and the deal can proceed.

Also bear in mind that the pace of some deals requires that a closing date be set when the parties are not ready. Depending on the personalities of the seller and buyer and the dynamics of the transaction, setting a closing and proceeding through a messy two-day process of finalizing documents, attaching schedules, finalizing balance sheets, etc., may be the only way a particular deal can ever be concluded. If that is the case, the lawyers must be as committed to closing as everyone else and willing to devote whatever effort is necessary to having documents finalized and the deal concluded within the timetable expected by the clients. It is axiomatic to say that where speed and quality of legal work conflict, quality must prevail, and no lawyer should be forced to proceed at a pace that runs the risk of overlooked issues and improperly drafted documents. Sometimes the only way to finish an acquisition is to force its conclusion, and the practitioner must use all his skills to insure both quality and speed in bringing about the closing.

The Closing Itself

A Lawyer's Utopia

In the ideal world, there really should be very little to a closing. The closing numbers should have been worked out, and other aspects of the deal buttoned down, in advance. Because the parties have been diligent in circulating copies of the closing documents, they should be ready to execute them without further discussion. A well-organized closing agenda will encourage this result by showing both the status of various items as well as the persons responsible. Even when all items are not quite ready at the time of closing, a carefully planned and successful pre-closing can promote the same result.

Is That All There Is?

A closing should not be a three-day boondoggle by lawyers and accountants to a foreign city in which persons of great importance spread documents around massive conference tables and display their sartorial skills to the delight of their clients. One of the major problems with closings is that people are gathering in a single place with the expectation that something important is happening. While expectations differ from client to client, all the participants expect some important occurrence. All will be disappointed if nothing more happens than a short and well-organized signing session. The ideal closing thus presents to the practitioner an objective that is totally at variance with the expectations of virtually everyone involved and which may actually be disappointing to many of the participants. "Is that all there is?" can be uttered at the closing in a sense of disappointment, but if in fact that is that all there is, the lawyers may have done a magnificent job for their respective clients. The objective is to close, and the faster and simpler the closing is, the more likely the transaction is to actually close. Clients should share a sense of pride when the closing is so quick and smooth that it hardly seemed worth the time to gather.

The Ceremonial Closing –Adding Some Necessary Theater

It is not uncommon for a closing to be conducted in a manner that includes some ceremonial aspects. This might be at the client's request, or simply because counsel senses that some degree of ceremony would be appropriate, if not expected by the client. Without some sort of formality, the streamlined closing can be a real let down. This can be particularly true for the sale of a business that has been owned by a family for generations or the sale of a business by an entrepreneur who feels a great sense of pride and accomplishment. Formal closings are also fairly common in cross-border transactions, when the parties are expected to be physically present.

Among the ceremonial elements that are often injected into the closing are counsel reading through portions of the closing memorandum while making reference to the various documents being delivered, having special pens for signing the documents that memorialize the occasion, leaving several of the key documents to be signed by the parties concurrently at the actual closing and physically delivering several of the documents between the parties with photographs. In the smaller transactions, the documents delivered physically would be the check and stock certificates or bills of sale. This is of course impractical in the larger transactions with wiring of funds and automatic stock transfers, in which case receipts can be used for this purpose. A final, legally insignificant, piece of paper for the two CEOs to sign before the photographer can sometimes serve this purpose.

The Closing Statement and Alternatives

Does the Closing Statement Matter?

This Guide will not go step-by-step through the various documents that are needed in a typical closing. However, the closing statement (sometimes called the flow of funds statement), if one is used, deserves special attention. A closing statement sets forth the source and application of funds needed to make a transaction happen. A familiar example is a real estate settlement statement where debits and credits are shown for each of the buyer and the seller. In the case of an asset acquisition agreement, the closing statement may similarly reflect the purchase price to be paid by the buyer, debits and credits to be allocated to the parties, and the disposition of funds to the seller and others, such as lenders to be paid off out of the purchase price. Simple transactions in which the price is specified in the acquisition agreement, with no other fees and expenses to be borne by one or the other parties, normally do not need a closing statement.

Sometimes the closing statement may be embodied in the closing agenda. For purposes of this discussion, we will refer to the closing statement even though it may be part of another document. Determining the funds flow becomes critical to the closing for a number of reasons. First, it requires information that is obtained from sources largely beyond the lawyer's area of focus, reducing that information to writing and having it summarized in closing statement form. Secondly, it often hides unresolved issues that must be dealt with at closing. Third, it is the single item that receives the most scrutiny from clients. This feature is both good and bad. Bad in that it holds the greatest potential for argument, but good in that clients rarely leave a closing with a statement like "I did not know the closing statement said that."

A commitment to furnish further documents could be included as well as the duty to cooperate in a newly discovered lawsuit or to assist in transitioning a critical customer or employee. Last-minute items are usually included in a separate post-closing agreement or side letter with the attendant formalities of a binding legal document.

If This Is So Important, Why Wait Until the End?

The finalization of the closing statement is like any other aspect of the closing process. The practitioner must identify the parties whose input is needed, communicate that responsibility to them, and then follow up to be sure the information is obtained in a timely manner. Particular attention should be paid to third parties whose information is needed. It is not unusual for lawyers to finalize and have the closing documents signed and then focus on the closing statement. Following this procedure can eventually result in a closing, but it may not happen quickly. A better strategy is to circulate a blank closing statement to all parties well in advance of closing and to assign each blank to a single person. Accountants might produce estimated working capital numbers, operations people might furnish inventory numbers, staff will show deposits and prepaids, bankers will furnish payoff numbers, etc.

Is It Binding?

What is the legal effect of the closing statement? It is most typical for a closing statement to recite that it is a mere non-binding summary of funds disbursed at closing. Under that structure, the acquisition agreement itself continues to represent the binding obligation of the parties, even as to funds owed at closing, so that should there be an inventory error or a failure to properly compute working capital, the aggrieved party could return to the other for a recomputation of the purchase price. More rarely, the closing statement represents the final decision of the parties as to the purchase price (particularly when there are subjective elements involved) and should, if properly documented, take priority over any conflicting provisions of the acquisition agreement or the other acquisition documents. The parties should acknowledge that it is binding, presumably as an amendment to the acquisition agreement.

Potential Waiver of Conditions

Counsel should remain aware of the status of closing conditions, some of which could be waived by the mere act of closing. Both the seller and buyer should remember to provide for retention on a post-closing basis of any conditions that have not been waived or satisfied and which should be satisfied during the post-closing period through an explicit binding agreement. A further assurances provision may not resurrect a waived condition. A recitation in the final closing agenda about what counsel agreed to do is not nearly as satisfactory as a binding agreement.

Mechanics of Closing

Did I Sign That?

Although this topic has been hotly debated in recent years, it is now universally recognized that a facsimile signature acts to bind the signatory and can be enforced for most purposes in all courts of law. The better practice is to begin the closing process in time for all signatures to be originals, but where facsimile signatures (including scanned documents sent by e-mail) are necessary to get a deal closed, they are acceptable. The custom is to accept facsimile signatures with the understanding that originals will be circulated post-closing and used in the final closing binders. Note the discussion on the challenge of establishing execution and what constitutes the agreement in Chapter 11.

All We Need Is Signatures

One of the most frustrating aspects of some closings is the unfettered use of signature pages during the closing process. The scenario goes something like this: The attorney drafts all the documents and has the signature pages signed by his client. He then enters the closing process with the apparent authority on the part of the client to make wholesale substitutions of pages that are necessary to reflect various further understandings of the parties. These modified pages are then attached to the original signature pages to form a complete document that is to be final and binding on the parties. Two years later the document is being litigated in court and the client is asked on the witness stand to authenticate the document. His response is unnerving but truthful: "I just signed the signature pages and my lawyer made some changes that weren't authorized." Is the document binding? The better practice is to have the document signed when they are completed and no sooner.

Lawyers sometimes recommend that the parties initial individual pages. The practice has much to commend it when something such as a closing schedule is comprised of many different documents, some of which have been revised in the negotiation process. Initialing does firmly indicate the final schedules or documents.

Although it is not generally the practice in the United States for the parties to initial every page of every closing document, there may be circumstances when it would be advisable to do so. However, if the parties agree on a discrete change in a particular document at the closing, especially where it is significant, and the change is made manually, it is customary to initial that change.

Paper Clips?

After two or three years of law practice, every lawyer knows that staples are your enemy. As soon as a document is stapled, it will inevitably need substitute pages. By the end of a complex closing, the more central documents can have upper left-hand corners resembling a piece of Swiss cheese. The prudent approach is to paper clip copies and keep all documents in folders until they are finally distributed. By the same token, it is best to avoid copying complete documents until after the closing—to be sure that the copies do include the substituted pages.

> ### Keep the Wrong Hands Out of the Machinery
>
> One of the pitfalls of in-person, live, real paper closings is that client executives, underutilized relationship partners, investment bankers expecting fee checks, and other participants with too little to do at the closing often feel compelled to start picking up folders, removing papers, reading things, and generally ruining the closing organization. A strong closing sheriff is needed to police the room. Our firm once had a paralegal with a commanding presence who told a litigator/relationship partner that if he touched one more closing document she would break his wrist. He believed her and retreated to the corner to read depositions.

Trust Me

In most closings, there is a single attorney in charge of the closing facilities. Typically the buyer's counsel will furnish the facilities and handle the details. That attorney is bound by the canons of ethics and subject to disciplinary action should he act improperly with respect to the documents, such as surreptitiously substituting a few critical pages. This framework is enough for most counsel to trust their counterparts with custody of documents overnight and during the various stages of the closing process.

The more difficult question relates to the custody of documents at the end of the closing process. A frequent practice is for the final act of closing to be the division of the documents into neat stacks, one of which is retained by buyer's counsel and one by the seller's counsel. This brings some finality to the transaction and puts each counsel in a position to prepare binders for his client. Another approach, not altogether infrequent, is for all documents to be left in the custody of one of the attorneys, who then undertakes to prepare closing binders and distribute the originals and copies to the various parties. The pitfalls of this procedure are obvious. Clients frequently need immediate access to some of the documents (the closing statement and assignments of contracts are frequent candidates). At its worst, nothing happens because the entrusted lawyer moves on to more pressing matters and never returns to the task, so that the trusting lawyer ends up with nothing. Clients also look unfavorably on an overly trusting attitude toward opposing counsel and feel more comfortable with closing documents in their own control. The better practice is to leave the closing with a complete set of signed documents, or at least some of the more important documents.

A variation of this theme is the ministerial act of filling in blanks and attaching exhibits. It is usually the case that parties will allow the closing to occur if those actions are truly ministerial. It is tempting to leave for another day completion of those actions. But because memories and intentions are frail, it is probably the best practice to complete these details while still at the closing.

Is That Really Your Signature?

Counsel should be mindful of the need to address particular jurisdictional requirements. Instruments of conveyance, such as deeds and mortgages, will need to be notarized and in some cases will need separate witnesses. State laws permit a single officer to bind a corporate entity where authorized by resolution, but an attestation by a secretary or other officer, at least on the instruments of conveyance themselves, can provide a further measure of the legitimacy of the signatures. Note, however, the cautions in the discussion on *Trust Me* above. In the interests of practicality, it is unusual to initial every page to avoid alterations. The existence of duplicate sets of documents, together with possible criminal penalties for improper conduct, addresses concerns over subsequent modifications.

Why Do We Need These Legal Opinions, Anyway?

One other specific area also deserves attention—the legal opinion. This is the one aspect for which the client likely has little interest and less appreciation, and even the most loyal of clients can lose patience with counsel when they learn that they are paying them to negotiate their way through five pages of redundant and meaningless qualifications. While the scope and content of legal opinions are the subject for other writers, lawyers should not wait until closing for resolution of opinion language. Time at closing is too precious and clients are too anxious. Given the multi-state nature of many transactions, the need for local counsel should be considered early. Attorneys should also be mindful of the proliferating (if not universal) institution of the opinion committee—a nameless, faceless group of attorneys cloistered somewhere in the corridors of opposing counsel's offices, which at times will appear to the opinion recipient to have as its purpose denying opinion requests on the eve of closing. The main issue with the opinion committee is the delay it can inflict on a closing. The attorney would be wise to inquire at an early point about the need for peer review and approval of opinions and to quantify any delays likely to arise from the opinion process. Counsel should be mindful of the need of opposing counsel to see original signatures on closing documents before the opinion is released. It is, of course, essential that the attorney understand and allow time to satisfy the requirements of his own firm's opinion committee.

Was I Supposed to Bring the Money?

Once documents are completed and the closing statement has been finalized, it would seem an easy task to pay the purchase price. However, given the time delays that can be encountered in wiring funds, counsel would do well to make special inquiry about the funding process. Wiring instructions should be solicited from recipients in advance and the buyer's bank alerted to the need to move promptly once instructions to fund are received and the seller's bank should be alerted to receipt of the funds. Counsel can encourage bankers to identify the person who will have physical possession of the wire transfer instructions and who will get the reference numbers from the FED. Where possible, those instructions should be completed in advance so that once the decision to fund has been made, money can be moved swiftly.

You Can't Be Too Careful

We represented the buyer of a business in a stock transaction. The closing was going smoothly and everyone focused on winding things up. Our client's only responsibility at the closing was to bring a corporate check for the purchase price. This was during the days when delivery of a check, rather than a wire transfer, was the norm. The check was delivered to the seller, who was thrilled, and everyone left the closing. That afternoon we received a frantic call from the seller's counsel. It appeared that the seller had attempted to deposit the check at his bank, only to find that it had been made payable to the company that he had just sold. We contacted our client, who had a check payable to the seller of the stock prepared and messengered to him. Even the simplest things can go awry.

Weekends Are for More Than Golf

A particular word of warning is in order for the Friday closing especially the last Friday of the month. In any transaction, it is usually critical for the buyer to both receive the funds and have the opportunity to invest them on the date of funding. It is entirely possible, where a wire has been initiated late in the day, that the funds have been debited from the buyer's account on a given date but not received by the seller on that date or received too late in the day to be invested. The funds then sit uninvested until the next business day. If that next business day is Monday after a Friday, significant earnings can be lost over the failure to invest. Recall also that sometimes key players leave the office early on Fridays to enjoy a longer weekend.

Facing the Funding Deadline

It inevitably happens: a few third-party consents or some other eventuality outside the control of the parties remains outstanding. Employee announcements are made. The auditors are scheduled to observe inventories. The world is watching. In order to be able to assure that funds will be received through the Federal Reserve system, the corporate treasurer insists that a wire transfer must be ordered within minutes. What is the buyer to do? Yes, there are further assurances language in the agreement, but the practical result is that closing at this juncture means that the buyer is at risk. The buyer will need to make a business decision that the disruption of not closing outweighs the risk of not receiving the third party consents.

Sometimes a Closing Prayer Doesn't Hurt

The CEO of our Midwest client had grown the wholesale coffee business started by his immigrant father into a very attractive regional target for a roll-up formed by a New York investment bank. At an early point in the closing, the beaming father asked principals, lawyers, bankers, paralegals and anyone else passing the conference room to hold hands and bow heads in prayer. The father blessed his good fortune in coming to America and thanked God for, among other things, introducing his son to his new friends with money from New York. After the "Amen," my partner leaned over and whispered, "I usually hold the prayer of thanks until after they fund and the wire hits."

Is It My Business Now?

While the attorney is focusing on documents and funding, the client should be forewarned to focus on those other business activities associated with the closing that must take place on and after the closing date. Insurance coverage must be in place for the business, the parties must attend to the physical transfer of possession (keys and combinations), announcements to employees must be made and third parties whose contracts have been transferred must be notified.

Deals Not Ready to Close

This Just Isn't Happening

Notwithstanding Herculean efforts by all involved, there are inevitably deals that cannot close on the designated closing date no matter what. In some cases, failure to close will give rise to a termination right, furnishing an opportunity for one party to hold out for better terms. In some cases, time constraints make the transaction no longer attractive to one party or the other, in which event the parties part ways. What to do when a deal is not ready to close and closing occurs anyway depends largely on the reasons for the failure. Where the parties have not finished taking inventories or compiling closing balance sheets (and these things do not usually occur until after the closing), a mere extension of the agreement may be appropriate. However, in some cases where the future conduct of one party or the other is in question, the parties may try to implement some sort of escrow arrangement in anticipation of closing. Escrow arrangements range from leaving the documents on a conference table (hopefully secured) for a few days, to executing a formal escrow arrangement in which documents and funds are placed with a third party in hopes of closing. Some lawyers are justifiably uncomfortable with serving as escrow agent, whether or not there are substantive issues outstanding, since even with an appropriate escrow letter it can, as a practical matter, inhibit the most vigorous efforts on behalf of the lawyer's client.

Who Do You Trust and for How Long?

Where a formal escrow agreement is used, the usual drafting considerations apply. The parties must choose an escrow agent and carefully outline in the document the condition or conditions that must be met in order for the documents to be released and funding to occur. Such a document should, like the acquisition agreement itself, contain a drop-dead date, at which time documents will be destroyed and funds returned if the transaction has not closed. The simplest approach for the triggering event is to require joint instructions from the parties on the date of funding. Another approach would be to permit the escrow agent to accept a verified statement from one party or the other as to the occurrence of an event or the satisfaction of a closing condition.

Yet Another Agreement to Draft

Another approach to the transaction not quite ready to close is the entering into of an agreement as to post-closing matters, sometimes including an escrow. Where conditions remain to be fulfilled by the seller, the buyer could easily place a portion of the purchase price in escrow pending satisfaction of those conditions. Where there is some seller financing of the transaction, an offset agreement can accomplish the same objective. Where it is known (or expected) that a transaction might be moving towards closing when it in fact is not ready, the practitioner would be well-advised to visit with the client on this topic. If the issues are well known, it might be appropriate to even draft a post-closing agreement or escrow agreement in advance so that it can be used for that purpose without delay.

Non-Legal Aspects of Closings

While You're at It

In addition to all the legal technicalities of closing, the most important of which is getting the documentation right, the practitioner must attend to the numerous issues involved every time human beings undertake activity together. Those include promoting courtesy among clients and counsel (even when it is not deserved), serving drinks and food and providing ample telephones and Internet access. Perhaps the food and drinks should be served in another room to avoid spilling coffee on signed closing documents. While luxurious accommodations are not necessary, comfortable surroundings do lessen stress and promote an attitude conductive to resolving issues. Bursts of emotion are permitted if part of some sort of perverse negotiating strategy, but otherwise emotions should be checked at the door, particularly for counsel, but hopefully for the other participants as well. One finer point of these discussions is the need for food. Among accomplished professionals, one of the most denied facts is hunger. Given the opportunity to work through lunch, every lawyer worth his salt will forge forward. About two hours after mealtime, attitudes deteriorate and the crowd becomes irritable for no apparent reason, except for the fact that no one has eaten. If your objective is to keep everyone on an even keel and in good spirits and moving smoothly towards the conclusion of the transaction, you must keep everyone eating. You must do this even if it appears a sign of weakness on your part. Hungry participants are irritable participants and irritability can cause deterioration of a closing for no apparent reason and in a hurry.

The second issue in the personal comforts category is the need for sleep. Your malpractice carrier would appreciate your getting adequate sleep each night, even when a deal is pressing. If you accept the thesis that lack of food causes irritability and threatens the progress of a closing, you must admit that lack of sleep is much worse. If your goal is to appear as the most macho lawyer in the room, you might well opt for an all night closing session. If your goal is to really get your deal closed, you should when possible opt to take a break, go home and get some sleep (and a shower), and return bright and early to attack the problems at hand. However, sometimes there is no choice but to stay all night.

Common Pitfalls

We can easily reiterate what makes closings successful. Foremost among these is adequate preparation. It matters far more what you do in advance of a closing than what you do once the parties are assembled. Here is a listing of the top reasons why closings fail:

- Extraneous factors entirely outside the control of counsel (this, of course, is our favorite)
- Too little time allocated for closing (a cheap and easy way to create unnecessary stress)
- Inadequate preparation (almost always deadly)
- Inattention to detail (equally deadly, not only to your client but to your career)
- Failure to control third parties (before you can control them you must identify them)
- Failure of counsel to finalize documents in advance (blame-shifting on this is not permitted)
- Unrealistic client expectations (some are unrealistic no matter what, but you can help adjust attitudes)
- Incomplete closing agenda ("you did not tell me you needed that. . .")
- Inexperienced counsel on one side or both (or worse yet, inexperienced counsel who does not realize he is inexperienced)
- Overly aggressive counsel (you get paid for being nice)
- Overly aggressive counsel who also happens to be inexperienced (maybe you do not get paid enough for this, but hang in there)
- Missing persons (if you are too important to attend, maybe the deal is too insignificant to proceed)
- Missing documents (lawyers, not paralegals, are responsible for eliminating chaos)
- Missing funds (the fed is not supposed to lose stuff)
- Unprepared bankers ("we will release the funds when we receive these 36 documents. . .")
- Surprises (any kind)
- Hunger (you must admit that you are a human being, despite media reports to the contrary, and accordingly need food)
- Temperature extremes (only the unprepared should be sweating)
- National emergencies (these may actually be outside of your control)

While you may note that many of these reasons are well beyond the control of counsel, a good lawyer with a passion for getting a deal closed does his best to overcome them all. The first reflexive impulse, that of saying it is beyond my control (a grown-up version of "Mommy, I didn't do it!"), should give way to an attitude of "we can get this transaction closed no matter what." The attitude itself will not bring about closing, but just the attitude, especially if it is contagious, could have more to do with a successful closing than you think.

What Is the Agreement?

Closings often take place long distance. The parties and their lawyers exchange faxed signature pages or e-mail pdf files or attachments bearing the required signatures, sometimes with the promise that the "original" signatures will follow by overnight delivery. How comfortable should deal lawyers and their clients be with signatures that one faxed or pdf'd or generated through some other electronic means? This subject is dealt with in Chapter 11.

APPENDIX 14-A
Closing Agenda

Regarding the
Purchase of the Assets of

by

ENTITIES

Seller:

Seller's Counsel:

Buyer:

Buyer's Counsel:

ACQUISITION DOCUMENTS

Item No.	Description Statue	Executing Parties	Party Responsible for Final Document Preparation
1.	Asset Purchase Agreement		Buyer
	Exhibits –		Buyer
	A Definitions		
	B Form of Bill of Sale and Assignment of Intangible Assets		
	C Form of Buyer Note		
	D Financial Statements		
	E Form of Side Agreements		
	F Form of Opinion of Counsel for Seller and Shareholder		
	G Form of Opinion of Counsel for Buyer		
	Schedules –		
	2(b) Excluded Assets Buyer;		Seller
	2(d) Assumed Obligations Buyer;		Seller
	4(a) Directors and Officers		Seller
	4(b) Issued and Outstanding Shares of Capital Stock		Seller
	4(e) Tangible Assets Purchased by Buyer		Buyer; Seller
	4(f) Subsidiaries		Seller
	4(k) Tax Matters		Seller
	4(l) Real Property Leases		Seller
	4(m)(iii) Intellectual Property		Seller
	4(m)(iv) License Agreements		Seller
	4(p) Contracts		Seller
	4(s) Insurance Policies		Seller

	4(t) Litigation		Seller
	4(x) Employee Benefit Plans		Seller
2.	Side Agreements [Specify Each Agreement]	Buyer; Seller	Buyer's Counsel
			Seller's Counsel
3.	Promissory Note	Buyer	Buyer's Counsel
4.	Opinion of Counsel		
	a. Counsel for Seller	Seller's Counsel	Seller's Counsel
	b. Counsel for Buyer	Buyer's Counsel	Buyer's Counsel
5.	Third Party Consents and Releases	Third Party	Seller's Counsel
6.	UCC/Lien Search		Seller's Counsel
	a. Termination Statements	Third Party	Seller's Counsel
7.	Bill of Sale and Assignment	Seller	Buyer's Counsel
8.	Instrument of Assumption	Buyer	Buyer's Counsel
9.	Estimated Purchase Price	Seller	Seller
	a. Preliminary Adjustments	Buyer; Seller	Seller's Counsel
10.	Secretary Certificate		
	a. Seller	Seller	Seller's Counsel
	i. Articles of incorporation		
	ii. Bylaws		
	iii. Director and shareholder resolutions		
	iv. Incumbency of officers		
	b. Buyer	Buyer	Buyer's Counsel
	i. Articles of incorporation		
	ii. Bylaws		
	iii. Director resolutions		
	iv. Incumbency of officers		
11.	Officer's Certificates		
	a. Seller	Seller	Seller's Counsel
	i. Representations and Warranties		
	ii. Performance of Covenants		
	iii. Litigation		
	b. Buyer	Buyer	Buyer's Counsel
	i. Representations and Warranties		
	ii. Performance of Covenants		
12.	Good Standing Certificates		
	a. Seller		Seller's Counsel
	b. Buyer		Buyer's Counsel
13.	Mutual Waiver of Conditions	Seller; Buyer	Seller's Counsel
14.	Closing Payment		
	a. Payment to Seller		Buyer

b. Instructions to transfer procedures (e.g. wire transfer instructions)		Seller

Post-Closing

15.	Seller's name change	Seller	Seller's Counsel

SUPPORTING DOCUMENTS

16.	Purchase Price Adjustment		
	a. Final Adjustment	Buyer	Buyer
	b. Adjustment Notice to Seller (if necessary)	Buyer	Buyer's Counsel
	c. Appeal of Adjustment to Buyer (if necessary)	Seller	Seller's Counsel
	d. Payment (if necessary)	Buyer; Seller	Buyer; Seller

CHAPTER 15

Handling Post-Closing Matters

Properly negotiating and structuring a transaction while shepherding it to closing is critical to ensuring that it comes off seamlessly. The less glamorous steps required after closing are often just as important to buttoning down the deal and making sure it works. The devil is in the details—if post-closing particulars are not attended to properly, problems and controversies may be the result.

Post-Closing Considerations

Expect the Unexpected

Once money, stock, or assets have passed hands, it may seem as if the important work (and in some cases all the work) is done. But the fun may have just begun. Filings need to be made, documentation assembled in final form, and post-closing relationships initiated and monitored. Although one can hope to avoid them, problems must be anticipated.

Expect the Unexpected

The watch words of any experienced M&A attorney are sure to be expect the unexpected. Businesses inevitably have their hidden risks, governmental agencies relish in creating red tape and circumstances in any industry are constantly in flux—problems are not the exception, they are the rule.

One excellent and particularly unnerving case study in expect the unexpected resulted from the acquisition by merger of an Internet business by a public company. The parties were organized under the laws of several states, requiring merger filings in multiple jurisdictions. These multiple filings also placed the transaction at the mercy of bureaucrats across the country. The closing went smoothly and the transaction went off without a hitch. Several months passed by, as did a Form 8-K, Form 10-Q, and Form 10-K filing by the buyer. When one jurisdiction (without any pre-clearance merger process) elected to give the merger an effective date corresponding to when it decided to get around to processing the filing (rather than the date of filing months earlier and conspicuously stamped on the officially filed merger certificate), the lawyers involved suffered through some sleepless nights. After a series of backroom meetings with Secretary of State personnel, starting with lawyerly explanations of why the date was wrong and ending with plaintive pleadings to simply do everyone involved a favor, the proper date was used, avoiding the task of determining how to treat a transaction that had been reported as closed months earlier in securities filings and financial statements. This is an example of an otherwise smooth transaction nearly falling victim to a hidden problem.

Post-closing work should not result in unexpected billings (and resultant controversies) for clients. Fee quotes should take into account clean-up activities and anticipate unknown issues. Attorneys are often paid out of the proceeds of the transaction at closing (particularly when representing a financially distressed seller). In those instances, it is important to be clear that the work and billing is not yet complete or to make provision through an escrow or hold-back of funds for the payment of additional fees.

Living with the Deal

The phrases buyer's remorse and seller's remorse were coined for a reason. Even in the M&A context, after closing, buyers and sellers often struggle to come to grips with just what they have agreed to do and what they have given up. M&A transactions are monumental events in the business and personal lives of those heavily involved and there is bound to be some fall out.

This struggle is particularly acute for the sellers of a closely held business. The sellers may feel guilt for having sold a business that has been in the family for generations or that they built with their own hands. This regret can be magnified when a former owner who remains with the business now reports to a superior, after years of being the boss. Even if an owner is not involved in the business post closing, watching another manage your business can be painful.

Buyers, while typically not having to deal with the more visceral issues a seller might deal with, still can be left scratching their heads after closing, wondering just what they got themselves into. Due diligence will not necessarily uncover every issue that might appear after closing. Sellers who remain employees of the business sometimes fail to take a back seat role in management, creating tensions at an operational level. These tensions may exist among rank and file employees, who remain suspicious of the new management. Integrating buyer and seller operations can be a lengthy, frustrating exercise that is only compounded when hoped for synergies fail to materialize.

Buyer and seller may need to address certain contentious issues left for after closing by the acquisition agreement. For instance, earnout calculations may need to be made, and certain tensions may arise relating to the methodology of the calculation itself or the seller's perceptions as to the buyer's post-closing operation of the business and its effect on the earn-out. Similarly, purchase price adjustment mechanisms (true ups) can be a source of post-closing angst, as the parties work their way through the prescribed procedures. While both earnout and purchase price adjustment provisions typically specify some dispute resolution procedure, whenever money is involved, controversy often follows and can impact the relationship of the buyer and seller and each party's perception of the transaction. Both earn-outs and true-ups are discussed in more detail below. The key for attorneys involved in an M&A transaction is to be aware of these tensions and emotions, prepare their clients and shepherd the parties through them.

Immediate Post-Closing Matters

Deal Cubes and Closing Dinners

While waiting for FED reference numbers or authorizations to release documents from escrow, the thoughtful lawyer may take a few minutes to reflect on some of the important post-closing matters: the deal cubes and the closing dinner. But care should be taken, since the first person to mention these matters often ends up paying for them.

With respect to the deal cube, attempts are often made to be creative in showing the character of the business sold. Expressing a hope for something more exciting than the names of investment bankers in Lucite is something best not said to or within earshot of the investment bankers who typically pay for the cubes. A corporate deal lawyer can never have too many deal cubes. Many team members are just starting their collections. Arrange for sufficient cubes to recognize the contributions of all members of the team.

Also suggest possible locations for the closing dinner. Regretfully, some are not that enthusiastic or generous about the post-closing festivities. Lawyers do not always have warm feelings for their counterparts on the other side (at least based on some of those comments lawyers have been known to make to clients as the latest markup arrived for their review at 9:00 p.m. on the night of their 20th wedding anniversary). But it is important to break bread together and tell everyone how enjoyable it was working with them. Socializing may take the edge off tensions that developed in the heat of negotiating or closing battles and develop needed goodwill down the road if post-closing issues arise.

Keep in mind one thing on timing of the closing dinner: it is better to hold the dinner fairly close to the actual closing date, before any post-closing indemnification claims arise. Moreover, to adopt a less cynical perspective, it is often helpful to stay in contact with those attorneys on the other side of the transaction (especially if the transaction went smoothly), particularly if they happen to be located in other states or jurisdictions. These attorneys can often become a key facet of a well-developed referral network.

The Closing Dinner

Apparently, the creative urges that M&A transactions tend to undervalue sometimes make their appearance at the closing dinner. Part celebration and part marketing opportunity, closing dinners range from champagne at the closing table to relatively elaborate events that can rival any formal affair. At the far end of the spectrum, foreign locations are always good if paid for by clients and guests are flown first class, accompanied by significant others and treated to private tours of local attractions, actors impersonating famous persons from the area, dinners held in castles, customized fireworks that spell the client's names and first class hotel accommodations (yes, to the amazement of many, this actually did happen in one private deal). One need not be a party planner to arrange a closing dinner, but failing to provide for such an event overlooks what is oftentimes the most memorable and enjoyable part of a deal.

Closing Documentation Clean Up

Many attorneys who have been working around the clock are tempted to uncork the champagne and take a much needed vacation in southern France the minute the money and/or stock are delivered. Resist the temptation until the parties agree on post-closing procedures to clean up the copies/documents, avoiding the embarrassment of not having a complete copy of the operative agreements when someone makes a claim after closing.

For starters, as is addressed in greater detail below, closing binders will need to be prepared and various filings made. In fact, it is common for final documents to be fully assembled after closing, as already agreed upon exhibits and schedules are finalized and trickle in. Often documents, certificates, and resolutions reference exhibits, schedules, or other types of attachments. In the closing frenzy, many forget to do the actual attaching. Before allowing documents to leave the room in a physical closing, or before assembling final documents for the closing binder, make certain that all documents, certificates, and resolutions are complete with all exhibits, schedules, and attachments. It is more important to agree on what the actual attachments are when the closing is done electronically. Make sure that everyone attached the proper draft, version, or final document.

If one or more parties will want multiple signed copies of the documents where the closing was primarily electronic, the attorneys should reach an understanding on who will take the primary responsibility to prepare and circulate those documents immediately following the closing. This post-closing work will add additional costs that will need to be included in the closing bill. Alternatively, the client should understand that this additional work is necessary and a subsequent bill will be delivered. Clients will not want this to drag out beyond the month following closing (absent some extraordinary situation of which the client is aware). The likelihood of being paid for post-closing work declines precipitously as the length of time between closing and completing this work increases.

Further complicating matters, more and more clients are convincing themselves that to send people to a closing is unnecessarily expensive and that remote closings are easier and cheaper. Clients may save on plane tickets and travel time, but attorneys will spend additional time post-closing trying to put together a final set of documents. Signature pages will not look alike, and many times will end differently. It will be hard to assemble a complete set. The client does not necessarily appreciate the time needed to sort this out. Nevertheless, remote closings are becoming increasingly common and have to be factored into deal planning. Also, if everyone is making changes remotely, it is best to put one person in charge of assembling the entire package so that all the copies are uniform. If there is any question about what the final schedules were, it is best to clear up that issue as soon as possible, while the parties are still fairly agreeable and the transaction is fresh in everyone's mind.

Announcements

While an impending acquisition may be kept confidential, once closed the parties must properly inform the public and the interested parties of the completed transaction. The parties may need to prepare and distribute a press release, call a company meeting, or prepare a memo to inform employees or make sure their customers, suppliers, and industry partners are up to speed on recent events. Failure to act quickly may result in rumors adversely affecting employee morale, customer and supplier trust, and general public perception.

Post-Closing Filings and Loose Ends

Once a transaction has closed, almost without fail a dizzying array of loose ends need to be tied down. While no two transactions will be alike with respect to the types of post-closing activities, a common trait is that post-closing details are overlooked. Whether they deal with a filing that is required by law or necessary to vest ownership of a purchased asset in the buyer or practical steps the parties need to take to inform their constituents of the transaction, post-closing details can directly affect the value of the deal to the buyer and seller.

Some of the most common post-closing clean-up items relate to borrowings and associated security interests. The seller may need to file UCC-1 financing statements to perfect any security interest granted by the buyer securing any deferred purchase price. Conversely, steps will often need to be taken to terminate security interests in the purchased assets securing debt paid off at closing pursuant to a pay-off letter. Given that these relatively mundane actions can go to the heart of the transaction (the security of the seller's purchase price and the buyer's unencumbered ownership of its purchased assets), inattention to these details can be nettlesome.

Assignments of registered assets, such as trademarks, domain names, and patents, should be filed immediately after closing. This is particularly important for intellectual property so that the buyer receives timely notices of renewals, maintenance fees, and other important correspondence. If the buyer bought the name of the seller in an asset transaction, the seller should change its name immediately following closing or in compliance with any contractually granted grace period. The better plan for buyer's counsel is to take responsibility and not rely on the seller or its attorney to file those documents. Many junior attorneys and even paralegals do not realize the importance of these post-closing steps, and senior attorneys should always make sure that assignments requiring filing to be effective are made as soon as possible following the closing. Costs for these filings (both legal and filing fees) should also be dealt with prior to closing so that substantial post-closing bills do not surprise the client.

Additional post-closing filings should be planned for if either the buyer or seller is a public company and the transaction is material. The buyer may be required to file audited financial statements for the business acquired. How can a buyer, practically speaking, cause an audit to be performed of an acquired business for periods of time prior to closing? The practical pointer in this situation is to be sure that the acquisition agreement requires that the seller provide the buyer with audited financial statements.

In addition to these more specific post-closing housekeeping items, any number of miscellaneous issues will need to be addressed. Examples include amending employee benefit plans, recording lease assignments, formally terminating unwanted contracts or vendor relationships, and updating employee handbooks. Regardless of whether a transaction is big or small or its closing smooth sailing or a bitter contest, issues will need to be addressed post-closing. Efforts should be made to identify those actions well in advance of closing, along with the parties responsible, and no loose end should be allowed to linger.

True-Ups

The negotiation of the true-up, by which the purchase price is adjusted based on the state of the balance sheet of the target on the closing date, is discussed in Chapter 8. Often a bogey is set at a specified amount of net worth or working capital, and payments may be made by either buyer or seller for variations from the bogey reflected in the accounts of the business purchased on the closing date. Often the true-up amount is payable from the standard escrow for the benefit of buyer (if the buyer is to receive a payment). The negotiated language of the true-up clause often depends on the use of accounting terms and summary procedures. The language may not be adequate when the rubber hits the road.

Unlike the general remedies provision (indemnification), if a true-up clause is specified in a deal, it will always be used. Unlike other post-closing matters, the true-up process needs to begin at closing. The true-up normally works off the closing date balance sheet, which one side or the other is to prepare. That may involve the physical observation of inventories, which may require the suspension of business operations. Often, because of the magnitude of the task of observing inventories (multiple plants and storage locations), planning is required because of the need to recruit outside help. But even without observing inventories, the designated party may have significant work to do and a limited time in which to prepare the closing date statement. The calculation to the true-up may be based on negotiated standards. Those are not necessarily standard accounting concepts. It may be necessary to educate the accountants preparing the numbers of the theory of the agreement. There is no precision in accounting. A presentation of net worth can vary widely depending up the reserves taken on the balance sheet. A buyer preparing a balance sheet would tend to present those items going into the calculation of the bogey conservatively, giving rise to a higher true-up to be paid by the seller. A seller having responsibility for preparing the calculation would take the opposite tact.

The party preparing the initial calculation will need to study the agreement carefully to assure that the proper presentation will be followed and the proper timing, notice and other information will be presented. The party will review the agreement to determine how tightly the party's position is framed by the agreement. Is it merely GAAP (with tremendous latitude) or the historical practices of the seller (probably tied down fairly tightly)? The notice and form of notice must be followed, as well as any other supplemental materials to be delivered.

Once the other side receives the initial calculation, it too will need to carefully consider the agreement in terms of its rights. It usually has a limited period to object and present its own calculations, but usually has a right to workpapers and calculations. If the seller has prepared the calculations, a buyer may be particularly disadvantaged because it has no prior experience in the preparation of interim financial statements of the business and the process or procedures used.

The hope of most lawyers is that the accountants will just work it out. In particular, if the measurement has been tied to historical practices and not to amorphous concepts such as GAAP, it may be easy for the accountants to quickly agree on how certain calculations are made. But the accountants on each side should be advised that their own thoughts about the principles to be applied may need to be adjusted to the precise language negotiated in the agreement. In all events, if there are time limits specified to negotiate the differences between the parties, the provisions for demanding arbitration, the appointment of an independent accountant or other arbitrator need to be observed. Counsel may prepare the necessary notice beforehand because of concern that discussions will carry until the bewitching hour. If the parties are making progress, it may be helpful to negotiate formal time extensions so that a party is not precluded from pursuing the specified remedy should negotiations extend beyond the stated date.

The true-up mechanics may contemplate that the determination of the actual true-up will just be handed over to an independent accountant to be selected by the parties. But those mechanics often fail to comprehend the elaborate engagement letters and broad protections now required by accountants before undertaking an engagement. Ultimately the determination of balance sheet line items is not nearly as precise as the lawyers may have believed. Each party will need to decide how to best advocate its position.

Closing Binders and Files

The preparation of closing binders (also referred to as closing books or bibles) is often delegated to the most junior attorney or paralegal on the team. While that may be viewed as educational and cost efficient, there may be some pitfalls with this strategy. The junior attorney or paralegal may not have been sufficiently involved with the entire transaction. Unless the compiler is provided with an overview and a complete list of the documents that should be included, many important documents may get lost in the shuffle. If there are multiple transactions (e.g., senior secured financing, mezzanine financing, equity financing, and the purchase or merger transaction), a junior may not be able to tell which documents go with which transaction. Time invested by a team member in logically arranging a comprehensive index to the documents will pay off when someone tries to locate a document for future reference or as a good working form.

Many clients have their own style preference for binding the final documents. Some like fancy leather bound volumes with their own color scheme, some like velobound copies and others like looseleaf or press board cover bindings for ease of copying in the future. It is always best to ask the clients how they would like the documents bound before sending them off for reproduction and binding. Some clients also appreciate a separate set of files with separate tabs that tie to each of the documents on the index. Especially when ordering the fancy leather version, it is much cheaper to determine the total number of sets the client would like in advance and if they want to pay for sets for any other parties. As obvious as this may seem, it is also good practice to double check the spelling of names (especially the client's) before the final order is made for personalized sets of bound volumes.

Preparation of the closing binders should be completed fairly quickly following the closing. There are pitfalls with failing to do this in that someone doing the assembling may forget about or not even be aware of side letters or documents that may have been created at the last minute. Also clients do not want to see bills for this work showing up months later. It is often best to include, in the final bill at closing, the cost to assemble and produce the closing binders and then to complete this work quickly after the actual closing. As a companion piece to the preparation of the closing binders, all attorneys working on the transaction should be certain to have their internal files and documents properly organized, indexed and filed.

Longer Term Post-Closing Matters

Implementing Lessons of Due Diligence

In larger and more complex transactions, the buyer often prepares a detailed integration plan. The buyer's interest in the target is the ability to enhance its present business through the acquisition. Crucial to that success is the process of integration, folding the newly acquired business into the buyer. Accordingly, the success of an acquisition is based not on the ease of the closing but a buyer's success in the years after the transaction closes. Integration takes on any number of forms, but typically addresses matters such as integrating employee benefit plans, information technology, logistics and facilities. The preparation and implementation of these plans is typically a matter directed by the businesspeople, but it is worthwhile for attorneys to be aware of these post-closing efforts, to be familiar with the plan and to ensure any post-closing legal matters make it on the short list of priorities.

Integration is difficult and often poorly done, although these are things not often observed by lawyers because once the deal closes they often fade from the picture. Successful buyers determine, as part of due diligence, the probability of successful integration. Planning for integration begins as an active part of due diligence. Within the bounds of law, implementation of an acquisition begins long before the deal is closed. Integration that is delayed risks employee malaise, customer defections and other bad outcomes. The elimination of redundancies is often part of the economics of a particular deal.

There are legal aspects of the integration process that may involve significant participation by the lawyers. For example, the alignment of employee compensation and benefits is often crucial, and the integration of various benefit plans involves significant legal talent. Compliance issues may need to be addressed, if the buyer is compliance oriented and the target's practices may have been marginal.

Even in transactions where no formal transition plan is followed, a buyer's due diligence review will often uncover issues that will need to be addressed after closing. These issues may range from mundane housekeeping items such as impending contract renewal dates and intellectual property maintenance filings, to more critical matters such as pending litigation. In both these formal and informal settings, implementing the lessons learned and fixing the unearthed problems is a key part of properly managing a transaction. Rather than remaining part of a buried due diligence file, these matters must be brought to the attention of the businesspeople dealing with the transition and ongoing business.

Document Retention and E-Discovery

With Enron, the demise of Arthur Andersen, Martha Stewart, and the escalating costs of litigation, a cottage industry, including many law-firm specialists, has sprung up. Some clients now require their attorneys to acknowledge and comply with their own document retention policies, many of which will affect not only hard paper but also computer document and e-mail storage. Those clients who have not yet focused on this issue may be in for a rude awakening in subsequent litigation or investigations. A good counselor will be pro-active in discussing these matters up front with clients and being certain post-closing that the firm (and all the attorneys, paralegals and even secretaries working on the transaction) follow the agreed procedures. Home computers and personal e-mail accounts where copies are frequently sent should also be reviewed for compliance with document retention policies.

Opinions differ regarding the wisdom of keeping old drafts following a successful closing. Some lawyers believe that holding onto all such materials is helpful if a subsequent need arises, whether as a result of a dispute or otherwise, to reconstruct the course of negotiations and the history how of the documentation evolved. For example, if the seller is arguing that an ambiguous provision should be read in a certain way, it would be helpful for the buyer to find that a seller proposal to include explicit language reflecting its view was expressly rejected during negotiations and never adopted.

Other lawyers, particularly litigators, take the view that on balance little good can come of retaining voluminous files. Most problematic are marginal comments or notes. They are often written spontaneously with little critical thought and so, when read out of context, can come back to haunt a party in litigation. There are also significant storage costs involved in maintaining voluminous files with an offsite storage firm. Some lawyers immediately purge all materials other than execution copies. Others save only those drafts that were exchanged between the parties. An intermediate approach is to retain only execution copies, original copies of intermediate drafts without marginal notations, correspondence and legal memoranda, but no informal notes or documents bearing marginal comments.

Computer systems keep versions, so even purging physical files will not solve all discovery issues down the road. In addition, circulation of drafts by e-mail is more common than ever. Frequently once the draft is sent off to cyberspace, someone may be able to produce copies of various versions even if the original drafter observes strict destruction or purging practices.

Regardless of the retention approach that is followed, organizing the files soon after the transaction closes is prudent so that when the need arises, the lawyer can put his hands on the materials as requested.

A client may expect its attorney to retain everything and will sometimes call years later to ask the attorney to produce or find a document, version or particular draft. That is one reason for document retention to be covered in the engagement or retention letter. Alternatively, this issue can be addressed in a post-closing letter to the client to avoid surprises.

If there are pending or threatened investigations, claims, or litigation, the landscape changes dramatically. Destruction of documentation or computer records in such circumstances can result in dire consequences. Spoliation of evidence could result in a judge's instruction that a jury be allowed to draw a negative inference as to the contents of the destroyed materials. Criminal charges, including obstruction of justice, are also a possibility depending on the situation. Because what is permissible or not will be highly fact sensitive and often involve judgment calls, attorneys and their clients should tread with great care and deliberation when they know of pending or threatened investigations, claims or litigation.

Expiration of Claim Periods and Termination of Escrows

Do attorneys have any responsibility to notify clients regarding deadlines for expiration of statutes of limitations for claims against other parties or to make claims as the escrow termination or survival deadlines approach? While most attorneys would say no, it is possible that clients think otherwise and assume their attorneys will provide notice when these dates are approaching. Some attorneys address this concern by sending a post-closing letter (at the same time or perhaps even before sending out the final documents) that sets forth specific post-closing dates and let the clients know that they will not be monitoring those dates unless requested to do so in writing. Others merely send copies of the documents and expect that the clients will appreciate and note those significant deadlines. The approach may also vary significantly depending on whether a client has in-house counsel sophisticated in handling transactions and familiar with the importance of the dates and timing for claims and releases from escrow. Even if attorneys inform their clients that they will not be monitoring or noting any significant deadline or action dates post-closing, some attorneys, in looking for reasons to periodically touch base with clients, may track those dates regardless and call clients as they approach. This may, however, lead to a precedent or at least an expectation that the attorney has some obligation to provide notice. Attorneys should think carefully about this practice.

Indemnification and Other Remedies

While M&A lawyers spend a great deal of time negotiating the indemnification provisions of acquisition agreements, crafting that precise language may be only a part of understanding the remedies available for a wronged party to an agreement after it closes. The full range of arrows in the quiver should be understood.

If there were no indemnification provisions, the parties would have the normal contract remedies. Remedies need not be specified in order to be available. Additionally, parties may have a variety of tort-based remedies available to them, such as fraud in the inducement and securities law claims. Any separate agreement (such as a covenant not to compete) may have its own set of remedies. The scope of the provision that provides that indemnification is the exclusive remedy must be examined to see if residual contract law remedies remain.

Indemnification should be understood for what it is: the right hand giveth and the left hand taketh away—that is, it is both a limitation on contract remedies but a potential expansion of other remedies. For example, MAPA, at section 11.2(c), contains a concept of indemnification on a "your watch/our watch basis" for operations of the target. An unexpected lawsuit based on actions taken while the sellers owned the target, even when it did not involve a breach of representation, would be covered by indemnification under the MSPA formulation.

The Aggrieved Buyer

A business is purchased with high expectations. If it fails to live up to those expectations, possible explanations include the buyer's expectations were unfounded, the business was poorly run after its purchase or the seller wrongfully induced high expectations (within the acquisition agreement or extraneous to it). The disappointed buyer of a purchased business may respond in various ways. Regardless of fault, as a matter of corporate face saving, a buyer may seek to blame the seller.

One problem faced in most acquisitions is that the team that did the due diligence and negotiated the agreement is not the team operating the business. Yet the team operating the business is the one that must determine in which manner the buyer was wronged. Often the exercise is to give the operating people (or an accountant) a copy of the representations to find out how a claim could be brought. The problem with this approach is that the representations, standing alone, may not really present an understandable snapshot of what was promised. Further, lawyers write them. While one hopes that their meaning is understood, they are often too complex and too subtle for the non-lawyer. In any event, there may be a basis for a claim outside the representations, which will not be identified by that process.

A different approach is for the buyer to identify the problems with the business and ask counsel to explore whether a claim is available for those deficiencies. That probably requires some sort of fact-finding investigation by counsel to probe any problems encountered. A beginning point might be to ask for an analysis comparing the financial projections of the business developed in the acquisition process with actual results, accompanied by an explanation of the differences.

This is not to say that there are many claims arising from M&A deals. The general experience is that a minor percentage of deals, but seemingly growing, give rise to an indemnification or other claim.

Preparing the Claim

While the parties should all be mindful of the survival period provided by the acquisition agreement, there may be a need for notifications pursuant to the acquisition agreement or applicable law at an earlier stage. Even though a claim outside the remedies provided in the acquisition agreement might be possible, the procedural aspects of the acquisition agreement would always be kept in mind. The form, content and manner of giving any notice should be complied with. One technique is to have a junior in-house lawyer become the keeper of a log so that the details of possible claims are preserved as they arise.

Careful reading of the acquisition agreement is required before a claim is prepared. Possible problems, even when no real damage has resulted as the claims period is expiring, would be listed. In order to gain leverage, a party may exaggerate claims, include claims only loosely supported by a breach of representation or schedule claims not supported at all. In particular, if a basket is of the threshold type (contrasted to the deductible), where coverage reverts to dollar one coverage once the threshold is reached, there may be a great stretch to top the threshold amount. In scheduling the claims, limitations on the types of damages pursuant to the acquisition agreement would need to be considered (the limitation on consequential damages so readily agreed to could have a real bite at this stage).

Failing to strictly comply with the deadlines and procedures may prejudice a claimant's ability to take advantage of those provisions and could turn into a significant financial exposure. Strict compliance with the notice provisions in any related escrow agreement is also imperative. It is best to be conservative and copy everyone and their attorneys if there is any doubt as to the nature of the notice procedures. Also, if there are pending escrow distributions in the short-term, it might be appropriate to call the escrow agent to be sure that it received the notice and is not wiring monies or sending checks to the other party. If representing a party with a right of set-off, the client should be made aware of this right and any steps that must be taken when availing itself of that right. If the client is a seller representative, before agreeing to any compromise, the attorney might make certain that the representative has the requisite authority to bind all sellers.

Responding to the Claim

The usual response by the seller to a notice of claim is predictable: denial and a demand for additional detail. Again, the procedures of the acquisition agreement should be understood and observed. The denial itself may trigger some form of ADR, such as mediation, before either litigation can be commenced or arbitration initiated. In some cases, the award of fees and costs may depend on the legitimacy of the claim and its amount (such as baseball style arbitration).

Third Party Claims

In addition to the claim for contract breach, most acquisition agreements will contain indemnification against third party claims, such as litigation. These usually require that the buyer provide notice to the seller and give it an opportunity to defend. Rarely is the buyer allowed to defend and then send the bill to the seller, although separate counsel may be used if there is a conflict. How third party claims get sorted out requires particular attention to the terms of the acquisition agreement and monitoring as the claim progresses to assure that the seller is acting in the buyer's best interests.

An interesting subset of third-party claims involves governmental investigations and product recalls, things that could have a significant reputational effect on buyer. Most buyers are reluctant, despite the indemnification provision, to turn over the reins to the seller's designated counsel in these circumstances. However, section 11.9 of MAPA allows a buyer to take over defense of a third-party claim if it has made a good faith determination that there is a reasonable probability that the claim may adversely affect it other than as a result of monetary damages for which it would be entitled to indemnification.

ADR or Litigation

If it becomes necessary to turn to the courts or arbitration to pursue a claim, the acquisition agreement must be consulted once again. If arbitration has been selected, the procedures specified in the acquisition agreement must be followed. If there is no arbitration provision, the forum selection clauses must be considered. At this stage, the litigators are undoubtedly all over the file. Tactical considerations will be brought into play.

Non-Indemnification Claims

The truly aggrieved buyer may seek counsel for what can be done in circumstances where the specified contractual procedures may be inadequate. This will involve review of the full range of claims that might be available, including

- Equitable relief, such as rescission or reformation
- Claims for damages based on tort, such as fraud or securities law claims
- Contract-based claims, such as a breach of the covenant of good faith and fair dealing

The M&A lawyer will need to provide guidance through the applicable portions of the document that might be a limitation on these rights, such as whether the acquisition agreement precludes other remedies (although even if present such provisions may not be effective) whether there is an effective non-reliance clause (the courts differ on the effectiveness of these clauses) and whether the indemnification claim is truly the exclusive remedy.

Earnouts

Earnouts, in which a portion of the purchase price is paid out based on the performance of the target business after the closing, are receiving increased use. The problem with earnouts is that buyers and sellers have absolutely diametric views on whether an earnout will in fact be achieved: sellers are convinced that their financial dreams will be satisfied with the earnout, while buyers believe that an earnout is merely wishful thinking. Earnout clauses are usually carefully crafted. Businesspeople, particularly corporate development officers, can fine tune the language about how the earnout will be paid. Often it is convoluted and difficult to understand but ultimately can be parsed through. Earnout provisions are discussed in Chapter 8.

The real problem with earnouts is that the buyer often ignores them after the deal is done. The operations people have a business to run. They know why a particular acquisition was made but are often unaware of the intricacies of the earnout, even though they may be vaguely aware of its existence. The tension is demonstrated by the case of *Horizon Holdings*.[184] In that case, a jury awarded about half of the potential earnout (which itself was twice what the initial cash purchase price had been), based on a finding of a violation of the implied covenant of good faith and fair dealing. In the case, the principal seller was able to present evidence of the promises that had been made in his operation of the business, which promises had not been honored. If an earnout is in place, it is prudent for those actually operating the business to understand the earnout and to be made aware of the legal parameters of not only the document but what may be implied by law.

Earnouts are often paid over extended periods, with partial payments based on annual or other periodic results. It is tempting to put the calculation into the hands of the accountants. The problem with that is that the junior accountant faced with the calculation may not understand the basis of the calculation and may not understand the procedures required to be followed.

The lapse of time is the problem with earnouts. Unlike the true-up, where the calculation needs to be done as of the very day of closing and memories are fresh, with the earnout the calculation may be done years later with vague recollections of how detailed calculations are to be made. Even so, the dispute resolution procedure required by the acquisition agreement may be akin to the true-up. In any event, strict compliance with agreement terms in the preparation of audits and calculations is important.

Post-Closing Covenants

Simply because a transaction has closed, does not mean the business relationship between the buyer and seller has terminated. Almost without fail, acquisition agreements provide for or anticipate some form of ongoing interaction among the parties. The arrangements can range from the mundane (e.g., an obligation to provide reasonable post-closing litigation support) to factors that are truly the impetus behind the deal (e.g., a long-term supply agreement that dwarfs the value of the acquisition itself). The common factor all these post-closing covenants share, however, is that they are ancillary arrangements that are often critical to the realization of the value of the transaction and should not be treated as afterthoughts.

Transition-Related Covenants

Acquisition agreements will quite often obligate the parties to take what might be viewed as fairly reasonable, common sense steps to aid in the smooth transition of the target business. In addition to the typical further assurances obligation, the seller will in all likelihood be required to provide all reasonable assistance requested by the buyer in connection with its transition efforts. Specific examples include communications with employees, customers and vendors, availability to answer routine questions regarding the business and the forwarding of inquiries from past or potential customers. Providing access to books and records can also be important. Similarly, litigation is a reality of operating any business and, unless cooperation and collaboration is specified, a buyer and seller might find themselves in the midst of a controversy without access to information, documents or witnesses critical to their cause. Just how, when and at whose expense that access is provided is a point of negotiation.

Covenants That Protect the Value of the Transaction

The post-closing covenants serve to protect the value of the transaction for the parties involved, most typically the buyer. In that sense, they can be as essential a component of the acquisition agreement as the purchase price provisions or the representations. Restrictive covenants, such as non-competition, non-solicitation, and confidentiality provisions, go to the heart of the transaction, in that they preserve for the buyer what likely motivated it to acquire the business in the first instance: its goodwill, proprietary information, customer base, position in the marketplace, and/or human capital. Without adequate restrictive covenants in place, there is little to stop the seller (or its shareholders) from taking the buyer's money and setting up shop across town as the buyer's now well-financed key competitor.

Diametrically opposed to the ease with which sellers accept confidentiality obligations, non-competition and non-solicitation provisions tend to create an incredible amount of consternation for sellers. The flash points are most often the duration of the obligation, its scope (both in terms of geography and the relevant market or industry) and the nature of activities restricted (i.e., ownership of a competing business versus providing consulting services within a related industry). The level of resistance by the seller to the non-compete has a direct relationship to the substance of any post-closing plans—retiring to a beach house as opposed to continuing to operate a related business that is not part of the transaction. Just as in any other context, the buyer needs to be careful not to be too greedy and attempt to expand the reach of the non-compete obligations (either temporally or in scope) beyond that which the relevant jurisdiction would deem permissible. That being said, courts have typically extended additional leeway to restrictive covenants that spring from an acquisition (as contrasted to an employment relationship), given the buyer's legitimate interests in protecting the value of the transaction and the typically large dollar amounts paid as consideration for the business.

From the buyer's perspective, the remedies tied to a breach of the restrictive covenants are fairly well settled: injunctive relief and the recovery of associated damages. What is often overlooked is that, from the seller's perspective, it will be important to push for the restrictive covenants to terminate if there is a material breach by the buyer of its obligations under the transaction (most likely the payment obligations). The threat of having the seller back in the market is quite often a better form of payment security than any collateral can provide.

Transition Services Agreements

In connection with a divestiture where the corporate seller centrally supported the infrastructure of the business sold, a buyer may negotiate for the seller to continue to provide those services for a short period for the benefit of the target. Because the services provided are fairly routine and the duration is short, transition service agreements are notorious for their simplistic drafting. They often provide that services can be terminated (usually only by the buyer) on a service-by-service basis.

Often these agreements take on a life of their own. Because performance is often at an operational level, terminations and renewals may not be adequately documented. Informal arrangements not supported by the language of the agreement creep into practice. Often buyers like the arrangements too well and may not have been properly incentivized to move to other independent or in-house services. This poses some risk to sellers who continue to provide services to a business that differs significantly from the business sold. The relationship shifts from one of being a well-understood accommodation to a commercial relationship unsupported by customary contractual protections.

The parties who continue these practices are responsible for their own behavior. But sometimes an informal inquiry whether the transition services agreement has run out will elicit a response that by itself may suggest the imprudence of continuing arrangements without a more fully documented contract.

Appraisal Proceedings

Under the laws of most states, in the sale of a target through a merger or, less prevalently, through the sale of all or substantially of all of the assets, shareholders objecting to the sale, in addition to any other legal remedies, have statutory dissenters' rights by which, in lieu of the consideration being offered, they have the right to have a court determine the fair value of their shares. State law needs to be consulted for the availability of, and the procedures to be followed in connection with, the assertion and defense of dissenters' rights.

A common scheme is a requirement that dissenters' rights be explained in the notice of the meeting called to approve the transaction. A shareholder wishing to assert dissenters' rights must then file a notice of that intention and refrain from voting for the transaction in question. In the case of a short-form merger or one done by consent without a meeting, the notice is given after the transaction is accomplished. Most acquisition agreements require that the buyer be given notice of any assertion of dissenters' rights and the right to conduct negotiations and handle any proceedings.

If the dissenter has preserved its rights, it may then seek appraisal by filing an action in the appropriate court. The perfection of dissenters' rights is not self executing—it is still necessary to go to court.

Whether appraisal is an adequate remedy depends on the substance of state law and the ease of the procedures. One famous case has involved numerous appeals and has bounced around for more than 20 years without being final.[185] On the other hand, some states require that the consideration in the transaction be paid out to dissenters, even as they seek additional money through the appraisal proceeding. In applying the tests of fair value, courts have historically been somewhat naïve, ignoring valuations found in the marketplace and applying principles out of the nineteenth century. See Chapter 7 for a further discussion of valuation.

Glossary

This Glossary is a compendium of the definitions of a number of technical and legal terms often encountered in the M&A practice in the United States, including some of the accounting and on financial terms used by professionals and business people involved with acquisitions. As with many things in this area of practice, some of the terminology is subjective and different practitioners may use the same terms, but not always with the same meaning.

This Glossary is focused primarily on terms used in acquisitions involving privately held businesses and some of the more technical terms used almost exclusively in acquisitions of or by public companies have not been included. Another Task Force of the Committee on Negotiated Acquisitions has been working on a more expansive Dictionary of M&A Terms that will be available through the Business Law Section of the American Bar Association, sometime after the publication of this Guide. This Dictionary will include terms used in both private and public company deals, as well as citations to statutes, rules, and cases that relate to those terms.

"A" reorganization: A reorganization under Section 368(a)(1)(A) of the Internal Revenue Code that is structured as a statutory merger or consolidation of two corporations and meets certain other tests, allowing for the deferral of recognition of income (or loss) for federal income tax purposes with respect to the buyer's stock (or stock of its parent) received by the target's shareholders.

ABA: American Bar Association.

Acceleration: Advancing of certain rights, such as the vesting of options or restricted stock, usually caused by an acquisition or other change in control.

Access covenant: A covenant in an acquisition agreement or letter of intent requiring the target to give the buyer access to the target's books, records and properties, generally for the purpose of conducting due diligence.

Accretion: See *Dilution.*

Acquiror: See *Buyer.*

Acquisition: A generic term referring to the acquisition of a business, whether the form is a purchase of assets, a purchase of stock, a merger or some variation.

Acquisition agreement: An agreement to consummate an acquisition that addresses all the essential terms and therefore is legally binding. The acquisition agreement will usually specify the consideration, structure, payment and other terms of the transaction, and will contain representations, warranties, covenants, and conditions. This is to be contrasted with a letter of intent, which is intended to create no legal rights other than as specifically provided with respect to a narrow range of matters. Sometimes called a definitive agreement or a purchase agreement and, less frequently, a purchase and sale agreement.

Acquisition sub: A subsidiary formed for purposes of facilitating an acquisition. See also *Triangular merger.*

Actual knowledge: Means that a person in fact knew about a particular fact or circumstance, as distinguished from constructive knowledge. Sometimes actual knowledge is elevated to a higher standard, such as conscious awareness of the consequences (e.g., that a particular fact constitutes a breach of representation). See also *Constructive knowledge.*

Add-on acquisition: An additional acquisition, usually involving a financial buyer, within the same line of business to add to a platform acquisition. See also *Platform acquisition.*

Affiliate: For purposes of the federal securities laws, an affiliate of a person is one who controls, is controlled by or is under common control with that person. This definition is frequently used in acquisition agreements, even those that do not implicate the federal securities laws.

Agreement in principle: A written document that contains many, but typically not all, of the essential terms of an acquisition. It may purport to be binding, but that will depend on whether it is legally enforceable under state law. Sometimes called heads of agreement. See also *Acquisition agreement* and *Letter of intent.*

Agreement of merger: An acquisition agreement for a transaction structured as a statutory merger, or a summary document required to be filed with a state official to effectuate a merger. Sometimes called articles of merger. See also *Certificate of merger.*

AICPA: American Institute of Certified Public Accountants.

Allocation of risk: The distribution of risk among parties to an acquisition as a result of the parties' bargaining and documented in an acquisition agreement as to which party will bear the financial or economic risk of certain conditions, events or occurrences. A buyer will attempt to shift to the seller the risk of any losses or damages that might be incurred after the closing. A seller will attempt to reduce its risk through use of qualifiers such as "material" and "actual knowledge."

Alternative dispute resolution (ADR): A provision in an agreement that provides for alternatives to litigation (such as arbitration or mediation) for the resolution of disputes arising under the agreement.

Amortization: An accounting concept in which the historical cost (or estimated value) of an intangible asset is systematically recorded as an expense over its useful life, resulting in a portion of the historical cost being charged to income for each financial reporting period, with a reduction in the carrying value of the asset in the amount expensed. This is distinguished from depreciation, which is a similar treatment for tangible assets.

Ancillary agreements: Agreements, other than the acquisition agreement (e.g., employment or consulting agreements, noncompetition agreements, leases, or escrow agreements), that are delivered in connection with an acquisition. Forms of the ancillary agreements typically are attached as exhibits to an acquisition agreement, and execution and delivery are conditions to closing. Sometimes they are signed and delivered concurrently with the execution and delivery of the acquisition agreement.

Anti-assignment provision: A provision in an agreement that prohibits a party from assigning the agreement (or its rights and obligations under the agreement) without the consent of another party or parties to the agreement.

Anti-dilution provision: The protection afforded holders of securities, such as warrants, options, convertible debentures or convertible preferred stock, against changes in the outstanding number of shares of common stock or of other classes or series of stock underlying such securities.

Antifraud rules: Rules that serve as the principal means of enforcing federal and state securities laws by generally prohibiting fraudulent or manipulative acts in connection with the purchase or sale of securities.

Anti-sandbagging provision: Generally, a seller-oriented provision in an acquisition agreement that either requires the buyer to inform the seller of any misrepresentation or breach of which it has knowledge prior to the closing, in order to provide an opportunity to cure the problem, or that precludes a buyer from recovery for a misrepresentation or breach by the seller if it had been known, actually or perhaps constructively, by the buyer prior to closing. See also *Sandbagging.* There can also be a buyer-oriented provision in an acquisition agreement where the buyer is making extensive representations.

Appraisal rights: A statutorily created right of shareholders to receive the fair value (or, in some states, fair market value) of their shares, in cash, as determined by a court in certain extraordinary transactions, such as a merger or sometimes a sale of assets or exchange of securities. In a merger, it will be in lieu of the merger consideration offered by the buyer. Also called dissenters' rights in some states.

Articles of merger: See *Agreement of merger* and *Certificate of merger.*

Asset acquisition: The acquisition of all or some of a target's assets, usually accompanied by the assumption of certain of its liabilities.

Asset-based financing: Financing provided on the basis of the security of assets that have commercial value, primarily equipment, inventory and receivables.

Assignment: The transfer by a party of intangible personal property or contract rights, as distinguished from a bill of sale, which is typically used to transfer tangible personal property. Sometimes an assignment and a bill of sale are combined in one document. See also *Bill of sale.*

Assumed liabilities: A term often used in an acquisition agreement to refer to those liabilities being assumed by the buyer.

Assumption (of liabilities): An undertaking to assume and discharge liabilities.

Auction: A process for the sale of a business, ranging from a controlled auction, in which negotiations are conducted with a limited number of potential buyers without any specific time constraints, to a formal auction, in which multiple potential buyers are approached or a proposed sale is publicly announced and the time parameters are highly structured.

Audit: An examination of the accounting books and records of a business by independent, outside auditors for the purpose of evaluating whether specified financial statements are fairly presented, in all material respects, in conformity with GAAP. An audit results in rendering an auditor's report on the financial statements. See also *Compilation* and *Review.*

"B" reorganization: A reorganization under Section 368(a)(1)(B) of the Internal Revenue Code that is structured as a "stock-for-stock" acquisition in which one corporation, solely in exchange for its voting stock (or voting stock of its parent), acquires stock of another corporation, such that immediately after the transaction the acquiring corporation has at least 80 percent control and meets certain other tests allowing for the deferral of recognition of income (or loss) for federal income tax purposes with respect to the buyer's stock (or stock of its parent) received by the target's shareholders.

Balloon payment: A final payment of principal at the maturity of debt that is significantly greater than other principal payments, if any, during the term of the debt.

Bank line: Typically, a line of credit, including a revolving line of credit, from a bank.

Basis: The value assigned to a taxpayer's investment in property that is used to compute gain or loss from sale of the property. The basis can be an outside basis, i.e., the basis of stock owned by a shareholder, or an inside basis, i.e., the basis of an entity in its assets.

Basis points: A unit for measuring yield (interest rate) that equals 1/100th of 1 percent. For example, a 1 percent change in rate equals 100 basis points.

Basket: A term describing a provision in an acquisition agreement dealing with indemnity obligations, so named because only certain types of claims or those exceeding in the aggregate a specified dollar amount are said to "hit" or "fill" the basket. Typically, recovery for indemnification is permitted only for the excess over the amount specified. Sometimes called a cushion, deductible, or deductible basket. A similar concept might be used for individual and unrelated claims. See *Mini basket* and *Threshold*.

Beneficial owner: Generally, a person having (alone or with others) the ultimate power to vote or dispose of securities, either directly or through the record owner of the securities.

Best efforts clause: A clause in an acquisition agreement that imposes a legal obligation on one or more parties to use "best efforts" to carry out the terms and intent of the agreement as a whole or specific terms of the agreement. Sometimes the clause is modified to apply a lesser standard, such as "reasonable efforts" or "reasonable commercial efforts."

Bid: An acquisition proposal submitted in an auction.

Bidders: Those who submit bids in an auction, a proposal in a negotiated acquisition or a tender in a tender offer.

Bidding procedures: Procedures developed and distributed to potential bidders to control the process and timing of an auction.

Bill of sale: An instrument for the transfer of title to tangible personal property, as distinguished from an assignment, which is typically used to transfer intangible property or contract rights. See also *Assignment*.

Blue Sky laws: The securities laws of the various states. Depending on the state, these laws may prohibit fraudulent activities in the sale of securities, require licensing of persons offering securities, or require the registration or qualification of securities with the state securities administrators.

Book (the): A marketing document, generally prepared by the seller with the assistance of its financial advisor, which is distributed to potential buyers and includes an overview of the seller's business and operations, limited industry information, management's background and selected historical and projected financial results. Also called an offering memorandum, a confidential memorandum or simply a memorandum.

Book value: The historical cost of an asset less accumulated depreciation, depletion and amortization. Also, in an aggregate sense, the excess of total assets (net of accumulated depreciation, depletion and amortization) over total liabilities of an enterprise as they appear on a balance sheet. In the latter case, also called shareholders' equity or net worth.

Boot: A term used in connection with a tax-free reorganization to refer to consideration other than stock and securities that are permitted to be received without recognizing gain.

Bootstrap: A term of art generally used in connection with a transaction whereby a financial buyer finances the transaction looking solely to the assets of the target.

Breach: A breach of a warranty or failure to perform or comply with a covenant or obligation in an agreement. Normally, also applies to the inaccuracy of a representation.

Break-up (break) fee: A payment promised by a target or its shareholders to the buyer if it loses the acquisition to another party. Usually a buyer is concerned about losing to higher bidders, but sometimes it asks for more general protection against termination of the acquisition agreement. Also called a bust-up or termination fee, although the latter may be payable if the deal is not completed for any reason. See also *Topping fee.*

Break-up value: See *Going concern value.*

Bridge loan: A short-term loan usually provided by an investment bank or commercial bank that is intended to be replaced quickly by permanent financing.

Bring-down: Usually refers to bringing down to the closing date the representations and warranties in an acquisition agreement by delivery of an officers' certificate (a "bring-down" certificate). May also refer to a representation in the acquisition agreement to the effect that all the representations by that party will be true and correct at the closing.

Broker: See *Financial advisor.*

Built-in gain: The fair market value of assets in excess of their tax basis at the effective date of an S corporation election, which may be subject to corporate level tax on a sale.

Bulk sale (transfer) law: Statutory provisions governing bulk transfers (Article 6 of the Uniform Commercial Code, versions of which are in effect in certain states) that require a buyer to give advance notice of a sale to avoid successor liability.

Business combination: A generic term that applies to the acquisition by one company of another or the consolidation of several companies, whatever the legal form.

Bust up: A transaction in which a company is sold in parts because the parts are worth more than the company as a whole.

Bust-up fee: See *Break-up fee.*

Buyer: The acquiring person in an acquisition, whether it be an entity, an individual or any combination, which may be the parent in an acquisition using an acquisition sub.

Buyer's market: The period during which economic and other conditions generally favor buyers rather than sellers.

"C" reorganization: A reorganization under Section 368(a)(1)(C) of the Internal Revenue Code that is structured as a "stock-for-assets" acquisition in which one corporation, solely in exchange for its voting stock (or voting stock of its parent), acquires substantially all of the assets of another corporation, and meets certain other tests, allowing for the deferral of recognition of income (or loss) for federal income tax purposes with respect to the buyer's stock (or stock of its parent) received by the target's shareholders..

Cap: A maximum limit on indemnity claims, generally of a certain type, in an acquisition agreement. Also called a "ceiling."

Capital expenditure (CapEx): Amounts expended to acquire or improve long-lived assets, such as buildings, machinery, furniture, leasehold improvements, and purchased intangibles.

Capital gain/loss: The profit or loss realized for federal income tax purposes upon the sale or exchange of a capital asset. If it is a long-term profit or loss, it ordinarily will be taxed at a rate less than the rate at which ordinary income is taxed, but that will not be the case if the profit or loss is short-term.

Capital lease: Generally, a lease that in substance represents a transfer of the risks and rewards of ownership to the lessee. If certain criteria are satisfied, the asset and liability are capitalized on the balance sheet.

Capital stock: The ownership interest in a corporation evidenced by stock, whether common, preferred or other special stock.

Capital structure: The debt and equity structure of a company, i.e., its permanent long-term financing, which includes capital stock, long-term debt and retained earnings.

Cash flow: A measure of the cash generated by a company, often calculated as net income plus depreciation, depletion and amortization. Earnings before interest, taxes, depreciation and amortization (i.e., EBITDA) are also frequently referred to as a measure of cash flow.

Cash merger: A merger in which the target's outstanding stock is converted only into cash.

Cash option merger: A merger in which the target's shareholders can elect to receive cash or stock, subject to limitations and allocation processes set forth in the acquisition agreement.

Cash-out merger: A merger at the second stage of a two-stage acquisition, whereby the target's remaining shares are converted into cash. See also *Two-step acquisition*.

Cash tender offer: A tender offer in which only cash is offered to the shareholders of the target. See *Tender offer*.

Cashier's check: A check drawn by a bank on itself, whereby it is the primary obligation of the bank. See also *Certified check*.

Ceiling: See *Cap*.

Certificate of merger: A written instrument typically filed with the officials of a state, in lieu of a merger agreement, to effectuate a merger. See also *Agreement of merger*.

Certified check: A check drawn by a customer of a bank that contains the bank's certification on its face, whereby the drawee's bank is required to honor the check when presented for payment. See also *Cashier's check*.

Change in (of) control provision: Usually, a provision in an agreement, charter, bylaws, or another document providing for payments or other entitlements, or in a security that provides for acceleration of vesting, on a change in control. Also, it is a provision in an agreement that treats a change in control as an assignment, requiring the consent of the other contracting party.

Choice of law provision: A provision that designates the governing law for the construction and interpretation of an agreement.

Class vote: Statutory or charter provisions (or certificates of designation) that entitle holders of individual classes or series of stock to vote as a class or series upon specified transactions, such as mergers or sales of assets, that may affect their rights.

Closing: Generally, the completion of the acts required to effect an acquisition or other transaction. At the typical closing of an acquisition, the buyer provides the consideration and the target delivers instruments of transfer (in an asset sale) or the shareholders deliver stock certificates (in a stock sale or merger). The appropriate parties will also execute and deliver ancillary agreements and other closing documents contemplated by an acquisition agreement. The date on which a closing occurs or is deemed to have occurred is called the closing date.

Closing balance sheet: Generally, a balance sheet for the target (or its successor) prepared as of the closing date that includes, in the case of an asset acquisition, only the assets of the target that were purchased and the liabilities that were assumed. It is usually prepared by the target or the buyer for the purpose of verifying information on which the purchase price was based or upon which a purchase price adjustment will be based.

Closing certificate: An officers' certificate or other certificate delivered at the closing of an acquisition. See *Officers' certificate.*

Closing conditions: Conditions in the acquisition agreement that must be satisfied or waived in order for the transaction to be consummated. A condition, for example, might be the absence of an event or the delivery of a document.

Closing date: The date on which the closing has occurred or is deemed to have occurred.

Closing memorandum/agenda: A document setting forth the various actions needed to be taken, and ancillary agreements and closing documents to be executed and delivered, at the closing to consummate the transaction, and other pre- and post-closing actions and documents to be executed and delivered.

Closing statement: A document setting forth the source and application of funds needed to consummate the transaction. Also called a flow of funds statement.

Closing time: The time on the closing date at which the closing has occurred or is deemed to have occurred.

Closing the books: The final recording of transactions in a company's accounts in anticipation of the preparation of financial statements.

COBRA: Consolidated Omnibus Budget Reconciliation Act of 1986, as amended.

Collar: Negotiated parameters for a flexible or floating exchange ratio in a transaction involving stock of a public company, designed to ameliorate the effect of price fluctuations.

Combined financial statements: Financial statements of companies that are economically linked because they are under common management or control, but there is no controlling equity interest of one in another, are often presented as combined financial statements.

Commission: See *Success fee.*

Commitment fee: A fee charged by a bank or other lender for agreeing to make a future loan under specified terms. See also *Commitment letter.*

Commitment letter: In the acquisition context, an agreement by a bank or other lender to provide funds for a buyer to effect an acquisition, subject to specified conditions.

Committee on Foreign Investment in the United States (CFIUS): An inter-agency committee chaired by the Secretary of the Treasury and responsible for conducting a national security review of filings under Exon-Florio.

Common stock: An equity security that represents the residual unit of ownership of a corporation and which will generally have voting and dividend rights.

Comparable companies method: A methodology for valuing a company by reference to companies that are comparable, in material respects, to the company to be valued.

Comparable transactions method: A methodology for valuing a company by reference to sales of comparable companies in transactions involving a change in control.

Compilation: The presentation of financial statements without an accountant's assurance as to conformity with generally accepted accounting principles. See also *Audit* and *Review*.

Conditions: See *Closing conditions* and *Walk rights*.

Confidentially agreement: An agreement or provision in an acquisition agreement, a letter of intent or an agreement in principle, whereby a party agrees to treat as confidential and neither use nor disclose non-public information received from another party, including in many cases the negotiations, the terms of the transaction or the fact that a transaction is being considered. Often, the agreement or provision is reciprocal. Sometimes called a nondisclosure agreement.

Conglomerate merger: A business combination of companies that neither compete nor are in a vertical relationship with each other, including product-extension mergers, geographic market-extension mergers and mergers between firms with no discernible commercial relationship.

Consent: In an acquisition agreement, permission granted in writing by a party to an action, event or condition.

Consolidated financial statements: Financial statements of a parent including the accounts of its subsidiaries in which it has a majority voting equity interest.

Consolidating financial statements: Financial statements showing separate line items for each member of a consolidated group.

Constituency laws: State statutes that allow directors to consider, in an acquisition context, the interests of employees, customers, suppliers, and local communities, in addition to the interests of shareholders.

Constituent corporation: A corporation that is merged with or into one or more other corporations or other business entities and includes a surviving corporation.

Constructive knowledge: Means knowledge that a person is legally charged with having, based on the totality of the related facts and circumstances that a person (or agent) knows, reasonably should have known or had available, even though the person lacked actual knowledge of the specific facts or circumstances in question. See also *Actual knowledge*.

Consulting agreement: An ancillary agreement providing for an individual (usually a member of management or owner of the target) to render consulting services after the acquisition for a specified period of time.

Contingent liability: A liability that arises only upon the occurrence of an uncertain future event.

Contingent payment: See *Earnout*.

Contingent payment rights: An instrument that entitles the shareholders of a target to additional consideration above the guaranteed minimum consideration received, based on various contingencies, such as the performance of the buyer's stock following the acquisition.

Contingent value rights: An instrument that entitles the shareholders of a target to a consistently valued state in the surviving company, such as a means by which the total proceeds to the shareholders are guaranteed to reach a certain value.

Control premium: A premium paid to obtain a controlling interest. See also *Minority discount.*

Controlled auction: See *Auction.*

Controlling interest: Generally, ownership of a majority of the voting stock of an corporation or ownership of enough voting stock to constitute, directly or indirectly, effective control or the power to control.

Conversion: A transaction whereby an entity is transformed directly into another form of entity, such as a corporation converting into a limited liability company, which for state law purposes is considered a continuation of the converting entity though in different form. This is distinguished from a merger, whereby the assets and liabilities of the merged entity become those of the successor and the merged entity ceases its existence.

Conversion ratio: The ratio between a share surrendered and the share into which it is converted in accordance with the terms of the convertible security.

Convertible preferred stock/security: Preferred stock or another security that can be converted, in whole or in part, into a specified class or series of stock in accordance with the terms set forth in the document evidencing the security.

Covenant not to compete: An ancillary agreement or provision in an acquisition agreement restricting competition by a seller and/or some or all the shareholders or employees of the seller, typically required by applicable law to be reasonably limited in terms of scope, geography and term. When contained in an ancillary agreement, provisions protecting confidential information and precluding hiring of employees are often included. Sometimes referred to as a noncompete or noncompetition agreement.

Covenants: Agreements of the parties in an acquisition or ancillary agreement to do (affirmative covenant) or not to do (negative covenant or forbearance) certain things. An example is an agreement of the target to, among other things, conduct the business in the ordinary course during the period between the signing of the acquisition agreement and the closing.

Cross-border transactions: Acquisitions involving buyers and targets in different countries.

Cross-species merger: A business combination in which different forms of legal entities are combined into a single entity.

Currency: The type of consideration in an acquisition, whether cash, securities, or a combination, provided by the buyer to the target or the target's shareholders.

Current assets: Assets that are reasonably expected to be realized in cash, sold, or consumed during the normal operating cycle of a business, which is usually one year.

Current liabilities: Liabilities that are to be paid or satisfied within the normal operating cycle of a business, which is usually one year, including the current portion of long-term liabilities.

Current ratio: The total amount of current assets divided by the total amount of current liabilities.

Cushion: See *Basket.*

D&O insurance: See *Directors' and officers' liability insurance.*

"D" reorganization: A reorganization under Section 368(a)(1)(D) of the Internal Revenue Code, in which a corporation transfers assets to another corporation if, immediately thereafter, the transferor or its shareholders is in control of the corporation to which the assets are transferred and stock or securities of that corporation are distributed in a certain manner. See *Spin-off*, *Split-off*, and *Split-up*.

Data room: The site at which documents relating to a party to an acquisition (generally the target) are placed for due diligence review by other parties and their advisors.

Debt financing: Borrowings, whether through the issuance of bonds, notes or other loan obligations (e.g., commercial paper). Companies typically use the proceeds from a debt issuance to finance general operations or specific projects, such as acquisitions.

Debt service: Schedule and amount of required payments on debt financing, including principal and interest.

Deductible: See *Basket*.

Definitive agreement: See *Acquisition agreement*.

Deposit: See *Good faith deposit*.

Depreciation: An accounting concept in which the historical cost (or estimated value) of a tangible (or fixed) asset is systematically (not necessarily linearly) recorded as an expense over its useful life, resulting in a portion of the historical cost being charged to income for each financial reporting period, with a reduction in the carrying value of the asset in the amount expensed. This is distinguished from amortization, which is a similar treatment for intangible assets.

Diligence out: A condition to the obligations of a party (usually the buyer) under an acquisition agreement requiring that the factual and other disclosures pertaining to the other party be satisfactory. The disclosures that are the subject of the condition are those made during the course of due diligence.

Dilution: Diminution in the proportion of net income and net assets to which each share is entitled. Transactions are often measured by the degree of dilution the buyer's common stock will suffer as a result of the transaction and the period of time until the transaction becomes accretive. Also, refers to the issuance of additional shares of a class or series of stock, thereby diluting the voting and other rights of the original shares (sometimes called "equity dilution"). Finally, the effect on net income or net assets per share if all convertible securities were to be converted and options and warrants were to be exercised.

Directors' and officers' liability insurance: Insurance that covers directors and officers for expenses, judgments and settlements arising out of lawsuits against them in their official capacities.

Disappearing corporation: In a merger, the entity that is merged into another entity and ceases to exist.

Disclosure schedules: Schedules accompanying an acquisition agreement in which the target or its shareholders are required to disclose specific aspects of the business operations, material agreements, and other matters, and to list exceptions and qualifications to their representations. Sometimes called a disclosure letter or simply schedules.

Discounted cash flow (DCF): A methodology for valuing a company that applies an appropriate discount rate to future projected cash flows to derive a present value for the company.

Dissenters' rights: See *Appraisal rights*.

Dissenting shareholder: Generally, a shareholder of a corporation who did not vote in favor of (but ordinarily need not have voted against) a transaction to merge with, or sometimes sell assets to, another corporation when the affirmative vote of the acquired corporation's shareholders is required. Dissenting shareholders are entitled to dissenters' or appraisal rights under state corporate law. See *Appraisal.*

Divestiture: Generally, the sale of a separate operating unit, whether a division or subsidiary, of a corporation.

Documentary tax: A tax imposed by local governmental authorities on the filing of certain documents, as for example a deed transferring real property.

Double materiality: A situation where the representations and warranties in an acquisition agreement are qualified by materiality and, in addition, the bring-down certificate reaffirms the representations as being true and correct in all material respects, thus doubling up materiality.

Double tax: Combined corporate-level and shareholder-level taxes incurred when a corporation sells assets and distributes proceeds to its shareholders.

Downstream merger: The merger of a parent into a subsidiary.

Drag-along rights: The contractual right of a controlling shareholder to compel minority shareholders to sell shares concurrently with any sale to a bona fide third party of the majority shares. See also *Tag-along rights.*

Drop-dead date: The date specified in an acquisition agreement on and after which either party may terminate the agreement if all conditions to closing have not been satisfied or waived. Also called the termination date or the outside termination date.

Drop down: Generally, the transfer of assets to, and assumption of liabilities by, a subsidiary, sometimes followed by the sale of the subsidiary.

Due diligence: The process by which a party assesses the benefits and liabilities of a proposed acquisition by reviewing all pertinent legal documents, contracts, intellectual property, financial statements, litigation, properties, etc., and interviewing selected employees and members of management.

Duty to defend: The obligation under indemnification provisions in an acquisition agreement of a party (usually the indemnifying party) to defend another party (usually the indemnified party) in the event of any claim, litigation or other proceeding.

Earnings per share (EPS): The amount of net income (earnings) related to each share of common stock, computed by dividing net income by the weighted average number of shares of common stock outstanding during the period. Sometimes this amount is reported on both a nondiluted and diluted basis, taking into account the conversion of convertible securities and the exercise of options and warrants.

Earnout: A term for a provision in an acquisition agreement giving the target or its shareholders the right to receive additional consideration after the closing if the target's (or its successor's) performance meets certain negotiated thresholds. Also called a contingent payment.

EBIT: Acronym for "earnings before interest and taxes."

EBITDA: Acronym for "earnings before interest, taxes, depreciation, and amortization."

Effective time: Sometimes acquisition agreements specify an effective time at a specific date (that may not be the closing date) and time. For example, the effective time may be when an agreement of merger is filed or, in an asset acquisition, when the transfer of assets and assumption of liabilities, and the related risk of loss, is to occur. The parties may also agree on an effective time for accounting and financial purposes that differs from the closing date.

Employee benefit plan: The term generally refers to any plan, program, arrangement, practice, or contract that provides benefits or compensation to or on behalf of employees, or former employees, of a company.

Employee stock ownership plan (ESOP): Defined in ERISA as a qualified stock-bonus plan or combination stock-bonus plan and money-purchase plan that is designed to invest primarily in qualifying securities of the employer and meets certain other requirements.

Engagement letter: An agreement with a financial advisor or other intermediary for services to be rendered in connection with a proposed acquisition and setting forth, among other things, the fees for the services and the basis on which they will be charged.

Enterprise value: A company's total value measured by the market value of its debt plus the market value of its equity. A common, but not universally accepted, variant to this calculation subtracts the company's cash balance. Also called "total intrinsic value."

Entire agreement clause: See *Integration clause.*

Environmental audit: An investigation or audit to evaluate environmental risks relating to cleanup of contaminated property and to operation of the business. The investigation or audit is undertaken usually by a buyer but sometimes by a target, using environmental consultants See also *Phase I* and *Phase II.*

Equity: Ownership interest in an entity that generally entitles the owner to benefit from the residual cash flows of the entity.

Equity accounting: An accounting method whereby a company having an investment in another company's stock can show on its income statement its pro rata share of the other company's earnings or losses.

Equity financing: The portion of acquisition financing that is obtained through the issuance of equity securities, usually designated as common or preferred stock.

ERISA: Employee Retirement Income Security Act of 1974, as amended, a federal law governing pensions and certain other employee benefits.

Ernest money: See *Good faith deposit.*

Escheat: Reversion of property to the state after remaining unclaimed for a specified period of time. For example, funds remaining in an escrow and unclaimed for the requisite statutory period may escheat to the state. Also called "unclaimed property laws."

Escrow: Usually, a portion of the purchase price, whether cash or securities, that is held by a buyer or a third-party in a separate account to secure the target's or its shareholders' indemnification obligations. See also *Holdback.*

ESOP: See *Employee stock ownership plan.*

Estoppel certificate: A certificate often required from a lessor as a closing condition to confirm, among other things, the terms of the lease, the current rental, and the absence of any defaults. Can also be required of any contracting party to an agreement.

Exchange Act: The Securities Exchange Act of 1934, as amended, a federal law that governs regulation of the securities markets and establishes reporting requirements for issuers, directors, officers and significant shareholders. Sometimes called the Securities Exchange Act, the 1934 Act or the '34 Act.

Exchange agent: The party appointed by the buyer to which shareholders are directed to submit their share certificates representing stock of the target, together with a letter of transmittal, in exchange for the acquisition consideration, whether cash or securities. Sometimes called a paying agent where the consideration is cash.

Exchange offer: A tender offer in which securities (sometimes together with cash) are offered by the buyer in exchange for the target's securities.

Exchange ratio: The ratio at which shares of stock of a buyer is offered for shares of stock in the target in a stock-for-stock transaction.

Excluded assets: A term used in an acquisition agreement to refer to assets that are not transferred to the buyer and retained by the target. Sometimes called "retained assets."

Excluded liabilities: A term used in an acquisition agreement to refer to liabilities that are not assumed by the buyer. Sometimes called "retained liabilities."

Exclusivity agreement: An agreement whereby a target provides a potential buyer a limited period of time to conduct due diligence and negotiate an acquisition agreement without soliciting or talking with other potential buyers.

Exercise price: The price per share at which an option or warrant is exercisable.

Exon-Florio: The Exon-Florio amendments to the Omnibus Trade and Competitive Act of 1988, as amended by the National Defense Authorization Act for Fiscal 1993, which permits the President of the United States or his designee to block acquisitions of U.S. enterprises by foreign persons on the basis of national security. See *Committee on Foreign Investment in the United States.*

Fair market value: Ordinarily, the amount for which an entity or specific property would change hands between a willing seller and a willing buyer, neither acting under compulsion and both with reasonable knowledge of the relevant facts.

Fair value: Ordinarily, the judicially determined value of an entity or shares in the context of the exercise of appraisal or dissenters' rights by shareholders.

Fairness hearing: A hearing before a court or certain governmental agencies (such as the California Department of Corporations) as to the fairness of an exchange in an acquisition, thereby permitting by the issuer to rely on the exemption from registration of securities under Section 3(a)(10) of the Securities Act.

Fairness opinion: A letter from a financial advisor to the effect that the consideration to be received in an acquisition is fair, from a financial point of view, to the target, the buyer or their shareholders, as the case may be.

FASB: See *Financial Accounting Standards Board.*

FED: A Federal Reserve Bank. Sometimes refers to Federal Reserve Board.

Federal funds: Funds deposited by banks at Federal Reserve Banks. Payment can be made by a federal funds check, which is a draft that a bank draws on its account at a Federal Reserve Bank, or by a wire transfer of federal funds by a bank, which is from the bank's account at a Federal Reserve Bank. Such a check or wire transfer represent funds that are immediately available. See also *Wire transfer.*

Fiduciary out: A term for a provision in an acquisition agreement that permits the seller's or the target's board of directors, in the exercise of its fiduciary duties, to take certain actions, such as dealing with competing bidders. These provisions may include the right to solicit other potential bidders, provide confidential information to other potential bidders or even terminate the agreement.

Financial Accounting Standards Board (FASB): A body charged with the responsibility of establishing and revising standards of accounting and reporting.

Financial advisor: An investment banker, broker or other professional intermediary engaged to value a business, to find a buyer or a seller, to advise on strategy and tactics, to render an opinion as to fairness or, in certain circumstances, to find capital to finance an acquisition.

Financial buyer: One that acquires a company for financial reasons and not to run the business over the long term. These are often funds sponsored by private equity firms formed for the purpose of acquiring, consolidating, expanding, and ultimately exiting businesses by reselling or taking them public for the benefit of their investors. See also *Strategic buyer.*

Financial statements: Statements setting forth in a quantitative fashion the financial results of a business for a specified period or its financial condition as of a specific date. Usually includes balance sheets, income or operating statements and sometimes cash flow statements.

Financial transaction: An acquisition pursued for financial reasons, and not for strategic or long-term operational purposes.

Financing out: A term for a provision in an acquisition agreement affording a buyer the right not to close if it does not obtain the necessary financing.

Finder: One who introduces parties to a proposed business combination, but is not involved in negotiations.

Finder's fee: The fee received by a finder normally in a completed transaction.

Fixed assets: Tangible assets held for business use and not expected to be converted into cash within the current and next fiscal year.

Flow of funds statement: See *Closing statement.*

Force majeure: An unanticipated or uncontrollable event or effect, the consequences of which are disregarded entirely or for a specified period of time, or that releases one from the fulfillment of a contractual obligation.

Foreign Corrupt Practices Act (FCPA): A U.S. anti-bribery and corruption law that, in general, prohibits the offering or giving of anything of value to a foreign official to use influence to assist in obtaining or retaining business.

Foreign Investment Real Property Tax Act (FIRPTA): A statute codified primarily in Section 897 of the Internal Revenue Code, which imposes a tax on gain recognized by a foreign person from the sale of a "U.S. real property interest."

Forward merger: A merger in which the target is merged into the buyer, with the buyer being the survivor. See also *Reverse merger.*

Forward triangular merger: A merger in which the target merges into a subsidiary of the buyer that is generally formed for purposes of the acquisition, with the subsidiary being the survivor. See also *Reverse triangular merger.*

4(c) documents: The documents required to be furnished pursuant to Item 4(c) of a Hart-Scott-Rodino filing. Generally includes documents prepared by officers and directors that address competition, markets and related antitrust topics.

Fractional shares: A unit of stock less than one full share, e.g., the fraction of a share to which a shareholder becomes entitled as a result of an exchange ratio applied in a business combination.

Fraudulent conveyance/transfer: A doctrine whereby creditors may void a transfer or seek satisfaction of their claims from a buyer if the transaction is found to be a fraudulent conveyance or transfer. The issue generally arises if a party makes a transfer or incurs an obligation without receiving fair or reasonably equivalent value and as a result is rendered insolvent, i.e., unable to pay its debts as they become due, or is left with unreasonably small capital in the business. The fraudulent conveyance laws are found in federal law (U.S. Bankruptcy Code) and state law (based mostly on the Uniform Fraudulent Conveyance Act or the Uniform Fraudulent Transfer Act).

Free cash flow: Generally, net income plus depreciation, amortization and other noncash charges, less working capital requirements and capital expenditures. Conceptually, the cash flow available to either service debt or pay dividends to equity investors.

Freeze-out: See *Squeeze out.*

Further assurance clause: A covenant in an acquisition agreement whereby the parties agree to cooperate to fulfill their respective obligations or to execute all documents and do all things that might be needed in the future to implement the transactions contemplated by the agreement.

Generally accepted accounting principles (GAAP): A series of accounting principles generally accepted by the accounting profession. GAAP is jurisdictional, e.g., U.S. GAAP, Canadian GAAP.

Generally accepted auditing standards (GAAS): Rules and guidelines established by the Auditing Standards Board of the American Institute of Certified Public Accountants for the conduct of an audit in the U.S.

Going-concern value: The value of a company, assuming that it continues to operate into the future in a manner that is viable and (typically) consistent with its current operations. This value is usually contrasted with break-up value, which assumes that the company is separated into multiple entities that operate independently, or liquidation value, which is the value of the company's underlying assets that can be realized in an orderly liquidation or an auction after taking into account the expenses and time of sale and the payment of liabilities.

Going-private transaction: A single shareholder or small group of investors acquiring all the shares of a public company. The form could be a merger, a tender offer or a reverse stock split.

Golden handcuffs: An agreement designed to bind an executive to a company by providing significant contingent compensation that would be lost if the executive left the company prematurely.

Golden parachute: An agreement or plan that provides benefits (in the form of severance pay, options, bonuses, or otherwise) to an executive if there is a change in control of the company (single trigger), or if there is a change in control and the executive's employment is actually or constructively terminated within a specified period of time following the change in control (double trigger).

Good faith deposit: A deposit in cash made to demonstrate a party's commitment to proceed with, discuss further or close a proposed acquisition.

Goodwill: When used in purchase accounting, the excess of the cost of the acquired business over the sum of the amounts assigned to identifiable assets acquired at their fair value less the liabilities assumed. See also *Purchase accounting.*

Gross margin: When used as an accounting term, the amount that results when gross profit (net sales minus cost of sales) is divided by net sales, expressed as a percentage. Also referred to as "margin of profit," "gross profit margin," or "profit margin."

Gross up: Calculation of the amount that would be required for an item subject to tax to be equal to that item as if it were not subject to tax.

H-10 election: See *Section 338(h)(10) election.*

Hart-Scott-Rodino (HSR): The Hart-Scott-Rodino Antitrust Improvements Act of 1976, as amended, a federal antitrust law that requires parties to a business combination meeting certain standards to give advance notice to the Federal Trade Commission and the Antitrust Division of the Department of Justice, and to wait a designated period before the transaction can be consummated.

Heads of agreement: See *Agreement in principle.*

Hell-or-high-water covenant: A covenant in an acquisition agreement that obligates the buyer to consummate the transaction even if the target is damaged or unable to satisfy certain specified conditions.

High-yield debt: Indebtedness with higher likelihood of default and associated higher returns. Also called *Junk bonds.*

Highly confident letter: A letter from an investment bank or commercial bank to a potential buyer stating that it is highly confident (or some similar formulation, such as "very likely") that funds can be raised for an acquisition. This is to be distinguished from a commitment letter.

Hold harmless: See *Indemnification.*

Holdback: Deferral of a portion of the purchase price as a means of financing the acquisition or as protection for the indemnification obligations of the seller or both.

Horizontal merger: A business combination involving companies in the same industry or companies that operate similar businesses.

Hostile bid: An effort to gain control of a target that has not been agreed to by the target's management and board of directors.

HSR: See *Hart-Scott-Rodino.*

Immediately available funds: See *Wire transfer.*

Impairment: A write off occurring when the carrying value of an asset exceeds its cash flows or other evidence of value.

In play: An entity is said to be "in play" when it is for sale or a change in control has become likely or inevitable.

In-the-money: A reference to an option, warrant, or convertible security or other right to purchase a security where the exercise or conversion price is lower than the current value of the security to be acquired on exercise or conversion.

Incentive stock options (ISOs): Employee stock options that conform to Section 422 of the Internal Revenue Code, thereby receiving favorable tax treatment subject to certain holding and other requirements.

Indemnity/indemnification: Terms for provisions generally included in an acquisition agreement whereby a target or its shareholders agree to indemnify and hold harmless (and typically defend) the buyer against any losses or damages suffered by the buyer based on any breach of the target's or its shareholders' representations, warranties or covenants contained in the acquisition agreement. Typically, the buyer also indemnifies the target or its shareholders, but on a more limited basis.

Indication of interest: A preliminary, nonbinding proposal submitted by a potential buyer or a bidder in an auction.

Inside basis: See *Basis.*

Installment treatment: A means of deferring a portion of the federal income tax to be paid on gains into later years to correspond with payments of the purchase price which has resulted in the gains.

Intangible assets: Assets that are not tangible assets (e.g., intellectual property and goodwill).

Integration: The process of combining the facilities, personnel, cultures, etc. of a target and buyer.

Integration clause: A standard clause that provides that the agreement in which it appears, together with all other agreements that are either entered into contemporaneously with the agreement or specified in the clause, represents the entire understanding of the parties regarding the transaction and, unless otherwise specified, supersedes all prior agreements, negotiations, communications and discussions among the parties relating to the transaction, whether written or oral. Also called an "entire agreement clause."

Intermediary: See *Financial advisor.*

Internal rate of return (IRR): A measure for determining the performance of an investment. It is the rate at which the discounted present value of future cash flows of an investment equal the cost of the investment.

Internal Revenue Code: The Internal Revenue Code of 1986, as amended.

Intrinsic value: The value of a company or an asset based on an underlying perception of value, as opposed to its market price or book value.

Investment bank (I-bank): The term encompasses a broad range of global, regional, and boutique financial services firms. Investment bank sometimes refers to the entity, and investment bankers to the individuals working at the investment bank, but the term "investment banker" is often used to refer to the entity as well. See also *Financial advisor.*

Joint and several: Generally, a reference to liability or responsibility among two or more parties being joint and several, meaning that recourse may be sought against one or more of the parties separately or all parties together. For example, certain of the representations by multiple sellers in an acquisition agreement may be made jointly and severally.

Junior lender: A lender whose debt is junior or subordinated to senior or other debt.

Junk bonds: See *High-yield debt.*

Knowledge qualification: A qualification to representations based on the knowledge of a party or of certain specified individuals. Knowledge can be actual or constructive, and can be conditioned upon an investigation or can expressly disavow any investigation obligation. See also *Actual knowledge* and *Constructive knowledge.*

LBO: See *Leveraged buyout.*

Lehman formula: A formula sometimes used by financial advisors to determine their compensation for an acquisition, which is based on 5 percent of the first million dollars of consideration, 4 percent of the second million, 3 percent of the third million, 2 percent of the fourth million, and 1 percent of the excess, or is based on some variation of that formula.

Letter of credit: A financial guarantee of performance issued by a bank. Payment is made on a standby letter of credit upon presentation of required documents. Sometimes used to back up indemnification obligations of parties to an acquisition.

Letter of intent (LOI): A document signed by the parties outlining the key aspects (price, structure and significant terms) of an acquisition. It is usually expressly nonbinding, except with respect to certain narrow issues such as confidentiality, nonsolicitation of employees and exclusive negotiations. Sometimes called a memorandum of understanding (MOU). See also *Term sheet.*

Level playing field: A set of rules applicable to all potential buyers or bidders, whereby they are treated on the same basis in terms of information provided and procedures employed.

Leverage: Debt expressed as a percentage of equity capital. Also, the use of borrowed money to increase return on investment.

Leveraged buildup: See *Add-on acquisition.*

Leveraged buyout (LBO): The acquisition of a business where a high percentage of the purchase price is financed by leverage (borrowing). If the management of the target has a large participation, it is also called a management buyout (MBO).

Leveraged buyout analysis: A methodology based on the value that could be paid if the target were to be acquired in a leveraged buyout, given a realistic range of debt service.

Leveraged recapitalization (recap): A transaction in which a company borrows a substantial amount of cash and distributes it to the shareholders by a dividend, self-tender, or otherwise.

Liability: A loan, expense or other claim on the assets that must be paid or otherwise satisfied.

LIBOR (London interbank offered rate): The rate that international banks dealing in Eurodollars charge each other for large loans.

Licklog: In the deal context, an important point of contention or decision (*e.g.,* an issue that must be resolved for the deal to go forward). The term probably derives from a salt lick for cattle, which at one time was a hollowed out place on a log. See *Random House Historical Dictionary of American Slang.*

Line of credit: An arrangement whereby a financial institution (usually a bank) agrees to lend a borrower funds from time to time up to a previously agreed maximum amount.

Liquidated damages: An amount contractually stipulated as a reasonable estimation of actual damages to be recovered by one party if another party breaches the agreement.

Liquidation value: The value of an entity's underlying assets in an orderly liquidation, after taking into account the expenses and time of sale and the payment of liabilities. See also *Going concern value.*

LOI: See *Letter of intent.*

Long-form merger: A statutory merger other than a short-form merger. See *Short-form merger.*

Long-term debt: Senior debt, including bonds, debentures, bank debt, mortgages, and capital lease obligations, but excluding payments within the next year (i.e., the short-term portion of long-term debt).

Long-term liabilities: Liabilities due in more than a year.

LTM: An acronym for last 12 months. Generally used in reference to financial measures or income statements for the immediately preceding 12-month period.

MAC clause: See *Material adverse change* and *Material adverse effect.*

M&A: A term used generally to refer to mergers and acquisitions.

Majority-of-the-minority: Conditioning shareholder approval on the affirmative vote of the holders of a majority of the shares held by the minority shareholders voting on the proposal or, in the case of a conflict of interest, the holders of a majority of the shares held by disinterested parties voting on the proposal.

Management buyout (MBO): Generally, a leveraged buyout in which management has a large participation. See also *Leveraged buyout.*

Management presentation: A formal presentation by management of a target to potential buyers, usually as part of the process in an auction. Sometimes called a "dog and pony show."

MAPA: The Model Asset Purchase Agreement included in Model Asset Purchase Agreement with Commentary (ABA Bus. Law Section 2002).

MSPA: The Model Stock Purchase Agreement included in Model Stock Purchase Agreement with Commentary (ABA Bus. Law Section 1995).

Material adverse change (MAC): A condition of an acquisition agreement to the effect that there has been no material adverse change in a party's business, operations, or other items since the signing of the acquisition agreement or some other specified date. The phrase is sometimes used as a representation of a party (usually referring to a recent balance sheet date) in lieu of a condition, which is then brought down to the closing. However, this concept necessarily involves a comparison between the state of the business as of two points in time. Often used interchangeable with material adverse effect.

Material adverse effect (MAE): A phrase used in an acquisition agreement usually to limit the scope of a party's representations, e.g., there is no litigation pending or threatened that might have a material adverse effect on the target or the transaction. Sometimes used as a condition of an acquisition agreement to the effect that there have been no events or circumstances that have had or might have a material adverse effect. See also *Material adverse change.*

Materiality qualification: A qualification to representations based on materiality. See also *Materiality standard.*

Materiality standard: An attempt to delineate or quantify materiality for certain purposes in the acquisition agreement. This may relate to materiality qualifications of the representations or to the determination of a material adverse change.

MBO: See *Management buyout.*

Memorandum: See *Book.*

Memorandum of understanding (MOU): See *Letter of intent.*

Merchant bank: A firm that offers a combination of advisory and investment banking and is able to use its capital to assist a client in achieving its objectives, including financing an acquisition.

Merger: A statutory combination of two corporations or other entities. One entity (called the disappearing entity) is absorbed by another (called the surviving entity) by operation of law, with the surviving entity acquiring the assets and liabilities of the disappearing entity.

Merger consideration: The consideration, whether cash, securities or both, received by shareholders of a target in a merger.

Merger sub: See *Acquisition sub* and *Transitory subsidiary*.

Mezzanine financing: See *subordinated debt*.

Middle market: Companies with revenues in the middle range, as to which there is no consensus. Often, those with revenues of $10 million to $25 million at the lower end of the range and $500 million to $1 billion at the higher end.

Mini basket: A term describing a provision in an acquisition agreement that excludes individual and unrelated claims under a specific dollar amount from an indemnification obligation. See also *Basket*, which is a term describing a provision that excludes claims in the aggregate below a specified dollar amount. Sometimes both concepts are used: each individual and unrelated claim has to exceed a specified amount and all claims that have not been so excluded in the aggregate have to exceed a specified amount for there to be an indemnification obligation.

Minority discount: A discount applied in valuing a minority interest, based on an inability to control governance of the entity. See also *Control premium*.

Minority shareholders: The shareholders that do not have effective control of a corporation.

Model: A buyer's computerized forecast of operating statements and balance sheets of the target after the acquisition, taking into account possible fluctuations in interest rates and other factors that may affect its results and financial condition.

MOU: See *Letter of intent*.

Negative goodwill: Situation that arises when the value of the net assets at the date of an acquisition exceeds the cost of the acquisition.

Negotiated acquisition: An acquisition in which the parties are willing participants, as distinguished from a hostile bid.

Net book value: See *Book value*.

Net earnings/income: Generally, total revenue less all expenses, including depreciation, amortization and taxes. Also called net profit.

Net operating loss (NOL): Tax deductions exceed taxable income for a specified fiscal period. NOL can usually be carried back and forward against taxable income, with some limitations.

Net present value (NPV): The calculation of the net present value of cash outflows and inflows using a given discount rate.

Net worth: See *Book value* and *net asset value*.

NLRA: National Labor Relations Act of 1935, as amended.

No-shop: A term for a provision in a letter of intent or an acquisition agreement that prohibits the target or its shareholders from soliciting or entertaining offers from any other prospective buyers for a certain period of time or until the acquisition is consummated or the agreement is terminated. See also *Exclusivity agreement*.

No-talk: A term for a provision in a letter of intent or an acquisition agreement that prohibits the target or its shareholders from providing information to or discussing a possible transaction with another party for a certain period of time or until the acquisition is consummated or the agreement is terminated.

Noncompete agreement (NCA): See *Covenant not to compete.*

Non-binding expression of interest: In an auction, a non-binding expression of interest is often sought by a certain date in order to narrow down the number of bidders.

Nondisclosure agreement (NDA): See *Confidentiality agreement.*

Nonqualified stock options: Options other than incentive stock options under Section 422 of the Internal Revenue Code, or options under an employee stock purchase plan under Section 423 of the Internal Revenue Code.

Non-solicitation agreement: An agreement in which a party (e.g., an employee, a shareholder, a seller or a buyer), for a specified period of time, agrees not to solicit customers or employees of the target or the buyer, as the case may be.

North American Industry Classification System (NAICS): An industry classification system developed by the U.S., Canada, and Mexico to provide comparability in statistics about business activity. It has largely replaced the Standard Industrial Classification (SIC) system developed by the U.S. Department of Labor.

Offering memorandum: See *Book.*

Officers' certificate: A certificate signed by an officer or officers of a party (usually at the closing) certifying to specific factual matters, such as the adoption of resolutions by the board of directors in the form attached to the certificate.

Operating lease: A lease that does not meet the criteria for a capital lease, although disclosure may be required in the notes to the financial statements. See also *Capital lease.*

Opportunity cost: The cost to a party of not obtaining the benefit of a transaction. Sometimes mentioned by a financial advisor as a reason for requesting a minimum success fee on a smaller transaction (i.e., by taking on the assignment, the financial advisor will be forgoing other potentially more profitable assignments).

Option: A right to purchase a security (usually common stock) for a stated period in the future at a determined or determinable price. Often, options are issued to employees, directors or consultants and are nontransferable. See also *Warrant.*

Ordinary income: Amounts taxed for federal income tax purposes at ordinary income, rather than at capital gains, rates.

Out-of-the-money: A reference to an option, warrant, convertible security or other right to purchase a security where the exercise or conversion price is higher than the current value of the security to be acquired on exercise or conversion. See also *In-the-money.*

Outside basis: See *Basis.*

Parachute: See *Golden parachute* or *Tin parachute.*

Pari passu: A Latin term meaning, for this purpose, "treated equally."

Paying agent: See *Exchange agent.*

PCAOB: See *Public Company Accounting Oversight Board.*

Phase I: An assessment of potential environmental contamination in property resulting from past or present land use. The assessment usually is based on site inspections and interviews, adjacent land use surveys, regulatory program reviews, aerial photograph evaluations, and other background research.

Phase II: A subsurface investigation of property through selected soil samples, laboratory analysis and testing.

Plan of reorganization: The plan providing for an acquisition intended to qualify as a reorganization for tax purposes. Often included in the title of an agreement for such an acquisition (i.e., Agreement and Plan of Reorganization).

Platform acquisition: The acquisition of one or more companies in the same line of business to use as a platform for other acquisitions within that same line of business. See *Add-on acquisition.*

Pooling-of-interests accounting: A method of accounting that was used only for a transaction in which the consideration consisted of common equity. The FASB eliminated this method of accounting for business combinations initiated after June 30, 2001.

Post-closing adjustment: An adjustment in the purchase price typically based on the increase or decrease in various items in the balance sheet as of the closing (e.g., working capital or net worth) as compared with those same items at a date or an average over a period prior to the closing (usually prior to entering into the acquisition agreement). Also called a true-up.

Post-closing covenants: Covenants that apply after the closing. See *Covenants.*

Pre-closing covenants: Covenants that apply prior to the closing. See *Covenants.*

Preferred stock: A hybrid security with some characteristics of both an equity security and a debt security. It usually contains preferences over common stock (and perhaps over other series of preferred stock), often including priority as to payment of dividends and distributions on liquidation.

Premium: In the acquisition of a public company, the value offered by the buyer in excess of the public market price of the target's stock (usually measured immediately prior to the announcement of the buyer's offer or the time, if earlier, the target became an candidate for an acquisition).

Price adjustment: See *Post-closing adjustment.*

Price-earnings (P/E) ratio: The ratio that the price for a share of common stock bears to the earnings per share for the prior year or the prior four quarters added together (sometimes called rolling 12 months).

Pro forma financials: Financial statements used to reflect the financial impact of certain significant transactions or events, such as a business combination, that have occurred or will probably occur after the date of the historical financial statements or that are not otherwise fully reflected in the historical financial statements. They may also reflect certain adjustments to the historical financial statements that will not be of a recurring nature following an acquisition (e.g., compensation of the founder).

Proration: Often, the method of allocating consideration (e.g., cash, stock, or a combination) among shareholders of the target in proportion to their respective interests and, if applicable, their individual elections.

Public Company Accounting Oversight Board (PCAOB): A board established by Sarbanes-Oxley to adopt auditing and related standards and rules that apply to public accounting firms that audit the financial statements of most publicly-owned companies.

Purchase accounting: The accounting treatment accorded all business combinations since the elimination of pooling-of-interests accounting. The buyer recognizes goodwill on its financial statements, which is measured by the excess of the cost of the acquired business over the sum of the amounts assigned to identifiable assets that are acquired at their fair value less the liabilities assumed. Intangible assets that do not have a finite life are also included in goodwill. See also *Pooling-of-interests accounting.*

Purchase price adjustment: See *Post-closing adjustment.*

Purchased assets: A term used in an acquisition agreement to refer to those assets being purchased by the buyer.

Rate of return: The annual return realized on an investment.

Recapitalization: A change in the capital structure of a company.

Record date: The date established by a board of directors to determine the shareholders entitled to receive notice of, and vote on or consent to, a particular matter, such as an acquisition. See also *Record owner.*

Record owner: The person named as owner on the books of the issuer of the security or its agent. A shareholder generally must be a record owner of the stock on the record date in order to receive notice of, and vote on or consent to, a particular matter.

Registration: The registration of securities on a registration statement with the Securities and Exchange Commission under the Securities Act.

Registration rights: Rights granted by a buyer in an acquisition or ancillary agreement to register under the Securities Act a buyer's securities issued to the target or its shareholders.

Registration statement: A disclosure document (including a prospectus) for registering securities with the Securities and Exchange Commission under the Securities Act for offering to the public.

Reincorporation: The process of changing a corporation's state of incorporation from one state to another.

Release: Often, a document required to be delivered at the closing by shareholders or other individuals associated with a target releasing any claims or causes of action (a general release) or specific claims or causes of action (a limited release) they may have with respect to the target.

Reorganization: A reorganization under Section 368(a) of the Internal Revenue Code allowing for the deferral of recognition of income (or loss) for federal income tax purposes with respect to the buyer's stock (or stock of its parent) received by the target's shareholders.

Representations (reps): Technically, statements that a target or its shareholders make in an acquisition agreement about various aspects of the business operations, material agreements, compliance with law, potential liabilities, and other matters. The buyer also makes representations, but they are generally much more limited. Often referred to in combination with warranties. The legal distinction between representations and warranties has been all but eliminated in the U.S., but the distinction is sometimes still recognized abroad. When recognized, the typical distinction made is that representations apply to past or existing facts, whereas warranties are promises that existing or future facts are or will be true.

Rescission: The undoing of an acquisition agreement or transaction to restore the status quo.

Restricted stock: Securities that have limitations on resale under the Securities Act, or are issued subject to vesting requirements.

Result fee: See *Success fee.*

Results of operations: An accounting term that refers to an entity's income or operating statement.

Retained assets: See *Excluded assets.*

Retained earnings: A balance sheet item for the accumulated earnings over a period of time.

Retained liabilities: See *Excluded liabilities.*

Retainer: A fee charged by an intermediary for taking on an M&A engagement; it is not dependent upon the closing of the transaction.

Retention bonus: A monetary incentive for personnel of a target to remain employed through a sale. Also called a "stay bonus."

Return on investment (ROI): A measure of profitability of an investment that can be calculated by taking net income as a percentage of net book value.

Reverse merger: A merger in which a buyer is merged into the target with the target being the surviving corporation. See also *Forward merger.*

Reverse triangular merger: A merger in which a buyer forms a subsidiary that is merged into the target, with the target being the survivor. See also *Forward triangular merger.*

Review: The presentation of financial statements with some assurances as to reliability of the financial data, but without an examination in accordance with generally accepted auditing standards.

Rollup: The acquisition of companies in the same line of business at or about the same time as part of a consolidation strategy.

Sales tax: A tax imposed by a state or local government on the sale of assets, usually tangible personal property other than inventory held for resale. See also *Documentary tax.*

Sandbagging: The situation where a buyer learns of a misrepresentation or breach prior to or at the closing but does not inform the seller of the problem until after the closing and then seeks indemnity. The buyer is sometimes said to "close over" the breach.

Sarbanes-Oxley: The Sarbanes-Oxley Act of 2002, a federal law enacted to restore and maintain the public's confidence in the capital markets.

Schedules: See *Disclosure schedules.*

Second request: A request for additional information and other documents by the Federal Trade Commission or the Antitrust Division of the Justice Department following a Hart-Scott-Rodino filing, triggering an additional waiting period depending on the type of transaction. See *Hart-Scott-Rodino.*

Second step transaction: The final phase of a two-step acquisition. See also *Two-step acquisition.*

Section 338(h)(10) election: An election to have a transaction governed by Section 338(h)(10) of the Internal Revenue Code, such that it will be treated for corporate law purposes as a stock acquisition but for tax purposes as if the target had sold all its assets and then liquidated.

Securities Act: The Securities Act of 1933, as amended, a federal law that governs the offer and sale of securities. Sometimes called the 1933 Act or the '33 Act.

Securities and Exchange Commission (SEC): The United States Securities and Exchange Commission.

Securities Exchange Act: See *Exchange Act.*

Seller(s): Generally used to refer to the shareholders of the target in a stock acquisition, the seller of assets in an asset acquisition and the target in a merger.

Seller financing: A means by which the seller can assist in the financing of an acquisition, normally by accepting a promissory note of the buyer for a portion of the purchase price or agreeing to installment payments of the purchase price.

Seller note: A promissory note delivered by a buyer to the seller in connection with seller financing.

Seller's market: The period during which economic and other conditions favor sellers rather than buyers.

Senior debt: Loans or debt that have a claim on assets prior to junior obligations and equity in the event of liquidation. Usually, senior debt is secured by assets of the borrower.

Senior lender: A lender (usually a bank) with the highest priority claim on a borrower.

Setoff: The right of a party, by law or agreement, to setoff amounts that are due from another party against other obligations of that party. For example, a buyer might setoff payments to which it is entitled under the indemnification provisions against amounts it owes the seller for the balance of the purchase price.

Severability: A term for a provision in an acquisition or ancillary agreement affirming the continued enforceability of the remaining provisions if some are held to be invalid, void or unenforceable.

Severance agreement: An agreement providing for payments upon termination of employment.

Share exchange: A means provided by the corporate laws of some states for an exchange of all the stock of a corporation by operation of law that is binding upon those who do not vote for or consent to the transaction.

Shareholder: A term to refer to the holders of common (and, depending on the context, preferred or special) stock of a corporation. Under the laws of some states, the term is stockholder.

Shareholder representative: One or more persons or entities designated by the shareholders involved in an acquisition to represent their interests in connection with any indemnification claims, post-closing adjustments, earnouts, or other matters.

Shareholders' equity: See *Book value.*

Short-form merger: A special kind of parent-subsidiary merger. In most states, if one company owns a large percentage (usually 90 percent) of another, the parent may merge with the subsidiary with only the approval of the parent's board of directors. This is often the second step of a two-step acquisition. See also *Two-step acquisition.*

Short-term assets: Assets expected to be converted into cash within the normal operating cycle (normally one year), such as accounts receivable and inventories.

Short-term liabilities: Liabilities that are to be paid or otherwise satisfied within one year.

Side letters: Separate arrangements made in writing between the parties to an acquisition that are not contained in the acquisition agreement or in the ancillary agreements.

Solvency opinion: An opinion as to a company's ability to meet its financial obligations.

Special committee: An ad hoc committee of a board of directors formed to consider a transaction, such as the sale of the company or an acquisition proposal. Such committees are usually formed where some of the directors have a conflict, in which case the committee consists of some or all of the disinterested directors.

Spin-off: A transaction in which a company distributes to its shareholders on a pro rata basis shares it owns in a subsidiary.

Split-off: A transaction in which some, but not all, of a parent's shareholders receive shares in a subsidiary in return for relinquishing their parent company shares.

Split-up: A transaction in which a parent spins-off all its subsidiaries to its shareholders and ultimately ceases to exist.

Squeeze-out: A transaction, usually a merger, designed to eliminate minority shareholders by converting their interests into cash.

Stalking horse: A colloquial term for a prospective buyer in a pending negotiated transaction that is being used principally to attract higher offers.

Standard Industrial Classification (SIC) system: A numerical coding system developed by the U.S. Department of Labor to group and classify products and services. It has largely been replaced by the North American Industry Classification System (NAICS).

Stapled financing: A pre-determined financing package that will be made available by a lender to the ultimate buyer in a controlled auction. See also *Auction.*

Statutory merger: See *Merger.*

Stay bonus: See *Retention bonus.*

Step-up (in basis): The increase of the tax basis of assets to the new cost in an acquisition, thereby allowing them to be depreciated from a higher tax basis. See also *Basis.*

Stock acquisition: A transaction in which the outstanding stock of a target is acquired directly from the shareholders, and the target continues to exist and maintains all of its assets, liabilities and contractual relationships.

Stock power: An instrument used to transfer ownership of stock evidenced by a certificate. Sometimes called an assignment separate from certificate.

Straight-line method: A method of calculating the depreciation of an asset that assumes the asset will lose an equal amount of value each year.

Strategic buyer: Typically an operating company that makes an acquisition for strategic business or long-term operational reasons, and not purely for financial reasons. See also *Financial buyer.*

Subordinated debt (sub debt): Borrowings from a junior lender that has agreed to subordinate its claims to senior lenders. Subordinated debt in LBOs is often called mezzanine financing. Seller financing in the form of the deferred portion of the purchase price normally will be subordinated to senior lenders and, with provisions that severely limit the rights of the seller, is referred to as being "deeply subordinated." Subordinated lenders often receive additional consideration for the loan in the form of warrants or securities, sometimes referred to as an "equity kicker."

Subsidiary merger: See *Triangular merger*.

Substantially all (of the assets): A term often used in corporate statutes to specify the circumstances in which a transfer of assets will require shareholder approval (i.e., the transfer of "all or substantially all" the assets). Depending on the statute or judicial interpretation, the determination may be made on a qualitative or quantitative basis. The term is also used in debt instruments and in the Internal Revenue Code in determining if an acquisition is tax free.

Substitution (of stock options): The substitution by the buyer of options to purchase its stock for options of the target that remain unexercised at the closing of an acquisition.

Success fee: A fee charged by an investment bank or intermediary based on the value of an acquisition that has closed. Also called a "result fee" or "transaction fee."

Successor liability: Liability imposed by statute or case law on a successor for claims against its predecessor (e.g., product liability claims with respect to products sold prior to the acquisition that the successor continued to manufacture).

Survival: Representations in an acquisition agreement can have continuing effect after the closing, and are said to survive the closing. The period during which claims for indemnification may be brought is often called the survival period. Usually, if the target is publicly held, the acquisition agreement will provide that the representations will not survive the closing.

Surviving corporation (or survivor): In a merger, the corporation into which another corporation is merged and which continues to exist as a separate entity.

Synergy: The overriding justification in many acquisitions that the performance of the combined enterprise will exceed that of its previously separate parts. Synergy will often exist where both companies have redundancies that can be eliminated.

Tag-along rights: The contractual right of minority shareholders to be included in any sale of shares or change in control by the majority shareholders. See also *Drag-along rights*.

Tail: The period following termination or expiration of the term of an engagement letter with an intermediary during which a target or its shareholders remain responsible for payment of a success fee if a sale occurs. Also the extension of the period under an insurance policy during which an insured remains covered for claims, which usually can be obtained under the original policy for payment of an additional premium.

Takeover: Usually, a hostile attempt by a bidder to acquire a target. See also *Hostile bid*.

Tangible assets: Normally physical assets such as inventory, land, buildings, and equipment.

Tangible book value: The net book value of assets less the net book value of intangible assets.

Target: The company being acquired or sought to be acquired.

Tax basis: The basis in an asset for tax purposes that is used for calculation of depreciation and to measure gain or loss on sale.

Tax-free: The opposite of taxable. Tax lawyers often avoid using the terminology "tax free" and rather tend to characterize such transactions as deferring recognition for tax purposes. See also *Reorganization.*

Tax representation letter: A letter or certificate from the parties to a reorganization required by tax counsel to support its opinion on the transaction.

Tax sharing agreement (TSA): An agreement between a parent and other members of the consolidated group governing the payment of, and reimbursement for, taxes among the group. Sometimes called a "tax treaty."

Taxable: A transaction is said to be taxable if it is immediately taxable to the target or its shareholders for federal income tax purposes.

Tender offer: An offer to shareholders of a target to acquire their securities.

Term loan: A loan (typically with a bank) with principal and interest payable over a fixed period pursuant to a specific repayment schedule. Interest may be payable at a fixed rate or in most cases at a floating rate.

Term sheet: A recital of general terms of a proposed transaction, typically intended to be nonbinding. Term sheets are usually unsigned, in contrast to letters of intent. See also *Letter of intent.*

Terminal value: The residual value of a business for the years beyond those projected in the determination of discounted cash flow.

Termination date: See *Drop-dead date.*

Termination fee: See *Break-up fee.*

Threshold: A term describing a provision in an acquisition agreement whereby once a threshold is reached or exceeded, the party seeking indemnification has the right to recover all amounts claimed from the first dollar. This is to be distinguished from a basket. Sometimes called a trigger, trip wire, first-dollar, dollar one, or tipping basket.

Time and responsibility (T&R) schedule: A schedule outlining action items, timing and responsibility among team members or all participants in an acquisition.

Tin parachute: Agreements providing variable parachute payments to a wide range of employees, rather then limiting them to executives. See also *Golden parachute.*

Topping fee: A type of break up fee paid to the prospective buyer in a negotiated transaction. Its purpose is to give the buyer some recompense where a seller terminates a transaction because of a higher price offered by another party. The fee is a percentage of the amount by which the final purchase price exceeds the price that is being topped.

Transaction fee: Sometimes a fee is payable to an intermediary on signing of an acquisition agreement, but most often on closing. See also *Success fee.*

Transfer tax: See *Documentary tax and sales tax.*

Transitional services: Services that continue to be provided after the acquisition on a transitory basis, often in a divestiture. For example, a corporate seller might continue to provide certain accounting and bookkeeping services for a business unit that it sells until the buyer can build the staff to perform these services.

Transitory subsidiary: A subsidiary that is formed for the purpose of facilitating a triangular merger, but is not the survivor in the merger.

Triangular merger: A merger in which the target is merged with a subsidiary of the buyer, thus becoming a subsidiary of the buyer. See also *Forward triangular merger* and *Reverse triangular merger.*

Trigger: Generally, an event or events that will trigger payment under a severance arrangement (including a golden parachute) with an employee. The arrangement can be structured as a single trigger, a double trigger or a modified double trigger.

True-up: See *Post-closing adjustment.*

Two-step acquisition: An acquisition completed in two stages—usually, the acquisition of a controlling stock interest followed by a merger in which the remaining shares are acquired.

Unaudited financial statements: Financial statements that have not been audited. See also *Audit, compilation and review.*

Unclaimed property laws: See *Escheat.*

Vertical merger: A business combination of firms that operate at different levels or different stages in the same industry.

Vesting: The circumstances under which (e.g., performance or continued employment) options become exercisable or restricted stock becomes free of repurchase provisions.

Voting agreement: An agreement whereby shareholders of a target agree to vote in favor of a proposed acquisition, usually signed concurrently with the acquisition agreement.

Waiver: An intentional or voluntary relinquishment of a known right or conduct that warrants an inference of the relinquishment of a right.

Walk rights: The ability of a party to terminate an acquisition agreement (or "walk away") for failure of a closing condition or otherwise.

WARN Act: The Worker Adjustment and Retraining Notification Act of 1988, as amended, a federal law which requires employers meeting certain threshold requirements to give at least 60 days advance written notice of certain plant closings and mass layoffs to the affected employees (or their union representatives) and certain local governmental officials. Some states have their own versions of the WARN Act.

Warrant: A right to purchase a security (usually common stock) for a stated period in the future at a determined or determinable price. Often, warrants are issued with another security and may be detachable from that security or nondetachable. See also *Option.*

Warranties: See *Representations.*

Wire transfer: Funds transmitted by electronic or other means through the Federal Reserve Wire Network (Fedwire) or similar network. Participants that maintain a reserve or clearing account with a Federal Reserve Bank may use Fedwire to send payments to, or receive payments from, other account holders. The transfer can be in clearinghouse funds or federal funds. A bank receiving a wire transfer of federal funds is required to make the funds available immediately on the date of receipt.

Working capital: The difference (whether positive or negative) between total current assets and total current liabilities on a balance sheet.

Bibliography

Kimberly S Blanchard, *The Tax Treatment of Earnouts in Business Acquisitions,* Tax Strategies for Corporate Acquisitions, Dispositions, Spin-Offs, Joint Ventures, Financings, Reorganizations & Restructurings, vol. 4, Practising Law Institute (2004).

Dennis J. Block, *Public Company M&A: Recent Developments in Corporate Control, Protective Mechanisms and Other Deal Protection Techniques,* Contests for Corporate Control 2005: Current Offensive and Defensive Strategies in M&A Transactions, Practising Law Institute (2005).

Arthur M. Borden and Joel A. Yunis, *Going Private* (2002).

J. Brooke Borden and Mark I. Merryweather, *Mergers and Acquisitions Practice Manual* (1999).

Committee on Negotiated Acquisitions, *Manual on Acquisition Review,* American Bar Association (1995).

Committee on Negotiated Acquisitions, *Model Asset Purchase Agreement with Commentary,* American Bar Association (2001).

Committee on Negotiated Acquisitions, *Model Stock Purchase Agreement with Commentary,* American Bar Association (1995).

Robert B. Dickie, *Financial Statement Analysis and Business Valuation for the Practical Lawyer,* American Bar Association (1998).

Christopher D. Dillon and Brett A. Pletcher, *The Acquisition and Sale of the Emerging Growth Company: The M&A Exit* (2004).

Byron E. Fox, Eleanor M. Fox, and Henry C. Su, *Corporate Acquisitions and Mergers* (2004).

James C. Freund *Anatomy of a Merger: Strategies and Techniques for Negotiating Corporate Acquisitions* (1975).

Martin D Ginsburg and Jack S. Levin, *Mergers, Acquisitions, and Buyouts* (2004).

Steven H. Goldberg and Philip Kruse, *Earnouts: Preserving a Stake in an Entity After the Acquisition,* NEW YORK LAW JOURNAL (October 18, 2002).

Joel I. Greenberg and A. Julia Haddad, *The Material Adverse Change Clause: Careful Drafting Key, but Certain Concerns May Need to Be Addressed Elsewhere,* NEW YORK LAW JOURNAL (April 23, 2001).

Mark W. Haller, Kevin D. Kreb, Benjamin W. Perks, and Thomas K. Riordan, *Mergers, Acquisitions, and Divestitures: The Nature of Disputes and the Role of the Financial Expert,* contained in *Litigation Services Handbook-The Role of the Financial Expert* (2001).

Robert T. Harper, *Financial and Accounting Provisions in Acquisition Agreements—Purchase Price Adjustment Mechanisms,* American Bar Association, Section of Business Law, 1998 Spring Meeting.

Jeffrey S. Isaacs and Stephen M. Wiseman, *The Pitfalls of Purchase Price Adjustment Provisions,* 22 No. 8 ACC Docket 86 (September 2004).

Kevin M. Keyes, *The Treatment of Contingent Consideration in Taxable Acquisitions*, Tax Strategies for Corporate Acquisitions, Dispositions, Spin-Offs, Joint Ventures, Financings, Reorganizations & Restructurings, Practising Law Institute (2004).

Lou R Kling and Eileen T. Nugent, *Negotiated Acquisitions of Companies, Subsidiaries and Divisions* (2004).

Cynthia Krus, *Annotated Confidentiality Agreement*, 4 THE M&A LAWYER 17 (March 2001).

Gary M. Lawrence, *Due Diligence in Business Transactions* (2004).

Henry Lesser, *Some Practical Suggestions for the M&A Due Diligence Process (Part 1)*, 46 No. 6 PRACTICAL LAWYER 47 (2000).

Henry Lesser, *Some Practical Suggestions for the M&A Due Diligence Process (Part 2 with forms)*, 46 No. 7 PRACTICAL LAWYER 47 (2000).

Martin Lipton, Erica H. Steinberger, and Henry Lesser, *Takeovers & Freezeouts* (1995).

Simon M. Lorne and Jay Marlene Bryan, *Acquisitions and Mergers: Negotiated and Contested Transactions* (2004).

R. Bradford Malt, *Selected Materials on Acquisition Basics*, ALI-ABA Course of Study Materials: Corporate Mergers and Acquisitions ALI-ABA 1 (2003) Westlaw: SJ061.

Harvey L. Pitt and Stephen I. Glover, *An Earnout—In Which Part of the Purchase Price Is Contingent on Performance Objectives—Can Rescue a Stalled Merger*, THE NATIONAL LAW JOURNAL (January 27, 1997).

Harvey L. Pitt and Stephen I. Glover, *When an Earnout Is to Be Used in an Acquisition, the Parties Must Resolve the Accounting, Tax and Securities Issues Involved*, THE NATIONAL LAW JOURNAL (February 3, 1997).

Pankaj Sinha and Erik Elsea, *Purchase Price Adjustments: A Survey*, 8 No. 5 THE M&A LAWYER 18 (October 2004).

Larry D. Soderquist, Pat K. Chew, Linda O. Smiddy, and A.A. Sommer, Jr., *Corporate Law and Practice* (1999).

Aaron D Rachelson, *Corporate Acquisitions, Mergers, and Divestitures* (2004).

Mark B. Tresnowski, *Working Capital Purchase Price Adjustments—How to Avoid Getting Burned*, 8 THE M&A LAWYER 14 (October 2004).

Leigh Walton and Joel I. Greenberg, *The Impact of Sarbanes-Oxley on Merger & Acquisition Practices*, 7 THE M&A LAWYER 6 (June 2003).

Leigh Walton and Kevin D. Kreb, *Purchase Price Adjustments, Earnouts and Other Purchase Price Provisions*, American Bar Association, Section of Business Law, 2005 Spring Meeting.

Maryann A. Waryjas, *Negotiating the Acquisition Agreement*, Drafting Corporate Agreements 2004-2005, Practising Law Institute (2004).

Maryann A. Waryjas, *Structuring and Negotiating Earn-Outs*, Acquiring or Selling the Privately Held Company, Practising Law Institute (2004).

Dennis J. White, *Work of the Devil? An Earnout Can Be a Tool That's Useful To Both Buyer and Seller—Or it Can Fail Miserably. The Key to Success Lies in Meticulous Planning and Crafting*, THE DAILY DEAL (April 8, 2003).

Endnotes

1. *See generally* 1&2 Hazard & Hodes, The Law of Lawyering (3d ed. 2005); ABA/BNA, Lawyers' Manual on Professional Conduct (2005); Gillers, Regulation of Lawyers (1998).

2. These are referred to as "waivers" or "consents" interchangeably in the text, as well as among experts in legal ethics, as there does not appear to be any distinction between these terms, at least as they apply to conflicts of interest.

3. *See* Model Rule 1.7 and accompanying comment.

4. *See, e.g.,* Model Rule 1.7 requiring informed consent, confirmed in writing. Model Rule 1.0(b) provides that if it is not feasible to obtain or transmit the writing at the time the person gives an oral informed consent, then the lawyer must obtain or transmit it within a reasonable time thereafter.

5. *See* ABA/BNA, *supra* note 1, at 55:307.

6. If a firm is disqualified from a proposed engagement, can it refer the inquiring party to a good deal lawyer in another firm who you know? After all isn't that how we build our practices, through courtesy referrals? At least in some jurisdictions, the referral of the inquiring party to a specific lawyer who could perform effective legal services for that party might be a breach of the duty owed to client whose interests are adverse to the inquiring party, even if the inquiring party is a client. *See* Flatt v. Superior Court, 9 Cal. 4th 275 (1994).

7. *See* Model Rule 1.18; Documenting the Attorney-Client Relationship: Law Firm Policies on Engagement, Termination and Declination pp. 27-28 (ABA Sec. Bus. L. 1999).

8. *See* Documenting the Attorney-Client Relationship: *supra* note 7 at 21-23, exhibit 8.

9. *See generally* Ratnaswamy, *Advance Waivers of Future Conflicts of Interest, The Bencher,* p. 8 (Amer. Inns of Court Nov./Dec. 2004).

10. *See* ABA/BNA, *supra* note 1, at 51:234.

11. *See* Model Rule 1.7(a); ABA/BNA, *supra* note 1, at 51:401-425.

12. *See generally* Documenting the Attorney-Client Relationship, *supra* note 7.

13. *See* Model Rule 1.5(b) (when the lawyer has not regularly represented the client, the basis or rate of the fee shall be communicated to the client, preferably in writing before or within a reasonable time after commencing the representation).

14. *See* the discussion of the role of the lawyer in Chapter 3.

15. *See* Model Rule 1.4(a).

16. For a general discussion of these issues, see the commentary accompanying MAPA § 12.6.

17. *See* Hickman v. Taylor, 329 U.S. 495, 511 (1947).

18. 8 Wright, Miller & Marcus, Federal Practice and Procedure: Civil § 2024, at 369 (1994); Behnia v. Shapiro, 176 F.R.D. 277, 279 (N.D. Ill. 1997).

19. *See, e.g.,* Venture Law Group v. Super. Ct, 118 Cal. App. 4th 96 (2004); Kenneth Gross v. SES Americom, Inc., 307 F. Supp. 2d 719 (D. Md. 2004).

20. *See generally* THE ATTORNEY CLIENT PRIVILEGE AND THE WORK PRODUCT DOCTRINE (Epstein ed., 4th ed. ABA Sec. of Lit. 2001) (4th ed. Supp. 2004); Simon & Braun, *Protecting Privileged Information in Transactional Negotiations,* 26 *Los Angeles Law.* 12 (Dec. 2003).

21. Union Carbide v. Dow Chemical, 619 F. Supp. 1036 (D. Del. 1985) (quoting Duplan Corp. v. Deering Milliken, Inc., 397 F. Supp. 1146, 1172 (D.S.C. 1974)).

22. *Compare* Hewlett-Packard Co. v. Bausch & Lomb Inc., 115 F.R.D. 308 (N.D. Cal. 1987), *with* Libbey Glass, Inc. v. Oneida. Ltd., 197 F.R.D. 342 (N.D. Ohio 1999). *See also* OXY Resources Cal. LLC v. Super. Ct., 115 Cal. App. 4th 874 (2004) (joint defense agreement).

23. MAPA § 12.6 attempts to allow a seller to furnish to the buyer confidential information without waiving any work-product, attorney-client and similar protections by demonstrating that the buyer and seller have or should be presumed to have common legal and commercial interests or are or may become joint defendants in litigation.

24. *See* THE ATTORNEY CLIENT PRIVILEGE AND THE WORK PRODUCT DOCTRINE, *supra* note 20, at 51-60.

25. *See* Hricik & Jueneman, *The Transmission and Receipt of Invisible Confidential Information,* 15 *Prof. Law.* 18 (Spring 2004); Krause, *Hidden Agendas: Unlocking Invisible Electronic Codes Can Reveal Deleted Text, Revisions,* 90 *A.B.A.J.* 26 (July 2004); Levitt & Rosch, *Making Metadata Control Part of a Firm's Risk Management,* 28 *Los Angeles Law.* 40 (March 2005).

26. N.Y. St. B. Ass'n Comm. on Prof. Ethics Op. 749 (Dec. 14, 2001).

27. N.Y. St. B. Ass'n Comm. on Prof. Ethics Op. 782 (Dec. 8, 2004).

28. *See, e.g.,* Harp v. King, 835 A.2d 953, 966 (Conn. 2003).

29. *See, e.g.,* Gray v. Bicknell, 86 F.3d 1472 (8th Cir. 1996).

30. *See, e.g.,* Lois Sportswear, USA, Inc. v. Levi Strauss & Co., 104 F.R.D. 103, 105 (S.D.N.Y. 1985).

31. *See* 2 HAZARD & HODES, supra note 1, §§ 38.1-38.10; ABA/BNA, *supra* note 1, at 71:301-318. Model Rule 4.2 prohibits communications by a lawyer with a party the lawyer knows to be represented by another lawyer in the matter without consent of the other lawyer or authorization by law or court order. By contrast, CAL. RULES OF PROF. CONDUCT 2-100 prohibits communications by a lawyer directly or indirectly with a party the lawyer knows to be represented by another lawyer in the matter without consent of the other lawyer.

32. *See* N.Y. LAW. CODE OF PROF. RESP. DR 7-104B, which provides that notwithstanding the general prohibition of communicating with a represented party, and unless prohibited by law, a lawyer may cause a client to communicate with a represented party, if that party is legally competent, and counsel the client with respect to those communications, provided the lawyer gives reasonable advance notice to the represented party's counsel that such communications will be taking place.

33. *See generally* ABA/BNA, *supra* note 1, at 5:101-110.

34. Attributed to Mark Twain.

35. *See, e.g.,* People v. Singh, 123 Cal. App. 365 (1932). A California lawyer may resign quietly or, in some instances, must resign where he knows or should know that continued representation will result in a violation of the California rules of professional conduct. CAL. RULES OF PROF. CONDUCT 3-700(B)(2). A noisy withdrawal is prohibited in the absence of preventing a criminal act that the lawyer reasonably believes is likely to result in death or substantial bodily harm to an individual. CAL. BUS. & PROF. CODE § 6068(e).

36. *See, e.g.,* Vega v. Jones, Day, Reavis & Pogue, 121 Cal. App. 4th 282 (2004).

37. Birbrower, Montalbano, Condon & Frank, P.C. v. Super. Ct., 17 Cal. 4th 119 (1998).

38. *See* McAuliffe & Voss, *Transactions Go Global: Can Lawyers Follow?*, 12 Bus. L. Today 17 (Jan./Feb. 2003).

39. Model Rule 8.5 contains a choice of law provision that establishes which rules of professional conduct are to be applied among various jurisdictions, but it is limited to the exercise of disciplinary authority.

40. It is often amazing the amount of information that can be obtained by simply searching for references to a company's name or product names through a search engine on the Internet.

41. The periodic reports filed by reporting companies with the SEC are available at http://www.sec.gov under Filings and Forms (EDGAR).

42. *See* discussion of such books in Chapter 5.

43. *See* discussion of transition agreements in Chapter 11.

44. *See* Chapter 8 regarding negotiating the deal.

45. *See* Chapter 10 for discussion of extranet sites.

46. *See* Chapter 5 regarding the engagement of an intermediary.

47. For a discussion of the Sarbanes-Oxley Act of 2002, *see* Chapter 10.

48. *See* Chapter 7 for a discussion of purchase accounting for acquisitions.

49. *See* discussion of Hart-Scott-Rodino filings in Chapter 12.

50. *See* discussion of work product and attorney-client privilege in Chapter 2.

51. Consideration might also be given to those attorneys and firms that have contributed to the MODEL ASSET ACQUISITION AGREEMENT WITH COMMENTARY: INTERNATIONAL ASSET ACQUISITIONS (ABA 2001).

52. The MODEL ASSET ACQUISITION AGREEMENT WITH COMMENTARY: INTERNATIONAL ASSET ACQUISITIONS (ABA 2001) is a useful guide and contains commentary on model acquisition agreements from 33 countries.

53. http://www.hcch.net/index_en.php?act = home.splash.

54. http://www.jus.uio.no/lm/un.contracts.international.sale.of.goods.convention.1980/doc.

55. *See* http://www.adr.org.

56. *See* http://www.iccwbo.org, where sample arbitration clauses can be found.

57. Although constituency statutes only came into existence beginning in the 1980s, their philosophical roots go back much further to a century old debate regarding the proper role of the corporation in society and the differences between those who believe that the sole role of the corporation is to maximize shareholder value, which in turn will benefit society by allocating resources in the most efficient manner (the shareholder primacy model), and those who believe that a corporation has broader social responsibilities and that, in exchange for the corporate franchise and limited shareholder liability, the corporation has responsibilities to the greater community and society beyond its shareholders.

58. Most states have adopted constituency statutes. Notably, however, Delaware does not have a constituency statute and, in fact, remains a bastion of the shareholder primary norm. Although there are many similarities among the various state constituency statutes, there is no model or uniform constituency statute. Accordingly, there are many variations. Almost all constituency statutes are phrased in permissive terms, and the board of directors, in taking or declining to take a particular action, is entitled but not required to take into consideration the interests of non-shareholder constituencies.

59. *See* Unocal Corp. v. Mesa Petroleum Co., 493 A.2d 946 (Del. 1985).

60. *See* Revlon, Inc. v. MacAndrews & Forbes Holdings, Inc., 506 A.2d 173 (Del. 1986).

61. The terms "financial buyer" and "strategic buyer" are defined in the Glossary and are discussed in Chapter 5.

62. *See* discussion of the WARN Act in Chapter 8.

63. An analysis of devices for retention of employees through employment agreements, stay-bonuses and change of control payments is contained in Chapter 5.

64. *See* discussion of transition agreements in Chapter 11.

65. *See* Ed Peters Jewelry Co. v. C & J Jewelry Co., 124 F.3d 252 (1st Cir. 1997); Askanase v. Fatjo, 130 F.3d 657 (5th Cir. 1997); *In re* Sharon Steel Corp., 871 F.2d 1217 (3d Cir. 1989); Am. Nat'l Bank v. MortgageAmerica Corp. (*In re* MortgageAmerica Corp.), 714 F.2d 1266 (5th Cir. 1983); Clarkson Co. v. Shaheen, 660 F.2d 506 (2d Cir. 1981).

66. *See, e.g.,* AES Corp. v. The Dow Chemical Co., 325 F.3d 174 (3d Cir. 2003), *cert. denied,* 540 U.S. 1068 (2003), in which the court considered an admonition to readers not to rely on the accuracy or completeness of information contained in an offering memorandum, as well as other provisions in the acquisition agreement, in the context of a securities fraud action.

67. Auctions also occur in the bankruptcy context, either when a proposed sale to an identified buyer evolves into a competitive process or a competitive process is proposed at the outset. These auctions are conducted by the bankruptcy court, and are beyond the scope of this discussion.

68. The directors may have a duty to achieve the highest possible short-term value for the target shareholders, the so-called *Revlon* duty. *See* Revlon, *supra* at note 60. For a discussion of the conduct of auctions under these circumstances, *see* Kling & Nugent, Negotiated Acquisitions of Companies, Subsidiaries and Divisions (2004).

69. *See The Deal,* p. 4 (July 28, 2003).

70. *See* AES Corp., *supra* note 66.

71. 36 Sec. Reg. & L. Rep. 1122 (May 21, 2004); Mass., No. SJC-09161 (June 10, 2004).

72. *See* Harsco Corp. v. Segui, 91 F.3d 337 (2d Cir. 1996).

73. Directors serving on special committees take this role very seriously. The committees usually engage their own independent counsel and advisors. In many situations where state law permits, they are delegated sole authority to conduct the process and to approve the final terms of the sale.

74. For example, the seller of the stock of an S corporation or of a consolidated subsidiary might illustrate the benefits from an election under Section 338(h)(10) of the Internal Revenue Code, which would allow a buyer to treat the transaction as the purchase of assets for tax purposes.

75. In Banner Industries, Inc. v. Schwartz, *N.Y.L.J.,* Jan. 11, 1990, at 24 (N.Y. Sup. Ct. County 1989), *rev'd on other grounds,* 581 N.Y.S.2d 184 (N.Y. Sup. Ct. 1992), the trial court refused to dismiss a claim that an auction was conducted in an unfair manner, but on remand the court in Banner Industries, Inc. v. Schwartz, *N.Y.L.J.,* Aug. 6, 1993, at 22 (N.Y. Sup. Ct. County 1993), *aff'd,* 612 N.Y.S.2d 861 (N.Y. Sup. Ct. 1994), *appeal denied,* 617 N.Y.S.2d 137 (1994), dismissed on the basis that the claim was controlled by a confidentiality agreement pursuant to which the seller had the right to limit access of any bidder to information and reserved the right to change the bidding process, thus avoiding having to decide whether a duty of fairness exists.

76. *See* MAPA §§ 3.4, 3.5, 3.11, 3.12 and 3.13.

77. A hierarchy for determining the relative priority of different sources of GAAP is set forth in Auditing Standards Board, Statement of Accounting Standards 69, *The Meaning of "Present Fairly in Conformity with Generally Accepted Accounting Principles" in the Independent Auditor's Report* (March 1995).

78. The most significant pronouncements are Financial Accounting Standards No. 141, *Business Combinations,* and No. 142, *Goodwill and Other Intangible Assets.*

79. *See* Annecca Inc. v. Lexent, Inc., 307 F. Supp. 2d 999 (N.D. Ill. 2004).

80. DICKIE, FINANCIAL STATEMENT ANALYSIS AND BUSINESS VALUATION FOR THE PRACTICAL LAWYER (ABA 1998).

81. *See* MAPA § 2.8.

82. *See* MAPA § 3.4.

83. *See* McLaughlin & Smith, *What Does Present Fairly Mean?* 16 INSIGHTS: CORPORATE & SECURITIES LAW ADVISOR, No. 6, at 2.

84. *See* MAPA § 3.5.

85. *See* MAPA § 3.13.

86. *See* MAPA § 3.11.

87. *See* MAPA § 3.12.

88. For a discussion of fairness opinions, *see* Chapter 5. The methodologies used in determining fairness are generally the same as are used in valuing a business.

89. *See* DICKIE, *supra* note 80; BRATTON, CORPORATE FINANCE CASES AND MATERIALS (2003). *See also* ZUKIN, FINANCIAL VALUATION: BUSINESS AND BUSINESS INTERESTS (1990, 1996 Supp.) for valuation methodologies as applied to various assets and types of businesses.

90. For a good explanation of discounting to present value, *see* BRATTON, *supra* note 89, at 30-39.

91. *See* BRATTON, *supra* note 89, at 24-32.

92. *See* BRATTON, *supra* note 89, at 49, 544-58.

93. *See* BRATTON, *supra* note 89, at 71-72 for a discussion of the confusion that can arise regarding this point.

94. 1990 WL 161084, at 28 (Del. Ch. 1990) at p. 28.

95. *See* BRATTON, *supra* note 89, at 677-93.

96. 1998 WL 44993 (Del. Ch. 1998).

97. *See* BRATTON, *supra* note 89, at 741-45.

98. Most state statutes use "fair value," but there are exceptions such as California that use "fair market value." CAL. CORP. CODE § 1300. As to appraisal rights generally, *see* BRATTON, *supra* note 89, at 741-57.

99. *See, e.g.,* Bell v. Kirby Lumber Corp., 413 A.2d 137 (Del. 1980).

100. *See, e.g.,* Cohen, *Valuation in the Context of Share Appraisal,* 34 EMORY L.J. 117 (1985).

101. 457 A.2d 701 (Del. 1983).

102. *See* 54 THE BUSINESS LAWYER 209, 215-17.

103. *See, e.g.,* cases cited by BRATTON, *supra* note 89 at 745.

104. Cunningham, *The Essays of Warren Buffett: Lessons for Corporate America,* 19 CARDOZO L. REV. 1, 180-87 (1997), reprinted in BRATTON, *supra* note 89, at 39-45.

105. Cede & Co. v. Technicolor Inc., 1990 WL 161084, at 8 n. 17 (Del. Ch. 1990).

106. *See generally* Walton & Kreb, *Purchase Price Adjustments, Earnouts and Other Purchase Price Provisions* (ABA Sec. Bus. L. 2005).

107. *See* Talegen Holdings, Inc. v. Fremont General Corp., 1998 WL 513066 (SDNY 1998). *See* the commentary following MAPA § 2.9.

108. *See generally* Walton & Kreb, *supra* note 106.

109. 244 F. Supp. 2d 1250 (D. Kan. 2003).

110. The introduction to MAPA contains an excellent analysis of the considerations in deciding upon an asset transaction.

111. *See* the discussion of the types of buyers in Chapter 5.

112. A simple example of where this can be seen would be an instance in which the buyer is concerned about the seller attempting to compete after the transaction is consummated.

This concern, presuming the seller does not have such an intent, can be alleviated by the addition of a covenant not to compete, with certain financial rewards to the seller included in the covenant not to compete which the seller will have to forego in the event it does not abide by the terms of the new aspect of the transaction. The purchase price may also be affected by the consideration contemplated by the covenant not to compete.

113. A change in control provision in some instances will prohibit a transaction in which a majority of the stock or a majority of the operating assets are conveyed by the seller. Other change in control provisions will grant to the third party the right to terminate the agreement. While, as a general proposition, contracts are freely assignable in the absence of a restriction, most substantive contracts now include limitations on assignment.

114. The use of a statutory merger or other methods may result in the granting of dissenters' rights to unwilling or objecting shareholders. State statutes address dissenter's rights and provide certain remedies to resolve these concerns.

115. For a discussion of successor liability, *see* MAPA (Appendix A).

116. For an example of a carefully drafted letter of intent, *see* MAPA. The letter of intent is divided into two sections, those provisions that are non-binding and those provisions that are binding.

117. No. 84-05905 (Dist. Harris County, Tex. Dec. 10, 1985), *aff'd in part,* 729 S.W.2d 768 (Tex. App. 1987), *cert. dismissed,* 485 U.S. 994 (1988), *appeal dismissed on agreement of the parties,* 748 S.W.2d 631 (Tex. App. 1988).

118. For a start on this subject, it is worth reading pages 9-51 of ANATOMY OF A MERGER: STRATEGIES AND TECHNIQUES FOR NEGOTIATING CORPORATE ACQUISITIONS by James C. Freund (1975). The entire work is noteworthy and very helpful reading for any M&A practitioner (or, for that matter, a client about to embark on a deal). It is, however, in these pages that Mr. Freund is able to capture and describe the chemistry of the human interplay of an M&A transaction.

119. There are many publications that address substantive due diligence, including the MANUAL ON ACQUISITION REVIEW (ABA 1995).

120. In re Insilco Corp., 125 F.T.C. 293 (1998) (acquiring company forbidden in future mergers from changing or seeking "non-aggregated customer specific information" unless provided to an independent expert).

121. These limitations are more fully discussed in the commentary to § 11.1 of MAPA.

122. The term "boilerplate" is thought by commentators to have two derivations. In shipbuilding, "boilerplate" referred to the standard identification plate attached to the steam boiler. In the newspaper business, "boilerplate" referred to the practice of newspaper syndicates sending plates with filler articles to the local syndicated papers. In both instances, the expression connoted standardized text. STARK, NEGOTIATING AND DRAFTING CONTRACT BOILERPLATE (2003).

123. ADAMS, A MANUAL OF STYLE FOR CONTRACT DRAFTING (ABA Sec. Bus. L. 2004).

124. 789 A.2d 14 (Del. Ch. 2001).

125. *See* Chapter 6 for a more in-depth discussion of the auction process.

126. This refers to Section 338(h)(10) of the Internal Revenue Code.

127. *But see* AIH Acquisition Corp. LLC v. Alaska Indus. Hardware, Inc., 2003 WL 21511921 (S.D.N.Y. 2003), where the court found that the plaintiffs' allegations supported a claim for specific performance of a stock purchase agreement where it alleged that the parties had a complete written agreement containing all the material terms in final form and for which signatures were a mere formality.

128. *See, e.g.,* FREUND, ANATOMY OF A MERGER: STRATEGIES AND TECHNIQUES FOR NEGOTIATING CORPORATE ACQUISITIONS, *supra* note 118.

129. *See* Adams, *supra* note 123.

130. *See, e.g.,* MAPA § 1.1.

131. *See* Prouty v. Gores Technology Group, 121 Cal. App. 4th 1225 (2004) (employees were intended beneficiaries and protected against termination).

132. A more thorough discussion of these issues is contained in Chapter 13.

133. Good examples of many of these typical clauses together with commentary can be found under General Provisions in MAPA. While drafted from a buyer's standpoint, MAPA is accompanied by commentary on the meaning and implications of commonly used general provisions.

134. For ease of reference, the term "schedules" will be used to encompass all these variations.

135. Not only would the inclusion of all the exceptions in the text of the representations tend to make the agreement unwieldy, but the exceptions are less likely to be subject to public disclosure when they are included on the schedules. Schedules are seldom, if ever, included with an acquisition agreement in a proxy statement to approve an acquisition or in governmental filings. This can be important to the parties because disclosure of some of this information can be very sensitive.

136. The schedules to an acquisition agreement played a prominent role in Vega v. Jones, Day, Reavis & Pogue, 121 Cal. App. 4th 282 (2004). In that case, it was alleged that a law firm representing the buyer had prepared a disclosure schedule detailing the terms of a financing that the buyer was planning to consummate after signing but before closing. The terms of the financing included "toxic" stock provisions that would result in significant dilution to the target shareholders. However, the plaintiff alleged that the schedule that was delivered was a "different sanitized version" without the "toxic" stock provisions. The appellate court concluded that the complaint properly stated a fraud claim based on concealment.

137. 789 A.2d 14 (Del. Ch. 2001).

138. MAPA § 13.8 contains general principles pertaining to a disclosure letter.

139. MAPA § 13.8 contains the following provision: "The statements in the Disclosure Letter, and those in any supplement thereto, relate only to the provisions in the Section of this Agreement to which they expressly relate and not to any other provision in this Agreement."

140. The following provision is suggested as some sellers might prefer in lieu of MAPA § 13.8: "Any disclosure under one Part of the disclosure Letter shall be deemed disclosure under all Parts of the Disclosure Letter and this Agreement."

141. A similar provision was included in the merger agreement discussed in IBP, Inc. v. Tyson Foods, Inc., *supra* note 137.

142. This is the approach taken in MAPA § 5.5.

143. *See* MAPA § 5.5.

144. *See* MAPA § 7.1 and related commentary. An exception is made in MAPA § 12.2(a)(iv) where the certificate reaffirming the accuracy of the representations at the time of closing expressly states that the matters disclosed in the supplement have caused a condition to closing not to be satisfied.

145. *See* the commentary to MAPA §§ 5.5 and 11.1.

146. *See, e.g.,* MAPA §§ 7.3 and 7.4.

147. *See, e.g.,* MAPA § 7.3.

148. *See, e.g.,* MAPA § 7.9.

149. *See* Chapter 14 for a discussion of the potential binding nature of such statements.

150. *See, e.g.,* MAPA § 7.12.

151. *See, e.g.,* MAPA § 5.7.

152. For an example of a noncompetition, nondisclosure and nonsoliciation agreement, *see* MAPA, Exhibit 2.7(a)(vii), and covenants of the seller contained in MAPA § 10.8.

153. *See* the commentary to MAPA § 10.8 and to the form of noncompetition, nondisclosure, and nonsolicitation agreement referenced in note 152 above.

154. For an example of an escrow agreement, *see* MAPA, Exhibit 2.7(a)(viii).

155. For an example of a transition services agreement see MAPA, Exhibit 2 to Appendix C.

156. For an example of a contribution agreement, *see* MAPA, Ancillary Documents.

157. *See* MAPA §§ 7.4 and 8.4.

158. Many of these documents, certificates and opinions are described in greater detail, with examples, in MAPA.

159. *See, e.g.,* Cal. Evid. Code § 1521 (permits the content of a writing to be proved by admissible secondary evidence provided, among other things, that no genuine dispute exists concerning the material terms of the writing and justice requires the exclusion); De Silva, *California's Best Evidence Rule Repeal: Toward A Greater Appreciation For Secondary Evidence,* 30 McGeorge L. Rev. 646.

160. Entering into a contract by electronic means is becoming increasingly common, but often creates concerns regarding security and the potential for fraud. Given that the creation of a contract requires only offer, acceptance and manifestation of assent, there is a risk that without a provision explicitly excluding the creation of a contract by electronic means an agreement or an amendment to the agreement could be entered into unintentionally.

161. The essential elements to the formation of a contract are an offer, acceptance and manifestation of assent or meeting of the minds. When an offer upon specified terms is accepted without conditions and acceptance is communicated to the other party without unreasonable delay, a contract arises. The offeror can prescribe conditions on the method of acceptance. Restatement (Second) of Contracts § 30. If a condition calling for a signature is not met, the contract does not come into being. *See* Kroeze v. Chloride Group Ltd., 572 F.2d 1099 (5th Cir. 1978). Like earlier cases dealing with telegrams and telexes, there is authority to the effect that the exchange of writings and acceptance by facsimile creates a binding contract. *See* Holbrook v. A C and S, Inc., 1997 WL 52060 (E.D. Pa. 1997); Coin Automatic Laundry Equip. Co. v. Pheasant Hollow Assocs., 1993 WL 267446 (E.D. Pa. 1993). In addition, a facsimile signature can satisfy the statute of frauds. *See, e.g.,* N.Y. Gen. Oblig. Law § 5-701 (written text produced by telefacsimile constitutes a writing and any symbol executed or adopted by a party with the present intention to authenticate a writing constitutes a signing); *see also* Restatement (Second) of Contracts § 134 comment b; Birenbaum v. Option Care, Inc., 971 S.W.2d 497, 502 (Tex. Ct. App. 1997) (statute of frauds not satisfied because acquiror signed a post-it cover memo rather than letter of intent that was sent by facsimile).

162. *See* The Uniform Electronic Transactions Act (1999).

163. *See* 15 U.S.C. § 7001 et seq. (2000).

164. The Uniform Electronic Transactions Act (UETA) provides "If a law requires a signature, an electronic signature satisfies the law." *See* UETA § 7, *supra* note 162. E-Sign states "a signature, contract, or other record relating to [a] transaction may not be denied legal effect, validity, or enforceability solely because it is in electronic form; and. . .a contract relating to such transaction may not be denied legal effect, validity, or enforceability solely because an electronic signature or electronic record was used in its formation." *See* 15 U.S.C. § 7001 (2000).

165. UETA §5(b) specifies that the Act only applies when parties have agreed to deal electronically (cf. E-Sign §101(b) which states it does not require anyone to deal electroni-

cally). UETA §5(d) specifies that parties have the power to vary its provisions by contract, §9 refers to the parties' agreement as a factor in determining the effect of an electronic record, and §10 refers to the parties' agreement to use security procedures. E-Sign confines itself to the legal effect, validity and enforceability of electronic records and signatures. It contains no provisions on variation by agreement. Moreover, UETA §§2(16) and 3(a) states that UETA applies only to electronic signatures that relate to a "transaction," which means "an action or set of actions occurring between two or more persons relating to the conduct of business, commercial, or governmental affairs." UETA §3(b) also specifically excludes certain transactions from its coverage, for example UETA does not apply to laws governing wills or trusts, the UCC (other than Articles 2 and 2A), or UCITA. Deal lawyers must also carefully scrutinize the jurisdiction in which the transaction occurs, because UETA §3(b) allows states to exempt certain types of transactions from the Act's coverage.

166. *See* 15 U.S.C. § 7002.
167. *See* Pond & Kump, *Virtual Deals: Electronic Contracting in the Current Legal Framework*, 683 PLI/PAT 897, 915 (2002).
168. *See* Electronic Signatures and Records Act (ESRA) § 101.
169. *See* Lesser, *The Validity of On-Line and Electronic Contracts*, 754 PLI/PAT 887, 915 (2003). *See also* New York State Office For Technology ESRA FAQ website at <http://www.irm.state.ny.us/esra/faq.htm>.
170. If a digital signature is desired, the drafter should consult the applicable state law and the ABA Guidelines for Digital Signatures which is available online at <http://www.abanet.org/scitech/ec/isc/digital_signature.html>. Several law review articles provide a good starting point for further research under both UETA and E-Sign. *See* Pond & Kump *supra* note 167; Smart, *E-sign versus State Electronic Signature Laws: the Electronic Statutory Battleground*, 5 N.C. BANKING INST. 485 (2001). Additionally, the "Global E-Commerce Law" page on Baker & McKenzie's website at <http://www.bakernet.com/ecommerce/uetacomp.htm> provides a state-by-state comparison table of those states that have (or have not) enacted a form of UETA.
171. 975 F. Supp. 1061 (N.D. Ill. 1997).
172. 2003 WL 21511921 (S.D.N.Y. 2003).
173. 2004 WL 1496864 (2d 2004).
174. *See* MAPA § 5.7, which provides that "Seller and shareholders shall use their Best Efforts to cause the conditions in Article 7 and Section 8.3 to be satisfied."
175. *See* MAPA § 13.9.
176. RESTATEMENT (SECOND) OF CONTRACTS § 237.
177. *See, e.g.,* MAPA § 9.1.
178. 789 A.2d 14 (Del. Ch. 2001).
179. CBS Inc. v. Ziff-Davis Publishing Co., 553 N.E.2d 997 (N.Y. 1990).
180. Galli v. Metz, 973 F.2d 145 (2d Cir. 1992).
181. Hendricks v. Callahan, 972 F.2d 190, 195-96 (8th Cir. 1992).
182. Appendix D to MAPA illustrates the operation and interaction among various provisions of MAPA, and analyses in that context whether the buyer can exercise a walk right or, if it proceeds with the asset purchase, whether the seller will be required to indemnify the buyer. *See also* the commentary to MAPA § 11.1 regarding the survival of an indemnification claim after the buyer's discovery during a preclosing investigation of a possible inaccuracy in the seller's representations.

183. *See* Rowley, *A Brief History of Anticipatory Repudiation in American Contract Law*, 69 U. Cɪɴɴ. L. Rᴇᴠ 565 (2001).

184. Horizon Holdings, L.L.C., v. Genmar Holdings, Inc., 241 F. Supp. 2d 1123 (D. Kan. 2002) and Horizon Holdings, L.L.C. v. Genmar Holdings, Inc., 244 F. Supp. 2d 1250 (D. Kan. 2003).

185. Cede & Co. v. Technicolor, Inc., 1990 WL 161084 (Del. Ch. 1990).